From Every Mountainside

From Every Mountainside

Black Churches and the
Broad Terrain of Civil Rights

Edited by

R. Drew Smith

Published by State University of New York Press, Albany

© 2013 State University of New York

All rights reserved

Printed in the United States of America

No part of this book may be used or reproduced in any manner whatsoever without written permission. No part of this book may be stored in a retrieval system or transmitted in any form or by any means including electronic, electrostatic, magnetic tape, mechanical, photocopying, recording, or otherwise without the prior permission in writing of the publisher.

For information, contact State University of New York Press, Albany, NY
www.sunypress.edu

Production by Eileen Nizer
Marketing by Michael Campochiaro

Library of Congress Cataloging-in-Publication Data

From every mountainside : black churches and the broad terrain of civil rights /
    edited by R. Drew Smith.
       p. cm.
    Includes bibliographical references and index.
    ISBN 978-1-4384-4725-4 (hardcover : alk. paper)
    1. African Americans—Civil rights.   2. African American churches—History.
3. Civil rights movements—United States—History.   4. United States—Church history.
5. United States—Race relations.   6. Civil rights—Religious aspects—Christianity.
7. Race relations—Religious aspects—Christianity.   I. Smith, R. Drew, 1956–

    E185.61.F9158 2013
    323.1196'073—dc23   2012027404

10 9 8 7 6 5 4 3 2 1

Land where my fathers died

Land of the Pilgrims' pride

From every mountainside

Let freedom ring

—"My Country, 'Tis of Thee"
Samuel Francis Smith, 1831

Contents

PUBLIC SPHERE CAPITAL AND
CONTEMPORARY RIGHTS EXPECTATIONS

PREVAILING BOUNDARIES OF SOCIAL DIFFERENCE

Acknowledgments

Many persons and institutions contributed to the successful completion of this volume. First of all, I would like to thank each of the volume's contributors for their chapters and for the convictions and expertise they brought to this exploration of church involvement with civil rights. Special thanks also go to the SUNY Press editors involved with this project: Larin McLaughlin who welcomed this project and was a source of encouragement during its initial stages, and Michael Rinella who provided strategic support throughout its final stages. I am indebted as well to the external reviewers for their detailed suggestions about ways for sharpening individual chapters and the book's overall focus. Also, many thanks to the Virginia Foundation for the Humanities and to Garrett-Evangelical Theological Seminary for providing intellectual spaces that helped facilitate my assembling and editing of the volume. Also, I convey here endless thanks to my family and to the many who have strived for what is good, and right, and just.

Introduction

R. Drew Smith

In both popular and academic understandings of the American Civil Rights Movement, the emphasis has generally been on the heroic activism mobilized from the mid-1950s through the mid-1960s against the segregationist juggernaut of the American South. It was on this historical stage that black churches were spotlighted for their substantial role in the black freedom epoch unfolding at the time—and it was a role that shifted perceptions in the minds of many about the potential political significance of black churches. This association between black churches, civil rights activism, and the mid-twentieth century South has become mutually reinforcing. When mentioning black churches and civil rights activism, one thinks of the mid-twentieth century South; when mentioning civil rights activism and the mid-twentieth century South, one thinks of black churches.[1]

A related orthodoxy has been that where civil rights activism may have occurred in the North and the West it was "secondary to the real struggle taking place in the South."[2] Activists who resided in the North and West often felt their connection to "the movement" was established more by whether they were involved in the southern struggle arena and, specifically, whether they marched with Dr. King, than by their activism within their own northern or western home contexts. Moreover, in the same sense that northern and western civil rights activism was deemed less important than that occurring in the South, black churches were viewed as contributing less within northern and western contexts of activism than they did within the southern context. One noted scholar suggests, in fact, that black churches were less central to northern civil rights activism than to the southern movement and that the lesser role they played in the North may account in some way for "the more episodic, relatively unfocused and physically explosive movement that developed in the North."[3]

While the conception of civil rights activism outside the South as less urgent, less central, and less effective has been strongly challenged by recent scholarship,[4] fewer studies exist that counter the view of black church civil rights activism as an almost exclusively mid-twentieth century southern phenomenon.[5] This volume adds to existing scholarship in emphasizing sociocultural and ecclesiastical factors specific to local contexts of civil rights activism in the North and West, while also examining ways local and national activism fed off each other within these contexts. With respect to the latter, as shown by an important study of black religion, not enough attention has been paid within scholarship on black churches to intersections between southern and northern black religious life, especially those occurring as a result of early- to mid-twentieth century black migration to northern cities.[6]

The volume also joins with other studies that have resisted a popular bracketing of the Civil Rights Movement which confines it largely to the South, from the 1955 Montgomery Bus Boycott to the passing of the 1965 Voting Rights Act.[7] The chapters here do not treat the quest for civil rights in America only as an historical theme, but also as an enduringly relevant framing of social injustices yet to be worked out within American polity and social practice. What the chapters do is point to multiple directions the quest for civil rights has extended beyond the mid-twentieth century southern movement—into the North and West during the Movement, and into policy areas left unresolved by the Movement, including immigrant rights, gay rights, health care entitlements, and persistent denials of black voting rights and school equality. In exploring these issues the volume's contributors shed light on distinctive regional dimensions of African American political and church life that bear in significant ways on both the mobilization of civil rights activism and the achievement of its goals.

Regional Dimensions of Black Church Activism in the Early- to Mid-Twentieth Century

While widespread southern black conversionist piety correlated well in the southern context with social change strategies utilizing nonviolence and moral suasion, there was a more worldly quality to the black church activism of northern and western cities that did not synchronize as well with the conversionist propensities and nonviolent methods of the southern movement. Milton Sernett, for example, points out black church regional contrasts between the "instrumentalism" of northern, "Social Gospel" clergy, and the "traditionalism" of southern clergy rooted in "old-time religion."[8] In this respect, black church life through the mid-twentieth century was commonly characterized by scholars as "other-worldly," especially the three-quarters of African American churches located in the South which Benjamin Mays and Joseph Nicholson referred to in a 1933 study as "uniformly" so.[9]

Meanwhile, scholars as early as W. E. B. Du Bois in his 1899 publication, *The Philadelphia Negro* have drawn attention to a stream of middle-class and secularizing black northern Christianity. Du Bois' analysis focuses mainly on the larger churches, which he describes as "the birthplaces of schools and of all agencies which seek to promote the intelligence of the masses," and as contexts where black audiences "quickly and effectively" received news and information and were introduced to celebrities, from bishops to poets.[10] Similarly, Mays and Nicholson pointed out that the urbanization of African Americans had led by the 1930s, especially in the North, to "definite demands upon the churches for a richer program" related to social and community services.[11] Both of these studies distinguished between more institutionalized black churches and a burgeoning sector of smaller black churches, which the Du Bois study characterized as "survivals of the methods of worship in Africa and the West Indies"[12] and the Mays and Nicholson study charged to combine into "fewer and better" churches attuned to the educational and economic imperatives of the context.[13]

Regionalist scholarship on early- to mid-twentieth century black church life, then, outlines a geographical black church repositioning from South to North and rural to urban, and a growing cultural receptivity to a mainstream secular mindset and its resistance to spiritualizations that could interfere with temporal problem solving. There were social class ramifications to this repositioning, with activism being more strongly associated with congregations possessing larger and more middle-class memberships.[14] These interlocking factors (along with the entrenched nature of black oppression in the South) favored the North as the center of black church activism, at least until the outbreak of the southern movement in the mid-1950s. In fact, it was in the early-twentieth century North and West that influential black pastors were counted among the most important political brokers in their respective cities, including Adam Clayton Powell, Sr. and Adam Clayton Powell, Jr. in New York City,[15] Archibald Carey, Sr. and Archibald Carey, Jr. in Chicago,[16] Marshall L. Shepard, Sr. in Philadelphia,[17] Rev. Wade McKinney in Cleveland,[18] and several pastors of Second Baptist Church in Los Angeles.[19] Black clergy also played crucial roles within early-twentieth century insurgent politics, including labor movement advocacy by San Diego's Rev. George

Washington Woodbey of Mt. Zion Baptist Church,[20] and Detroit's Rev. Charles Hill of Hartford Avenue Baptist and Rev. Horace White of Plymouth Congregational.[21]

Moreover, the North was where key African American institutions with regional and national reach were launched and based. The oldest (and most politically active) African American denominations were founded in northern cities—the African Methodist Episcopal (A.M.E.) denomination founded in Philadelphia in 1787 and the African Methodist Episcopal Zion (A.M.E.Z.) denomination founded in New York in 1820. Also, the first black Baptist associations (precursors to the National Baptist Conventions) were organized during the 1830s and 1840s in northern states such as Ohio, Illinois, and Michigan.[22] The third oldest black Baptist Convention, the Progressive National Baptist Convention (PNBC), was founded in Cincinnati in 1961 (sixty-six years after the parent Baptist Convention from which it split). Unlike the predecessor Convention it broke away from and from which many of its member churches came (the National Baptist Convention USA, Inc.), the PNBC drew noticeably more on congregations outside than inside the South. Suggestive of the PNBC's geographic profile is that twelve of its eighteen presidents between 1961 and 2010 were pastors of prominent churches in the North, the West, or the District of Columbia.[23]

It is not surprising that politically active black churches through the mid-twentieth century would be concentrated in the North or West. With the primary black political organizations and post-Reconstruction-era black governmental leaders also in those parts of the country, there was strength in numbers and a greater sense of black political possibilities in those contexts than in the South.[24] The two preeminent black civil rights organizations, the National Association for the Advancement of Colored People (NAACP) and the National Urban League (NUL), were both founded in the state of New York—the former in 1909 and the latter in 1911. The NUL expanded rapidly, with eighty-one paid staff members operating in twenty cities by 1919, increasing to affiliates in fifty-eight cities by 1943 and with an operating budget of $2,500,000 (a one-hundred-fold budgetary increase from its 1919 amount).[25] That NUL activities had a northern concentration is evident in the fact that forty-five of fifty-six NUL affiliates established between 1910 and 1950 were in northern cities.[26] The NAACP also experienced pronounced growth, achieving 62,000 members by 1919 and 600,000 members by 1946. Roughly half of its members in 1919 were located in the South, with NAACP branches chartered in every southern state.[27] Nevertheless, the NAACP's membership growth in the South did not appear to keep pace with its northern growth given that its southern membership was less than one-quarter of its national membership by the mid-1950s and declined noticeably more in the next few years as southern states cracked down on NAACP activities during the Movement.[28]

There were other organizations located in the North of great importance to black civil rights, although with a less exclusively black focus and operations staff. The Fellowship of Reconciliation, a pacifist group formed in Europe in 1914, inspired the formation a year later of Fellowship of Reconciliation (FOR) in the United States. Headquartered in the state of New York, the organization championed war resistance, civil liberties, and racial justice. Its racial justice work was primarily through its collaborations with the Congress of Racial Equality (CORE), founded in 1942 by several of its Chicago branch members, and later through the Civil Rights Movement involvements of its staff member, Bayard Rustin, who helped guide the nonviolent resistance strategies employed in the 1955 Montgomery Bus Boycott and served as a principal organizer for the 1963 March on Washington. CORE, under the team leadership of University of Chicago students, James Farmer and George Hauser, focused initially on desegregating public housing in the North. In 1947, it initiated protests of segregated interstate bus travel in the upper South, devoting significantly more attention to this in the form of "Freedom Rides" during the early 1960s, and also became strongly associated with student sit-ins across the South during the movement. Nevertheless, by the mid-1960s it refocused its attention primarily on the North and West where two-thirds of its fifty-three affiliate chapters were located.[29]

Black nationalist organizations such as the Moorish Science Temple of America (MSTA), the Universal Negro Improvement Association (UNIA), and Nation of Islam (NOI) were also forces within black politics during the first half of the twentieth century—and their strongholds were in the North and West. The MSTA, a racial uplift organization steeped in Islamic and Near Eastern mystical teachings, began in 1925 when Timothy Drew (a North Carolinian) founded its first temple in Chicago. By the late-1920s, Drew (who became known as Noble Drew Ali) had established seventeen temples in the North (including in Philadelphia and Detroit) as well as in the upper South, and had a membership of approximately 35,000 persons. The UNIA, founded by Marcus Garvey in Jamaica in 1914 as a global black unity initiative, organized a U.S. division in New York City in 1917 that attracted 3,500 members in its first three months and served as the base city from which it reached out internationally. By 1920, the UNIA was reported to have 1,100 divisions in forty countries and attracted 20,000 participants to its international conference held that year at New York's Madison Square Garden. The organization declined by the late-1920s and, in 1940, five years after Garvey's death, the organization relocated its headquarters to Cleveland under new leadership.

The NOI, a group committed to black self-determination, was founded in Detroit in 1930 by W. D. Fard Muhammad who disappeared in 1934 and was succeeded as leader of the group by Elijah Muhammad. In 1935, Elijah Muhammad relocated to the Chicago mosque, which was the second mosque established by the NOI, and it became the NOI national headquarters. By the mid- to late-1950s, NOI had a membership estimated at between fifty to one hundred thousand persons, and mosques in at least fifteen cities—only two of which were in the South (Baltimore and Atlanta).[30]

Organizational leaders such as Garvey, Farmer, Elijah Muhammad, Drew Ali, and others certainly influenced black political praxis in the early- to mid-1900s, but the black political leaders most able to broker public decision making and resources during this period were black Congressmen, all of whom were from the North or West. From the 1929 election of Oscar DePriest (R-IL), the first black elected to Congress after the Reconstruction era, until the passing of the 1965 Voting Rights Act, eight African Americans were elected to Congress.[31] Several of these men gained a following nationally as a result of their advocacy on civil rights matters, including William Dawson (D-IL) who fought against poll taxes, Charles Diggs (D-MI) who was outspoken on civil rights matters and helped bring national attention to the murder of Emmett Till by attending the 1955 Mississippi trial of his accused killers, and Adam Clayton Powell, Jr. (D-NY) whose protests against discriminatory practices within New York City and within the federal government and his ascendance in 1961 to the chairmanship of the House Education and Labor committee helped keep him in the national spotlight throughout his twenty-five years in Congress.

With the onset of the southern protest movement in the mid-1950s, black leadership momentum clearly shifted to persons and organizations in the South, including Martin Luther King, Jr. and the Southern Christian Leadership Conference (SCLC) network of activists, emergent activist organizations such as the Student Nonviolent Coordinating Committee (SNCC), local activist networks in key struggle sites such as Birmingham and Nashville, and thousands of laypersons and clergy drawn from congregations across the South. In some respects, Dr. King's summons to lead this southern political movement after his years of graduate-level theological studies in the North symbolized a convergence at the heart of the movement between the South's relational, conversionist culture and a northern secular-humanism that privileges individual reason. Harold Cruse interprets the significance of the southern movement along these lines in arguing for the southern movement's usurpation of northern black leadership authority:

Prior to King, the class interests of the civil rights spokesmen in Montgomery had coincided with the goals of the secular NAACP. When King mobilized the boycott, he also mobilized the church along with other sectors of black life. Thus, the NAACP, essentially northern-based, had to take a backseat to the new southern middle-class self-assertion.[32]

Cruse goes on to connect King's importance as the "standard-bearer" of the movement to his embodiment of an emerging "middle-class secularization of the black church" that emphasizes "moral" reasoning and social ministries in response to black social needs.[33]

Although King and other movement leaders in the South achieved national black spokesmanship status almost from the outset of the southern movement, and although King and SCLC networks and allies provided the activist church model with momentum that would reach far beyond the southern movement, the newly gained authority of southern movement leaders met with reversals beginning in the early 1960s via challenges from entrenched and emerging black leadership sectors throughout the North and West. Key black leaders in the North engaged in noticeable pushback against the authority of southern movement leaders such as Dr. King, with NAACP leaders Whitney Young and Roy Wilkins frequently criticizing King, and Congressman Adam Clayton Powell, Jr. often referring to Dr. King contemptuously as "Martin 'Loser' King."[34] Moreover, black identity and black self-reliance politics, already enjoying a strong following, increased its support base in the 1950s and 1960s as a result of the leadership of Malcolm X. After Malcolm's death in 1965, "Black Power" activists such as Stokely Carmichael built upon Black Nationalism's emphasis on blackness, though pushing Nationalism further in the direction of a modern, rational politics and away from its more "mythological" aspects.[35] A related development in the late-1960s was the emergence of Black Theology, a critical reading of mainstream (read white) religion and culture. Black Theology, which was positioned as an intellectual heir to both the church-led Civil Rights Movement and the secular Black Power Movement, traces to James Cone, who like other of his contemporary Black Theology proponents, was based in and drew most support from northern ecclesiastical institutions and networks. By the end of the 1960s, then, southern black leadership authority was declining, giving up ground to new and resurgent black leadership sectors in the North and West. Nevertheless, black leadership sectors within all three regions (including the church sector) were well-positioned to vigorously compete for leadership authority and standing at the beginning of the 1970s.

Post-Movement Activist Geographies
and Leadership Camps

Regional tensions between black leaders over spokesperson status, political strategy, and ideology were pronounced by the 1960s,[36] but lessened in
subsequent decades as barriers to black social cooperation across regional
boundaries were struck down. In short, the geographies of black leadership authority begin to blur during the 1970s and 1980s. Where tensions
did persist within post-movement contexts, two significant forms have
been competition between electoral and protest leaders, and competition
between activist churches and "new paradigm" megachurches.

With mass action civil rights protests dying down across the country
by the late-1960s, black electoral activism was achieving a critical mass of
its own on the heels of the electorally empowering 1965 Voting Rights Act.
The numbers of black elected officials climbed from roughly 100 in 1965
to almost 1,500 by 1970, increasing again to almost 7,500 by 1990.[37] During the period dating from 1967–1990, this included one person elected
to the U.S. Senate and thirty-three elected to the House of Representatives
(joining six already serving in the House in the mid-1960s). Twenty-four
of these thirty-three Representatives, as well as the Senator, were elected to
Congress from states in the North or the West. Also, by 1973, forty-eight
African Americans were serving as mayors (including mayors elected in
recent years to cities such as Los Angeles, Detroit, Hartford, Gary, Atlanta,
and Birmingham). By 1983 there were 223 black mayors, with the vast
majority (143) located in the South.[38] As the comparisons between black
Congressional and mayoral leadership suggest, black electoral politics was
becoming national during the 1970s and 1980s in ways that included a
newly mobilizing black electorate in the South.

Prospects for a national black electoral politics were tested by efforts
during the 1970s to establish a National Black Independent Political Party
(NBIPP) and during the 1980s by Jesse Jackson's impressive presidential
campaigns. Both of these initiatives also represented attempted conver-
gences as well as sources of contention between black clergy activists,
black elected officials, and Black Nationalists. The idea of an independent
black political party was a matter of serious discussion as early as 1967,
when Congressman Powell proposed it during a Black Power conference
he convened in Newark, New Jersey. Political Scientist, Ronald Walters
notes, "by 1971, the idea of a Black political party had become an expression of Black independence in electoral politics."[39] The formation of a
Party was a primary topic of conversation at gatherings in 1972 and 1974
of what was called the National Black Assembly (a pre-party structure),
and in 1976 the National Black Assembly took steps to field a black can-

didate for the U.S. presidency. When unsuccessful in recruiting Georgia State Senator, Julian Bond, as its candidate, the Assembly recruited an African American clergyman, Rev. Frederick Douglass Kirkpatrick. The NBIPP was finally established at a 1980 Assembly meeting on a motion made by Rev. Benjamin Chavis and over the next year established forty-six chapters in twenty-seven states and a national office in Washington, DC. The entire initiative quickly stalled, leaving the NBIPP with little more to show for its efforts than fourteen years of symbolic accomplishments riddled with conflict between black elected officials, clergy, and nationalists.[40] Jesse Jackson's presidential candidacies attempted to appeal, at one level, to the same base of black elected officials, clergy, and nationalists the NBIPP was unable to hold together, while also reaching out to the Democratic Party's multi-racial constituency. His efforts produced an impressive coalition from across these various constituencies, resulting in 3.15 million votes and 400 delegates in the 1984 Democratic primaries and 6.6 million votes and 1,200 delegates in 1988. Jackson's candidacies also signaled that black clergy civil rights activists and their successors had been bridged, once and for all, into the growing black consensus around an electoral emphasis for black activism.

A form of black clergy activism tapping historic black emphases on entrepreneurialism and community-based social development began blossoming in force in the early-1990s. A cadre of talented black clergy who came of age after the Civil Rights Movement and who, in many cases, were resistant to black church reliance on outmoded, top-heavy denominational structures and on black community dependence on government largess began transforming preexisting and newly founded congregations into socially and religiously dynamic megachurches. By embracing innovative approaches to worship style, preaching, teaching, utilization of technology, programmatic service delivery, and church administration and governance, these congregations developed into user-friendly, multi-dimensional, high-growth ministries. Based upon recent estimates, there are between 100 and 150 congregations headed by African American pastors where weekly attendance averages 2,000 or more persons (the widely accepted numerical designation for "megachurch").[41] The largest concentrations of black megachurches are in metro-Atlanta and in two metro areas bordering the South: Washington, DC and Dallas.[42] The denominational ties of many of these congregations have been weak or nonexistent, the political alignments of their high-profile pastors have tended to be conservative and Republican as much as liberal and Democrat, and the activism promoted by these churches has been inspired more often by economic growth principles than by social justice principles. The combination of these factors has created competition and conflict between

black megachurch pastors and civil rights clergy activists over strategy
and support bases.

Post Movement Ideological Context

Calls for the ideological broadening of civil rights activism were increasingly heard by the latter-1960s from black activists concerned with the
inadequacies of a politics of racial integration and black empowerment
in addressing forms of discrimination and oppression related to econom-
ics, gender, and sexual orientation. Martin Luther King, Jr. became one
of the forceful critics of the Civil Rights Movement's inability to account
for the economic oppression of blacks and others. Campaigns to end
poverty in America (and to end U.S. military and human rights atrocities
in southeast Asia) were his primary concerns toward the end of his life.
Black nationalists such as Malcolm X and Black Power advocates such
as Stokely Carmichael, though framing black struggle in ways strongly
emphasizing discriminatory racial practices, did not necessarily promote
racial integration as the desired solution.

Racial framings of civil rights activism have certainly been challenged, with some arguing that the black civil rights agenda, as emanating
from the U.S. Constitution's Fourteenth Amendment, has run its course.
As one prominent scholar on American race and politics states: "Civil
rights justice, for all intents and purposes of the United States Constitution, has been won; there are no more frontiers to conquer; no horizons
in view. . . ."[43] The argument in this instance pertains to the absence of
additional legal remedies, within our existing constitutional framework,
for social inequalities plaguing blacks and others in the years since Civil
Rights Movement legislation was passed to address urgent social inequalities. Accordingly, contemporary denials of equal rights and opportunities (addressed within the scope of the Constitution and subsequent civil
rights legislation)[44] are technically addressed through the courts. Thus,
while referencing "civil rights" paradigms may attract attention to ongoing
denials of rights in these instances, "civil rights" paradigms are of little
relevance where social deprivations are not addressed by the Constitution
(as in the case of economic opportunity). Consequently, as the argument
goes, we are in a "post-civil rights era."

The term "post-civil rights era" may be accurate as a way of capturing exhausted constitutional possibilities, but it seems far from an accurate
description of the African American mindset. In a 2004 Gallup poll, 84
percent of African Americans still express strong concerns about civil
rights issues. In a 2006 Associated Press/Ipsos poll, 32 percent of African American respondents felt there has not been significant progress

toward Martin Luther King's dream of racial equality.[45] Thirty-one percent of African American clergy surveyed in a 1999–2000 Black Churches and Politics (BCAP) survey indicated that their congregations were
involved with civil rights issues, which was among the highest percentage
of involvement from among a list of high profile social policy issues.
Congregational involvements on two other policy issues with civil rights
dimensions were also relatively high: affirmative action policies were cited
by 24 percent of the clergy and criminal justice policies were cited by 23
percent. When asked about congregational involvement with advocacy
organizations, 16 percent of these clergy indicated that their congregations
were involved with the NAACP, which was twice the frequency of any
other organization.[46] Also, when asked in an open-ended question about
the most important issue facing their community, 11 percent of BCAP
survey respondents indicated they believed racial justice to be the most
important issue.[47] While the policy concerns of African Americans, and of
African American churchgoers, do not center exclusively on race-related
civil rights, that category of issues continues to represent a significant
policy priority—even outside of the South.

Meanwhile, American feminism was gaining strength as a social
movement and a critical discourse, challenging gender roles and assumptions with unprecedented sweep. African American women, whose gender
empowerment had given way historically to male-brokered racial empowerment claims, were repositioning in light of 1960s and 1970s feminism
and 1980s black womanist scholarship. Black womanist writings directly
indicted the idea that black empowerment agendas carried forward from
the 1960s were necessarily inclusive of an empowerment agenda for black
women.[48] Advocacy and critical discourse on the empowerment of wom-
en, and concurrent advocacy and discourse on social tolerance and the
legal rights of non-heterosexuals, gained increasing traction within black
church contexts, challenging what black churches meant by civil rights
and the extent to which they could claim to champion such rights. Black
church alignments with civil rights ideals were also called into question on
matters related to discrimination against illegal immigrants and religious
minorities, especially in the wake of the September 11, 2001 attacks. The
expansion of civil rights activism beyond concerns with racial exclusion,
and tensions and debates over how black churches have or should position
around these matters, are central foci of the present volume.

Structure of the Volume

Each section of the book explores ways the struggle for civil rights was
broadened and functioned conceptually to mobilize black church activism

as it moved geographically and chronologically beyond the Jim Crow South. The first section examines mid-twentieth century civil rights activism in northern and western cities, where black grievances were expressed and heard within contexts somewhat less singularly absorbed with race matters than in the South. Chapters in this section outline challenges black clergy and lay leaders had in adapting civil rights activism to local arenas of struggle in Chicago, New Haven, Philadelphia, New York, and the Bay Area. Several of these chapters emphasize black church concerns over what they perceived to be ideological or methodological radicalism by activist leaders who advocated black power, economic development, socialism, disruptive protest, female leadership, and close collaborations with government.

The second and third sections of the volume explore black clergy responses to various public policy concerns within the post-Civil Rights Movement context that extend and broaden conceptions of civil rights prevailing within the Movement. The four chapters within section two explore expectations about the extension and enforcement of rights within a post-movement context marked by expanded black and minority claims on government capital. As these chapters point out, those expectations of government, and of a continuous and systematic pursuit of rights by black churches, have produced achievements along with many frustrations. This mixed assessment comes through clearly in the chapters on educational fairness, on voting rights, and on health reform, while the chapter on religious groups' hiring rights points to tensions in some instances between conceptions of social rights and conceptions of religious freedom.

That "civil rights" is not a completely uncontested idea, even in the wake of the Civil Rights Movement, is at the heart of the analysis in chapters within the final section of the volume. The chapter on black church burnings, for example, draws attention to continued racist assaults on civil rights symbolism in the form of black church buildings. Most of the chapters in this section though document black church reluctance and sometimes refusal to embrace civil rights causes which they view to be at cross-purposes with their religious convictions or with African Americans' historic race-centered civil rights agenda. Examples of this covered within the chapters include immigrant rights, gay rights, rights of religious minority groups, and concern for persons with HIV/AIDS.

Chapters throughout this volume show that there are critical social justice issues within the post-Movement context where the potential or, at least, the need, exists for persons of all racial groups, faith traditions, and political perspectives to find common cause. Although the discussions here will make evident that there is yet distance to travel toward the goal of commonly applied inalienable rights, a supposition and hope underlying this volume is that pointing out persistent social justice needs and potential for responsiveness increases prospects for realizing our common cause.

Notes

1. Some scholars have certainly argued effectively against too close an association between black churches and civil rights activism, e.g., Gary Marx, *Protest and Prejudice: A Study of Belief in the Black Community* (Harper Torchbook, 1967); and Adolph L. Reed, Jr., *The Jesse Jackson Phenomenon: The Crisis of Purpose in Afro-American Politics* (New Haven: Yale University Press, 1986).

2. For this critique, see Jeanne Theoharis, "Introduction," in Jeanne Theoharis and Komozi Woodard (eds.), *Freedom North: Black Freedom Struggles Outside the South, 1940–1980* (New York: Palgrave Macmillan, 2003).

3. Vincent Harding, *There is a River: The Black Struggle for Freedom in America,* (New York: Vintage Books, 1981), 87.

4. Angela Dillard, *Faith in the City: Preaching and Radical Social Change in Detroit,* Ann Arbor: University of Michigan Press, 2007; Martha Biondi, *To Stand and Fight: The Struggle for Civil Rights in Postwar New York City* (Cambridge: Harvard University Press, 2006); Randal Jelks, *African Americans in the Furniture City: The Struggle for Civil Rights in Grand Rapids* (Urbana: University of Illinois Press, 2006); Thomas Sugrue, *The Origins of the Urban Crisis: Race and Inequality in Postwar Detroit;* (Princeton: Princeton University Press, 2005); Matthew Countryman, *Up South: Civil Rights and Black Power in Philadelphia* (Philadelphia: University of Pennsylvania Press, 2005; Douglas Flamming, *Bound for Freedom: Black Los Angeles in Jim Crow America,* Berkeley: University of California Press, 2005; Jeanne Theoharris and Komozi Woodard (eds.), *Groundwork: Local Black Freedom Movements in America* (New York: NYU Press, 2005); Richard Pierce, *Polite Protest: The Political Economy of Race in Indianapolis, 1920–1970,* Bloomington: Indiana University Press, 2005; Theoharis and Woodard (eds.), *Freedom North,* op cit.; Gretchen C. Eick, *Dissent in Wichita: The Civil Rights Movement in the Midwest, 1954–72* (Urbana: University of Illinois Press, 2001); Quintard Taylor, *The Forging of a Black Community: Seattle's Central District, from 1870 Through the Civil Rights Era* (University of Washington Press, 1994); James R. Ralph, Jr., *Northern Protest: Martin Luther King, Jr., Chicago, and the Civil Rights Movement* (Cambridge: Harvard University Press, 1993).

5. Important studies of civil rights activism by black churches in the North and West include, Dillard, 2007; Jelks, 2006; Eick, 2001; and Ralph, 1993.

6. This point is effectively argued by Milton Sernett, *Bound for the Promised Land: African American Religion and the Great Migration,* Durham: Duke University Press, 1997, especially pp. 3–4

7. Some have argued, for example, that the Movement dates from the black union strikes, or other forms of protest, during the interwar years (e.g., Beth Tompkins Bates, *Pullman Porters and the Rise of Protest Politics in Black America,*

1929–1945, (Chapel Hill, UNC Press, 2001); Jeanne Theoharis, "Introduction" in, *Freedom North* (New York: Palgrave MacMillan, 2003) edited by Jeanne Theoharis and Komozi Woodard), while others have argued that the black freedom struggle needs to be viewed along a longer continuum, dating from abolitionism and culminating in mid-twentieth century mass protest activities (Vincent Harding, *There is a River: The Black Struggle for Freedom in America* (Harvest/HBJ Books, 1993). It has also been argued that the Movement did not effectively end until the 1968 assassination of Martin Luther King, Jr. or that it has not ended at all and continues through the present.

     8. Sernett, 1997: 4.

     9. Benjamin E. Mays and Joseph W. Nicholson, *The Negro's Church* (New York: Institute of Social and Religious Research, 1933), 230, 249.

     10. W. E. B. Du Bois, *The Philadelphia Negro: A Social Study*, (Philadelphia: Published for the university, 1899), 207.

     11. Mays and Nicholson, 119.

     12. Du Bois, 220.

     13. Mays and Nicholson, 227.

     14. Du Bois, 1899; Mays and Nicholson, 1933; Sernett, 1997.

     15. Adam C. Powell, Sr. was pastor of Abyssinian Baptist Church in Harlem from 1908 to1936 during which time the congregation became one of the largest black churches in the country. Adam C. Powell, Jr. succeeded his father as pastor of Abyssinian and represented Harlem in the U.S. House of Representatives from 1945 to1970.

     16. Archibald Carey, Sr. was an A.M.E. Bishop who held several appointive positions within Chicago politics. Archibald Carey, Jr. served as pastor of Quinn Chapel A.M.E. Church in downtown Chicago from 1949 to 1967, served as a Chicago alderman from 1947 to 1955, an alternate U.S. delegate to the U.N. from 1953 to 1956, and a circuit court judge from 1966 to 1978. See Dennis C. Dickerson, *African American Preachers and Politics: The Careys of Chicago* (Jackson: University of Mississippi Press, 2010).

     17. Rev. Marshall Lorenzo Shepard Sr., pastor for forty years of Mt. Olivet Tabernacle Baptist Church, was a three-term state representative, city councilman, and recorder of deeds.

     18. Rev. Wade H. McKinney, who was pastor of Antioch Baptist Church from 1928 to 1963, headed multiple clergy associations, helped organize several important civic groups, and served on the mayor's committee. See Mittie O. Chandler, "Black Clergy Electoral Involvement in Cleveland," in R. Drew Smith and Fredrick C. Harris (eds.), *Black Clergy and Local Politics: Clergy Influence, Organizational Partnerships, and Civic Empowermen*, (Lanham, MD: Rowman & Littlefield Publishers, 2005), 137–38.

     19. Especially the nationally connected Rev. H. D. Prowd (pastor from 1915–1920) and Rev. Chester Anderson, who twice served as the Moderator of the Western Baptist Association. See, Flamming, 2005: 111–12.

     20. Philip Foner, "Reverend George Washington Woodbey: Early Twentieth Century California Black Socialist," *Journal of Negro History*, 61/2, April 1976.

21. Angela Dillard, "Religion and Radicalism: The Reverend Albert B. Cleage, Jr. and the Rise of Black Christian Nationalism in Detroit," in Theoharis and Woodard, 158, 160

22. C. Eric Lincoln and Lawrence Mamiya, *The Black Church in the African American Experience* (Durham: Duke University Press, 1990).

23. Dr. T. M. Chambers, Los Angeles; Dr. Gardner C. Taylor, Brooklyn; Dr. Earl L. Harrison, Washington, DC; Dr. L. Venchael Booth, Cincinnati; Dr. Thomas Kilgore, Jr. Los Angeles; Dr. William A. Jones, Brooklyn; Dr. Charles W. Butler, Detroit; Dr. Marshall L. Shepard, Philadelphia; Dr. J Alfred Smith, Oakland; Dr. Charles Adams, Detroit; Dr. Bennett W. Smith, Buffalo; and Dr. Major L. Jemison, Oklahoma City.

24. Scholars refer to this as "political efficacy." See, for example, Elizabeth Ananat and Ebonya Washington, *Segregation and Black Political Efficacy,* Cambridge, MA: National Bureau of Economic Research, 2007; and Lawrence Bobo and Franklin Gilliam, Jr., "Race, Sociopolitical Participation, and Black Empowerment," *American Political Science Review,* 84/2, June 1990.

25. National Urban League, *The National Urban League: 100 Years of Empowering Communities,* 2010, 8.

26. New York (1910), Richmond, VA (1913), Detroit (1916), Chicago (1916), Brooklyn (1916), Cleveland (1917), Newark (1917), St. Louis (1918), Englewood, NJ (1918), Columbus, OH (1918), Pittsburgh (1918), Westchester County, NY (1918), Boston (1919), Milwaukee (1919), Springfield, MA (1919), Kansas City, MO (1920), Atlanta (1920), Fort Wayne (1920), Los Angeles (1921), Louisville (1921), Canton, OH (1921), Tampa (1922), St. Paul (1922), Baltimore (1924), Akron (1925), Minneapolis (1925), Springfield, IL (1926), Buffalo (1927), Omaha (1928), Toledo (1928), Seattle (1930), Warren, OH (1930), Massillon, OH (1936), Little Rock (1937), New Orleans (1938), Washington, DC (1938), Providence (1939), Anderson (1940), Cincinnati (1940), Memphis (1943), Flint (1943), Grand Rapids (1943), Miami (1943), Elizabeth (1944), Morris County, NJ (1944), Phoenix (1944), Gary (1945), Portland, OR (1945), Oklahoma City (1946), San Francisco (1946), Denver (1946), Jacksonville (1947), Dayton (1947), Winston Salem (1948), Muskegon (1949), Pontiac (1950). See National Urban League, op cit.

27. See Gilbert Jonas, *Freedom's Sword: The NAACP and the Struggle Against Racism in America, 1909–1969* (London: Routledge, 2004), 21–22.

28. NAACP membership in the South was reported to be 128,716 in 1955, declining to 79,677 in 1957 (http://nedv.net/community/blackhx/stanford-mlk-chronolgy.html).

29. CORE, "The History of CORE," (http://www.core-online.org/History/history.htm).

30. Mosque No. 1 (Detroit), Mosque No. 2 (Chicago), Mosque No. 3 (Milwaukee), Mosque No. 4 (Washington, D.C.), Mosque No. 5 (Cincinnati), Mosque No. 6 (Baltimore), Mosque No. 7 (New York), Mosque No. 8 (San Diego), Mosque No. 9 (Youngstown), Mosque No. 11 (Boston), Mosque No. 12 (Philadelphia), Mosque No. 13 (Springfield, MA), Mosque No. 14 (Hartford), and Mosque No. 15 (Atlanta).

31. Oscar DePriest (R-IL), 1929–1935; Arthur Mitchell (D-IL), 1935–1943; William Dawson (D-IL), 1943–1970; Adam C. Powell, Jr. (D-NY), 1945–1970; Charles Diggs (D-MI), 1955–1980; Robert Nix, Sr. (D-PA), 1958–1979; Augustus Hawkins (D-CA), 1963–1991; John Conyers (D-MI), 1965–present.

32. Harold Cruse, *Plural But Equal: Blacks and Minorities in America's Plural Society* (William & Morrow, 1988); Peter Paris, *The Social Teachings of Black Churches* (Philadelphia: Fortress Press, 1985); and Manning Marable, *How Capitalism Underdeveloped Black America* (Boston: South End Press, 1983), 228–29.

33. Ibid, 242–43.

34. "Adam Clayton Powell," a documentary directed by Richard Kilberg, (1989).

35. On mythological aspects of black nationalist teachings, see Herbert Berg, "Mythmaking in the African American Muslim Context: The Moorish Science Temple, the Nation of Islam, and the American Society of Muslims" *Journal of the American Academy of Religion,* 73/3, September 2005; R. Drew Smith, "Black Religious Nationalism and the Politics of Transcendence," *American Academy of Religion,* 66/3, 1998: 533–547; and E. U. Essien-Udom, *Black Nationalism: A Search for Identity in America* (Chicago: University of Chicago Press, 1962).

36. See, for example, Theoharis op. cit., 2003; Dillard, op. cit., 2003; and Adolph Reed, Jr., *The Jesse Jackson Phenomenon: The Crisis of Purpose in Afro-American Politics* (New Haven: Yale University Press, 1986).

37. *Statistical Abstract of the United States,* 1990, p. 260; *Statistical Abstract of the United States,* 1992, p. 267.

38. "Taking Over City Hall," *Black Enterprise Magazine,* June 1983: 155–160.

39. Ronald Walters, *Black Presidential Politics in America: A Strategic Approach* (Albany: State University of New York Press, 1988), 143.

40. Walters, 142–150.

41. A 2005 study by Hartford Seminary places the number of African American megachurch pastors at roughly 100, and a 2011 study by Tamelyn Tucker-Worgs places the number at 149. See Tamelyn Tucker-Worgs, *The Black Mega-Church: Theology, Gender, and the Politics of Public Engagement* (Waco: Baylor University Press, 2011).

42. Tucker-Worgs, op. cit.

43. Cruse, 385.

44. Key pieces of civil rights legislation include: the Civil Rights Acts of 1957, 1962, 1964, 1968, and 1991; the Civil Rights Restoration Act of 1988; and the Voting Rights Acts of 1965, 1975, and 1982.

45. Associated Press/Ipsos poll was conducted by Ipsos-Public Affairs. Jan. 9–12, 2006. N = 1,242 adults nationwide (margin of error ± 3), including, with an oversample, 312 blacks (MoE ± 5.5).

46. The BCAP Survey was conducted by Morehouse College's Public Influences of African American Churches Project, 1999–2000. N = 1,956. For further details about the BCAP survey and these specific variables, see R. Drew Smith, "Assessing the Public Policy Practices of African American Churches," in *Long March Ahead: African American Churches and Public Policy in the Post-Civil Rights Era* edited by R. Drew Smith (Durham: Duke University Press, 2004), 12–13.

47. R. Drew Smith (editor), *New Day Begun: African American Churches and Civic Culture in Post-Civil Rights America* (Durham: Duke University Press, 2003).

48. See Alice Walker, *In Search of Our Mother's Gardens* (San Diego: Harcourt Brace Jovanovich, 1983); and Jacquelyn Grant, *White Women's Christ and Black Women's Jesus: Feminist Christology and Womanist Response* (Atlanta: Scholar's Press, 1989).

MID-TWENTIETH CENTURY CHURCH ACTIVISM BEYOND THE SOUTH

1

Black Church Divisions and Civil Rights Activism in Chicago

James R. Ralph, Jr.

In the mid-1940s, Richard Wright wrote, "no other community in America [has] been so intensely studied, [nor] has had brought to bear upon it so blinding a scrutiny as" black Chicago.[1] Since then, scholarly interest in black Chicago has not slackened. Yet surprisingly, the role of African American churches in civil rights activism in the Midwest metropolis has never been comprehensively addressed.[2]

The dynamics of power relations in the city of Chicago in the second half of the twentieth century have defined the shape of African American protest in the city and the complex relationship of black churches to that activism. The structure of politics in the city has generally served to compromise the independence of black churches, one of the community's most important institutions, and shape its participation in public life.[3] Historically, the influence of activist, progressive clergy, though notable at times, has been, on the whole, limited. Nevertheless, the story of black churches and the struggle for racial equality in Chicago is as significant and revealing as anywhere in the country.

While scholars have recently cautioned against viewing the black church within a protest/accommodationist framework, black churches, black congregations, and black clergy were not unified in response to civil rights activism. That was especially true in Chicago.[4]

By 1940, black Chicago had become a black metropolis, the home to more than a quarter of a million black people, most of whom lived on the South Side. In 1900 the city's black population had barely topped 30,000.[5] On the eve of World War II, black Chicago was a city of churches, numbering roughly 500. There were a few large churches with congregations over 2,000 members, but there were many more of the "storefront" variety. While most of the churches were affiliated with the two major Baptist conventions, there was a wide range of faith communities. These churches also reflected class divisions within the city, but the Great Migration had infused a southern sensibility in virtually every congregation.[6]

Spatial segregation was a fact of life for black Chicagoans in the middle of the twentieth century. Yet, unlike most black southerners, black Chicagoans had access to the ballot. They were increasingly playing an important role in their city's political life. By the early 1940s, the majority of black voters had swung into the Democratic camp, and they now regularly elected an African American to Congress and blacks to the City Council, including for a time Archibald Carey, Jr., the pastor of the Woodlawn A.M.E. Church and later of the Quinn Chapel A.M.E. Church. The most influential politician was William Dawson who was the head of a powerful black political machine and served as a United States Congressman.[7] The political trends were toward greater inclusion. Democratic Mayor Edward Kelly had embraced the coalition-building of New Deal urban liberalism, and African Americans were part of his coalition. Black politicians, led by Dawson, focused on securing material advantages and extending opportunities for their constituencies.[8]

Racial discrimination remained potent in Chicago, however, and some black Chicagoans aggressively attacked the color line. In the 1930s, the National Labor Relations League, the Council of Negro Organizations, and the Chicago chapter of the National Negro Congress sponsored picketing, boycotts, and other strategies to confront discriminatory employers and rapacious landlords. The Congress of Racial Equality (CORE) began on the city's South Side in 1942. Inspired by Gandhian tactics and by A. Philip Randolph's March on Washington Movement, a small group of black and white Chicagoans pressured restaurants and recreational centers that refused to admit and serve blacks. Later in the decade, the United Packinghouse Workers, whose members included large numbers of African Americans who toiled in the stockyards, pressed for equal service in restaurants and stores on the South Side.[9]

Black churches and black clergy were not, however, in the forefront of these protests.[10] Assertive activist clergy like J. C. Austin of the Pilgrim Baptist Church, one of the largest in the country, were rare. In the 1930s, Austin delivered sermons with pointed social messages, opened his church to National Association for the Advancement of Colored People (NAACP) activists, and supported protest initiatives. But the vast majority of black clergy in the city did not aggressively pursue social justice. They did not want to jeopardize potential resources that came from the dominant political establishment, and many did not link religious concerns with civic activism.[11]

In 1947, Mayor Kelly was displaced as the head of the local Demo-cratic Party in part because of his liberal views on race and public policy. For the next few decades, Chicago politics tended to reinforce, if not accentuate, racial divisions in the city. In 1954, William Dawson used his clout to keep businessman Martin Kennelly from gaining a third term as mayor. Dawson felt that Kennelly lacked respect for African American interests. Kennelly's successor as mayor, Richard J. Daley, then consolidated political control over Democrats across the city, including Dawson's political fiefdom. Daley saw no need to take special steps to aid black Chicagoans and did not want controversial racial issues to upset his city.[12]

Black Chicagoans continued to go beyond established political chan-nels to confront blatant racial injustice. When in the mid-1950s, city authorities failed to protect an African American family assigned to an all-white public housing project, the Trumbull Park Homes, on the city's far South Side from assaults by whites, thousands of African Americans marched on City Hall demanding action. The African American popula-tion mobilized too in the face of southern barbarity. The 1955 funeral of Emmett Till, a fourteen-year-old Chicagoan who was murdered while visiting relatives in Mississippi, was a defining episode in the black com-munity's collective consciousness. Over 50,000 persons passed by his open casket in Roberts Temple Church of God on the South Side.[13]

These were episodic protests, however, and they did not represent a sustained local movement. Most Chicagoans, including most black clergy, viewed direct action suspiciously, especially in the intense anticommunist environment of the early 1950s. Later in the decade, the Chicago branch of the NAACP, the most important civil rights organization in the city, was essentially defanged. In 1957, the critics of labor activist Willough-by Abner, who had reenergized the local NAACP, ousted him from the presidency. More generally, most blacks (and whites) believed that racial progress would evolve organically over time. "[F]ull-time fighting against discrimination and segregation" was, St. Clair Drake and Horace Cayton wrote in 1961, "considered a specialist activity—the job for Race Leaders and Race Heroes . . ." rather than the mission of a mass movement.[14]

It was disaffected parents and their children on the far South Side of Chicago's Black Belt who in the early 1960s ignited a local civil rights movement. Distressed by the unequal and segregated public schools, they demanded change. They first turned to legal action and then direct action. One of those parents was James Webb, the pastor of the Bethlehem Pres-byterian Church, the central plaintiff in a legal suit against discriminatory school practices. Webb also rallied a group of ministers to support the citizen protests.[15]

Aggrieved residents turned to direct action in other parts of black Chicago, especially Woodlawn on the South Side. Starting in 1960, the famed community organizer Saul Alinsky and his field staff worked with local residents and community groups and churches to develop The Woodlawn Organization, TWO. Members of TWO formed "truth squads" and turned to boycotts to pressure school officials. The president of TWO for much of its early history was the Reverend Arthur M. Brazier, pastor of the fast-growing Apostolic Church of God.[16]

Nevertheless, black churches played only a modest role in the ignition of the Chicago civil rights movement as was evident in the formation in 1962 of the Coordinating Council of Community Organizations (CCCO), which became the central engine behind local civil rights activism during the 1960s. Its founding organizations were the Chicago Urban League, the Chicago NAACP, TWO, and the Chatham Avalon Park Community Council. Ministers and religiously minded people were a part of this umbrella organization, but the institutional black church was not formally represented. In 1963, more religiously inspired groups joined the CCCO—including the Presbyterian Interracial Council, the Interracial Council of Methodists, the Episcopal Society for Cultural and Racial Unity, and the Catholic Interracial Council—but they tended to be interracial organizations affiliated with predominately white faith communities.[17]

The leadership of the CCCO reflected its secular tilt. While the Reverend Brazier served as convenor for a few months in 1963, his predecessor, Charles Davis, the executive secretary of the local NAACP, was a public relations executive and his successor, Al Raby, was a public school teacher.[18] The CCCO's most controversial protests—two massive school boycotts in October 1963 and February 1964—ultimately divided the black clergy. Some black clergy publicly identified with the goals of these protests, and a number of churches like J. C. Austin's Pilgrim Baptist Church opened their doors for Freedom Schools during the boycotts.[19]

But not a few black ministers doubted the wisdom of school boycotts. In February 1964, for instance, 800 persons, including Claude Holman, an African American alderman loyal to the Daley political machine, attended an antiboycott rally at the Bethesda Baptist Church. At the same time, the Reverend Joseph H. Jackson of the famed Olivet Baptist Church denounced the protest. "It is not," he said, "in the best interests of the children and the community to conduct this boycott."[20]

The CCCO targeted the policies of Superintendent of Schools Benjamin Willis, yet it did not monopolize civil rights activity in the city. In 1962, the synergetic linkage between the burgeoning southern civil rights movement and Chicago activism was illustrated when a number of local African American ministers—including W. L. Lambert of the Greater Mount Hope Baptist Church, Stroy Freeman of the New Friendship Baptist Church, and John R. Porter of Christ Methodist Church—joined a broader Chicago delegation, many of whom were affiliated with the Catholic Interracial Council, that traveled to Albany, Georgia, to support Martin Luther King, Jr., the Southern Christian Leadership Conference (SCLC), and the civil rights campaign there.[21] The following year, Freeman and Lambert led a group of black ministers who initiated selective buying campaigns to boost black employment in white-owned firms. The Clergy Alliance of Chicago was, however, short-lived.[22]

As Chicago's school leaders fended off policy reforms, the CCCO reached out in 1965 to African American clergy in the hope of enhancing its power. The Reverend S. S. Morris, pastor of the Coppin Memorial A.M.E. Church (and a past president of the Chicago branch of the NAACP) organized Clergy for Quality and Equality in Education to bring to bear ministerial power against segregationist school policies. This new group took to the streets to picket and march on City Hall during Lent in March 1965. They were clearly energized by the outpouring of clerical witnesses in the wake of Martin Luther King's and the SCLC's campaign for the vote in Alabama.[23]

Overall, however, the involvement and impact of African American clergy was limited in the Chicago civil rights insurgency. The CCCO remained the central force in the Chicago civil rights movement, and it escalated its tactics in order to force city authorities to address the schools question. Starting in June 1965, the CCCO sponsored marches against segregationist school policies through the Loop or downtown Chicago. These marches initially attracted hundreds of participants, including white and black clergy and actively religious people. Al Raby and the comedian Dick Gregory were generally at the head of these marches, but John Porter, the pastor of a movement church in Englewood, occasionally led them.[24]

However, even this escalation did not budge local school officials, and the CCCO began to court the intervention of Martin Luther King and the SCLC. King and the SCLC toured Chicago for three days in late July 1965 as part of their "People to People" tour. King wanted to build a "coalition of conscience," and he sought out the support of clergy. Fittingly, his first appearance was before a large group of ministers. He then spoke at neighborhood rallies on the city's South and West Sides (a number of which were coordinated by black ministers) and presided at Sunday services at the Quinn Chapel A.M.E. Church, home of the oldest African American congregation in the city.[25]

The CCCO leadership relished the energy that King generated. It now wanted King and SCLC to come to Chicago and help lead a campaign against northern racial injustice. In late summer 1965, one of King's lieutenants, James Bevel, accepted a position with the West Side Christian Parish, an inner-city outreach ministry with a predominately white staff on Chicago's West Side. That September, the CCCO and SCLC announced their partnership in what would become known as the Chicago Freedom Movement.[26]

The Chicago Freedom Movement threatened the status quo in the city, and powerful African Americans rose to try to deflect Martin Luther King and his team from working on their home turf. "This is no hick town," declared Ralph Metcalfe, a former Olympic sprinter and now a South Side alderman. "We have a lot of intellect and can take care of these situations ourselves." Metcalfe joined with Bishop Louis Henry Ford of the Church of God in Christ, a renowned African American minister, to form their own civil rights organization, the Chicago Conference to Fulfill These Rights.[27]

The Chicago Freedom Movement was also the target of criticism from the Nation of Islam, which was headquartered in Chicago. The long-time head of the Nation of Islam, Elijah Muhammad, met with Martin Luther King in the winter of 1966, but that meeting did not lead to active participation by the Black Muslims. Not long after their meeting, Muhammad told his followers, who were not especially numerous, "King does not understand the Negro problem. The white people want to buy King. He loves the white folks and the white people know it."[28]

The main site of the SCLC organizing initiative took place on the city's growing West Side ghetto. Here James Bevel reunited with his friend and fellow activist Bernard LaFayette, who had studied with Bevel at the American Baptist Seminary in Nashville and who had been tapped by the American Friends Service Committee to introduce southern strategies of social change to the northern ghetto. Bevel believed that African Americans on the West Side would be more receptive to the new initiative. It was the less established area of African American settlement and the port of entry for many recent southern migrants. The West Side, Bevel stated, was "very much Mississippi in terms of the ethos of black people—church and life."[29] But Bevel and his fellow activists did not find many West Side ministers who were willing to welcome them to use their churches as sites for grassroots organizing. It was telling that the headquarters of their operations was the Warren Avenue Congregational Church in East Garfield Park, which had a small congregation and a white minister, William Briggs.[30]

As Bevel and Chicago Freedom Movement activists tried to build unions to end slums on the West Side in late 1965 and during the first half of 1966, Martin Luther King asked Jesse Jackson to develop a Chicago chapter of Operation Breadbasket. King knew the importance of the support of the black church for the Chicago Freedom Movement, but he also recognized, given the nature of the politics of the city, that few black ministers were likely to throw themselves into a campaign destined to launch protests against racial injustice. A divinity student at the Chicago Theological Seminary, Jackson had been a student leader in protests in Greensboro, North Carolina, in the early 1960s, and had headed south in 1965 to assist with the Selma campaign.[31]

Starting in the fall of 1965, Jackson worked closely with the Reverend Clay Evans of the Fellowship Baptist Church to cultivate support for the Chicago Freedom Movement among African American clergy. King himself appealed to black ministers to back the Chicago initiative and met with a core group, including Lambert, Porter, and the Reverend Frank Sims of the Ebenezer Baptist Church, to consider how to institutionalize clergy support. Shortly thereafter, roughly forty ministers, most of whom were black, began to work to expand employment opportunities for African Americans, thus marking the emergence of Chicago's Operation Breadbasket.[32]

Under Jesse Jackson's direction, Operation Breadbasket scored victories in its selective buying campaigns against dairies and then soft-drink bottlers in the summer of 1966. Later in the year, it took on supermarket chains that marketed their wares to blacks but failed to employ many. It lived up to its motto, "Your Ministers Fight for Jobs and Rights."[33] Although the successes of Operation Breadbasket were substantial, they did not represent the main thrust of the Chicago Freedom Movement. In light of mounting frustrations among African Americans and the upsurge of Black Power rhetoric, King and the Chicago Freedom Movement leadership needed to prove that nonviolent direct action could bring about social change outside of the South. During the summer of 1966, the Chicago Freedom Movement launched a campaign to end housing discrimination in metropolitan Chicago.

The turn to direct action and then in early July the rioting in the city's West Side ghetto exposed more dramatically than ever the deep divisions among African American clergy over the Chicago Freedom Movement. While a few black ministers publicly identified with the open-housing campaign, the Reverend Joseph H. Jackson, the powerful president of the National Baptist Convention (and no relation to Jesse Jackson), openly questioned its value. The legendary pastor of the large Olivet Baptist Church on the city's South Side had clashed with King before over the proper approach in achieving social change. Jackson had even kept black Baptists in Chicago from participating in the historic Conference on Religion and Race held in his home city in January 1963. But now that King had set up operations in his city, Jackson intensified his critique of King's methods. "There is a danger," he said at the time of the West Side uprisings, "of using nonviolence in such a way that it will create violence."[34]

Black ministers did not control the thoughts and actions of their congregations, but it is significant that two ministers who welcomed the Chicago Freedom Movement to use their churches as action centers on the South Side during the open-housing campaign—Stroy Freeman and W. L. Lambert—were affiliated with the Progressive National Baptist Convention, which had formed in response to the conservative leanings of the Reverend Joseph H. Jackson and the National Baptist Convention. Freeman and Lambert both had deep histories of social activism. A graduate of Morehouse College, Freeman was the long-time pastor of the New Friendship Baptist Church, a big edifice in Englewood. This close identification with the Chicago Freedom Movement led, however, to threats against Freeman's family and congregation, and in early August 1966, the South Side Action Center was moved to Lambert's church, the Greater Mount Hope Baptist Church.[35]

For more than a month, these two churches, the staging grounds for open-housing marches, were the sites of vibrant mass meetings. These meetings closely resembled the rousing gatherings that helped defined the modern civil rights movement in the South. They generated a spiritual fervor that fortified the foot soldiers of the open-housing marches, many of whom viewed themselves as part of a larger moral undertaking. Women were particularly well represented at these meetings.[36]

Chicago Freedom Movement activists had even more difficulty finding action centers on the West Side and ultimately relied on the Warren Avenue Congregational Church. The reluctance of black clergy to support the Chicago Freedom Movement did not just reflect the ideological differences that the Reverend Joseph. H. Jackson articulated, but also the hard-ball politics of the Daley regime. The Reverend Clay Evans directly felt the cost of supporting the Chicago Freedom Movement. In 1965, he discovered that he could no longer secure financing to continue the construction of a new church for his congregation because of his activism.[37]

The Reverend A. P. Jackson, pastor of the Liberty Baptist Church on the South Side, a church which did open its doors to Martin Luther King and the Chicago Freedom Movement, knew what determined the allegiances of many black ministers in Chicago during the regime of Mayor Richard J. Daley. Daley, Jackson noted, "had a large number of ministers at City Hall eating from the king's table. You don't talk against the king when you are eating at his table." And so "when Dr. King came to Chicago," Jackson continued, "these ministers were afraid of inviting Dr. King to their churches because they were afraid they would alienate the feelings of Mayor Daley. . . ."[38]

In late August 1966, the Chicago Freedom Movement's open-housing campaign came to a conclusion. Its marches against housing discrimination brought the city's political, civic, religious, and business leaders to the negotiating table and produced a "Summit Agreement." While Martin Luther King and Al Raby hailed the agreement as a clear victory, some activists insisted it was a "sell out." In early September, a large group of disaffected activists followed through on the Chicago Freedom Movement's unfulfilled declaration that it would march on Cicero, a bastion of white supremacy that bordered the city of Chicago. There was little formal involvement by Chicago's black clergy in this march.[39]

While in retrospect, the "Summit Agreement" is rightly viewed as the climax of the Chicago Freedom Movement, at the time King and Raby believed that it marked the end of an important phase of their initiative. In September and October 1966, Chicago activists focused their attention on urban renewal plans in Englewood. The Reverend John Porter's church served as the meeting place for these efforts. It was clear, however, that disillusionment and recriminations over the "Summit Agreement" had sapped the strength of the Chicago Freedom Movement. King had other commitments, and by the late spring of 1967, most of the SCLC's staff had left Chicago. The CCCO, weakened as well, dissolved within six months.[40]

Jesse Jackson's Operation Breadbasket was the most significant product of the organizing efforts of the Chicago Freedom Movement.[41] It built on its earlier successes and expanded its programs. It sought black economic development and focused on expanding opportunities for black-owned businesses and black-owned banks and savings-and-loan associations. Ultimately, in 1969 Operation Breadbasket would host a "Black-Minorities and Business and Cultural Exposition," or a "Black Expo," to boost awareness of African American business initiatives.[42]

The emergence of Operation Breadbasket as the center of social activism in Chicago flowed, according to one of its early organizers, from a conscious effort to stress its church-like features. By 1968, Operation Breadbasket's Saturday morning meetings had come to resemble a church service. There was music from the Breadbasket Choir and passionate sermons from Jesse Jackson. The ministerial backgrounds of Breadbasket's leaders—Calvin Morris, George "Ed" Riddick, Willie Barrow, and, of course, Jesse Jackson—were emphasized.[43]

In the aftermath of the assassination of Martin Luther King in April 1968 and the cataclysmic inner-city disorders, Jackson drew national attention for his many initiatives. In 1969, he was, along with the Reverend C. T. Vivian, a veteran civil rights activist, a leading force in the Coalition for United Community Action that helped shut down construction sites in Chicago to protest the lack of black construction workers. That same year, he led a campaign against hunger in Illinois that was an extension of the Poor People's Campaign. And increasingly, Jackson became involved in national politics.[44]

The proliferation of Operation Breadbasket's activities raised Jackson's profile, but they also stretched the organization's resources to the breaking point. Jackson found himself at odds with the leadership of the SCLC. In late 1971, he broke with the SCLC and his Chicago organization was rechristened Operation PUSH (People United to Serve Humanity). Operation PUSH continued to have a strong religious orientation, but it never represented the collective black church in Chicago. It was a successful vehicle for promoting Jesse Jackson and his work. It served as the foundation for Jackson's historic campaigns for the presidency in 1984 and 1988.[45]

In general, however, black churches in Chicago were essentially supportive of status quo, even after the death of Richard J. Daley in 1976. But in the early 1980s, African American activists saw a historic opportunity to elect a black mayor. The incumbent Jane Byrne was vulnerable politically, and the old Democratic machine was not nearly as strong as it once was.[46] The black population—and black churches—increasingly rejected the old exchange of modest benefits for political support of the white-led Cook County Democratic organization.

The story of the election of the city's first African American mayor, Harold Washington, is complex, but black clergy played a significant, if not decisive, role. Evidence that large numbers of black clergy were ready to support progressive politics came when Harold Washington, an African American Congressman who had come up the ranks in Chicago politics but who had broken from the machine, declared his candidacy for mayor. His campaign was more a movement than a traditional quest for office.[47] The Reverend John Porter tied Washington's campaign with earlier activism with a benediction at Washington's mayoral announcement in 1982: "Lord, we thank you, for the man, the moment and the movement have come together."[48] And after 150 black ministers endorsed Richard M. Daley, the late mayor's eldest son, the Reverend Jesse W. Cotton of the Greater Institutional African Methodist Church organized black ministers behind Washington. Over 200 signed a public "Washington for Mayor" statement which read, in part, "the black church which stands firmly in the tradition of Martin Luther King, Jr. (and not that splinter group that backs the 'Daley regime.' Who opposed Dr. King). . . ."[49] Among those signing the statement were the Reverends Porter, A. P. Jackson, Clay Evans, Al Sampson, pastor of the Fernwood United Methodist Church and an organizer for the SCLC during the Chicago Freedom Movement, and Jeremiah Wright, pastor of Trinity United Church of Christ, later the home church for many years of Barack Obama.[50]

To an extent, Washington's supporters among the black clergy were simply following the preferences of their congregations. African Americans turned out in record numbers to catapult Washington beyond Byrne and Daley to victory in the Democratic primary in February 1983. Two months later, Washington swept to victory in the general election, largely because of remarkable support from black voters.[51]

This was a dramatic time in black politics in the city and for many black clergy. Well-known African American ministers like Bishop Louis Ford openly acknowledged that their independence had been trimmed during the Daley years. Shortly after Washington's election, Ford declared, "From now on I'm a free man, a free pastor of a great church."[52] But this unconventional era did not last. Harold Washington died shortly after winning a second term, and Richard M. Daley gained control of the top spot in City Hall. The younger Daley ultimately surpassed his father as the longest serving mayor in Chicago's history. He did not govern in the same fashion as his father. Even if he had so desired he could not revive the old Daley machine with its thousands of foot soldiers indebted to it because of patronage jobs. But the younger Daley skillfully courted the black clergy, including those like Bishop Louis Ford and the Reverend Wilbur Daniel of the Antioch Missionary Baptist Church who had worked within the old political machine and some of the most activist ministers in the city such as the Reverends Arthur Brazier and Clay Evans.[53]

Chicago is, and has been for many decades, a capital of black America. It has launched innovative new civil rights groups like CORE, nurtured the strongest local civil rights movement in the North, featured the most notable northern campaign of Martin Luther King, and been the base for remarkable black politicians like Harold Washington, Jesse Jackson, and Barack Obama. The role of black church people and clergy in these developments has been central, though by no means unified.

Notes

1. St. Clair Drake and Horace C. Cayton, *Black Metropolis: A Study of Negro Life in a Northern City*, rev. and enlarged edition, vol. I (New York: Harcourt, Brace & World, 1970), ixx.

2. Wallace D. Best has recently explored the changing face of the black church in Chicago for the first half of the twentieth century. His important study does not, however, address in detail the protest activities of the church. Best, *Passionately Human, No Less Divine: Religion and Culture in Black Chicago, 1915–1952* (Princeton: Princeton University Press, 2005). Fredrick C. Harris has written a searching meditation on the black church and postwar Chicago politics. See Harris, "Black Churches and Machine Politics in Chicago," in R. Drew Smith

and Fredrick C. Harris, eds., *Black Church and Local Politics: Clergy Influence, Organizational Partnership, and Civic Empowerment* (NewYork: Rowman and Littlefield, 2005), 117–136.

3. Drake and Cayton, *Black Metropolis*, II, 412–429.

4. For a classic examination of the relationship of the black church to politics and civil rights militancy, see C. Eric Lincoln and Lawrence H. Mamiya, *The Black Church in the African American Experience* (Durham and London: Duke University Press, 1990), 196–235. For a cautionary assessment, see Curtis J. Evans, *The Burden of Black Religion* (New York: Oxford University Press, 2008), 275–280.

5. Drake and Cayton, *Black Metropolis*, I, 8.

6. Drake and Cayton, *Black Metropolis*, II, 412–429; Best, *Passionately Human*, 71–117; Milton C. Sernett, *Bound for the Promised Land: African American Religion and the Great Migration* (Durham: Duke University Press, 1997), 154–179.

7. Drake and Cayton, *Black Metropolis*, I, 350–360; William J. Grimshaw, *Bitter Fruit: Black Politics and the Chicago Machine, 1931–1991* (Chicago: The University of Chicago Press, 1992), 40–44, 65–67, 78–82. The black church does not figure in prominently in discussions of black politics in mid-twentieth-century Chicago. See, for example, Christopher Robert Reed, "A Study of Black Politics and Protest in Depression-Decade Chicago, 1930–1939," PhD dissertation, Kent State University, 1982. Harold F. Gosnell, *Negro Politicians: The Rise of Negro Politics* (Chicago: The University of Chicago Press, 1935) devotes only a few pages to the involvement of African American clergy in Chicago politics.

8. Drake and Cayton, *Black Metropolis*, I, 350–360; Arnold R. Hirsch, "The Cook County Democratic Organization and the Dilemma of Race, 1931–1987," in Richard M. Bernard, ed., *Snowbelt Cities: Metropolitan Politics in the Northeast and Midwest since World War II* (Bloomington: Indiana University Press, 1990), 63, 66–69; Grimshaw, *Bitter Fruit*, 56–57.

9. August Meier and Elliott Rudwick, "The Origins of Nonviolent Direct Action in Afro-American Protest: A Note on Historical Discontinuities" in *Along the Color Line: Explorations in the Black Experience* (Urbana: University of Illinois Press, 1976), 314–315, 327–328, 338–339; Rick Halpern, *Down on the Killing Floor: Black and White Workers in Chicago's Packinghouses, 1904–1954* (Urbana: University of Illinois Press, 1997), 240–241. For an overview of activism in the 1930s, see Drake and Cayton, *Black Metropolis*, II, 716–744; Reed, "A Study of Black Politics," 305–371, and Oliver Cromwell Cox, "The Origins of Direct Action Protest Among Negroes," unpublished manuscript, 1973. Beth Tompkins Bates describes the role of A. Philip Randolph and the Brotherhood of Sleeping Car Porters and "protest politics" in black Chicago in the 1920s, 1930s, and 1940s in *Pullman Porters and the Rise of Protest Politics in Black America, 1925–1945* (Chapel Hill: University of North Carolina Press, 2001), 63–105, 138–142, 167.

10. This was in keeping with the pattern elsewhere. See Meier and Rudwick, "Origins of Nonviolent Direct Action," 313–344, although Adam Clayton Powell, Jr., in New York City was a notable exception.

11. Harris, "Black Churches and Machine Politics in Chicago," 120–123. Randall K. Burkett highlights the ministry of Austin in order to counter the portrayal of the African American church between the two world wars as essentially on the sidelines in the fight for economic opportunity and civil rights. Burkett, "The Baptist Church in Years of Crisis: J. C. Austin and Pilgrim Baptist Church, 1926–1950," in Timothy E. Fulop and Albert J. Raboteau, eds., *African-American Religion: Interpretive Essays in History and Culture* (New York: Routledge, 1997), 311–340. Burkett seeks to counter the theme of the failure of the African American church to confront racial injustice developed by E. Franklin Frazier, *The Negro Church in America* (New York: Schoken Books, 1962). A. Philip Randolph also worked with a few black clergy such as Austin and William Cook of the People's Church and Metropolitan Community Center to advance his union movement. But Bates notes, "the majority of Chicago's black clergy either ignored the Brotherhood or actively opposed it." Bates, *Pullman Porters*, 75–76. In the 1940s, there were examples of African American clergy standing up for civil rights. See *Chicago Defender* (CD) (national ed.), November 1, 1947, 5. In 1943, Archibald Carey, Jr., hosted the first national conference of CORE at his church in Woodlawn.

12. Grimshaw, *Bitter Fruit*, 82–86, 97–110; Hirsch, "The Cook County Democratic Organization and the Dilemma of Race," 69–81; Adam Cohen and Elizabeth Taylor, *American Pharaoh: Mayor Richard J. Daley: His Battle for Chicago and the Nation* (Boston: Little, Brown and Company, 2000), 212–215.

13. Adam Green, *Selling the Race: Culture, Community, and Black Chicago, 1940–1955* (Chicago: The University of Chicago Press, 2007), 186–187, 201–202; Halpern, *Down on the Killing Floor*, 241.

14. Christopher Robert Reed, *The Chicago NAACP and the Rise of Black Professional Leadership, 1910–1966* (Bloomington: Indiana University Press, 1997), 184–187; Drake and Cayton, *Black Metropolis*, II, xxvi. See too James Q. Wilson's assessment of the black church in *Negro Politics: The Search for Leadership* (New York: The Free Press, 1960), 127–130.

15. James R. Ralph, Jr., *Northern Protest: Martin Luther King, Jr., Chicago, and the Civil Rights Movement* (Cambridge: Harvard University Press, 1993), 15–16; CD (daily ed.), January 17, 1962, 1, 3. It is important to distinguish, as Charles M. Payne points out, the difference between the institutional church and the religious spirit that shaped the motivation of protesters. Payne, *I've Got the Light of Freedom: The Organizing Tradition and the Mississippi Freedom Struggle* (Berkeley: University of California Press, 1995), 271–275.

16. Arthur M. Brazier, *Black Self-Determination* (Grand Rapids: William B. Eerdmans Publishing Company, 1969), 23–49; Dr. Sammie M. Dortch, *When God Calls: A Biography of Bishop Arthur M. Brazier* (Grand Rapids: William B. Eerdmans Publishing Company, 1996), 49–56; Ralph, *Northern Protest*, 17.

17. Alan B. Anderson and George W. Pickering, *Confronting the Color Line: The Broken Promise of the Civil Rights Movement*, (Athens: University of Georgia Press, 1986) 90, 106.

18. Anderson and Pickering, *Confronting the Color Line*, 121, 129. All three convenors were African American.

19. *CD* (city ed.), February 24, 1964, 4; February 25, 1964, 2. For a full listing of churches, see *CD* (city ed.), February 24, 1964, 2.

20. *CD* (city ed.), February, 25, 1964, 2; *Chicago Tribune* (*CT*), February 22, 1964, 2.

21. Stephen C. Rose, "Albany Georgia—A Report," *New City*, Oct. 1, 1962, 7–9; *CD* (daily ed.), August 29, 1962, 1. Porter, whose church was located in Englewood, was particularly active in the protests against Superintendent Willis and his policies. See *CD* (daily ed.), June 18, 1963, 8; August 15, 1963, A6.

22. *CD* (daily ed.), September 3, 1963, 4; October 1, 1963, 1.

23. Anderson and Pickering, *Confronting the Color Line*, 152; *CD* (daily ed.), March 15, 1965, 3. For more on the relationship of CCCO to black clergy, see George W. Pickering, "The Issue of the Color Line: Some Interpretative Considerations," vol. 2, PhD dissertation, University of Chicago, 1975, 621–622, 627–630, 633–634.

24. *CD* (daily ed.), June 22, 1965, 3; *CT*, June 17, 1965, D12; June 25, 1965, 18. Porter, in fact, had established the Englewood Christian Leadership Conference which was affiliated with the Southern Christian Leadership Conference. *CD* (national ed.), September 12, 1964, 5; Porter interview with author, August 12, 1986. Arrest records in these demonstrations reveal the scarcity of black clergy as participants. *CT*, November 2, 1965, A1. For a listing of Chicago churches in the mid-1960s, see Church Federation of Greater Chicago inventory, November 20, 1964, Church Federation of Greater Chicago Papers, Chicago History Museum (CHM).

25. Ralph, *Northern Protest*, 34–35; Anderson and Pickering, *Confronting the Color Line*, 161.

26. Ralph, *Northern Protest*, 40–41. Another important activist group was the West Side Federation, whose leaders included the Reverends Shelvin Hall and Arthur Griffin. Hall's Friendship Baptist Church was used for CCCO meetings. Griffin's Mozart Baptist Church was a site for organizing on the West Side. Pickering, "The Issue of the Color Line," vol. 2, 775; Ralph, *Northern Protest*, 137.

27. *CT*, September 8, 1965, B4; "By-Laws of Chicago Conference to Fulfill These Rights," pamphlet file, Municipal Reference Library, Chicago; Lori G. Waite, "Divided Consciousness: The Impact of Black Elite Consciousness on the 1966 Chicago Freedom Movement," in Jane Mansbridge and Aldon Morris, eds., *Oppositional Consciousness: The Subjective Roots of Social Protest* (Chicago: The University of Chicago Press, 2001), 183–189.

28. Ralph, *Northern Protest*, 76–77.

29. Ralph, *Northern Protest*, 40, 48–49; James Bevel interview with author, 11 August 1988.

30. Ralph, *Northern Protest*, 44, 48.

31. "Southern Christian Leadership Conference in Chicago: An Analysis of the Strategic Response of the Churches," 11 October 1965, Msgr. Daniel Cantwell Papers, Box 35-7, CHM; Gary Massoni, "Perspectives on Operation Breadbasket," in David J. Garrow, ed., *Chicago 1966: Open Housing Marches, Summit Negotiations, and Operation Breadbasket* (New York: Carlson Publishing, 1989), 194–195.

32. *CD* (national ed.), February 5, 1966, 1; Massoni, "Perspectives on Operation Breadbasket," 197–198.

33. Massoni, "Perspectives on Operation Breadbasket," 198–207, 273.

34. *CT*, July 16, 1996, 2; Wallace Best, "'The Right Achieved and the Wrong Way Conquered': J. H. Jackson, Martin Luther King, Jr., and the Conflict over Civil Rights," *Religion and American Culture: A Journal of Information* 16 (Summer 2006): 195–226; Sandy Dwayne Martin, "Uncle Tom, Pragmatist, or Visionary?: An Assessment of the Reverend Dr. Joseph Harrison Jackson and Civil Rights," in Peter Eisenstadt, ed., *Black Conservatism: Essays in Intellectual and Political History* (New York: Garland Publishing, 1999), 169–200. The clash between Jackson and King flowed in large part from Jackson's determination not to lose any control over the National Baptist Convention, which King hoped to use as an instrument to advance civil rights. Jackson's authoritarian streak and his willingness to engage in power politics predated his arrival in Chicago in 1941, but his domination of the NBC uncannily mirrored that of Mayor Daley over politics in Chicago. See Best, "'The Right Achieved,'" 198–205.

35. Waite, "Divided Consciousness," 198; Mary Lou Finley, "The Open Housing Marches: Chicago, Summer '66," in Garrow, ed., *Chicago 1966*, 16–17; Ralph, *Northern Protest*, 138; Elbert Ransom, Jr., *I Shall Not Pass This Way Again* (Longwood, FL: Xulon Press, 2004), 55–56. For more on the Progressive National Baptist Convention, see William D. Booth, *A Call to Greatness: The Story of the Founding of the Progressive National Baptist Convention* (Lawrenceville, VA: Brunswick Publishing, 2002).

36. One survey suggests that among church-going African Americans those who regularly attended church were more likely to support civil rights actions than those who attended infrequently. Donald J. Bogue and Richard McKinlay, *Militancy for and against Civil Rights and Integration in Chicago: Summer 1967* (Chicago: Community and Family Center, 1967), 31. The black church never became, however, the heart of the civil rights movement in Chicago as it was in many southern cities. See the discussion of "local movement centers" in Aldon Morris, *The Origins of the Civil Rights: Black Communities Organizing for Social Change* (New York: Free Press, 1984), 73–76.

37. Dorothy June Rose, *From Plough Handle to Pulpit: The Life Story of Rev. Clay Evans, "A Man with A Mission"* (Ivyland, PA: Neibauer Press, 1981), 44–47. As an example of Martin Luther King's effort to reach out to clergy, see King to the Reverend Leon Davis, June 1, 1966, King Papers, Box 5-30, King Center, Atlanta.

38. A. P. Jackson interview with author, January 3, 1992; Waite, "Divided Consciousness," 193–200.

39. Ralph, *Northern Protest*, 149–171, 195–200.

40. Ibid., 200–219, 223–224.

41. The Summit Agreement gave birth to the Leadership Council for Metropolitan Open Communities, which for the next forty years fought against housing discrimination in metropolitan Chicago.

42. Massoni, "Perspectives on Operation Breadbasket," 202–224.

43. Ibid., 253–254, 281–283.

44. Ibid., 227–229, 232–233. For a recent account of the 1969 protests, see Erik S. Gellman, "'The Stone Wall Behind': Chicago's Coalition for United Community Action and Labor's Overseers, 1968–1973," in David Goldberg and Trevor Griffey, *Black Power at Work: Community Control, Affirmative Action, and the Construction Industry* (Ithaca: Cornell University Press, 2010), 112–133. The Black Panthers, an important manifestation of black radicalism in Chicago in the late 1960s and early 1970s, were not grounded in the black Protestant church. They had closer connections with Catholic churches in African American neighborhoods. Jon Rice, "The World of the Illinois Panthers," in Jeanne Theoharis and Komozi Woodard, eds., *Freedom North: Black Freedom Struggles Outside the South, 1940–1980* (New York: Palgrave Macmillan, 2003), 51, 57.

45. James Melvin Washington, "Jesse Jackson and the Symbolic Politics of Black Christendom," *The Annals of the American Academy of Political and Social Science* 480 (July 1985): 89–105. Interestingly, Jesse Jackson never broke with the National Baptist Convention, and when J. H. Jackson was defeated as its president in 1982, the civil rights leader took on an important role within the NBC.

46. Paul Kleppner, *Chicago Divided: The Making of a Black Mayor* (DeKalb: Northern Illinois University Press, 1985), 118–133, 143–144.

47. The Reverend Al Sampson noted that he "saw the Harold Washington story as an extension of Martin King's beginning here in Chicago, with the whole question of housing, voter registration and political and economic empowerment." Sampson, "The Importance of the Black Church and Community Organization in the Harold Washington Story," Henry J. Young, ed., *The Black Church and the Harold Washington Story: The Man, the Message, the Movement* (Bristol, IN: Wyndham Hall Press, 1988), 121.

48. John R. Porter, "Historical Overview of Harold Washington's Political Career: Beginnings of "The Man-the Message-The Movement," in Young, ed., *The Black Church and the Harold Washington*, 80–94.

49. Dempsey J. Travis, *An Autobiography of Black Politics* (Chicago: Urban Research Press, 1987), 577–584; Jesse Cotton, "The Role of the Clergy in the Harold Washington Story," in Young, ed., *The Black Church and Harold Washington*, 67–72; Harry B. Gibson, "Harold Washington and the Politics of Inclusiveness: The Black Church Then and Now," ibid., 73–79; Willie Barrow, "The Black Church as Agent of Social Change: The Harold Washington Story," ibid., 109–113. Cotton interestingly concludes, "The Black Church should *never* divorce itself from politics." And, he notes, "If we are to have true Black Power in this country, it *must* come through the ballot box." For a suggestive overview of the role of African American women, especially those affiliated with the black church, see Addie Wyatt, "The Role of Women in the Harold Washington Story," ibid., 95–108. Al Sampson tells how one woman in his congregation, Fernwood United Methodist Church, registered 2000 persons to vote. Sampson, "The Importance of the Black Church, ibid., 124.

50. Jeremiah Wright, "Church Growth and Political Empowerment: The Significance of Harold Washington," in Young, *The Black Church and the Harold Washington Story*, 1–19.

51. Kleppner, *Chicago Divided*, 216–224.

52. *CT*, April 29, 1983, 21. In this column by Vernon Jarrett, Ford discusses the realities facing ministers in a city with a dominant political regime.

53. Harris, "Black Churches and Machine Politics in Chicago," 129-134. For a broader overview of the role of the African American church in Chicago politics in the late twentieth century, see Harris, *Something Within: Religion in African-American Political Activism* (New York: Oxford University Press, 1999).

2

The NAACP, Black Churches, and the Struggle for Black Empowerment in New Haven, 1955–1961

Yohuru R. Williams

When the Reverend Edwin Edmonds passed away in November of 2007, the city of New Haven, Connecticut mourned the loss of the man rightfully described by the *New Haven Independent* as the city's "premier civil-rights" leader. Over the course of his nearly fifty years of service to the Elm City, Edmonds spearheaded efforts to address many of the problems impacting the African American community, from substandard housing to quality education. During the tumultuous decade of the 1960s, however, Edmonds willingness to work within the system often put him at odds with other civil rights leaders who worried about the clergyman's close ties to city hall and the implications for independent black leadership. Edmonds put a good deal of his faith in Mayor Richard C. Lee whom he saw as an ally in his quest to build a vibrant black middle class in New Haven, which is something Edmonds believed to be the answer to the black community's problems.

As a recent migrant from the south, Edmonds was less skeptical than many of his northern born counterparts within the NAACP about a close alliance with the Mayor. As it turns out, Edmonds walked a fine line between maintaining cordial relations with the mayor's office and pursuing his own agenda of creating a vibrant black middle class within the city; an agenda often at odds with the goals and objectives of other leaders. His role in the struggle for black empowerment within New Haven illustrates some of the deep divisions that beset African American civil rights organizations outside the South as they sought to confront black marginalization in the North, and the often conflicted and contradictory

39

role black ministers and black churches played within the mid-twentieth
century civil rights and Black Power Movements. The chapter will focus
especially on internal power struggles and divisions within the New Hav-
en NAACP branch and within the black clergy sector, and on the often
problematic alliances actors from both groups sought to forge with ambitious politicians in their respective quests for power and primacy of ideas.[1]

Competing Voices, Conflicting Strategies, and Compromised Leadership

Edwin Edmonds was born and raised in Texas, where he felt the bitter
sting of southern racism while growing up in a completely segregated
community. A gifted student he graduated from high school at the age of
fifteen, only to struggle at Morehouse College where a debilitating eye dis-
order made his studies more difficult and eventually robbed him of most
of his sight. Despite the trouble with his sight, Edmonds completed his
undergraduate studies in 1938 and went on to earn a bachelors of sacred
theology degree and a doctorate in social ethics from Boston University.
In 1950, his youthful ambition and spiritual calling was realized when he
was ordained as a Methodist minister.

In addition to the ministry, Edmonds pursued a career in education and in 1950 accepted a job teaching sociology at Bennett College
in Greensboro, North Carolina. It was at Bennett that the Reverend
Edmonds first became deeply involved in the Civil Rights Movement.
Elected president of the Greensboro chapter of the National Association
for the Advancement of Colored People (NAACP), he became an outspoken advocate for civil rights in the city, earning him the praise and
friendship of the Reverend Dr. Martin Luther King, Jr., whom he first
met in 1958.

As president of the NAACP Edmonds took on the role as adviser
to the "Greensboro Four," a group of black college students who would
eventually lead the celebrated sit-in at a whites-only Woolworth's department store lunch counter. Edmonds would not remain in Greensboro long
enough to realize the fruits of his efforts because his political activities
created problems at Bennett which eventually cost the energetic pastor his
job. As Joe Mitchell, a member of the NAACP and Greensboro Citizens
Association was to recall:

> . . . at that particular time the NAACP was a pretty bad word
> in the community . . . And of course . . . Edmonds was presi-
> dent . . . I knew that they put pressure on him. Bennett is a

college that is mostly funded by gifts from big donors and from churches. So the Methodists at that particular time didn't see fit to keep Dr. Edmonds because they needed, I guess, they needed to move forward with what they were doing. He was very outspoken.[2]

Greensboro's loss proved to New Haven's gain after Edmonds accepted a position as the pastor of the Dixwell Congregational Church on Dixwell Avenue. His arrival in the Elm City coincided with a shakeup in the local branch of the NAACP that left the organization in need of new leadership. Edmonds proved an ideal candidate. His doctorate made him one of only a handful of such persons of color in the city. Furthermore his bona fides as a southern movement activist presented him as a seasoned and informed leader. This was a key issue given the prominence of the Dixwell position.

With more than 300 members, the Dixwell Church was one of the largest and most prominent in the city. Purported to be the oldest black Congregational church in America, it was a church born of activism. The church was founded in protest in 1820 after the Center Church on the Green required its Black members to sit in the balcony, away from its white members on the main floor. Dixwell church's founding pastor, white abolitionist Simeon Jocelyn, continued that activism through the congregation's deep involvement in the plight of the enslaved Africans at the center of the Amistad affair.[3] Over the years the Dixwell church remained an integral part of the African American community, its ministers and influential members often serving in community leadership roles on issues related to community development, race, and social justice. Edmonds selection to head up the church instantly provided him with a position of leadership in the city—one that he used to promote his vision of a vibrant and politically active black middle class.

That Edmonds's idea about how best to steward the city's black population might be at odds with some long-time residents is of little surprise. As historian Donna Murch has proposed, the story of civil rights and Black Power in the urban north is very much the story of black migrants and their efforts to survive the city. By the same token, these migrants brought with them a unique perspective on how best to achieve political equality and economic self sufficiency—experiences at times very different from those whom they joined in the city. In the case of the Reverend Edmonds, his political agenda was defined by a firm conviction in the necessity of building a strong black middle class, coupled with his belief that the best way to achieve this goal was through a close working relationship with the mayor.[4] Such a relationship with City Hall, he reasoned, would open up possibilities for political patronage and opportunities to impress upon city officials the need to provide minorities with private sector jobs and lucrative city contracts. At the time such thinking was a departure from the way local civil rights leaders and activists envisioned the black community's relationship with the city's chief elected official.

In the years leading up to Edmonds arrival in New Haven, black leaders (especially within the NAACP) had been divided over the branch's relationship with New Haven Mayor Richard C. Lee. Elected in 1953, Lee would serve a record sixteen years in office and preside over one of the most ambitious and well-funded urban renewal programs in the nation. Unlike the Reverend Edmonds, Lee was no scholar. He made his way up the political ranks, first serving as an Alderman and later capturing the Mayor's office after losing in two close previous elections. The deciding factor in 1953 was the African American vote which easily put Lee over the top. The new Democratic mayor reached out to the African American community in a way few had before, but his policies and programs also threatened the rapidly expanding black community—hemmed in as they were by de facto segregation and later the bulldozers of urban renewal deployed in effort to meet to the mayor's goal of ridding the city of slums within ten years.

During his campaigns for mayor, Lee actively courted support from the NAACP,[5] promising to appoint blacks to important city positions and to address issues of police brutality. Recognizing the political value of the association, after he became mayor, Lee prompted his Redevelopment Director, Ed Louge, to join the branch and provided financial support to the association through his participation in various branch initiatives including its annual fund raiser. The mayor's interest in the branch was appreciated if not always welcomed by its members. As the older group of leaders, generally more welcoming of the mayor's involvement within the organization became less active or in some cases passed away, Lee's hold on the branch began to diminish. After the death of branch Secretary Charles Hubbard in 1957, the debate within the organization intensified with opponents of the mayor's involvement arguing that it hurt the NAACP in two concrete ways: by preventing the chapter from expressing any substantive criticism of the mayor or his policies and by splitting loyalties among members into pro-Lee and anti-Lee factions.

This would prove especially problematic in 1957 as the strategies and tactics of the national movement and its local manifestations began to change. First and foremost, a younger and more vocal group of leaders emerged with a broader agenda than maintaining cordial relations with the mayor. In addition, between 1954 and 1957 the Civil Rights struggle began to shift from the NAACP's legal attack on segregation to direct action protest. While the New Haven chapter's original approach of working with the city government was fine for the late 1940s and early 1950s, the national attention afforded to direct action protests including the Montgomery Bus Boycott of 1955–1956 and the Little Rock, Arkansas school desegregation battle of 1957 had a distinct appeal among local branches and chapters, including New Haven.

Importantly, throughout the late 1950s and early 1960s a parade of leaders from the southern civil rights movement, such as Little Rock NAACP President, Daisy Bates, came through New Haven on various speaking tours and fund raising endeavors. Their accounts of the struggle in the South inspired some members to be more proactive in identifying targets of protest in the Elm City. At about the same time, the Dixwell Ministerial Alliance, a group of local ministers and church leaders who were committed to improving the quality of life for African Americans in New Haven, were becoming more radical. In most instances the Ministerial Alliance proved to be far more radical than the NAACP in addressing issues of inequality in New Haven. An issue involving the New Haven police and the Reverend Edmonds predecessor the Reverend Theodore S. Ledbetter drove that point home.

In the winter of 1957 the branch chapter had become embroiled with the police over the demotion of Clarence Jacobs, New Haven's only black detective. Jacobs was removed after he was arrested during an incident of domestic violence. The situation struck an uneasy chord with Ledbetter, who was head of the Dixwell Ministerial Alliance and served on Lee's Human Relations Council. John Daniels, a lifelong NAACP member and member of the Dixwell Congregational Church notes that this was not surprising since the Dixwell Church had always been closely associated with the NAACP. According to Daniels, a number of leaders of the NAACP had come out of the Dixwell Church and the two organizations had worked closely together in the past.[6]

During a meeting with New Haven's four police commissioners and Chief of Police Francis McManus on February 26, 1957, Ledbetter ruffled the feathers of some influential persons when he requested that police review Jacobs's dismissal. Frustrated by the Commissioner's stubborn refusal to reconsider Jacobs' punishment, Ledbetter warned, "New Haven is building up for an explosion." When asked what he meant Ledbetter replied, "I mean a race riot. Unless you come up with the right solution there will be trouble and it will be on your conscience."[7] Such militant posturing, especially peppered with the threat of violence was rare in New Haven and it set into motion the events that would eventually bring the Reverend Edmonds to the Elm City.

Interestingly, just as Edmonds had been forced out of North Carolina for his activism, soon after the meeting, Ledbetter resigned or was forced to leave his position on the Human Relations Council. In response Mayor Lee had aides draft a report on the number of blacks appointed by his administration and privately met with members of the NAACP to remind them of his close relationship and attentiveness to the black community. He declined to mediate the Jacob's affair, however, citing the need for police to determine their own personnel decisions. In the end, Ledbetter proved the only casualty of the affair. Jacobs was never re-promoted and Ledbetter subsequently left New Haven to take over the Plymouth United Church of Christ in Washington, DC.

Despite the Jacobs affair, the mayor's relationship with the NAACP continued to blossom, especially after Edmonds began his leadership of Dixwell Congregational Church. The two men seemed to share compli-mentary visions of the future of the black community in New Haven. However, both would be challenged in the years after Edmonds's arrival with a new energy in the association that sought a degree of political independence perceived as threatening to the mayor and those closest to him in the branch.

The most significant change in the New Haven branch took place with the election of James E. Gibbs as branch president in 1959. A native of New Haven, Gibbs had been active in the NAACP for five years. Having served on the Executive Board of the branch for four years, he organized the local youth council, and in 1955 headed the branch's Political Action Committee for which he received praised for his "diligent and faithful work."[8]

Gibbs was also a labor organizer employed by the Seamless Rubber Company and an active member of Local 338, United Rubber Workers of America. Gibbs served as a Union Steward for four years and also served on the Grievances Committee, Negotiating Committee, and Fair Employ-ment Practices Committee. He was also a member of the Greater New Haven Industrial Union Council for three years and at the time of his election was a delegate to the Greater New Haven Central Labor Council.[9]

Gibbs proved to be a very radical influence on the chapter. A great deal of his radicalism grew out of his involvement with other social groups, including the Communist Party. In a confidential report, the New Haven police noted that from 1953 to 1954 Gibbs was active in the Dixwell Avenue branch of the Communist Party and that in 1954 he was a member of a "cell" consisting of six persons whose purpose was to recruit black members. The police further suspected that Gibbs had been advised to join the NAACP by Simon Silverman, a prominent Connecticut Communist, who had been convicted under the Smith Act in the early 1950s.[10] When the NAACP began to emerge nationally as a direct action protest group within Montgomery and Little Rock, Gibbs may have seen possibilities for the New Haven branch and began channeling his energies in that direction. A report by the New Haven police confirmed this, indicating: "Although Gibbs was never openly active in the Communist Party; at this point (when he joined the NAACP) he became completely inactive."[11]

As president of the branch, Gibbs immediately began to move the chapter in the direction of more substantive issues including housing, poverty, and labor concerns. This inevitably meant challenging city officials, most notably the mayor. Breaking from the tradition of his predecessors in the office, Gibbs was not as apt to take advantage of the mayoral committee as past chapter presidents. In clear defiance of the union between the NAACP mayoral committee and Lee's Citizen's Action Committee, Gibbs appointed several new committees to deal with a myriad of problems affecting blacks in New Haven. Furthermore Gibbs sought to challenge the mayor's influence on the branch through direct confrontation.

Gibbs's activities alienated Lee's supporters within the branch including the Reverend Edmonds and also led to a very public rift with the Dixwell Ministerial Alliance early in 1959. In February, for instance, Branch Secretary Andrew Harris wrote to the national office to update Gloster Current, national director of chapters, on the status of problems within the New Haven branch. Harris warned Current that the members of the branch were being denounced as radicals by local clergy. In addition, Harris complained that Mayor Lee and the Chief of Police, Francis V. McManus, were attempting to play the two groups against one another by staging a meeting to which they invited the Ministerial Alliance without the knowledge of the NAACP. Both the New Haven branch of the NAACP and the Dixwell Ministerial Alliance placed the majority of the blame for the incident on New Haven Chief of Police McManus and the President of the Board of Police Commissioners. In a joint statement the organizations declared: "We deplore such actions as detrimental to the best interest of our community, and we strongly urge that the necessary steps be taken to prevent such a reoccurrence." Furthermore, the two groups declared their mutual respect for one another reaffirming their "common struggle for justice and truth in the Greater New Haven area, and our united struggle for equal opportunity and equal protection under the laws for all the people of this community."[12]

In a subsequent letter to the national offices of the NAACP, Harris told Current that the incident had been "confined to our colored community" and that the NAACP would not respond in the press to the "very silly statements made by the clergy." Pressure from these members brought about a conciliatory meeting between the Alliance and the NAACP which produced the joint statement. Harris concluded his letter with an assurance that the Ministerial Alliance would "never openly attack the Branch again" and that the NAACP "believed the matter closed."[13]

On March 10, 1959, Current responded, noting: "The organizations in the Negro community should be kept fully advised of our activities." He added that, "It is not a bad policy to educate the clergy, although they would resent the term 'educate,' by meeting with them frequently and bringing them up to date on what is going on." He thought it was "unfortunate when any segment of the community has a disagreement with the NAACP over matters in which they should have a common interest." He acknowledged that, "The ministers are a potent force in any community and the NAACP could not exist without their aid."[14]

Although Harris was confident that the NAACP had minimized fallout from the situation, in the months to come, the New Haven branch of the NAACP would split over support of the mayor. Gibbs continued to agitate Lee supporters through his activities as president. When Lee rejected several proposals made by the newly created NAACP branch delegation on housing, in September 1959 Gibbs dispatched an angry letter to the mayor. "Your answer to their request and your attitude towards them did not resemble that of a candidate seeking reelection, but of one who already has the Negro vote in his hip pocket," Gibbs complained. "Based on six years of the Lee administration," he continued, "and especially the past year, it is my opinion that the time has come to unseat the popular myth that Dick Lee is concerned about the Negroes' problems." Gibbs further lectured Lee: "I also take this opportunity, Mr. Mayor; to terminate this you-tell me and I'll take care of it relationship between us. We shall resume our tried and trusted ways of the past for they bring results."[15]

For Gibbs, tried and trusted ways meant applying pressure on the mayor to make lasting changes within New Haven. It also meant adopting direct action protest as a means of bringing attention to problems in the city. Lee's supporters were critical of Gibbs for placing too much emphasis on Lee. The mayor worried about what impact the Gibbs presidency would have on the branch as a whole and what prospects the negative attention might have on the city as well. Lee was quick to alert his allies within the branch to stay abreast of the latest news. In addition, Lee was not beyond instructing his supporters to express their disapproval of Gibbs. In this manner Lee helped to create a rift in the local branch. One of his primary agents at least initially would be a young, black, law student named John Barber; the other would be the Reverend Edwin Edmonds.

Gibbs's election coincided with Barber's arrival from Detroit. Barber had been invited to apply to Yale Law School and was first introduced to Mayor Lee in 1958. Lee wrote a letter of recommendation for Barber in which he described Barber as a "very impressive chap" who "seems to be very sharp." Lee also wrote, "He is someone I feel confident you would likely consider, and I wanted to send this note to endorse him to you."[16]

Barber was similarly impressed with Lee and contacted the Mayor the following week to express his "sincerest thanks" for Lee's endorsement. "Needless to say," Barber added, "I look forward to being able to put into practice the human values you exemplify in community service." Several months later Barber joined the New Haven branch of the NAACP and began reporting on the activities of the group to the mayor. Barber joined several older members of the branch who remembered Lee's openness, thereby constituting a pro-Lee faction within the NAACP which greatly compromised the organization's effectiveness.[17]

During the preparation for the local NAACP's annual membership and fund raising event, the Freedom Fund Drive, Gibbs made Barber the fund's Promotional Director. Barber immediately approached Lee about writing a letter inviting Daisy Bates, president of the Little Rock Arkansas branch of the NAACP, to speak at the Freedom Fund dinner scheduled for October 19, 1959. Lee agreed and extended an invitation to Bates which she accepted. In the meantime, Gibbs was engineering a modest protest campaign aimed at getting the mayor to act on a long standing demand of the NAACP, that blacks be appointed to the New Haven Board of Education. Gibbs decided that one of the most effective ways to reach Lee would be through postcards to the mayor's office from citizens who supported the demand for a black board member.[18]

In the aftermath of the postcard campaign, Barber wrote Lee in an attempt to distance himself from the branch's actions. In a letter dated September 11, 1959, Barber affirmed his loyalty to Lee as he explained: "If I had known what was developing I would have surely decided hands off for me." Barber claimed that his actions would not have been motivated by a desire to avoid controversy or avoid negative repercussions but because: "I have too much to learn about many things to pop off ill considered demands and besides I am increasingly acquiring implicit faith in you which more and more precludes me allying with transient and subverting causes."[19] Barber continued his apology:

> My civic loyalties are with the Negro cause, the Democratic party and your political stature . . . I think of you as a political hero . . . and my acquired adulation of you is to a great extent independent of the fact that you have helped me in my academic and employment situations for which I am eternally grateful. I like you as the epitome of the liberal politician for what I consider your sincere interest in the progress of the long underprivileged of this community.[20]

Barber concluded:

> If I sincerely believed my loyalties to my race, the party and
> you were conflicting; I would be beset by dilemmas which I am
> not sure how I would resolve. Perhaps, integrity would impel
> me to step one way, perhaps another. One factor in my choice
> in such a hypothetical situation would be my consideration
> of two occasions in which you counseled me on my youthful
> proclivity toward impetuousness and on the virtues of patience.
> I appreciated your considered opinion as in large measure
> correct and worthy of implementation in terms of its value.[21]

In the meantime, Gibbs followed up the postcard protest with an
all-out assault on Lee's civil rights record in the pages of the NAACP
newsletter. In a biting editorial, entitled, "Just a little Mail," Gibbs attacked
Lee for refusing to place a black on the Board of Education. Gibbs wrote,
"It seems that for the past six years, since Mayor Lee has been in office,
we have been trying to get a Negro on the Board of Education. During
these six years we have pleaded, we have reasoned, we have worked and
yes we have begged. But like the stone and mortar and concrete of the
buildings that are new, New Haven, Mayor Lee has been unmoved."[22]

Gibbs related the events of the September meeting between Lee and
the NAACP noting: "This time the Mayor was furious . . . because more
than 250 of you dropped the Mayor a card asking him to consider a Negro
for the Board of Education." Gibbs recounted how Lee had informed the
branch that the selection of a member of the school board was a political
issue and that "We Negroes haven't earned any appointments and that
WE haven't worked hard enough for HIM." To this Gibbs' responded,
"Well now didn't he carry the Negro wards in 1953, 1955, and 1957 with
a healthy majority?" Gibbs added, "In fact in 1957 the 19th and 22nd
Wards were the only wards to overwhelmingly support his pet projects
the Charter Reform."[23]

"So deep is our concern for the future of our children," Gibbs
observed, "that a spontaneous movement has emerged within the Negro
community to elevate a member of our race to the Board of Education."
Gibbs further castigated Lee, "We may well be on the verge of fighting
our Battle of Little Rock, in any event the New Haven NAACP is 1000%
behind this movement." He concluded, "Coincidental as it may seem, the
very woman who symbolizes the Negro's fight for Educational Equality
will be our keynote speaker in just a few weeks. How will Mayor Lee
appear to us standing there on the stage next to Daisy Bates of Little
Rock."[24]

Juxtaposed to the Gibbs editorial was a short article by John Barber on the upcoming mayoral election in New Haven entitled "Political Scene." Barber surveyed the field of candidates but subtly reminded voters of the branch's special relationship with Lee. In an attempt at humor, Barber noted, "personally this writer is going out and vote for . . . Oops, pardon me. I almost slipped up there and named my choice"; not really a slip since Barber had emerged as one of Lee's chief supporters within the branch. Despite the tenor of Barber's comments, he had cause to be concerned about the placement of his article in relation to the Gibbs's editorial.[25]

Barber sent Lee a Western Union Telegram on September 22, 1959 explaining that he had been out of town at the time the newsletter was published. As he explained, "I had written the page 3 article and tried to make explicit what I thought was the organization's nonpartisan role in politics, notwithstanding my own dedicated partisan commitment." Barber claimed that after reading Gibbs' article on the opposite page, "I resigned my position as Freedom Fund Director." Barber further explained, "I regard the article as an outright and unjustified political slap. More importantly personally it was a slap in my face since I had in good faith turned to you in behalf of the organization for Ralph Bunche, for ads and to appear on program with Mrs. Bates."[26]

After Barber's resignation the Branch's Freedom Fund drive ended abruptly. This brought the emerging conflict in the local chapter to the attention of the National Director of Branches, Gloster B. Current. In December of 1959, branch secretary Andrew Harris sent a letter to NAACP Executive Director, Roy Wilkins, in reply to a special inquiry by Current concerning New Haven's Freedom Fund campaign. As Harris conceived the problem, "A group of enthusiastic people, and some older ones, all members of the Branch became overzealous in their support of our Mayor Lee during the past year. Also, during this year the New Haven Branch has had reasons to inquire very closely into some of the policies of the Mayor."[27]

Harris noted that the root of the disagreement was the effort of this group to prevent the branch from taking any action or raising any issue which might embarrass the mayor during his reelection bid. Harris further explained that the branch administration did not agree and that, as a result, Lee's supporters attempted to elect a slate of their group to head the branch in 1960. Harris believed the danger had passed noting that the leader of this group, John Barber, realized he had been "used" by the mayor. Harris explained: "He is very sincere in his desire to help our Branch and its policies but more than that he was influenced that the way to achieve progress was through close and quiet cooperation with the city administration."[28]

Despite these problems, Harris noted that with the help of the Reverend Edwin Edmonds, the situation actually brought the branch together. Harris credited Edmonds as a calming influence within the organization. Initially though, Edmonds was viewed as a militant, based upon his participation in civil rights protests in the South. He was much in favor of direct action and shared Gibbs's belief that the mayor held the key to changing conditions in New Haven, especially with regard to political appointments. As Edmonds recalled:

> He [Lee] had a scheme that any promotion on the police force had to take a two-part examination. Forty percent of its core was a written exam. Sixty percent was an examination by the Mayor orally and there was space enough in there to manipulate anyone's score. So we said we have to put pressure on you if we are going to have any officers or promotions in the police department.[29]

Like Barber, however, Edmonds eventually was convinced by Lee that he had a genuine interest in seeing the black community prosper. As Edmonds explained, Lee was "not free of prejudice but . . . he was an astute politician; he saw the political worth of an amicable and productive agency with the Black community." In addition, Edmonds believed that the local branch often proved too militant in dealing with a mayor and city government who were willing to communicate with them, something Edmonds had not experienced in the North Carolina. According to Edmonds, Lee supported his idea of building a black middle class in New Haven. Working behind the scenes Edmonds quietly steered the branch and the alliance in directions favorable to Lee. Interestingly, though, the mayor's two closest "friends" within the branch, Barber and Edmonds, had an intense dislike for each other, often clashing with one another while working independently toward the same goal of supporting the mayor.[30]

With two of the branch's most influential members on his side, Lee continued to work behind the scenes through Barber and Edmonds to have Gibbs removed from the NAACP leadership. One of the means of discrediting Gibbs was by bringing up his past. On June 15, 1960, Roy C. Jackson, the First Vice President of the NAACP's New England Regional Conference received an anonymous letter concerning the NAACP's outspoken branch president. The letter recounted how the leftist views of Gibbs had first come to attention in New Haven when he was identified during 1956 hearings before the House Un-American Activities Committee. During that inquiry, Gibbs was identified as a possible associate of the Negro Commission of the Communist Party. Raising the specter of a communist infiltrator the writer concluded: "In these days we are engaged in an all important struggle for equality for members of our race, can we afford to continue to offer our enemies such a justifiable basis for criticizing our organization?" The letter further indicated that Gibbs should be removed by a "self-imposed house cleaning" rather than "exposure from enemies of the NAACP."[31]

The letter was the first in a series of events which effectively destroyed the NAACP as a viable organization in New Haven. Jackson forwarded the letter to Gloster Current who subsequently contacted Gibbs. Upon receiving the letter, Gibbs informed the national office that he had distributed copies to the New Haven Executive Committee. He explained: "It is their opinion that since the writer did not see fit to sign his or her name; no great importance could or should be placed on the letter." Gibbs further informed Current that he would be in New York in September and would be willing to meet with him then. Current responded a few days later thanking Gibbs for his response and acknowledging that a meeting in September would be fine.[32]

While Lee's supporters were working to get rid of Gibbs from the inside, Lee attempted to demonstrate his new sensitivity to the problems facing black people by proposing a controversial protest in the early spring. As Allan Talbot recorded the events, Lee had been given a draft of a speech he was to deliver which called for New Haven blacks to stage a sit-out and obstruct late afternoon traffic to demonstrate to homeward bound suburbanites the poor conditions in which urban blacks lived. The mayor's proposed sit-out served two purposes: to identify with the problems of urban blacks and also to drum up support for urban renewal projects which would obliterate those conditions.[33]

The speech, delivered in August of 1960 evoked the desired response from the local radical element, namely James Gibbs, who assured the mayor that as a result of his proposal: "The relationship between you and the branch can develop into a much stronger and healthier one, and I am sure this is what we both want, if you just deal with us directly on matters of importance."[34] Lee was not prepared, however, for the intense backlash against his proposal from seemingly disinterested elements. Especially from those who saw it as unwise and untimely. Typical was a letter penned by New Haven resident Arthur Irwin accusing the Mayor of "buttering up the minority groups for their dubious political support." Irwin asked the Mayor to consider carefully the impact of a sit-out on the taxpayers of "your community" and accused him of sounding more like a "left wing radical" than a "responsible, intelligent adult, with a great responsibility to the local and state communities."[35] Attempting damage control, Lee distanced himself from his previous announcement and returned to the place where he delivered the speech. There he promised to create an urban renewal program aimed at the slums within New Haven.

Tempered by this experience, Lee made use of his friends within the NAACP, Barber and Edmonds, to see to it that Gibbs was kept in check. Edmonds and Barber began reporting to the Mayor at regular intervals about events in the chapter, and marshaled support against what they termed Gibbs's abuse of power with regard to the local chapter. For example, in November of 1960 the members of the Dixwell Ministerial Alliance drafted a protest letter to the national offices of the NAACP charging Gibbs with bringing disgrace on the chapter. The issue this time was the Dewitt Jones Housing Case, a local cause célèbre involving a middle-class Black couple who were attempting to purchase a home but were refused by real estate agents. On November 4, 1960, Gibbs distributed a letter criticizing Edmonds and the Dixwell Church for not supporting the NAACP in the Jones's case. In particular, Gibbs accused Edmonds of making a "concerted effort" to restrict information on NAACP activities and for not allowing him to speak before the congregation to announce news relative to the NAACP.[36]

At the same time Gibbs was circulating his letter, the national offices of the NAACP received a letter from Dixwell Congregational Church signed by eighteen members who accused Gibbs of abusing his powers as the New Haven Branch President. The signers, which included the Reverend Edmonds, complained that Gibbs had also embarked on an "irresponsible and unauthorized public letter writing campaign which was the source of much embarrassment for the organization." The signers invited Current to attend a proposed meeting by the Dixwell Church scheduled for November 17, 1960 as an official observer from the national offices.[37]

Current responded personally to Edmonds and advised him that he would be present and that Gibbs had been apprised of his visit as well. From Edmonds perspective he was only pursuing a moderate course which had worked during his tenure as head of the NAACP in North Carolina. While Edmonds was not opposed to direct action protest he felt that in order for any protest to be effective it needed to speak directly to the issue and not simply function as a show of disapproval for elected officials. While this may have been a prudent course, it failed to satisfy those within the branch, namely Gibbs who began to see Edmonds as an impediment to the more militant course of action he proposed. Even if Edmonds imagined himself as staking out the moderate course, his pro-Lee stance fueled speculation about his loyalties to the community. Nevertheless, Gibbs was clearly at a disadvantage in his dispute with Edmonds given that Dixwell Church remained one of the key black power bases within the city and it was unquestionably under the control of Edmonds.[38]

Lee, in the meantime, was not beyond exploiting the situation for his own benefit. A report on an NAACP meeting from one of Lee's aides, Barry Passett, illustrates the Mayor's attempt to micro-manage the affairs of the branch. Passett wrote: "It was obvious that your spokesman was Edmonds. He was sharp, brilliant and effective." Critiquing the performance of Lee's other "friends," Passett accused Barber of taking "the easy way out" by abstaining from the reverend's motion to censure Gibbs. Revealing the politicized nature of Lee's interest in the matter, Passett recorded how the "Republicans, with one exception voted for Gibbs." But Passett also warned the mayor not to view the situation in purely political terms. As he explained: "The problem is that all of these people with the exception of the rich and the secure city employees-are angry about housing conditions, especially rent gauging, and expect something to be done." "They are not necessarily mad at you," he continued. "They do not however, feel the Dixwell Project is benefiting them and they have the strong feeling that they must do something active, like down South, to win support for their cause."[39]

The power struggle between Edmonds and Gibbs came to a head in 1961 after a young black Republican alderman named Blyden Jackson organized a local chapter of the national civil rights organization, Congress of Racial Equality (CORE). Motivated by a desire to see direct action protests against unfair housing practices and other social ills in New Haven, Jackson sought to make the New Haven CORE chapter the most radical group in New Haven. As one of his first acts as president of the new CORE chapter, Jackson renewed Lee's call for a sit-out to dramatize poor housing conditions in New Haven.

Eager to expand his own calls for a direct action protest, Gibbs endorsed Jackson's call and further announced plans for the NAACP to participate in the CORE sit-out. Horrified by the specter of his mistake coming back to haunt him, Lee began to put pressure on his contacts within the NAACP to oppose Gibbs' call. In addition, Lee's supporters within the NAACP inundated Gloster Current, the national NAACP director of branches, with dozens of letters questioning the legality of Gibbs's actions. Current was also contacted directly by Mayor Lee, who telephoned the NAACP headquarters the week before the protest was to take place. The conference call which, according to the NAACP typed transcripts, included Reverend Edmonds, focused on the "James Gibbs problem." Lee complained to Current that Gibbs was a radical who was only proposing the sit-out to embarrass the mayor and highlight problems that did not exist. During the conversation Lee reminded Current of his record on civil rights and that he was running for reelection as New Haven mayor "seven weeks from Tuesday." Lee explained: "Gibbs is doing nothing more to us than attempting to embarrass me with the most scurrilous kind of tactics."[40]

As a result, Current contacted Gibbs by telegram that afternoon, September 18, 1961. Dispensing with the usual pleasantries, Current informed Gibbs that before any action could be taken the national office needed to be advised. Current also warned Gibbs of the potential consequences of an ill-conceived protest without a sound basis in fact. Finally, he urged Gibbs to respond by telephone that evening, thus placing the national office directly in the conflict between the Mayor and the New Haven branch.[41]

The following evening the branch held a two-hour meeting, which the local press characterized as "stormy," to decide on possible postponement of the sit-out. As the *New Haven Register* reported: "In the wake of shouted demands for action now, contrasting pleas for observance of NAACP procedure, and two challenged votes on a motion for further deliberation," the meeting finally ended with the provision that the protest would be reconsidered at another meeting scheduled for September 29. Not surprisingly, it was Reverend Edmonds who succeeded in tabling the discussion of the proposed sit-out by calling for the submission of the proposal to the Executive Committee for further consideration.[42]

Current, in the meantime, continued to try to make contact with Gibbs. In a letter dated September 20, 1961, Current reminded Gibbs that the NAACP could "ill afford" to have the organization proceeding on some highly complex matters, such as in the field of housing, without the benefit of advice from "the National Housing Secretary or even our General Counsel." Current again strongly advised that Gibbs contact him or postpone the protest until more information was available.[43]

While he was attempting to contact Gibbs, Current continued to receive pressure from people within the chapter to have Gibbs removed. On September 26, Gibbs finally replied to Current's letters noting that reports of the proposed sit-out in the New Haven press were grossly exaggerated. He also noted that the New Haven branch had acted in accordance with organizational procedure. Gibbs explained that the proposed protest was "merely one small part of our Housing campaign to develop community awareness and support for our program." Underscoring Harris's concerns about undue influence from the mayor's office, Gibbs added: "Some people, politically motivated have been attempting to discredit our housing campaign by attacking our sit out." Gibbs maintained that the sit-out would still take place that Saturday afternoon and offered Current an invitation to observe it.[44]

Current drafted a response to Gibbs and made plans to attend the planning meeting for the sit-out. In his response, Current sharply criticized Gibbs's actions noting: "We have engaged in direct action, such as sit outs, where legal remedies are not available or where duly constituted authorities fail, neglect or refuse to act. None of these factors are present here." Current attended the meeting and delivered his statement which received wide coverage in the local press. In addition, Current threatened to revoke the New Haven branch's charter if it proceeded to carry out the protest. The Minutes from the meeting reflected the growing tension and partisanship within the local NAACP and that the will of the majority was being repressed by the national office.[45]

Following the meeting Current called for a meeting of the New Haven Executive Board on October 5, 1961 to consider the fate of President Gibbs, who Current clearly blamed for the volatile atmosphere in the local chapter. In official charges brought against Gibbs by the national office for conduct "inimical to the best interest of the National Association for the Advancement of Colored People," Current concluded:

> The entire attitude of the president reflects disrespect for the organization which he supposedly represents and indifference to the most effective and orderly ways of taking advantage of the progress already made and of insuring community cooperation in future progress. Obviously he is more concerned with his own position and with colorful demonstrations and newsletters than action in keeping with the organization's reputation for reliance on lawful channels.[46]

On October 3, 1961, three members of the New Haven branch came to the national offices to press for Gibbs' removal. In a confidential memorandum, Current noted that Bishop C. H. Brewer, a Mr. Ullman, and John Barber visited his office to impress upon him the necessity of removing Gibbs from the presidency. Although Current told them that the national office had made no determination he noted that the trio continued to insist that the chapter would only survive if Gibbs was no longer president.[47]

On October 7, 1961, the day that his fate was to be determined, Gibbs resigned; but not before drafting a letter to Roy Wilkins, the NAACP national executive director, outlining his concerns for the future of the NAACP. In that letter Gibbs expressed his frustration with the way Current handled the sit-out meeting but more importantly chastised the national offices for sending mixed messages. Gibbs wrote:

> At the Philadelphia Convention sit-outs and sit-ins were endorsed. Now one is told that endorsement was only for the

South and not for the North. Further one is told that only with
the support of a segment of the political community and segment of the white community could a direct-action program
be carried out." Gibbs charged, "This latter comes as a complete
surprise since the announced policy of the National office in
the past has been not to become involved in politics to the
degree of aligning itself with one political party or another.[48]

Gibbs noted further: "It is felt that a grave danger exists as far as
the success of the NAACP projects is concerned if a branch must depend
upon the support of a segment of the political element in the community—especially when the segment is directly opposed and worked to
prevent the success of the project." He concluded:

> It is necessary to point to the growing disillusionment among
> intelligent Negroes in the community at the obstacles placed in
> the path of those who wish to protest discriminatory practices.
> Indeed many within the New Haven Branch have become so
> disillusioned with the response of the National Office that
> it becomes impossible to work within the framework of the
> NAACP.[49]

In his official report to Roy Wilkins on problems within the New
Haven branch, Current betrayed much of the backward thinking that
Gibbs complained about. As he explained: "I am beginning to conclude
that some of our northern branches are infiltrated and the line is calling
for demonstrations and other protest activities, the success of which is
questionable, but which stirs up confusion and brands the NAACP as an
irresponsible organization. This has happened in San Francisco where the
group picketed the Fairmont Hotel and in Los Angeles where a boycott
has been called against the *Los Angeles Times* and the large hotels." Current concluded, "I am planning to take strong action in every instance
where this situation crops up."[50]

Meanwhile, speculation about who was responsible for undermining
Gibbs was rampant in the local chapter. Reverend Edmonds was singled
out as one of the persons who had opposed Gibbs and the sit-out. In the
aftermath of Gibbs's public censure a controversial newsletter entitled, *The
Bee Sting Spark*, attacked Edmonds for the, "Sit out sell out," and accused
Current of high-handed tactics in dealing with the local chapter. The
Sting reserved its strongest venom for Reverend Edmonds who, it argued,
engineered the whole debacle. Prior to the removal of Gibbs, Edmonds
had moved into a new home which critics dubbed "Mt. Carmel Plan-

tation." Rumor circulated that Edmonds had purchased the home with money provided by Lee. In addition, just a few months before the sit-out fiasco, in July of 1961 Lee had invited Edmonds to attend the NAACP convention all expenses paid, as a fraternal delegate of the City of New Haven. Many saw a direct connection between Edmonds's willingness to see Gibbs removed and what they termed his selling out to the Mayor.[51]

Current's conclusion concerning the changes in northern chapters helps to explain the NAACP's problems as a grass roots protest organization. The national office denied indigenous leadership the right to exercise meaningful protest specific to their locale. Even though both Current and the NAACP noted that the majority of those present supported Gibbs and some form of protest in New Haven, Current dismissed them as the "Gibbs clique." The NAACP was not the organization for new leaders and did not relate well to local issues. CORE promised to deliver where the NAACP had failed.

Gibbs joined CORE, which despite the problems in the NAACP continued to push for a sit-out in New Haven. Two days after his resignation, Gibbs participated in the first of a series of pickets staged by CORE to dramatize the plight of New Haven blacks. Furthermore, on October 17, 1961, CORE announced plans to stage a massive sit-out on Grand Avenue to protest housing discrimination.[52]

The NAACP, meanwhile, went through the motions of selecting a new president. In a highly charged election in December of 1961 *The New Haven Register* reported that the NAACP was a battle ground divided between conservative, moderate, and extremist influences. The *Register* identified Sam Dixon, the acting president of the NAACP, as a conservative candidate. It labeled John Barber as the moderates choice and Walter Henderson, who was also a member of CORE, as the militant selection. Underscoring the personal feud between the two men working on Lee's behalf within the organization, the *Register* noted that Henderson was backed up by the local chapter of CORE and the Reverend Edmonds.

During the meeting to select the new president, Henderson and Barber bitterly attacked one another, with Barber calling Henderson a "faceless man" propped up by Edmonds and Blyden Jackson. Referring to Barber's summer job with the Redevelopment Department, Henderson charged: "The mayor is not paying my tuition." Henderson further implied that if Barber were elected he would take orders directly from the mayor. Although Henderson and Barber tied in a vote of 38 for Barber, 38 for Henderson, and 10 for Dixon, Barber ultimately won the election, only to then preside over the NAACP's further decline.[53] In the following decade the NAACP would be eclipsed by new civil rights and black power organizations in New Haven.

While Edmonds would continue to exercise important community leadership, he was increasingly on the other side of the fence as an appointed member of various mayoral committees and commissions. From this vantage point Edmonds would be instrumental in pushing for change that resulted in more patronage jobs for African Americans, better housing, and better schools. In 1979, for example, he was elected as chairman of the school board and served in that position until 1988. By the time of Edmonds's death in 2004, the 1950s and 1960s power struggles within the local branch of the NAACP and the divisive influence of Mayor Lee seemed long forgotten. Nevertheless, the case remains very instructive in analyzing northern black churches and mid-twentieth century civil rights activism.

While churches served as an important conduit for social change, the internal politics reveal a great deal about the struggle for black equality and the various means by which African Americans sought to attain it. In her essay "Upon This Rock: The Black Church, Nonviolence, and the Civil Rights Movement" political scientist Allison Calhoun-Brown notes how congregational-specific characteristics "such as socioeconomic background, educational achievement, age composition, ministerial disposition, and theological orientation" played a key role in determining the type of activism, or lack thereof emanating from among the various churches during the Civil Right Movement.[54] It is fair to say that these same forces were often at work within the churches themselves, especially larger ones like the Dixwell Church, and that disagreements over the best way to achieve racial equality exacerbated these tensions often dividing the membership and driving a wedge between the church and black civic organizations as they did in New Haven. Ministers like the Revered Edwin Edmonds and Theodore Ledbetter were not immune from the fallout from these splits and the sectarian politics that emerged when their personal views, augmented by their divine calling, ran a-foul of more conservative or radical influences both within and outside the church. The church's close relationship, not only with black civic organizations like the NAACP, but also local government left a wide field of political land mines for local pastors to negotiate. In Edmonds's case, what appeared as a sellout to some was interpreted by Edmonds himself as evidence that the mayor endorsed his view. While Edmonds may have lost the initial public relations campaign, his vision won out eventually helping to shape the course of the civil rights and post-civil rights struggle for racial equality in New Haven. A struggle that continued to privilege politics and development of a black middle class over other more community based forms of action and protest.

Notes

1. This chapter is derived from my book, Yohuru Williams, *Black Politics/ White Power: Civil Rights Black Power and Black Panthers in New Haven* (Wiley-Blackwell, 2006; Brandywine Press, 2000) which chronicles the Civil Rights and Black Power Movements in New Haven. See also "No Haven: From Civil Rights to Black Power in New Haven, Connecticut" in *The Black Scholar* 31:3–4 (Fall/ Winter 2001): 54–66; on the struggle for civil rights in New Haven see also Robert A. Dahl, *Who Governs?* (New Haven: Yale University Press, 1961) 60–66; Jane Jacobs, *The Death and Life of Great American Cities* (New York: Vintage, 1961), 411; Fred Powledge, *Model City: A Test of American Liberalism: One Towns Efforts to Rebuild Itself* (New York: Simon & Shuster, 1970), 16–20; Allan R. Talbot, *The Mayor's Game: Richard Lee of New Haven and the Politics of Change* (New York: Harper & Row, 1967), 11; William Lee Miller, *The Fifteenth Ward and the Great Society: An Encounter with a Modern City (Cambridge: Riverside Press, 1966),*

2. Oral history interview with Joe Mitchell. Available at http://library.uncg. edu/depts/archives/civrights/detail-iv.asp?iv=105. On the Greensboro sit-ins see Frye Gaillard, *The Greensboro Four: Civil Rights Pioneers: A Profile.* Charlotte (NC: Main Street Rag Publishing Company, 2001); Lorraine Hansberry, *The Movement: Documentary of Struggle for Equality* (New York: Simon and Schuster, 1964); Sally Avery Bermanzohn, *Through Survivors' Eyes: From the Sixties to the Greensboro Massacre* (Nashville: Vanderbilt University Press, 2003); William H. Chafe, *Civilities and Civil Rights: Greensboro, North Carolina, and the Black Struggle for Freedom* (New York: Oxford University Press, 1980); Otis L. Hairston, Jr. *Greensboro, North Carolina* (Charleston, SC: Arcadia Publishers, 2003); H. A. Sieber, *Holy Ground: Significant Events in the Civil Rights-Related History of the African-American Communities of Guilford County, North Carolina, 1771-1995* (Greensboro, NC: Tudor Publishers, Inc., 1995).

3. On the Amistad case see Howard Jones, *Mutiny on the Amistad: The Saga of a Slave Revolt and Its Impact on American Abolition, Law, and Diplomacy.* (New York: Oxford University Press, 1987); Yohuru Williams, *Black Politics/White Power: Civil Rights, Black Power, and the Black Panthers in New Haven* (St. James, NY: Brandywine Press, 2000), 4–6; Robert Austin Warner, *New Haven Negroes, A Social History* (New York, NY: Arno Press, 1969 (c 1940)), 53–61; Iyunolu Folayan Osagie, *The Amistad Revolt: Memory, Slavery, and the Politics of Identity in the United States and Sierra Leone* (Athens: University of Georgia Press, 2000); Clifton Johnson, "The Amistad Case and Its Consequences in U.S. History," *Journal of the New Haven Colony Historical Society,* Vol. XI. 36, No. 2 (Spring 1990), 3–22.

4. Donna Murch, "The Campus and the Street: Race, Migration, and the Origins of the Black Panther Party in Oakland, CA" in *Souls: A Critical Journal of Black Politics, Culture, and Society,* (October-December 2007) 9:4, 333–345. See also Donna Murch, *Living for the City: Migration, Education, and the rise of the Black Panther Party in Oakland, California* (forthcoming from the University of North Carolina Press, 2010); Reverend Edwin Edmonds, interview by author,

tape recording, 23 July 1997; Reverend Fred Harris, interview by author, telephone tape recording, 9 April, 1999.

5. The local NAACP chapter was founded in 1917 and at its peak boasted nearly 500 members.

6. John Daniels, interview by author, tape recording, New Haven, CT, 25 July 1997.

7. Report by Bishop Brewer to Mayor Lee. Richard C. Lee Papers, RG 318 Series I, Box 113, Folder 2018, Manuscripts and Archives, Yale University Library.

8. "Gibbs's heads 59 Slate," *NAACP Newsletter*, February 1959 contained in NAACP Papers Group III, Box I 6, Manuscript Division, Library of Congress.

9. Confidential Police Report re: James E. Gibbs. Dated [1961?]. Richard C. Lee Papers, RG 318 Series II, Box 107, Folder 1911, Manuscripts and Archives, Yale University Library.

10. Ibid.

11. Ibid.

12. Andrew R. Harris, Secretary of the New Haven Branch, NAACP to Gloster B. Current, National Director of Chapters, NAACP, 15 February 1959, NAACP Papers, Group III, Box C18, Manuscript Division, Library of Congress; News Release from New Haven Branch, NAACP and Dixwell Ministerial Alliance, News Release dated 16 February 1959, NAACP Papers, Group III, Box C18, Manuscript Division, Library of Congress.

13. Andrew R. Harris, Secretary of the New Haven Branch, NAACP to Gloster B. Current, National Director of Chapters, NAACP, 15 February 1959.

14. Gloster Current, National Director of Branches, NAACP to Mr. Andrew R. Harris, Secretary of the New Haven Branch, NAACP, 10 March 1959, NAACP Papers, Group III, Box C18, Manuscript Division, Library of Congress.

15. James E. Gibbs, President of New Haven Branch, NAACP, to the Honorable Richard C. Lee, Mayor, City of New Haven, 18 September 1959, Richard C. Lee Papers RG 318, Series II, Box 113, Folder 2016, Manuscripts and Archives, Yale University Library.

16. Mayor Richard C. Lee to Gene Rostau, 10 February 1958, Richard C. Lee Papers RG 318, Series II, Box 113, Folder 2016, Manuscripts and Archives, Yale University Library.

17. John Barber to Mayor Richard C. Lee, 19 February 1958, Richard C. Lee Papers RG 318, Series II, Box 113, Folder 2016, Manuscripts and Archives, Yale University Library.

18. *NAACP News*, 18 September 1959, contained in NAACP Papers, Group III, Box I 6, Manuscript Division, Library of Congress.

19. John Barber to the Honorable Richard C. Lee, 11 September 1959, Richard C. Lee Papers RG 318, Series II, Box 113, Folder 2016, Manuscript and Archives, Yale University Library.

20. Ibid.

21. Ibid.

22. James E. Gibbs, "Just a little Mail," *NAACP Newsletter*, February 1959, contained in NAACP Papers. Group III. Box I 6, Manuscript Division, Library of Congress.

23. Ibid.

24. Ibid.

25. John Barber, "Political Scene," *NAACP Newsletter*, February 1959, contained in NAACP Papers. Group III. Box I 6, Manuscript Division, Library of Congress.

26. John Barber to Richard C. Lee, via Western Union Telegram, 22 September 1959, Richard C. Lee Papers RG 318. Series II. Box 113. Folder 2017, Manuscript and Archives, Yale University Library.

27. Andrew R. Harris, Secretary of the New Haven Branch, NAACP to Mr. Roy Wilkins, Executive Secretary of the NAACP, 13 December 1959, NAACP Papers. Group III. Box C18, Manuscript Division, Library of Congress.

28. Ibid.

29. Reverend Edwin Edmonds, interview by author, tape recording, New Haven CT, 23 July 1997.

30. Ibid.

31. "Discouraged" to Mr. C. Roy Jackson, First Vice President of New England Regional Conference of the NAACP, 15 June 1960. NAACP Papers. Group III. Box C18, Manuscripts Division, Library of Congress; A Jimmy Gibbs is mentioned in the text of the Hearings before the Committee on Un-American Activities, New Haven, September 1956, U.S. Government Printing Office, Washington, DC, 1956: 5607.

32. James E. Gibbs, President of the New Haven Branch, NAACP, to Mr. Gloster B. Current, National Director of Chapters, NAACP, 23 August 1960, NAACP Papers, Group III, Box C18. Manuscript Division, Library of Congress; Gloster B. Current, National Director of Chapters, NAACP, to James E. Gibbs, President of the New Haven Branch, NAACP, 29 August 1960, NAACP Papers, Group III, Box C18, Manuscript Division, Library of Congress.

33. Talbot, 170–171.

34. James E. Gibbs, President New Haven Branch of the NAACP to Mayor Richard C. Lee,

7 August 1960. Richard C. Lee Papers RG 318, Series II, Box 114, Folder 2040, Manuscript Division, Library of Congress.

35. Arthur E. Irwin to Mayor Richard C. Lee, 29 July 1960, Richard C. Lee Papers RG 318, Series II, Box 114, Folder 2040, Manuscript Division, Library of Congress.

36. Open Letter addressed Dear Friend and Fellow Member of Dixwell Congregational Church: from James Gibbs, 4 November 1960, NAACP Papers, Group III, Box C18, Manuscript Division, Library of Congress.

37. Dixwell Congregational Church to Gloster Current, National Director of Chapters, NAACP from the Dixwell Congregational Church, New Haven, CT, 9 November 1960. NAACP Papers, Group III, Box C18, Manuscript Division, Library of Congress.

38. Gloster B. Current, National Director of Chapters, NAACP to Dr. Edwin R. Edmonds, 15 November 1960. NAACP Papers, Group III, Box C18, Manuscript Division, Library of Congress; Reverend Edwin Edmonds, interview by author, tape recording, New Haven, CT, 23 July 1997.

39. Barry Passett to Mayor Richard C. Lee, Re: Last night's NAACP meeting, 19 September, 1961, Richard C. Lee Papers RG 318, Series I, Box 35, Folder 771.

40. Transcript of telephone conversation between Mayor Lee, Dr. Edmonds and G. Current Re: James Gibbs Problem, Five-page typed transcript, 18 September 1961, NAACP Papers, Group III, Box C292, Folder: New Haven, Connecticut Branch Problems 1961, Manuscript Division, Library of Congress.

41. Gloster B. Current to James Gibbs, via Western Union 18 September 1961, NAACP Papers, Group III, Box C292, Folder: New Haven, Connecticut Branch Problems 1961, Manuscript Division, Library of Congress.

42. "NAACP Postpones Sit-Out Action after Stormy Two-Hour Meeting," *The New Haven Register*, 19 September 1961, 1–2.

43. Gloster B. Current, National Director of Chapters, NAACP, to James E. Gibbs, President of the New Haven Branch, NAACP, 20 September 1961, NAACP Papers, Group III Box C292, Folder: New Haven, Connecticut Branch Problems 1961, Manuscript Division, Library of Congress.

44. James E. Gibbs, President of the New Haven Branch, NAACP, to Gloster Current, National Director of Chapters, NAACP, 26 September 1961, NAACP Papers, Group III, Box C292, Folder: New Haven, Connecticut Branch Problems 1961, Manuscript Division, Library of Congress.

45. "Sit-Out Plan is blocked at city Meeting," *The New Haven Register*, 29 September 1961, 1–2.

46. Gloster B. Current, Official Charges, Findings of Fact, and Conclusions Re: James Gibbs, undated report, NAACP Papers, Group III, Box C292, Folder: New Haven, Connecticut Branch Problems 1961, Manuscript Division, Library of Congress.

47. Confidential Memorandum for the files New Haven (Gloster B. Current), 4 October 1961, NAACP Papers, Group III, Box C292, Folder: New Haven, Connecticut Branch Problems 1961, Manuscript Division, Library of Congress.

48. James Gibbs et al. to Roy Wilkins, 5 October 1961, NAACP Papers, Group III, Box C292, Folder: New Haven, Connecticut Branch Problems 1961, Manuscript Division, Library of Congress.

49. Ibid.

50. Gloster B. Current to Roy Wilkins, 29 September 1961, NAACP Papers, Group III, Box C292, Folder: New Haven, Connecticut Branch Problems 1961, Manuscript and Archives, Library of Congress.

51. Sam Carruthers, "Doc Ed Stung As Uncle Tom Par Excellence," *The Bee's Sting Spark*, 10 October 1961, Vol. 1 Edition 4, contained in Richard C. Lee Papers RG 318, Box 44, Folder: 922, Manuscript and Archives, Library of Congress.

52. "First Sit-Out Is Staged Along Dixwell Ave Curb," *The New Haven Register*, 7 October 1961, page unknown, clippings file, local history collection, New Haven Public Library, New Haven, Connecticut; "CORE Pickets Stage March At City Hall," *The New Haven Register*, 10 October 1961, page unknown, clippings file, local history collection, New Haven Public Library, New Haven, CT; "CORE to Picket Pavilion to Protest Housing," *New Haven Journal Courier*, 18 October 1961, page unknown, clippings file, local history collection, New Haven Public Library, New Haven, CT.

53. Ibid.

54. Allison Calhoun-Brown, "Upon This Rock: The Black Church, Non-violence, and the Civil Rights Movement," *Political Science and Politics*, Vol. 33, No. 2. (June, 2000), 174.

3

Ruby Hurley, U.S. Protestantism, and NAACP Student Work, 1940–1950

Rosetta E. Ross

Ruby Hurley, the competent and beloved organizing director of the National Association for the Advancement of Colored People's (NAACP) Southeast Region, is most well known for strategic work in the South during the height of the Civil Rights era. As regional director, from 1951 until her retirement in 1978, Hurley coordinated membership drives and school desegregation campaigns; organized protests; investigated lynchings/murders, rapes, and beatings; negotiated relations between state councils and NAACP national headquarters; organized women's auxiliaries; supervised a staff of primarily male state field secretaries (including Medgar Evers, Vernon Jordan, Charles Evers, I. DeQuincey Newman, and others); administered regional work and conventions; and conducted a variety of other activities. Similar to, and in collaboration with, more well-known women movement leaders such as Ella Baker, Septima Clark, Fannie Lou Hamer, and a host of black male leaders, Ruby Hurley conducted civil rights work not only as her professional occupation, but also as a vocational endeavor emerging from her identification with African American Christianity, especially Protestantism. Movement veterans are well acquainted with Hurley's important regional work, even though civil rights literature does not substantially recognize her contributions.

While she is most well known for her role as NAACP Southeastern Regional Director, for a decade before moving south, Hurley distinguished herself as a successful NAACP youth worker, whose leadership of the Washington, District of Columbia, NAACP youth council (1940 to 1943) and the NAACP's national youth programs (1943 to 1951) not only helped form a cadre of leaders who supported civil rights efforts

as youths then adults, but also developed and nurtured interracial collaborations that supported evolution of the U.S. student movement. From
1943 to 1951 Hurley built a reputation and helped form the substructure
for later Movement activity as Director of NAACP youth work. Under
her leadership, youth and college chapters grew from 97 with approximately 4,100 members in 1943 to over 380 chapters, with memberships
topping 22,000 by 1946.[1] Taking up NAACP youth work in its fifth year
of national presence, Hurley developed a program that included regular
leadership training; critical analysis of current events; interracial collaboration; legislative instruction and lobbying; exposure to a wide range of
political leaders, government officials, scholars, and other professionals;
engagement with international and labor issues and groups; and practical
experience organizing protests. Her collaborations also nurtured cooperation among national and international youth organizations.[2] Relationships
Hurley developed helped ensure interracial emergence of the National
Students Association,[3] and solidified as they helped intensify momentum
of the Civil Rights Movement through participation of students from
across the nation.

Born 1909 in Washington, DC, Ruby R. Hawkins Hurley is among
a cadre of women whose leadership helped engender and structure the
modern Civil Rights Movement. Hurley's collaborators—peers on the
NAACP staff and leaders beyond the NAACP—included persons such
as Mary B. Talbert, Addie W. Hunton, Ella J. Baker, Septima Clark, and
Anna Arnold Hedgeman, among others.[4] These women shared in common birth near the turn of the century, "middle class" social origin, a
professional identity derived from access to post-secondary education,
employment as organizational administrators at some point during their
careers, and Christian religious affiliation. As administrators within racial
uplift and civil rights organizations, Hurley and her contemporaries (and
their predecessors) were "formal" activists who conceived, translated, and
disseminated ideas about freedom, citizenship, democracy, and justice;
initiated, organized, and oversaw actions that became regular elements
of African American activism; innovated new practices as needed; and
followed (sometimes being challenged by) the directives of senior administrators in organizations within which they worked.

The social location and experiences of Hurley's closest collaborators does not mean activist work of black Christian women is exhausted
by considering only similarly situated persons. As Betty Collier-Thomas
observes, women from a variety of stations and contexts made contributions; it "was through the collective efforts of African American church
women and their organizations, and the work of individual black women
in race-specific, gender-specific, biracial, and interracial associations, that

the struggle for the rights of women and blacks was conducted."[5] From their stations in an array of primarily Protestant contexts, Hurley and her women colleagues helped lay the foundation, develop strategic initiatives, orchestrate campaigns, and initiate collaborations that challenged and changed, as Collier-Thomas notes, racial and gender norms in the United States. At the same time, because their work on behalf of African Americans often disrupted long-established practices of cronyism, corruption, and exploitation affecting all citizens, these women also helped restore, and in some instances supported development of, the public trust.

Similar to many of her predecessors and contemporaries, Hurley incorporated "religion" as a constituent of self-representation and self-understanding, as a strategic element in constructing black womanhood, and as a source of and resource for activism.[6] Women's varied interactions with Christianity contributed to a goal of changing political and cultural norms and constructing the society they envisioned. This chapter explores Hurley's 1940 to 1950 contributions to this goal as a youth worker for the National Association for the Advancement of Colored People. Noting the intentionality with which Hurley constructed her identity as a Protestant Christian laywoman in the tradition of Methodism, the chapter begins by examining Hurley's early life and her continuous relationship with the Method Episcopal (now United Methodist) Church. Through her Methodist identity, Hurley engaged various religious institutions and personalities, particularly within Protestant Christianity, in undertaking her work. From the standpoint of an educated, professional Protestant laywoman, Hurley entered community organizing work that led to her post with the NAACP. While she used her Protestant Christian identity and relationships derived from it to help develop her work, the overall character of Hurley's contributions as NAACP National Youth Director is similar to organizing activities practiced in a variety of contexts. A final section of the chapter considers the meaning of Hurley's youth work for the broader U.S. student movement. Each section of the essay introduces the areas discussed, pointing toward more full explication to come in a longer work on Hurley. I conclude by examining linkages to youth work Hurley maintained as she transitioned to taking on the role as NAACP Southeast Regional Director.

Setting Her Course: Hurley's Allegiance to Methodism and Protestant Christianity

Ruby Ruffin was born November 7, 1909, in Washington, DC, the same year the NAACP was formed. In a 1968 interview, Hurley reflected on her

youth and described herself as growing up "shielded" from segregation
"as most middle-class or so-called middle-class Negroes were shielded
in Washington."[7] An element of this shielding would have included her
time as a youth and young adult at the historic Asbury Methodist (now
United Methodist) Church. Founded in 1836 to protest the humiliation of
segregated worship within a white congregation,[8] Asbury Church permitted Ruffin to become acquainted with the generation of black Christian
women activists before her since Mary McLeod Bethune was a member of
the congregation. Ruffin attended Washington's Miners Teachers College,
then Terrell Law School. Because, she said, she learned early on that she
"didn't want to be a teacher," Ruffin began professional life working at
the Industrial Bank, a black business, located in the U-Street corridor, a
once prominent residential and business district of Washington's African
American residents. She attended law school in the evenings while working for the bank. Ruffin eventually left the Industrial Bank for better pay at
the U.S. Treasury Department.[9] While working at the bank, however, she
was tapped to join the Marian Anderson Citizens Committee, organized
in response to Daughters of the American Revolution denying Anderson
the opportunity to perform in Constitution Hall. Perhaps the invitation
to join the committee came, she later said, "because I was working in the
bank and coming into contact with the many Negroes who had business
in the bank."[10]

After the committee's successful work coordinating Anderson's concert on the steps of the Washington Memorial, Ruffin helped reconstitute
the then-defunct Washington NAACP branch. She served on the executive committee, and became a stand-out because of her work enrolling and
organizing a local NAACP youth council. Performance on the Anderson
Committee and work with the Washington branch soon led to her full-
time employment as an NAACP organizer.[11] In addition to facilitating a
professional transition, work on the Anderson project accompanied two
personal transitions. During this time, Ruffin married William L. Hurley
of the U.S. Army Corp of Engineers. Also, she says, as a result of the
Anderson Committee work, "I started getting interested in us. . . . [A]fter
the performance of Marian Anderson at Lincoln Memorial on that Easter
Sunday, I suppose the spirit moved because in hearing her sing 'Climb-
ing Jacob's Ladder' and other numbers, I really felt moved."[12] Prior to
that time, Hurley described herself as "like most young people, I couldn't
decide what I wanted to do."[13]

Hurley uses religious references—"the spirit moved," hearing "Climb-
ing Jacob's Ladder," "I felt moved"—to characterize her heightened social
consciousness and becoming "interested in us." For many of her predecessors and contemporaries, identifying themselves as religious, more

precisely as Christian, and engaging churches were central to work they set out to do. In spite of the need to challenge patriarchy found in black churches, these institutions affirmed many black women activists. They sustained black women "emotionally and provide[d] 'theological space' for black women's faith expression."[14] They also were institutional spaces of "relatively safe discourse" for "Black women [to] construct independent self-definitions," find their own voices, and develop forms of "Black women's resistance."[15] As they confronted racism and sexism, black women were conscious of and intentional about representing themselves as Christian, especially in an era when it was necessary to combat stereotypes about black people, generally, and black women, in particular. Many black women consciously constructed Christian identities to make larger spaces in which they could create themselves, transgress boundaries, and shape society. They also were conscious of using Christian identity and church contexts as mechanisms to both legitimate women's public engagement and draw in civil rights participation by others.

Similar to many of these women, Ruby Hurley engaged Protestant Christianity to validate her black humanity, to inform her personal identity, to construct a space for and legitimate her female public engagement, and to encourage civil rights participation. Hurley took care in developing her identity not only as a Protestant church woman, but particularly as a Methodist Episcopal laywoman, a denominational identity she held onto throughout her life. When Hurley left Washington and Asbury Church to take her NAACP post in New York, she maintained her relationship with Methodism by joining the historic St. Mark's Methodist Church in Harlem. Hurley joined and was a leader at St. Paul Methodist Church in Birmingham, when she started regional coordination work in 1951.[16] Finally, she joined Warren Memorial United Methodist Church when she left Alabama and moved to Atlanta.[17] In and beyond these congregations Hurley was an active laywoman serving, for example, as president of the congregational women's group (the Wesleyan Service Guild, later the Women's Society of Christian Service, then United Methodist Women), as a member of the local congregational personnel committee, and as Christian Social Involvement Mission Coordinator for the North Georgia Conference of United Methodist Women.

Hurley used churches and church networks to advance her civil rights agenda in a variety of ways including to organize strategy sessions, protests, regular NAACP meetings; to publicize her work; to share her views; and to advance interracial collaboration, such as by organizing legislative training for religious leaders.[18] As National Youth Director, Hurley scheduled public relations activities through congregations from a wide range of denominations (and sometimes other faith traditions), celebrating for example a nationwide youth week, as in 1945 when she called for observance of "Sunday, April 8 [as] youth and religion [day] in all churches under the heading of True Christianity is Unity." As a part of that observance, Hurley spoke at an afternoon event of the youth council at Dixwell Congregational Church in New Haven, Connecticut.[19] While she focused primarily in Christian communities as she engaged religious institutions to support her work, Hurley did not relate exclusively to Christianity. In September, 1949, she was principal speaker at a program of the National Conference of Christians and Jews in Croton-on-Hudson, New York, developing plans for a college-age conference on opposing racial bigotry. The NAACP's November 1949 Youth Conference included an Armistice Day memorial service which paid tribute to "three noted civil rights leaders"—Mr. Oswald Garrison, Rabbi Stephen S. Wise, and Mr. William Staton—at Dayton's Temple Israel. Hurley regularly included rabbis as speakers and workshop leaders during national youth conferences.[20]

Ruby Hurley: NAACP Youth Worker and National Director of Youth Councils

Shortly after reorganization of the Washington NAACP chapter, Hurley was assigned by its executive committee to develop a local youth council. Thirty-five persons signed up as charter members in response to her initial attempt to organize District of Columbia youth. Within six months of the group's February 1940 chartering, membership grew to 150 and a representative attended the NAACP Youth Annual Conference in Texas. Having worked with the local Washington NAACP youth chapter in the early years of World War II, Hurley said youth

> were concerned with the treatment of our men in the Armed Forces. One of the projects that our youth council in Washington was involved in was raising funds to get cigarettes for the boys in camps. The youth council took that position because one of the local newspapers was sponsoring a "Smokes for the Boys Overseas," and at that time, there were relatively few Negroes overseas. The youth council, recognizing that the NAACP was against segregation or discrimination even then, said they would raise money to get smokes for the boys in camps and give them to both Negro and white soldiers, which they did.

The Washington youth chapter also worked with adult NAACP members who engaged the Federal Fair Employment Practices Commission to improve African American employment and preparation for employment.[21]

Hurley's success with the local chapter led Federal Judge William Hastie to recommend her to Walter White, Executive Secretary of the NAACP, for the post as national NAACP Director of Youth Councils when Madison S. Jones, Jr., left. Having had three years to recognize, test, and successfully hone her skills as a leader and youth organizer, Hurley wrote a May 5, 1943 application letter to Walter White that not only made a case for employment on the basis of her successes, but also recommended reorganization of the national youth division, identified activities for youth councils, and included plans she intended to undertake in directing youth programs. While completing youth work, Hurley wrote, she would "at the same time [permit] the ideas and ideals of the N.A.A.C.P. to filtrate into some untouched channels."[22]

On July 15, just over two weeks after she started her position as Director of Youth Councils, Hurley sent Walter White a more detailed memorandum (three single-spaced pages) outlining sixteen specific recommendations for NAACP youth work and identifying how the NAACP should respond to the needs of "Negro" youth of the day. Taking the post in the middle of World War II, Hurley paid particular attention to the meaning of black youth's citizenship in the context of a country at war.[23] Her memorandum argued that black youth felt excluded from the "Four Freedoms and the Democracy" originally identified in President Roosevelt's 1941 State of the Union Address. She called for training youth to know about and take responsibility for their citizenship; a campaign to eliminate negative discursive depictions of black persons and to develop "more favorable material"; "added pressure" to enlist ministers in supporting NAACP efforts with youth; a national youth program aimed at providing youth constructive outlets and training youth for cooperative social interaction and healthy living; developing youth institutes on leadership and civic engagement; youth correspondence with service men and women to support them and learn their experiences of discrimination; youth preparation for "participation in post-war world affairs"; legislative training for youth; instructing branches to engage youth councils in their work; supervision of youth councils by branches; a variety of fundraising activities for youth councils; field staff encouraging youth as well as adult memberships; and "a meeting of the National Committee on Youth Work be called immediately." Hurley also recommended mechanisms for publicizing NAACP youth activities and greater emphasis on junior youth councils (ages 12 to 16).[24] As the work developed, Hurley undertook these recommendations as her own agenda.

Hurley's work as national youth secretary required that she help build the NAACP's youth organization. From headquarters at the NAACP national offices in New York, she traveled across the country organizing, enhancing, and supporting youth work. This included a substantial portion of her first months of NAACP employment which Hurley spent preparing for and traveling extensively to generate interest in the annual youth conference (already scheduled for the fall). Signaling the heightened visibility Hurley would bring to her work, that October 29–31, 1943, Annual NAACP Student Conference, at Lincoln University in Pennsylvania, featured an address by Eleanor Roosevelt and was, at that point, the largest NAACP student conference ever held. Though the numbers of councils had not reached their peak, the racially diverse group of attendees came from as far south as Florida to as far midwest as Michigan. In addition to Mrs. Roosevelt, 1943 youth conferees heard addresses from Regional National Labor Relations Board Director Charles Douds, Scomburg Library Curator Lawrence Reddick, NAACP Special Council Thurgood Marshall, NAACP Executive Secretary Walter White, Review and Analysis Director of the Federal Fair Employment Practices Commission John A. Davis, progressive Actress Jean Muir, Ms. Hurley, and others. Delegates elected officers, primarily from Washington and the Southeast, though the chairperson, Gloria Morgan, was a student at Wayne State in Detroit. The meeting culminated with adoption of a 10-point statement calling for

> (1) the end to all discrimination and segregation in the Armed Forces, (2) the abolition of discrimination by the American Red Cross, including especially the segregation in the blood plasma banks, (3) Federal Law to aid the states in education, the funds thus made available to be distributed without discrimination on account of race, color, or national origin, (4) closer association between NAACP College Chapters and white student groups on the various campuses, (5) Congressional legislation that will make permanent the President's committee on Fair Employment Practice, (6) activities by the entire youth section of the NAACP to instruct the use of the ballot and to work for the removal of restrictions on the exercise of the franchise, (7) consultation and cooperation with organized labor in every community, (8) freedom for subject peoples of the world, (9) the pardoning of Alton Levy, now confined to the guard house at the Lincoln, Nebraska Air Base after conviction on charges which included protest by him on the treatment of Negroes at the base, (10) the inclusion of NAACP Youth Councils with College Chapters in one Youth Conference annually.[25]

Although early in Hurley's tenure as Youth Secretary, topics of the Lincoln meeting overlapped and combined with her 16-point memo to Walter White and indicated the range of conference topics and year-round projects she was to undertake with youth. Successive annual conferences, for example, engaged issues of racial segregation and subordination, including voting rights; discussed "methods of combating the Ku Klux Klan, mob violence, lynching and police brutality, and obtaining freedom from terror for all citizens"; considered the range of issues impediments to the fourteenth and fifteenth amendments to the U.S. Constitution; examined the relationship of "Negro Youth" to international minorities; considered issues of labor relations; and more.[26] Though Hurley opposed "ill-advised" use of direct action tactics,[27] annual youth conferences and day-to-day youth work also included protests and demonstrations. In 1947, following the Michigan Supreme Court ruling that opposed segregated accommodations on excursion steamers, Hurley urged youth councils "to form interracial picnic parties and attempt to secure accommodations on ocean, lake and river steamers carrying passengers on moonlights, picnics and other excursions this summer."[28] In 1949 she wrote to Pennsylvania Governor James H. Duff urging that he convene a grand jury to investigate failure of police officials who arrested members of the Lincoln University youth chapter for a protest campaign against segregated public accommodations. Hurley maintained attention on the role of persons from the armed forces, noting in her letter to Governor Duff that the *largely veteran* student body "are determined to secure their full rights in the enjoyment of various accommodations in the Borough of Oxford."[29] Other protest activities peppered Hurley's work with youth.[30]

In 1946, Hurley initiated the NAACP's legislative conferences which trained youth to engage legislative processes. The three-day spring meeting, held in Washington, supplemented the fall annual conference in its focus on lobbying techniques, attending hearings on Capitol Hill, visiting congressional majority and minority leaders, and youth discussing their legislative program with respective senators and representatives. Speakers for these conferences included a range of civic, legislative, and government leaders such as Booker T. McGraw, deputy assistant director of the National Housing administration, Clarence R. Mitchell, NAACP labor secretary, Charles H. Houston, director of NAACP litigation and dean of the Howard University Law School, A. Powell Davies, pastor of All Souls Unitarian Church, Ms. Hurley, and others.[31]

In some instances, Hurley specifically sought to further the NAACP youth agenda through interracial/race relations work. Her intentionality in undertaking interracial work reflected Hurley's perspective that some

challenges of racial discrimination could be overcome only through exposure, collaboration, and cooperation. In a 1945 speech she encouraged
black youth to participate in cross-racial exposure. "White people don't
know you," she said; "they only know what they may have read in history books, many of which have erroneous and misleading statements
about the race." Hurley added that such misconceptions also existed in
black communities about white persons.[32] She made alliances with and
founded youth chapters on campuses of majority institutions, and pursued her youth agenda through these chapters. At Columbia University,
chapter goals included "work toward the elimination of textbooks con-
taining passages derogatory to minority groups, abolition of the college
'quota system,' improvement of student and teacher attitudes toward race
problems."[33] In early January, 1948, Hurley met in New York with area
representatives of youth councils (from Long Island, Columbia, and New
York universities; Queens and Hunter colleges; and youth councils in
Yonkers, Port Washington, Jamaica, Manhattan, Brooklyn, Far Rockaway,
Plainfield, and Elizabeth) to discuss "increased contact with interracial
colleges and . . . outlining a program for college chapters." A permanent
NAACP youth work Faculty Advisory Committee formed at that gather-
ing included faculty and administrative representatives from New York,
Wilberforce, Cornell, Bucknell, and Howard universities.[34]

Ruby Hurley and the U.S. Student Movement

Ruby Hurley's leadership of the NAACP's youth department was pre-
scient in clearly incorporating two elements that would prove substantially
important to shaping work of U.S. students and U.S. interracial collaborations during the mid-twentieth century and beyond. First, Hurley recognized both the need to address and the energy potential of soldiers
disenchanted during and returning after World War II. As early as her
1940 coordination of the Washington youth council, Hurley led young
people in engaging both segregation and morale of U.S. World War II
troops. Second, throughout her time as Director of Youth Work, Hurley
fostered and built interracial collaborations among young people. She felt
this engagement was essential to changing the society. Both these emphases fed growth of the mid-century U.S. student movement which, though
it sometimes diverged from, frequently overlapped and aligned with African American efforts in what became the U.S. Civil Rights Movement.

In her earliest NAACP work, Hurley explored with youth the status
of black soldiers, morale of all soldiers, and issues of segregation in the
U.S. Armed Forces. Hurley reflected on this element of her work with the
Washington youth council in an interview conducted by John Britton:

We were concerned with the treatment of our men in the Armed Forces. One of the projects that our youth council in Washington was involved in was raising funds to get cigarettes for the boys in camps. The youth council took that position because one of the local newspapers was sponsoring a "Smokes for the Boys Overseas," and at that time, there were relatively few Negroes overseas. The youth council, recognizing that the NAACP was against segregation or discrimination even then, said they would raise money to get smokes for the boys in camps and give them to both Negro and white soldiers, which they did. We worked over a Thanksgiving weekend and raised some seven or eight hundred dollars. The kids bought a number of the huge cartons, you know the big things of cigarettes, took them out to Fort Belvoir, and shocked the Southern white boys in camp out there by giving them cigarettes as well as the Negro soldiers who were stationed out at Fort Belvoir.

We were interested then in the same kinds of things. I remember too, what with all the noise being made about Vietnam, that A. Philip Randolph and Grant Reynolds, as I remember, raised questions about Negroes serving in World War II. With the assistance of—I can't remember his name now; one of the professors of Columbia University—we conducted a survey on the college campuses to see how Negro students on college campuses really felt about serving in segregated Armed Forces. The results of our survey were published in *Newsweek*. This was back during World War II.[35]

When she began youth work at NAACP national offices in New York, as one of her sixteen recommendations to Walter White, Hurley included explicit emphasis on engaging military personnel, recommending that "youth councils formulate their programs to include members and potential members in the armed forces." In addition to letter-writing to lift the troops' morale, Hurley said youth council correspondence with soldiers could "serve as a source of material from which the NAACP may learn of cases of segregation, discrimination, and other bigotrous practices effecting them, and take measures to adjust or correct them."[36] Emphasis on the U.S. armed forces persisted throughout her NAACP youth work. The 1944 annual youth conference at Virginia Union University discussed world peace and included resolutions calling for "postwar planning." Its recommendation for "appointment of a Negro to the Veterans' Administration Bureau" offered a mechanism to begin such planning.[37] In 1945, Hurley gave a Kansas speech encouraging black youth at Sumner High School to take up the work of improving race relations, saying if discriminatory practices in the United States did not change before the war ended, she expected returning soldiers to make changes once they arrived. She urged young people to recognize significance "of the problem of segregation so as to be ready to aid in its solution when Negro soldiers return." "A changed attitude on the part of young Negroes returning from military service is to be expected," Hurley continued, and added "a changed attitude on the part of whites was needed to meet" that of the soldiers. That same year Hurley discussed "What Negro Youths Expect in a Post-War World" with students at Smith College.[38]

After the war ended, Hurley's youth work continued to include a focus on the military with the tenth NAACP Youth Conference, meeting in St. Louis resolving to request that President Truman eliminate segregation in the Armed Forces.[39] By the time she transitioned out of the post as Director of Youth Work and into the position as Southeastern Regional Coordinator, Hurley framed her assertions about the military as consistent with the view of members of the armed forces and World War II veterans. Calling for school desegregation across the South, Mrs. Hurley said young people have long advocated equality and asserted "that this is true especially of young men in the armed forces during World War II." With many World War II veterans, Hurley called for the country to live up to its creeds and its role in global politics: "These walls of segregation have got to come down if America is going to stand in a position of leadership in the world," she said.[40]

Near the war's end, changes occurred in the United States that helped connect returning veterans and Hurley's interracial work and helped solidify the relationship of Hurley's work to the mid-century U.S. student movement. Passage of the GI Bill (formally the Servicemen's Readjustment Act of 1944) included a benefit providing college or vocational education for returning veterans. This bill alone, some persons assert, accounts for doubling enrollment in U.S. colleges and universities. As they entered or returned to higher education, World War II veterans carried with them "international" perspectives and concerns they took up as a result of military service. In addition to generalized opposition to segregation, many felt the United States should be a global leader by adhering to its founding principles. Miriam Haskell Berlin observes that the changed international position of the United States after the war was the context out of which these ideas and the U.S. student movement emerged. The "United States emerged from the conflict not only physically intact," Berlin writes, "but enormously transformed in economic and physical power. Our sense of responsibility for leadership in maintaining the peace had developed commensurately."[41] Adding to other changes they advocated, World War II veterans also opposed the hitherto ordinary practice of colleges serving *in loco parentis*. The combat and international experience returning service persons brought made them unlikely candidates for customary restrictions they faced on college campuses. Many became campus leaders. In some instances, as Hurley asserted of Lincoln University in 1950, student bodies were comprised "largely of veterans."[42] U.S. college students in the mid-century had a decidedly international and adult perspective.

Hurley supported students internationalizing their agenda. Within the NAACP, she helped youth focus on international issues. Annual NAACP youth conferences regularly included resolutions in support of all subjugated peoples of the world and attention to issues in transnational relations. The 1944 Virginia conference issued a call for the United States to participate in "world-wide cooperation with international student groups." Among speakers at the 1944 NAACP youth conference was Aziz Pabani, Indian member of the All India Students Federation, who was studying engineering at Columbia University.[43] Beyond the NAACP youth program, Hurley supported and influenced U.S. student engagement with international student meetings. She is listed in the booklet "The Bright Face of Peace" as "a sponsor of the U.S. Participation in the World Youth Festival, Prague, July–August, 1947" (where the U.S. exhibit included a large poster showing a Negro hanging from a tree; the caption said 70 Negroes had been lynched in the U.S. since V-J Day.).[44] Hurley also is identified in 1949 as related to 175 U.S. students attending the World Federation of Democratic Youth, August 14–28, 1949, in Budapest. These two relationships landed Hurley in reports of the U.S. House Committee on Un-American Activities.[45]

During World War II, Eugene G. Schwartz observes in *American Students Organize*, "American college students went to war. On their return, they elected to pursue peace and justice at home and abroad with renewed commitment. The U.S. National Student Association (NSA) reflected this resolve."[46] Carrying the peace and anti-militarism perspective that had emerged among students internationally and rising from remnants of previous student organizations in the United States, the NSA was founded in 1947 "as a direct response to the formation of the International Union of Students after the postwar birth of the United Nations."[47] In addition to emphases on peace, the NSA retained the commitment of more radical elements of earlier national students groups to overcome racism. Hurley's intentional interracial work allowed her to engage persons that would form the NSA, which originated as a substantial ally to the NAACP's youth and civil rights agenda. Assessing Hurley's role in this regard, Swartz writes that the

> NSA's national leadership, strongly committed to desegregation and to integration, originally showed their support of the NAACP's efforts through mutual appearances at each other's

conventions and in informal information sharing. When the first NAACP Youth Secretary to work with NSA, Ruby Hurley, left her position after her appearance at the NSA 1950 Congress, the groundwork had been laid for a good working relationship on civil rights issues which her successor, Herbert Wright built on during the following years. NSA's interest in integration culminated in NSA's 1958 Southern Student Human Relations Project and its involvement in the formation of the Student Non-Violent Coordinating Committee (SNCC) in 1960 after the Greensboro sit-ins.[48]

Hurley served on the Southern Student Human Relations Project's advisory committee (alongside National Council of Churches representative Will Campbell, Atlanta University President Rufus Clement, Morehouse College President Benjamin Mays, and Atlanta Journal Constitution publisher/editor Ralph McGill). As a relative newcomer to Atlanta, Hurley's appointment to the advisory committee obviously derived from previously established relationships. The committee encouraged Project Director Constance Curry to share southern student work with other student groups. Curry developed a monthly newsletter that went to the National Federation of Christian College Students as well as the NSA which was her sponsor.[49] Hurley's near ten-year investment in interracial student collaborations paid dividends for years after she left the Youth Director post.

Transition to the South and Southeast Regional Work

Less than 35 years old when Hurley took the post as national youth director, the NAACP required staff members to share responsibility for helping develop the organization while performing their other assigned work. This was especially the case in recruiting members as the Association sought to build its base. Early in her NAACP career Hurley spoke at membership drives and attended membership strategy sessions. In 1950, as the NAACP undertook a new membership recruitment campaign, Ruby Hurley was assigned to coordinate membership drives in five southern states (Alabama, Florida, Georgia, Mississippi, and Tennessee). By 1951 the initial unfolding of the Civil Rights Movement and requests from Mississippi and Georgia state NAACP presidents led to Hurley's being appointed permanently to the South.[50] She initially set up offices in Birmingham in 1951, then, after the Association's activities were outlawed in Alabama, moved her work to Atlanta in 1956. As she transitioned to Southeast Regional coordination, Hurley maintained a relationship with youth work.[51] Soon, however, she was consumed with the demands of coordinating NAACP activity across the seven-state region.[52] When Hurley began regional work, she continued using relationships with religious institutions, particularly churches to support her agenda. In addition to maintaining connections with Methodist churches as she relocated, Hurley frequently held rallies, strategy sessions, state and regional meetings, and other events in church facilities. She also regularly collaborated with ministers in completing her work. This emphasis developed so substantially that in April, 1959, Hurley coordinated (with Rev. Edward J. Odom, Jr., NAACP national church secretary) a Southwide Interracial Conference of Religious Leaders at Morehouse College.[53] Though many persons understood Christianity as opposed to the very causes for which Ruby Hurley worked, her relationship with and assessment of Christianity identified the tradition with overcoming segregation and discrimination. In addition to holding this view as a Christian moral imperative, Hurley asserted that the general quality of life is negatively impacted when segregation and discrimination are practiced. "[A]ctive racial prejudice is unsound in dollars and cents and community prestige," Hurley once wrote. She continued, asking, "When will all the people see that this malignant, cancerous growth must be cut out before it destroys us economically, physically, mentally, morally and spiritually?"[54] Hurley's life work sought to make this change. The legacy of "racial prejudice" in continuing discrimination and class subordination makes Hurley's question relevant in our time.

Notes

1. "NAACP to Sponsor World-Wide Fight against Exploitation, White Reports," *Baltimore Afro-American*, January 12, 1946, 11; Hurley Memo to Walter White, September 8, 1944, NAACP Files.

2. Memo, NY 100-7629 Sub-C, June 1958, Unnamed Recipient, Ruby R. Hawkins Hurley FBI File 1154910-000.

3. Eugene G. Schwartz, editor, *American Students Organize: Founding the U.S. National Student Association after World War II: An Anthology and Sourcebook*, (New York: Praeger, 2006), 452.

4. August Meier and John H. Bracey, Jr., "The NAACP as a Reform Movement, 1909–1965: 'To Reach the Conscience of America'" *Journal of Southern History*, Vol. 59, No.1 (Feb., 1993), 19–20; Zina Rodriguez, "Legends: NAACP Women Who Have Made a Difference," *The New Crisis*, March/April 2000.

5. Bettye Collier-Thomas, *Jesus, Jobs, and Justice: African American Women and Religion* (New York: Knofp, 2010), xxxiii.

6. See Evelyn Brooks Higginbotham, *Righteous Discontent: The Women's Movement in the Black Baptist Church, 1880–1920* (Cambridge: Harvard, 1993), especially chapter seven, "The Politics of Respectability."

7. Hurley interview by John Britton, 2.

8. Founded in 1836 when a group of black persons left the majority white Foundry Methodist Church to protest of racial segregation, Asbury served as a part of the Underground Railroad network. See *Asbury, Our Legacy, Our Faith, 1836–1933: The History of Asbury United Methodist Church, Washington, D.C.* (Washington, District of Columbia: Asbury Church, nd).

9. Britton Interview, 1, 5; "Mrs. Hurley Addresses Freedom Fund Dinner Tuesday Evening" *Atlanta Daily World*, May 14, 1961, 2; Wallace H. Terry, "Troubleshooter Was 'Outsider': Now She's a Voice for the Silent South" *The Washington Post*, August 27, 1963, a1.

10. Britton Interview, 1.

11. Ruby R. Hurley to Walter White, May 5, 1943, Papers of the National Association for the Advancement of Colored People, Group II, Box J41; John H. Britton, Interviewer, A Transcript of a Recorded Interview with Mrs. Ruby Hurley, Director, Southeastern Regional Office of the National Association for The Advancement of Colored People, Atlanta, Georgia, January 26, 1968, The Civil Rights Documentation Project; Venue: 1527 New Hampshire Ave, NW. Washington, DC, 20036, The Moorland-Spingarn Research Center, Howard University, Washington, District of Columbia, 1–2, 4–5.

12. Britton Interview, 2.

13. Britton Interview, 5.

14. Delores Williams, *Sisters in the Wilderness: The Challenge of Womanist God-Talk* (New York: Orbis, 1993), xiii.

15. Patricia Hill Collins, *Black Feminist Thought: Knowledge, Consciousness, and the Politics of Empowerment* (New York: Routledge, 1991), 95; also see Evelyn Brooks Higginbotham, *Righteous Discontent: The Women's Movement in the Black Baptist Church, 1880–1920* (Cambridge: Harvard, 1993), 185.

16. "Mrs. Ruby Hurley Speaker at Centenary"*Atlanta Daily World*, April 19, 1964, 2.

17. On June 1, 1956, the state of Alabama served Hurley with a restraining order, enjoining the NAACP from operating in the state and holding the Association in contempt for failure to surrender names of the state's members and contributors. Hurley immediately left Alabama and soon set up regional offices in Atlanta. See "Ala. Will Hear NAACP after 5½ Years Delay" *Atlanta Daily World*, June 1, 1956, 1; John H. Britton Interview, 16.

18. Rosetta E. Ross, interview, Thomasina Daugherty, Atlanta, Georgia, October 29, 2009.

19. "NAACP to Observe Youth Week, April 8–14" *The Negro Star*, April 6, 1945, Vol. 37, Iss. 48, 1.

20. "Plan Bigotry Fight on Neighbor Level" *Atlanta Daily World*, Sept. 14, 1949, 2; "Youth Group Wins Citation: Milwaukee Unit Named for Honor" *Baltimore Afro American*, November 12, 1949, A20; Program, 6th Annual Youth Conference, NAACP, Virginia Union University, Richmond, Virginia, Papers of the National Association for the Advancement of Colored People, Library of Congress, General Office File, Box II: A587, Folder 2, Staff, Ruby Hurley, 1943–1954.

21. Britton Interview, 6–7.

22. Ruby R. Hurley to Walter White, May 5, 1943, Papers of the National Association for the Advancement of Colored People, Library of Congress, General Office File, Group II, Box J41.

23. In work with the Washington Youth Council Hurley both affirmed youth support of the young men in the armed forces (with a "smokes for the troops" campaign) and led the youth to consider the issue of segregation in the U.S. Armed Forces. See Britton Interview, 7.

24. "Memorandum to Mr. White from Mrs. Hurley," July 15, 1943, Papers of the National Association for the Advancement of Colored People, Group II, Box J41.

25. "Mrs. Roosevelt Addresses Largest NAACP Student Annual Conference" [Kansas City] *Plaindealer*, November 12, 1943, Vol. 45, Iss. 44, 2; "Youth Call for Jobs, Freedom, and Opportunity" Atlanta Daily World, November 9, 1943, 1; "Digest of Speeches at the NAACP Student Session" *Baltimore Afro-American*, November 6, 1943, 6.

26. For examples see, Program, 6th Annual Youth Conference, NAACP, Virginia Union University, Richmond, Virginia, Papers of the National Association for the Advancement of Colored People, Library of Congress, General Office File, Box II: A587, Folder 2, Staff, Ruby Hurley, 1943–1954; "NAACP to Observe Youth Week, April 8–14" *The Negro Star*, April 6, 1945, Vol. 37, Iss. 48, 1; Civic Youths Plan 8th Conference," *Baltimore Afro-American*, November 16, 1946, 15.

27. For an example of Hurley's view of using protests judiciously, see Wallace H. Terry, "Troubleshooter Was 'Outsider': Now She's a Voice for the Silent South" *The Washington Post*, August 27, 1963, 1.

28. "NAACP Youth Urged to Use Excursion Steamers" *Atlanta Daily World*, May 17, 1947, 2.

29. "Asks Governor to Probe Bias in Oxford, Pa." *Atlanta Daily World*, April 5, 1950, 1.

30. For two other examples see "Savannah Youth Week Closes" *The Negro Star*, June 7, 1946, Vol. 29, Iss. 5, 1; "NAACP Presses for Halt to Filibuster" *Atlanta Daily World*, March 8, 1949, 1.

31. See "Negro Teen-Agers Here to Learn Lobbying Technique" *Atlanta Daily World*, April 11, 1947, 1; "NAACP Youth Head for Capitol Hill" *The Negro Star*, March 25, 1949, Vol. 41, Iss.48, 1; "NAACP Youth Head for Capital City" *Atlanta Daily World*, March 22, 1949, 3; "Davies Keynotes NAACP Youth Lobbying Meet" *Atlanta Daily World*, April 6, 1949, 2; "NAACP Youth Planning Lobbying Sessions" *The Negro Star*, April 1, 1949, Vol. 41, Iss. 49, 1.

32. "Students Hear Mrs. R. Hurley" *Plaindealer*, February 9, 1945, Vol. 47, Iss. 5, 2.

33. "Youth Chapter Set Up at Columbia U" *Atlanta Daily Wold*, Dec. 22, 1946, 6.

34. "NAACP Youth Groups Hold New York Meet" *Atlanta Daily World*, Jan. 23, 1948, 2.

35. Britton Inteview, 6–7.

36. "Memorandum to Mr. White from Mrs. Hurley," July 15, 1943, 2.

37. " 'Total Peace' Up To Youth and Unity, Are Findings of NAACP Conference" *The Negro Star* (Wichita, Kansas), December 1, 1944, Vol. 37, Iss. 30, 1.

38. See "Students Hear Mrs. R. Hurley" *Plaindealer*, February 9, 1945, Vol. 47, Iss. 5, 2 and "Smith College Concerned about Post-War Negro Expectations" *The Negro Star*, March 16, 1945, Vol. 37, Iss. 45, 1.

39. "End Armed Forces Segregation; NAACP Youth Asks President" *The Negro Star*, December 31, 1948, Vol. 41, Iss. 36, 1.

40. "Ala. Miss. Targets of New NAACP Suits" *Atlanta Daily World*, Apr. 5, 1951, 2.

41. Miriam Haskell Berlin, "American Society and American Students: A Historical Perspective" in *American Students Organize: Founding the U.S. National Student Association after World War II: An Anthology and Sourcebook*, Eugene G. Schwartz, editor, Praeger, 2006, 10.

42. "Asks Governor to Probe Bias in Oxford, Pa." *Atlanta Daily World*, April 5, 1950, 1.

43. "Mrs. Roosevelt Addresses Largest NAACP Student Annual Conference" [Kansas City] *Plaindealer*, November 12, 1943, Vol. 45, Iss. 44, 2; " 'Total Peace' Up To Youth and Unity, Are Findings of NAACP Conference" *The Negro Star* (Wichita, Kansas), December 1, 1944, Vol. 37, Iss. 30, 1.

44. Eugene G. Schwartz (Other Contributors include Wiliam Wellsh, William Dentzer, jr., Norman Holmes, Richard J. Medalie, Richard G Heggie), "Covert U. S. Government funding of NSA International Programs, Attachment 2: American Students in Postwar International Affairs" *American Students Organize: Founding the U.S. National Student Association after World War II: An Anthology and Sourcebook* (New York: Praeger, 2006), 571.

45. Memo, NY 100-7629 Sub-C, June 1958, Unnamed Recipient, Ruby R. Hawkins Hurley FBI File 1154910-000.

46. Eugene G. Schwartz, *American Students Organize: Founding the U.S. National Student Association after World War II: An Anthology and Sourcebook*, Praeger, 2006, 3.

47. Berlin, 9.

48. Schwartz, 452.

49. Faith S. Holsaert, Martha Prescod Norman Noonan, Judy Richardson, Betty Garman Robinson, Jean Smith Yount, Dorothy M. Zellner, editors, *Hands on the Freedom Plow: Personal Accounts by Women in SNCC*, University of Illinois, 47–48.

50. "Establish Temporary NAACP Headquarters IN Southeast" *Atlanta Daily World*, March 27, 1951, 3; Britton Interview, 9.

51. "Organize Michigan State NAACP Youth Conference" *Atlanta Daily World*, September 10, 1950, 2; Alice A. Dunnigan, "Dr. Dorothy Ferebee Keynotes Democracy at White House Meet" *Atlanta Daily World*, December 7, 1950, 1; "Ala. Miss. Targets of New NAACP Suits" *Atlanta Daily World*, April 5, 1951, 2; "NAACP Launches Full Scale Selective Buying Drive" *Kansas Sentinel*, September 22, 1960, 9. Also see, Annette Jones White, "Finding Form for the Expression of My Discontent" in *Hands on the Freedom Plow: Personal Accounts by Women in SNCC*, Faith S. Holsaert, Martha Prescod Norman Noonan, Judy Richardson,

Betty Garman Robinson, Jean Smith Young, and Dorothy M. Zellner, University of Illinois, 2010, esp., 106, 108.

52. South Carolina and North Carolina were added to Hurley's portfolio as the new region took shape.

53. "Clergymen to Meet Here" *Atlanta Daily World*, April 5, 1959, 1.

54. Marion E. Jackson, "Sports of the World" *Atlanta Daily World*, Oct. 2, 1953, 7.

4

Black Churches, Peoples Temple, and Civil Rights Politics in San Francisco

James Lance Taylor

The black freedom struggle in Northern California conflated around persistent problems of residential segregation, job discrimination, education policy, police brutality, and housing which African Americans across the region faced in the decades between World War II and the turbulence of the Black Power phase of the struggle. In cities such as Richmond, Alameda, Berkeley, Oakland, and San Francisco, local leaders, assorted groups and organizations, and community institutions confronted many of the challenges taken up by the larger effort. As the region's African American population increased from less than 18,000 in the 1940s to more than 235, 000 in Oakland and San Francisco by the 1960s,[1] the black migrant population took center-stage in at least three distinct but overlapping phases of the Civil Rights Movement. The first was developed between 1945 and 1963 as these emergent populations sought to define the terms of community engagement with a hostile political establishment dominated by white reactionaries and moderate African American leaders whose forebears migrated during the nineteenth century.[2] African American church and community institutions served in critical capacities, sponsoring a tepid but effective activism and establishing the National Association for the Advancement of Colored Peoples (NAACP) and the Congress of Racial Equality (CORE), which respectively engaged in moderate and more confrontational tactics between the 1940s and 1960s. In addition to the NAACP, the political career of future California Speaker of the House and San Francisco Mayor Willie Brown was launched at Jones United Methodist Church in San Francisco under the leadership of the highly influential Rev. Hamilton Boswell.[3] Boswell served as the Chairman of Willie Brown's unsuccessful 1962 State Assembly campaign and the Rev. Frederick Douglas Haynes, Sr.,—who sought elective office himself three times between 1947 and 1951—served on Brown's campaign committee.[4] By some accounts, Jones's United Methodist Church and Third Baptist Church, where Rev. Haynes served as pastor, spearheaded the local Civil Rights Movement in concert with other churches and surrogate institutions.[5]

The second phase largely mirrored the southern Civil Rights Movement as leading pastors engaged increasingly in social movement activism around perennial issues consistent with integrating existing white institutions. For instance, local leaders picketed Woolworth's in San Francisco for one year in solidarity with the 1960 Student Nonviolent Coordinating Committee (SNCC) sit-ins in Greensboro, North Carolina.[6] In fact no major downtown businesses that openly denied service or job opportunities to African Americans in the region were immune from protests in the middle of the decade. Daniel Crowe insists, "African Americans in northern California felt that their struggles for racial equality in the urban West were fundamentally connected to their brethren's efforts in the rural South."[7] In the early 1960s the adults, children, and especially the youth of the first generation of southern émigrés unleashed a succession of boycotts, sit-ins, strikes, walk-offs and work stoppages that stunned Northern California's legal and political establishment and more conservative organizations such as the NAACP. Yet since the 1940s, intense factionalism between elites in the civil litigation-oriented NAACP and the fledgling CORE—which reemerged in the 1960s with a white-led direct action program based in San Francisco and Berkeley—characterized the dispersive character of black politics in the region. Most established African American congregations in Northern California failed to take the lead in fighting the loss of church and community members resulting from "urban renewal" in the Bay Area. According to Rev. Wilbur Hamilton, the Director of SFRA Project Area 2 (A-2), several major African American churches actually benefitted from urban renewal and therefore were reluctant to oppose it.

Lastly, during the middle 1960s to 1970s, with the Free Speech Movement (1964), the emergence of Black Power (1966), the "Summer of Love" (1967), and opposition to the Vietnam War, Bay Area cities instigated an intense shift away from religiously motivated and moderate approaches to protest politics and nonviolence. The issues which precipitated the earlier struggles persisted and yielded a record of mixed results. The opportunity structure remained largely closed off to African Americans in the region, and reactionary political and law enforcement establishments hardened against younger activists who took up the rhetoric and ideologies of militancy. Accompanying this shift was a general critique of the Black Church as a movement institution. Crowe for instance, notes, "the crises and policies of the 1950s had by the 1960s produced isolated ghettos in San Francisco and the poverty populations they contained grew more restless as conditions worsened and the rest of the city seemed to leave them further behind."[8] Yet African American churches were never fully out of step with a majority of black people in the region or country who rejected the new militancy. Huey P. Newton understood, in hindsight, that dismissing black churches and black religion for the purpose of politics was equal to "defecting from the black community."[9] The emergent milieu of New Left and Black Power movement activism culminated in the Christian Socialist project of the Peoples Temple movement, the self-consciously "beloved community"[10] inspired by Martin Luther King, Jr., and Huey P. Newton, who Jim Jones imagined he channeled (and exceeded) in his leadership among the African American communities. With the death of Martin Luther King, Jr., Jim Jones and Peoples Temple were able to project their movement as a local successor to Civil Rights Movement ideals, tapping effectively into receptivity to those ideals among black churchgoers in the Bay Area (and Los Angeles).[11] Peoples Temple reverberated the complex set of ideological, political, social, leadership, and migration struggles of the San Francisco Bay Area's African American communities. For all of the scholarly and journalistic interrogation of Jim Jones, Peoples Temple, and Jonestown, it becomes apparent that there is hardly a feature of this movement that was original; it was mostly parasitic of the overarching black freedom struggle.[12] Peoples Temple self-consciously understood itself to be seizing on the failure of many local black clergy (and many black political leaders) to appreciate and capture the potential of a black church-centered militancy in the Bay Area. Jim Jones and Peoples Temple adopted the intra-communal criticisms by segments of the African American community aimed at church institutions as a recruiting pitch to build its movement. The draw of Peoples Temple was not merely affirmative, that is, attractive on the merits of its outreach and social service programs, rather it ambushed unsuspecting pastors and churches steeped in traditions poorly suited for the emergent consciousness and expectations of their constituencies. The two decades between the Birmingham boycott movement and the mass destruction of Jonestown, exposed the vicissitudes of local black church mobilization against the particular issues facing their communities. How to be relevant and to remain so, at a time and place where radical was chic and "revolutionary," and where anyone under thirty years old wanted to be described in this way, was the task of older black church leaders in the Bay Area. Jones was approaching his forties. How to *appear* vital to the community in a region dominated by young, charismatic, and activist personalities like Huey P. Newton, Bobby Seale, Angela Davis, Eldridge Cleaver, George Jackson, Stokely Carmichael, Willie Brown, and Rev. Cecil Williams is where most of the

Bay Area's black clergy and churches fell off, and Jim Jones and Peoples Temple stepped in.[13]

This chapter is based on person-to-person interviews of community members—including several Peoples Temple survivors—and leading men and women who were active in the Bay Area church community in the 1960s and 1970s.[14] It is also based on participant observation of the annual commemoration of the Peoples Temple massacre where principal survivors (and a rival group of remaining supporters of Jones) meet annually in East Oakland on November 18th—to mourn the murdered children of Jonestown whose remains are buried there. Sociologist Judith Mary Weightman, who provides a good summary of pertinent literature, counted nineteen books written within five years of the massacre.[15] They vary from the investigative and conspiratorial,[16] to sympathetic and repudiationist survivor accounts, including that of journalist Tim Reiterman who co-authored *Raven: The Untold Story of the Rev. Jim Jones and His People* (1982), which is a definitive work for many. John R. Hall and David Chidester have separately written excellent studies that improve on the early works, particularly as they take seriously the theological content of Peoples Temple and its relationship to the African American churches in the Bay Area and the United States more generally.[17] Rebecca Moore, Anthony Pinn, and Mary R. Sawyer have collaborated in *Peoples Temple and Black Religion in America* (2004), which is the only work that explicitly details the religious dimensions of Peoples Temple and black religiosity.[18]

This chapter builds on narratives of black church civil rights activism in Northern California cities and the experiences of African American communities which precipitated Peoples Temple's appeal as a movement in the 1960s and 1970s. The chapter argues that the 913 mostly black Bay Area residents who succumbed at Jonestown, while drawn in the United States to Peoples Temple for many different reasons, were essentially disappointed with most of the area churches' failure to sustain them as they confronted social problems being addressed by progressive groups, including (arguably) Peoples Temple. The few churches and leaders who did address social problems, however, waged a fierce battle that would transform social and political relations in the region.

Black Churches in Illiberal San Francisco

African American churches in Northern California took the lead in linking the region's political activism to the larger movement led by southern clergy. Well before the seminal *Brown v. Board of Education, Topeka* (1954) decision, African American church leaders in the Bay Area instigated a struggle for rights that encompassed three decades after World War II. Consistent with local movements elsewhere, Northern California clergy were instrumental in reform efforts concerning residential segregation, housing and job discrimination, public education, and police brutality. Some church leaders supported the Brotherhood of Sleeping Car Porter's union movement in the region, while others sought or recruited persons to seek public office. Dr. Howard Thurman cofounded and served as pastor of the first interracial and interfaith church in the United States, Church for the Fellowship of All Peoples in San Francisco, from 1944–1953.[19] The idea of an intentionally interracial church was novel even in liberal San Francisco and was not widely accepted outside of its Russian Hill neighborhood. At the core of his religious teachings was the feeling that "I believe that before God there are no men or women, no races, no Protestants, Catholics, or Jews. We are all Spirits who are His children."[20] Thurman represented an important presence in the city of San Francisco, and Fellowship Church anticipated King's "beloved community," Cecil Williams's Glide Church in San Francisco, and Peoples Temple—which thought it had invented the idea of interracial community in Indiana and California.

Other pioneer progressive church leaders included Third Baptist Church pastor Frederick D. Haynes, Sr., Bethel A.M.E. pastor J. Austell Hall, Rev. George Bedford of Macedonia Missionary Baptist Church, L. S. Rubin, Pastor of Olivet Baptist Church, Rev. Hamilton T. Boswell of Jones Memorial United Methodist Church, and L. Roy Bennett of First A.M.E. Church, who were leaders at the center of the principal policy battles of civil rights in the San Francisco Bay Area. In 1947, Haynes was the first African American to seek election to the San Francisco Board of Supervisors, earning 60,000 votes in a losing effort. Considered the oldest African American Baptist church in the western United States, under Haynes, Third Baptist was at the fore of African American life and politics in San Francisco.[21] As the local movement intensified in 1963, Rev. Haynes and NAACP leader Thomas Burbridge formed the United San Francisco Freedom Movement in order to give the local movement independence from the NAACP's national office and Roy Wilkins.[22] For his part, Bethel's Rev. Hall was an astute organizer and visionary among Bay Area African Methodists who built credit unions, congregations, and a federally funded housing unit named "Freedom West" in the Western Addition. And Bedford supported CORE's sit-ins and protest activity targeting hiring among local auto dealers. Before coming to San Francisco in 1955, Rev. Roy Bennett was president of Montgomery Alabama's Interdenominational Ministerial Alliance, hosting a meeting of local pastors at Mt. Zion A.M.E. Church one day after the arrest of Rosa Parks to plan a one-time boycott. According to its founding minutes, the group selected King as its chairman and Bennett as its vice chairman. During the boycott Bennett was assigned to the First A.M.E. Zion Church in San Francisco where he worked for a decade. Hamilton T. Boswell was an important linkage figure between the Southern movement, California's emergent black elected officials, and the regional struggle. He was an important ally of King's and the SCLC. Willie Brown became the youth director at Jones Methodist because it was for him, "a church with a strong civil rights commitment even in the early 1950s."[23] As Brown emerged as an important attorney for poor black San Franciscans, indigents, prostitutes, and Jones Methodist, the congregation sponsored the political careers of a group of young-turk attorneys who used the NAACP as a political fulcrum. The NAACP was nearly synonymous with the African American church in the region. So much so that when internecine conflicts led to splits between moderate and more militant elements, respectively, the factions aligned as Catholics versus Protestants. Along with Brown, persons such as his one-time ally Terry Francois[24] and their rival Joe Kennedy (who was also a member of Jones Methodist) were at the center of the city's black political establishment. Factionalism was characteristic of the region's politics. An alliance of black ministers, for instance, disassociated from the Richmond branch of the NAACP when it was associated with Communism.[25] Moreover, African Americans in CORE rejected its white leadership and became the most radical civil rights organization in the region. In Oakland, the Rev. C. C. Bailey pulled Allen Temple Baptist Church out of a segregated white fellowship known as The General Baptist Association of the American Baptist Family and joined a regional association located in Oakland.[26]

The challenges which the San Francisco Bay Christian community confronted centered on open schooling through busing, political appointment representation, housing dislocation, job hiring discrimination, and police violence.[27] The congregations also provided the African American community with much-needed social service assistance, credit unions,[28] leadership, political education, and communal and social bonds. The region's black churches from Richmond, Oakland, San Francisco, and Berkeley financed public rallies and provided thousands of dollars in legal defense funds for thousands of arrested demonstrators. In the East Bay congregations like Allen Temple Baptist Church and surrogate organizations such as CORE placed women in primary leadership positions.[29] But the most important legislative breakthroughs of their efforts included supporting the fight for passage of the 1959 Fair Employment Act and the Fair Housing Act in 1963, which were both sponsored by William Byron Rumford of Oakland. As churches and clerics led the firestorm of protest activity, which for its time, was considered militant, white Californians responded angrily to this activism with the passage of Proposition 14 in 1964, which eliminated the Rumford Fair Housing Bill.

As with cities elsewhere, simultaneously in 1959, San Francisco's African American community was confounded by a massive removal and gentrification project—led by Redevelopment Agency (SFRA) director Justin Herman and Republican Mayor George Christopher—that devastated its population of nearly 44,000 residents.[30] In discussing his plans at the outset, Herman insisted, "without adequate housing for the poor, critics will rightly condemn urban renewal as a land-grab for the rich and a heartless push-out for the poor and nonwhites." The expansion of Geary Street (to Boulevard) literally and psychologically became the unnatural barrier dividing black San Francisco from the more affluent and white Pacific Heights and borderline Japantown.[31] Geary Blvd. marked the containment of African Americans in the declining Fillmore/Western Addition and the formation of the social dreg Tenderloin district.[32] As the West Oakland and San Francisco, African American communities experienced the decade-long dismantling of the 7th Street[33] and Fillmore/Western Addition communities and entertainment and business districts,[34] a coalition of white pastors encouraged a grassroots effort to respond to the SFRA, through the Western Addition Community Organization (WACO), after an earlier organization known as Freedom House was unable to halt demolition.[35] A powerful demonstration of grassroots democracy led by residents Mary Rogers, Inez Andry-Frazier and Hannibal Williams—who immediately rejected its white church leadership—successfully sued Herman's agency and won concessions allowing short-lived community input in 1968. In West Oakland, the United Tax Payers and Voters Union was likewise successful only in stalling city planners' Project ACORN which uprooted thousands of families in the mid-1960s.[36] While Rev. Cecil Williams of Glide Memorial (Methodist) Church joined them in seeking to prevent dislocation in San Francisco, most churches did not. Many were preoccupied with the city-wide struggles, while others benefitted from the second phase (A-2) of the redevelopment plan.[37] As a concession to the WACO movement, A-2 was headed by an African American Pentecostal minister, the Rev. Wilbur Hamilton. His father, the Bishop E. Hamilton, was pastor of the Emanuel Church of God in Christ, the first African American fellowship to build its own church facility in San Francisco. Contrary to strongly held belief in the community that the SFRA's plan meant "Negro removal," Hamilton insisted that it staved off a total razing of the Western Addition's black population. He argued,

It's naïve to say that blacks were better off 30 years ago—especially where housing is concerned. Thirty years ago real estate people actively boycotted blacks. They wouldn't sell to them or rent to them, except in certain circumscribed districts like the Western Addition. Had redevelopment not been in the Western

Addition, the following scenario would have occurred: Blacks would have remained huddled into overcrowded, underutilitied apartments into the mid-1950s. Then Pacific Heights money would have begun to nibble away at the edges of the ghetto, reclaiming block by block. As Victorians became desirable to whites, blacks would have been forced out by higher and higher rents. The Victorian craze of the 1960s would have driven every black person from the Western Addition."[38]

Where the earlier phase, A-1, indiscriminately targeted the African American community for removal, Hamilton insists further that despite this legacy, African American churches in the city benefitted from a special agreement with the SFRA allowing sponsored housing for the elderly and families needing affordable housing. He explains, "we visited a number of churches. Redevelopment, . . . has helped six black churches rebuild themselves in the Western Addition. . . . [W]e like to think by promoting the black church, we've promoted community stability."[39] The African American community never fully recovered from the two large-scale phases of the plan, however, despite reaching a population peak of 96,000 (13 percent of San Francisco's population) in 1970. In the end, there was widespread agreement among pedestrian African Americans in San Francisco that "the era that closed with [George] Moscone's election [1975] has come to be seen as a model of the devastation, rather than improvement, that came out of urban renewal projects in the 1950s and 1960s."[40] More to the point, Hannibal Williams captured the sentiment of San Francisco's African American community in suggesting:

> The times were right to produce a man like Jim Jones. The circumstances of a community that is broken up, when the relationships that bind people together fall apart, the time is always right for a religious scoundrel to take advantage of our credibility. Justin Herman literally destroyed the neighborhood and in the process he made the neighborhood ripe for anybody with any kind of solution. People were desperate for solutions, something to follow. Jim Jones was another solution. He had a charismatic personality that won the hearts and souls of the people.[41]

Many of the pastors and congregations noted above were past their primes in the mid-1960s and viewed as conservative (or worse) on pressing social issues by Black Power militancy, and altogether nonexistent among New Left activism in the region. These factors facilitated Peoples

Temple. The sharp criticisms of Malcolm X toward King, Bayard Rustin, and toward SCLC techniques and political philosophy provided a rationale for rejecting the Christian sponsorship of the modern Civil Rights Movement. Malcolm X spoke to and for younger blacks when he said, "the day of the sit-in, the lie-in, the crawl-in, the cry-in, the beg-in is outdated." Across the Bay Bridge in Oakland, the Black Panther Party, led by Huey P. Newton, eclipsed the Christian churches beginning in October of 1966. Newton and his comrades castigated the progressive black churches in deference to a general Marxian critique of all religion and tended to downplay the consciousness-raising activity of the southern and local civil rights struggles led by the community's churches.[42] Key members of the Christian liberal integrationist organization SNCC (Student Nonviolent Coordinating Committee), including H. Rap Brown, James Forman, Kathleen Cleaver, and Stokely Carmichael, joined forces with the Black Panthers. According to Vincent Harding, King, too, "was deeply influenced by the courageous and militant shock troops of the freedom movement, the [Student Nonviolent Coordinating Committee] . . . helped to radicalize him. . . ."[43] King seemed to understand (and Newton later concedes bypassed himself in the urgency of constant battle) that the church "has been going through phases of development. It too has found itself somewhat isolated from the community. Today, the church is striving to get back into favor with the community. Like the church, the Black Panther Party is also trying to reinstate itself with the community."[44]

In the mid-1960s, the Bay Area could be characterized as having a perfuse issue pluralism which overshadowed the Civil Rights struggle. Rufus Browning and his colleagues provided a useful assessment of Bay Area cities where they outlined factors that contributed to the political incorporation of underrepresented populations—meaning "the extent to which group interests are effectively represented in policymaking."[45] For them, the degree of political incorporation of these populations rested on the size of the minority population, liberal white support in biracial or multiracial coalitions, electoral organization, and the role of political leadership. Based upon these criteria, they observed relatively strong incorporation of African Americans during the 1960s and 1970s in some cities (Berkeley and Oakland); considered them subordinate partners in liberal or progressive coalitions that controlled city governments in others (San Francisco, Sacramento, San Jose, Richmond); and weak incorporation (Hayward, Vallejo, Daly City, and Stockton) where African American populations were smallest.[46] Despite marked progress in the first two categories, the study concluded it was "unevenly achieved, however, and many problems were not effectively alleviated by it. Widespread unemployment and poverty and terrible health problems associated or intensified with poverty remained."[47] These lingering challenges were reinforced by what Richard DeLeon calls San Francisco's "hyperpluralism." An atmosphere dominated by the "politics of everything," not only muted the hard fought gains of African Americans, but it actually facilitated the "deincorporation" of the city's black population. DeLeon insists, "the politics of race must compete for public attention with gender politics, gay and lesbian politics, neighborhood politics, environmental politics, labor politics, and the politics of land use and development."[48] While Archie Smith, Jr., adds, "the relative success of the Peoples Temple movement in San Francisco and Jonestown is not difficult to explain when we consider the influence of these movements in the 1960s did not take significant hold in established black religious institutions and consciousness of the majority of black churches in the San Francisco Bay Area."[49]

African American residents of San Francisco concur with the sentiments of a former President of the San Francisco NAACP as she stated, "to the outside world San Francisco touts itself as a very liberal city. My own perception is that it is probably one of the most racist cities in the country," and of another African American woman who stated, "this town is not as progressive as its image might suggest. When it comes to things that have nothing to do with ethnicity, we are progressive. But when it comes to race and cultural issues, we're not as progressive as Mississippi."[50] These reflect the sentiments of a generation that witnessed the planned destruction of the city's African American community in the 1950s. They witnessed the federal government remove and intern more than 120,000 Japanese citizens and nationals during World War II who were mainly from the Bay Area and Fillmore/Western Addition district. It partially explains why older black women, who first fled the South and later fled San Francisco with Jim Jones, were the largest segment of Peoples Temple and victims at Jonestown.[51] One of them, Christine Miller, was the only person to confront Jones as the cyanide was being readied.

The Black Church as the Source of Religion in Peoples Temple

Peoples Temple became *fin de siècle* of the African American church in the region and the most marginal within its constituent community. The extent to which Peoples Temple, with its Christian Leninist ideology was a church, scholars contend, was found expressly in its black membership coming from black congregations in the Bay Area.[52] Of its three primary cohorts, the working-class idealists who came with Jones from Indianapolis in 1965; the young, white radical "hippieish" utopians who were embracing the different movements in the West Coast; and the majority black cadre of elders and young children stirred by the Civil Rights and Black Power phases of the freedom struggle, the latter sourced its religiosity.

Blacks made up more than 80 percent of Peoples Temple membership in Los Angeles and San Francisco, and more than 70 percent of those who died in Guyana, South America.[53] But Jones's racial utopia was top heavy in white elite leadership—especially white women[54]—and bottom heavy in rank-and-file African Americans and others who were patronized in the tradition of a caring slave master and his family. Jones was in essence an "antiracist racist," (a phenomenon that had precedence in the other major black movement led chiefly by white Christian radicals, that of the abolitionists and William Lloyd Garrison). Garrison stridently employed Christian imperatives against slavery during the nineteenth century in what was essentially an antiracist social movement funded by blacks, even as most abolitionists rejected "social equality" for them.[55] And John Brown, a white Christian abolitionist who led his sons and a handful of slaves and their allies to certain death in trying to overthrow the system of racial slavery, is also pertinent.

On one of many occasions, speaking before an audience of Father Divine's Peace Mission followers in Philadelphia—after Divine's passing—the swarthy Jones stood before the congregation, with his several adopted children present, and declared, "I'm a nigger," prompting many people to walk out in disgust, while the white socialists of Peoples Temple in the audience, hailed it as revolutionary. Rev. J. Alfred Smith, Sr., notes, "Jim Jones was a white man. *Especially for his elderly followers, there was an authority that a white leader has that the most educated black man can't have.* It is a thriving vestige of racism that damages the black community and—to my way of thinking—damages the white community too."[56] This is not to suggest that the black people of Peoples Temple were without agency in the movement.[57] Their presence signified the authenticity of the Peoples Temple as a grassroots movement even though its leadership structure contradicted its egalitarian claims. Blacks were on the outside of Jim Jones's inner-circle, looking in, while to an outsider their presence was the most phenomenal proof of Jones's sincerity. He predicted that the deaths of nearly one thousand black people and their allies in a foreign country would make a powerful statement about U.S. capitalism, racism, and inequality.[58]

Peoples Temple sampled "the black ethic of resistance to oppression as the basis for making strong appeals for justice [which] has always been a part of the black protest tradition."[59] Jones cites that his attendance at a "Paul Robeson event" in Chicago, which resulted in FBI interrogations of

Jones and his mother, helped him realize that he could never accept capitalism. He claimed, "down the road I became even more alienated by that event." I decided how can I demonstrate my Marxism? The thought was *'infiltrate the church.'* "[60] Peoples Temple also minstreled Negro Spirituals, rhythm and blues, freedom songs, and the Glide Church. In his formative years, Jim Jones would visit a little known Negro school in Hanover, Virginia, the Hanover Industrial School, which taught its students socialism in the middle to late 1940s.[61] A driving premise concerning Peoples Temple and its relationship to the Bay Area's African American churches is that the movement was mimetic of black religious production and originality and black politics in the city and region, and that it was for the most part only *original in this way*. Like blackface Jewish comedian Al Jolson in the 1920s,[62] 1930s jazz musician Benny Goodman, Elvis Presley in the 1950s and 1960s, and white hip-hop rappers, Jim Jones mastered a cultural craft traditionally performed by black people. Rev. Smith notes for instance, "if you closed your eyes and just listened to him preach, you would swear you were listening to a black man."[63] David Chidester writes,

> In light of the predominantly African American membership of the Peoples Temple, one way out of the 'cult controversy' might be to recover the legacy of Jonestown as part of a broader, deeper tradition of black religion in America. Although Jones was white, he claimed to have a black soul, a black heart, and a black consciousness. Consistently, he identified himself as a black messiah advancing black liberation. . . . Jones, the Peoples Temple, and Jonestown requires sustained attention to black religion in America.[64]

Jones performed a Father Divine routine in white face as he emulated the Peace Mission in every detail. C. Eric Lincoln and Lawrence Mamiya suggest that the concept of mass suicide may have occurred to Jones first in his study of the Peace Mission's loyalty to Divine. To this end they enlist a citation, which Jones may have encountered, that stated, " 'if Father Divine were to die, mass suicides among the Negroes in his movement could certainly result. They would be rooted deep, not alone in Father's relationship with his followers but also in America's relationship with its Negro citizens. This would be the shame of America.' "[65]Aside from mimicking black religiosity, there is nothing in the record of Peoples Temple that shows it actually engaged in political struggle around the critical issues of jobs, housing, police brutality, education reform, or anything that the black churches had been struggling against for three decades before it arrived in California. The meager resources of the different classes of African Americans were actually pooled by Peoples Temple in order to empower Jones's minstrel in their ranks as the Great White Father.

If Jim Jones (and Peoples Temple) embodied the problem of "bad religion," there was nothing in his movement that could not be found in the black religious styles and content which he minstreled, or ideological formations such as Huey P. Newton's "revolutionary suicide" trope. Newton meant something more akin to *martyrdom* resulting from confronting the brutal conditions, not dying to evade them. Indeed among the last words Jones spoke in life were those taken from Newton's autobiography, *Revolutionary Suicide* (1973), claiming the acts of mass murder and suicide were "revolutionary," and "protesting the conditions of an inhumane world." But Jones and his cadre of elites actually enacted what Newton understood to be "reactionary suicide," where leaders, individuals, or entire groups surrender to the slow death of self-destruction in the face of "social conditions that overwhelm [people] and condemn [them] to helplessness."[66] Self-murder, resulting from evasion through drug abuse, alcoholism, religion, sex, and violence was reactionary, not revolutionary.

If Jim Jones and Peoples Temple represent "religious madness," they refract the turbulence of the national and local milieu in which they emerged. If it seems irrational to leave twentieth-century United States to flee racism for life in a country described at the time as one where "it was not easy to find meat, milk, fish, flour, potatoes, rice, cooking-oil, sugar," and where "hungry children and adults combed the refuse dumps,"[67] it also reflects an "exoduster" tradition among African Americans—from the early emigrationist projects of the nineteenth century to the domestic migration movements from the South. Much of the Bay Area's black population was already a migrant one when Peoples Temple arrived, purchasing its building in the Fillmore district in 1970. Those who followed Peoples Temple to Jonestown, Guyana were likely unaware that they participated in the most notorious of several notorious migrations of blacks from San Francisco beginning with the April 1858 flight of up to 800 black people to Victoria British Columbia after attempts to enact the 1850 Fugitive Slave Clause targeting the state's nominally free black population and Negro exclusion measures in the California legislature. The first public meeting for this exodus was held in the First A.M.E. Zion Church, built in 1852.[68]

Among the two dozen churches that served the African American community in San Francisco's Fillmore/Western Addition district, a few extended fellowship to Jones and Peoples Temple, granting instant standing in the community. None were more influential in this than Third Baptist Church trustee, physician, and *San Francisco Sun-Reporter* publisher

Carlton B. Goodlett,[69] Glide Memorial Methodist Church pastor Cecil Williams, Rev. George Bedford of Macedonia Missionary Baptist, and the San Francisco Nation of Islam under Wallace Muhammad who was assigned to the Bay Area temples.[70] J. Alfred Smith, Sr., of Allen Temple Baptist Church in Oakland also precipitously accepted Jones and has written, that "the 1970s were a dark age for the black church in San Francisco," which made Peoples Temple more appealing to the black community. He insists that most of the churches were steeped in a middle-class otherworldly orientation, with no outreach to poorer individuals. He argues only a minority of churches held a grassroots commitment such as "Glide Memorial United Methodist Church and nearby Third Baptist Church, where the Reverend Amos Brown presides, but once you turn the corner past these churches, you might have to look a long time to find another."[71] The more conservative churches altogether ignored Jones and Peoples Temple, as did most people in the city. The theologically and socially progressive congregations (allied in the black liberation theology-oriented Alamo Clergy),[72] took Jones as he presented himself, as a white anti-racist. Rebecca Moore and her collaborators insist, for instance, that while the ministers of even this alliance were skeptical, they "saw Jones and his congregation functioning in accord with the prophetic biblical tradition."[73] Throughout the latter stages of the Peoples Temple movement, Jim Jones did not just betray the local Democratic Party leadership and his unwitting supporters and followers in the catastrophic murder-suicides, he betrayed a burgeoning progressive black church movement. Those congregations that were not considered "dead" churches endorsed Jones's work in the Bay Area and in its move to Guyana. For instance a prominent Oakland pastor wrote Guyana's Prime Minister Forbes Burnham, just days after Jones fled to Guyana in July, 1977, extolling ". . . the elements of radical faith which Rev. Jones and his congregation have translated into actions. Their success has inspired *and challenged church and community leaders throughout California* and the United States; they have shown conclusively that Christian socialism is a viable alternative to the rapidly deteriorating fabric of our highly competitive, acquisitive society."[74]

Anthony Pinn rejects the premise that black participation in alternative religious organizations or movements such as Peoples Temple refracts, "not the value of these communities for their members but a short-coming with respect to the Black Church that pushes people away." He urges, "must we think about the movement of African Americans into Peoples Temple as a negative statement about the Black Church?"[75] Under Jones, Peoples Temple actively campaigned against black churches and their leaders in California and throughout the country even as it mimicked traditional black worship styles, demands for social justice, and gained acceptance among these key black clergy. Indiana's black population in1950 was a mere 4.4 percent (174, 168),[76] and between the World Wars, it was surrounded by the largest contingency of the terrorist Ku Klux Klan anywhere in the United States. Thus in its Indiana years, Peoples Temple was an anomaly not well received by many blacks there. What becomes clear is how its acceptance among black Californians began exponentially with the siphoning of black church members in 1968 and a concerted mocking especially of its more traditional and conservative congregations and ministers. Rebecca Moore notes that it was precisely in the year of King's death, 1968, that "the Temple began establishing relations with black churches in San Francisco by attending special events at those churches, winning the trust of the local black ministers, and inviting their congregations to visit Peoples Temple in Redwood Valley in an exchange of fellowship."[77] It was just after King's assassination that Jones approached Rev. Bedford who had written an article calling for a greater ecumenical fellowship between African American and white Christian congregations. Jones soon arrived at the doors of Macedonia with a contingency of Peoples Temple members asking Bedford for a pulpit exchange agreement and to allow him and his members to sleep in the lobby of the church facility.[78] When Bedford declined the request and invited Peoples Temple members to the parsonage, Jones later publicly claimed that Bedford sexually propositioned two young white women while before his own wife and church members. Macedonia lost more than 200 members to Peoples Temple. Jones had a reputation as a "sheep stealer" who also drew members away from L. S. Rubin's Olivet Baptist Church on Ellis Street; Friendship Institutional Baptist and Third Baptist Church also lost members to Jones. Like the Nation of Islam before it, Peoples Temple leaders "fished" from the black churches, derided leaders, distorted theology, and downplayed their avant-garde role in stirring many of the contemporary movements that followed. John R. Hall insists, "Jones himself pointed to the problem in his sermons: many black ministers were still promoting an essentially conservative and spiritualistic theology of heavenly compensation after death, while popular black sentiments increasingly were directed toward concrete social change in 'this' world."[79] Hugh Pearson's critical study of the Panthers Breakfast Program led him to argue to the contrary: "[O]ne would think that no African American had ever thought of feeding people for free before the Panthers. What do they think African-American churches had been doing for so many years?"[80] The struggles waged in the Bay Area by the churches and clerics since the 1940s seemed to go unnoticed amid the maelstrom of radicalism. Despite the support which student radicals received from congregations such as West Oakland's St. Augustine's Episcopal Church and Sacred Heart Catholic Church in the Fillmore district which launched the Panthers' successful breakfast program at their facilities, the idea that the area's churches were disengaged prevailed.[81]

Rev. Cecil Williams notes, "the promise of death was a cornerstone of all churches in black communities across the country. Freedom, liberation, and salvation, we were told, would be ours after life, not during it. In a sense, our church was a call to death. . . ." When Williams began his ministry in the poor Tenderloin district of San Francisco in 1966, he caused the first of many great controversies by removing the church's large stone cross from its roof. This act was driven by Williams's belief that the cross "kept getting in the way of the power of the people, people who have freedom to choose . . . 'I took down the cross because I am convinced that the cross will not save humanity—humanity will redeem the cross."[82] Glide Church would be at the center of the Hippie movement's 1967 "Summer of Love," gay rights, anti-Vietnam events; it also hosted the Hookers' Convention for prostitutes,[83] and was principally involved in negotiating with the Symbionese Liberation Army for the release of kidnapped heiress Patty Hearst. Williams's theological and humanist commitments derived from his sense that "the essence of mystery is revealed in action, not detachment, and that human life is a community of connection fulfilled not by insulated worship but through a struggle that must be continually renewed. "I wanted a church that merged with the world, a church so authentic to human life that it neglected no facet of that life."[84] Glide supported the dissident elements in the American Indian Movement, farm workers struggles, and the Black Panther Party, making it "a haven for radicals and a sanctuary for those in rebellion."[85] It was precisely in this atmosphere that Jim Jones entered the religious and political communities of San Francisco in the 1970s. Cecil Williams embraced Jones and Peoples Temple during the few years that they were in San Francisco. Glide Church modeled what Peoples Temple imagined itself to be in the city and in U.S. society. The national, state, and local Democratic Party and black leadership establishments nurtured Jim Jones's prominence in the black community. When deposed, one survivor who left Jonestown on the morning of the massacre stated, "I mean, there was a lot of things being said about [Peoples Temple], but then put yourself in my place. If you sit there and watch the congressmen and the chief of police and the governor and people like that come to visit a place, you kind of think it's a choice place to be. . . . Assemblyman Willie Brown was there on several occasions. He made speeches about how the program was an accepted program. I figured if these people—if anybody should know, they should know, you can't be fooling these people."[86] Part of the support that Jim Jones received from key political and religious figures, (including Good-

lett, Willie Brown, and Cecil Williams) grew expressly from these individuals' sense that most of the black churches in the city were irrelevant
and ineffective in mobilizing in the mode of the Southern movement.[87]
Williams included his relationship with Jones in his autobiography, *I'm
Alive!* where he expresses anger toward Jones because he *"didn't die first."*
Directing his thoughts to Jones, Williams insisted,

> they had a need because they were poor and black. . . . You
> exploited their weaknesses to strengthen your own institution.
> The poor will always be exploited, because their needs are so
> great. There will always be room for you, Jim, and I am angry
> at that. How badly did you want to be black, Jim? . . . You used
> me for that, I realize it now. You traded on my blackness as a
> calling card to open certain doors in the community. . . . Look
> at what you did to them at your *last communion*, mounds of
> black bodies paying homage to the Father, the Great White
> Father. Hundreds of black corpses on that jungle floor, dead at
> your insistence. I am not belittling the white people who died in
> Jonestown. Human life is human life. But you advanced your
> self as champion of the poor and it was all the basest deceit.[88]

Jones's supporters remained mostly silent and obtuse about the
subsequent annihilation at Jonestown, Guyana.[89] Obtuse because former
Supervisor and future San Francisco Mayor Willie Brown hardly mentions
Jones or Peoples Temple (less than a page) in his autobiography.[90] And
he called the entire Peoples Temple debacle "irrelevant." Brown also notes
that Jones was a "strange person," who "was a marginal figure in San Francisco church circles." After being appointed by Mayor George Moscone
to the Public Housing Authority, he "essentially made him one of the
largest landlords in San Francisco." But the relationship was much deeper
according to biographer James Richardson and San Francisco journalist
Tim Reiterman, who was shot in Guyana by Jones's security.[91] Less than
a month after the massacre, Brown moved forward with plans to host a
fundraiser for Peoples Temple.[92] Brown's ally, Carlton B. Goodlett—then
the most influential Black person in San Francisco—defended Jones when
defectors exposed Peoples Temple practices.[93] A *Sun-Reporter* editorial
chastised San Francisco's black churches *after* the murder-suicides. In an
anonymous editorial written five days later, the paper stated,

> The churches of the land, and especially the Black churches of
> San Francisco, *might well emulate* the commitment of Peoples
> Temple, which brought so many people together under their

banner because they believed this religious institution was totally committed to changing the sordid circumstances of their lives. Peoples Temple members . . . thought they might *leave a legacy of hope and inspiration to the oppressed of the world.* The Black churches, which in ages past have served as a refuge in the dark days of the Black experience, must hold high the banner of the Christian faith, proclaiming through action that the gospel of Christ is a vibrant, dynamic, life-giving concept, and especially that Christianity is a commitment that men live for, rather than one that they die for.[94]

It is impossible to know if Peoples Temple and Jim Jones would have appealed to its black members and supporters had a majority of black churches in the region been predisposed to more socially conscious outreach efforts. Peoples temple had achieved no major policy initiative as had established black churches which led the charge for civil rights in the state and region. It offered not a single aspect of ministry that was not already in place in the most progressive of the established African American churches. Perhaps it was the "one-stop shop" feature of Peoples Temple where it harbored a sampling of all the core activist churches in the Bay Area. Peoples Temple represented the best in black religious tradition to the extent that it extrapolated from its centuries-long social service commitments of tending to "the least of these" elements in society. Peoples Temple represented the worst of black religious tradition to the extent it and Jim Jones fused the movement with charismatic personality of a single leader. It also engaged in a sadistic, paternalistic and racist manipulation of black peoples' cravings for dignity, in the name of antiracism. What is certain is that Jim Jones and Peoples Temple massacred black people who had escaped a racist U.S. society in the name of black liberation. It was a feat that was without precedent in the black religious experience.

Notes

1. Daniel L. Crowe, *Prophets of Rage: The Black Freedom Struggle in San Francisco, 1945-1969* (New York: Garland Publishing, Inc., 2000), 24-35.
2. Ibid.
3. James Richardson, *Willie Brown: A Biography* (Berkeley: The University of California Press, 1996), 49.
4. Series 1 Haynes Family Papers, 1935-1980, *Frederick Douglas Haynes Family Papers*, MS 3355A. California Historical Society
5. Daniel L. Crowe, *Prophets of Rage*, 62, 78.
6. James Richardson, *Willie Brown*, 71.

7. Daniel L. Crowe, *Prophets of Rage*, 121–122.

8. Ibid., 155.

9. For an explanation of the Black Panther Party's rejection of the black church and Huey P. Newton's acknowledgment that rejecting the church was tantamount to rejecting the black community, see "On the Relevance of the Church," in Huey Newton, *To Die for the People*, Toni Morrison, ed. (San Francisco, CA: City Lights Books, 2009).

10. King's conceptualization of the beloved community reflected his understanding of the Christian mandate found in Galatians 3:28 that believers are "all one in Christ Jesus." Drawn on the ideal that Christianity is a race transcendent community, King imagined that the United States. and larger global societies could partake of a world where capitalism, war, and racism could be undermined. For James Cone, King's ideal community was based on "justice, love, and hope" and "black Christianity [that believes] we are all sisters and brothers because 'God made of one blood all nations of people to dwell on the face of the earth.' As God's justice is grounded in God's creative and redeeming love, so human justice is grounded in love. Neighborly love, especially for the enemy, defines the means by which justice is established and also the goal of the struggle for freedom, namely *the beloved community*." See James H. Cone, *Martin and Malcolm and America: A Dream or A Nightmare* (Maryknoll, NY: Orbis, 1991), 126.

11. Peoples Temple opened its Los Angeles facility in 1972. It also had meeting places in the Central Valley of California where Fresno is located. See Tim Reiterman and John Jacobs, *Raven: The Untold Story of the Rev. Jim Jones and His People* (New York, Penguin Books, 1982), 156.

12. This is the case with their eclectic plagiarism of Father Divine's and Howard Thurman's interracial church movements; of King's "beloved community"; of Huey Newton's "revolutionary suicide," concept, and of the idea of emigration from the United States, to flee its racism. It also adapted the defiant clenched Black Power fist as a symbol of unity; though Peoples Temple members raised the left fist, where the Black Power symbol was right-handed.

13. There were many other local individuals who actually shaped and influenced the tactics and strategies of the region's younger activists, namely, Curtis Lee Baker and Mark Comfort who founded the Oakland Direct Action Committee (ODAC) from which Huey Newton and Bobby Seale liberally borrowed. For instance, Comfort and Baker were the first in the city of Oakland to follow the Oakland Police Department to monitor police brutality in 1966. Comfort accompanied Seale and Bobby Hutton to the Sacramento State Capitol building in their famous gun-toting incident in 1967. See Daniel L. Crowe, *Prophets of Rage*, 210–212.

14. I also reviewed audio and video material and autobiographical accounts of key religious and political figures who facilitated Jones's acceptance among segments of the African American community. The literature that has emerged since the 1970s concerning Jim Jones, Peoples Temple, and Jonestown presents a wide range of topics too disparate to specify here.

15. Judith Mary Weightman, Making *Sense of the Jonestown Suicides: A Sociological History of Peoples Temple* (New York: The Edwin Mellen Press, 1983), 1–13.

16. See for instance, Peoples Temple attorney and Jonestown massacre survivor Mark Lane's *The Strongest Poison* (New York: Hawthorn Books, 1980). See also John Peer Nugent, *White Night: The Untold Story of What Happened Before and Beyond Jonestown* (New York: Rawson, Wade Publishers, Inc., 1979); and Shiva Naipaul, *Black And White* (London: Sphere Books, 1980).

17. See John R. Hall, *Gone From the Promised Land* (New Brunswick, NJ: Transaction Publishers, 2001); David Chidester, *Salvation and Suicide: Jim Jones, The Peoples Temple, and Jonestown* (Bloomington, IN: Indiana University Press, 1988).

18. Moore has written extensively on Peoples Temple and her otherwise excellent research and scholarship are tempered by, the at times, sanitized interpretations of source material which reiterate an apologetic on behalf of Jones and Peoples Temple. She lost three members of her family, including two sisters (Carolyn and Annie) who were at the highest ranks of its white elite inner-circle. It is well known that her sister Carolyn was Jones's mistress and Chief of Staff. Annie, who was allegedly "healed from suicide tendencies" by having sex with Jones, was a nurse who helped administer the cyanide poison. Her Father, the Rev. John V. Moore was Superintendent of the local United Methodist Church who allegedly provided surveillance, spied for, and defended Jones against an early critic seeking to expose him and the hierarchy's abusive practices, Lester Kinsolving. Three months before the massacre, Rev. Moore assured British freelance journalist Gordon Lindsay, who was considered a media enemy of Peoples Temple, that "Jim Jones is in touch with the pain and suffering of people . . . I think that anyone who can lead 1,200 people from their country to settle in a new country has got it together." Moore's research and maintenance of the *Jonestown Report* are subject to fierce criticism by Mr. Kinsolving's son Tom Kinsolving. See for instance his blog at http://jonestownapologistsalert.blogspot.com/. Last accessed 1/22/10. See also Tim Reiterman, *Raven*, pp. 179 and 479. Rebecca Moore and Fielding M. McGehee III edit and publish the Peoples Temple propaganda annual, *The Jonestown Report*, at San Diego State University. At the 2009 commemoration of the massacre, there was a clear division between the "pro" and "anti" Jim Jones cliques. Those who were sympathetic to interpreting Jim Jones as a "victim" of government and his own psychological maladies, handed out *The Jonestown Report*. Those who considered Jones a "racist deceiver" of his followers refused to take them. The author was in conversation with Laura Johnston Kohl, a "pro" Jones survivor of Peoples Temple at the very moment that she and Jynona Norwood and Yulanda Williams engaged in a very tense and emotional discussion concerning whether Jones should be memorialized with the others who perished.

19. Thurman operated behind the scenes during the early stages of the Civil Rights Movement locally and in the South—counseling a young Martin Luther King, Jr., on the thinking and tactics of Gandhi, who Thurman met in the 1930s.

20. Cited in Susan Hendrickson, "Howard Thurman: A Personal Journey with His Words," in *Creation Spirituality*, Vol. VII, No. 2 March/April 1991, 24.

21. Despite the scrutiny of the House Un-American Activities Committee (HUAC) it publicly hosted Paul Robeson in 1956 during his persecution by the U.S. government under the 1950 Internal Security Act. The church also hosted

W. E. B. Du Bois' 90th birthday years after his trial for violation of the Foreign Agents Registration Act earlier in the decade. Haynes remained a vital presence among the region's active clergy even as he approached sixty years old at the peak of the local movement.

22. James Richardson, *Willie Brown*, 81–84.

23. Willie Brown, *Basic Brown: My Life and Our Times* (New York: Simon and Schuster, 2008), 71.

24. Francois, for instance, became the first black supervisor (City Council) and Joe Kennedy, his nemesis, was appointed as a municipal judge by Gov. Pat Brown in 1963.

25. James Richardson, *Willie Brown*, 114.

26. Daniel L. Crowe, *Prophets of Rage*, 102.

27. In November 1963, the local CORE and W. E. B. Du Bois Club organized pickets at Select Realty, a rental firm that served whites only, and three of the city's popular Mel's Drive-In restaurants; in March, 1964 for instance, white student activist, and future San Francisco District Attorney Terence Hallinan led a two-day protest against the Sheraton Palace Hotel for racial discrimination in hiring; April, 1964 over 200 protesters were arrested for sit-ins targeting the Motor Car Dealer's Association which spread to cities throughout the country; in 1960, the San Francisco Police Department included only six black officers in a department of 1,700. In 1969 local black truckers protested discrimination in the construction of the BART. They chained trucks to a local BART job site and subsequently won jobs concessions. Events compiled by Algis Ratnikas at http://timelines.ws. Accessed 1/10/10.

28. Jones's United Methodist Credit Union was founded in 1952 as a response to red-lining, the common practice of offering credit with exorbitant interest rates, and other discriminatory practices against blacks. Bethel A.M.E. has also housed a credit union for decades.

29. Ibid., 102–103.

30. Herman also served under mayors John Shelley and Joseph Alioto.

31. In the early 1970s, Peoples Temple's main facility was located in the heart of the African American community at 1859 Geary Boulevard and Fillmore.

32. The Ingleside district and Bayview Hunters Point sections have also had significant African American working-class and middle-class populations since World War II.

33. 7th Street in West Oakland, like Central Avenue in Los Angeles, was a thriving Blues district in the 1940s and 1950s. It was home to supper clubs and restaurants and every bit an equal to the Fillmore across the Bay Bridge. 7th Street was lined with upscale and "dive" type juke-joints and African American owned records shops. Bob Geddins, who is considered the father of Oakland Blues owned a recording studio on the corners of 7th and Center Streets. Please see www.bayareabluessociety.net, which is hosted by the City of Oakland. Accessed 2/2/2010. The general area of 7th Street in West Oakland is now known locally as "the bottoms."

34. San Francisco African American historian John Templeton locates its boundaries "from Van Ness to Baker Streets from Hayes to Sacramento, [where]

hundreds of blacks owned residences dating from the 1890s to current times such as the Frazier-Toombs House in the 1300 block of Baker Street, built in 1900. See http://www.blackpressonline.com/Californiablackhistory.com.html. Accessed 2/4/2010.

35. The ministers and churches included Rev. Tom Dietrich of Howard Presbyterian Church, Rev. Dave Hawbecker of Christ United Presbyterian Church, and the Rev. Ed Smith of St. Cyprian's Episcopal Church (founded by blacks in 1870s). See Tanya M. Hollis, "Peoples Temple and Housing Politics in San Francisco," in *Peoples Temple and Black Religion in America*, Rebecca Moore, Anthony B, Pinn, and Mary Sawyer, eds. (Bloomington, IN: Indiana University Press, 2004), 88.

36. Daniel L. Crowe, *Prophets of Rage*, 71–72.

37. Among them was the First Union Baptist Church on the corner of Golden Gate and Webster, Hannibal Williams' New Liberation United Presbyterian Church on Divisadero and Turk streets, and The Queen Adah Chapter of the Order of the Eastern Star. This organization of 5,000 black women sponsored a housing development for the elderly known as the Royal Adah Arms on the corner of Turk and Fillmore Streets. See, Kevin Starr, "In Historical Perspective: Is Redevelopment of the Western Addition A-2 A Rip Off? Or Is it Worth It?" pp. 1–10. It is an unpublished manuscript of the San Francisco Redevelopment Agency located at the Main Branch of the San Francisco Library.

38. Ibid., 5.

39. Ibid., 9.

40. Tanya M. Hollis, "Peoples Temple and Housing Politics in San Francisco" in *Peoples Temple and Black Religion in America*,.89.

41. Ibid., p. 82. Cited originally in Peter L. Stein, *The Fillmore*. Videorecording (1999), produced for KQED-TV.

42. David Hilliard and Lewis Cole, *This Side of Glory: The Autobiography of David Hilliard and the Story of the Black Panther Party* (Lawrence Hill Books, 1993). Newton sought to radicalize the black church with exotic, internationalist solutions of the very sort for which he and the Panthers derided the Los Angeles-based U.S. organization "cultural nationalists," who sought African "dashiki" solutions to the problems facing the black community.

43. Vincent Harding, *Martin Luther King: The Inconvenient Hero* (Maryknoll, NY: Orbis Books, 2008), 6.

44. Huey P. Newton, *To Die For the People*, 61.

45. Rufus P. Browning, Dale Rogers Marshall, and David H. Tabb, eds., *Racial Politics in American Cities*, 2nd ed. (New York: Longman Publishers, 1997), 9.

46. Ibid., 24.

47. Ibid., 25.

48. Ibid., 140.

49. Archie Smith, Jr., "An Interpretation of Peoples Temple and Jonestown: Implications for the Black Church" in *Peoples Temple and Black Religion in America*, 47.

50. Dale Rogers Marshall and David H. Tabb, eds., *Racial Politics in American Cities*, 141.

51. Rebecca Moore, "Demographics and the Black Religious Culture of Peoples Temple," Anthony Pinn, and Mary Sawyer, eds., *Peoples Temple and Black Religion in America*, 62–63.

52. Mary R. Sawyer, "The Church in Peoples Temple" in *Peoples Temple and Black Religion in America*, 169.

53. Muhammad Isaiah Kenyatta, "America Was Not Hard to Find" in *Peoples Temple and Black Religion in America*, 161.

54. Mary McCormick Maaga, *Hearing the Voices of Jonestown: Putting a Human face on an American Tragedy* (Syracuse, NY: Syracuse University Press, 1998).

55. Donald Jacobs, ed., *Courage and Conscience: Black and White Abolitionists in Boston* (Bloomington, IN: Indiana University Press, 1996). Jacobs argues Garrison was dependent on the appeals and legacy of David Walker for accessing Black Abolitionists in Boston who were leery of his early support for colonizationism and for the African American readership—which constituted the overwhelming majority of subscribers—and financing of Garrison's *Liberator* publication.

56. J. Alfred Smith, Sr., "Breaking the Silence: Reflections of a Black Pastor" in *Peoples Temple and Black Religion in America*. 152. Emphases added.

57. Many suborned the interracial socialist project from its beginnings in Indianapolis where Archie James played a vital role in integrating Jones's flock, to Jim McIvane's fateful words assuring those holding the cyanide drinks, that reincarnation awaited them after death. When a black woman, Christine Miller, challenged Jones's suicide plan, McIvane talked her down of the microphone. See John R. Hall, *Gone From the Promised Land: Jonestown in American Cultural History*, 284.

58. Interview with Mr. William Wade, former member of Peoples Temple who joined the organization in Indianapolis. Interview conducted November 23, 2009.

59. Judson Lance Jeffries, *Huey P. Newton: The Radical Theorist* (Oxford, MS: University of Mississippi Press), ix.

60. See for instance, Denise Stephenson, ed., *Dear People: Remembering Jonestown*, 77. Emphasis added.

61. In several person to person interviews, according to former Peoples Temple member Mr. William Wade (who is a seventy-nine-year-old African American living in Alameda, California) he and young Jim Jones would occasionally visit the school and Jones was impressed with its organization and operations. He insists it was an early influence of Jones's burgeoning interest in socialism. The papers of James Hoge Ricks at the University of Virginia School of Law and those of African American historian Luther Porter Jackson at the Virginia State University Johnston Memorial Library, there is discussion of the Hanover School. Dr. Jackson was an associate of Carter G. Woodson, John Hope Franklin, W. E. B. Du Bois, E. Franklin Frazier, Charles S. Johnson, and Rayford Logan. Cedric J. Robinson's *Black Movements in America* (New York: Routledge, 1997), identifies similar institutions in Southern states such as Tennessee's Highlander Folk School. Civil Rights icons Septima Clark and Rosa Parks attended Highlander Folk School. See pages 139–140.

62. For an interesting discussion of Jolson, please see Matthew Frye Jacobson, *Whiteness of A Different Color: European Immigrants and the Alchemy of Race*, Cambridge, MA: Harvard University Press, 1999, 119–122.

63. J. Alfred Smith Sr., "Breaking the Silence: Reflections of a Black Pastor" in *Peoples Temple and Black Religion in America*, 144.

64. David Chidester, *Salvation and Suicide: Jim Jones, The Peoples Temple, and Jonestown* (Bloomington, IN: Indiana University Press, 1988), xxi.

65. C. Eric Lincoln and Lawrence H. Mamiya, "Daddy Jones and Father Divine" in *Peoples Temple and Black Religion in America*, 41.

66. Huey P. Newton, *Revolutionary Suicide* (New York: Penguin Books, 1973), 2.

67. Siva Naipaul, *Black and White*, (London: Abacus, 1981), 27.

68. According to historian John Templeton, who is widely regarded as a foremost historian of black San Francisco, The church, originally on Stockton Street, is where black businessmen Mifflin Gibbs and Peter Lester hosted a meeting in 1858 to discuss the passage of the Fugitive Slave Act, which declared that all runaway slaves must return to their masters. Faced with intense discrimination in California, more than 800 black people decided at that meeting to leave San Francisco and seek a better life in Vancouver, British Columbia. The church was destroyed during the earthquake of 1906 and opened again on Geary Street in 1915. See http://www.blackpressonline.com/Californiablackhistory.com. Accessed 1/10/2010.

69. Dr. Carlton Goodlett (1915–1997) joined Dr. Daniel A. Collins as owners of the *Reporter* in 1948 serving the black community. They then absorbed the *Sun*, to become the *San Francisco Sun-Reporter*. To indicate his influence in the City, today the San Francisco City Hall is located at 1 Carlton B. Goodlett Drive after being christened as such by then mayor Willie Brown. His patients included Jim Jones, W. E. B. Du Bois, and Paul Robeson. He was the biggest of the "big Negroes" in the San Francisco Bay Area. Goodlett was also one time president of the San Francisco NAACP.

70. The Nation of Islam temple and People Temple buildings were adjacent. After initial conflict that bordered on violence, the Nation of Islam and Peoples Temple held a joint gathering at the Los Angeles Convention Center with many prominent individuals in attendance and where Jones was venerated by Peoples Temple members.

71. J. Alfred Smith, "Breaking the Silence: Reflections of a Black Pastor," 140. Rebecca Moore, Anthony B. Pinn, and Mary R. Sawyer, eds., *Peoples Temple and Black Religion in America*. Rev. Brown, who has granted multiple interviews during the writing of this article, arrived in San Francisco on 1976 and confronted Jim Jones in a meeting at Carlton Goodlett's office calling Jones a "cult leader" and demanding that he remove his trademark dark sunglasses in the meeting.

72. James H. Cone, *For My People: Black Theology and the Black Church* (Maryknoll, New York Orbis, 1984), 11, 111. ALAMO CLERGY is an acronym for Alameda Oakland Clergy.

73. Rebecca Moore, "The Church in Peoples Templs," Anthony B. Pinn, and Mary R. Sawyer, eds., *Peoples Temple and Black Religion in America*, 184.

74. Siva Naipaul, *Black and White* (London: Abacus, 1981), 33. The name of the Oakland pastor of a Baptist congregation is not listed. Emphasis added.

75. Antony Pinn, "Peoples Temple in Black Religion: Re-imaging the Contours of Black Religious Studies," in *Peoples Temple and Black Religion in America,* Ibid., 9, 10.

76. Campbell Gibson and Kay Jung, U.S. Census Bureau, Population Division, "Historical Census Statistics on Population Totals by Race, 1790 to 1990, and by Hispanic Origin, 1970 to 1990, for the United States, Regions, Divisions, and States." Working Paper Series, No. 56. Posted online at www.census.gov/population/www/documentation/twps0056/twps0056.html.

77. Rebecca Moore, Anthony Pinn, and Mary R. Sawyer, eds., *Peoples Temple and Black Religion in America,* xi.

78. Tim Reiterman, *Raven: The Untold Story of Jim Jones and His People* (New York: Penguin Books, 1982), 138.

79. John R. Hall, *Gone from the Promised Land: Jonestown in American Cultural History* (New Brunswick, NJ: Transaction Publishers, 2001), 70.

80. Cited in Daniel L. Crowe, *Prophets of Rage,* 254; see Hugh Pearson, *The Shadow of the Panther: Huey Newton and the Price of Black Power in America* (Reading, MA: Addison-Wesley Publishing Company, 1994).

81. Rev. Neil, an African American, was Rector of St. Augustine where Newton's girlfriend, LaVerne Anderson, was enrolled in the Afro-Haitian dance course taught by Mrs. Ruth Beckford-Smith, who facilitated the program, despite reservations concerning the Black Panther Party. After Neil visited Newton in the Alameda County Jail following his arrest for charges of killing Oakland police officer John Frey, the relationship strengthened. He was considered the "pastor of the Black Panther Party"—having conducted the funerals of Bobby Hutton, Captain Franko, Alprentice "Bunchy" Carter, Jonathan Jackson, George Jackson, and in 1989, the funeral of Huey P. Newton—even after he left the Bay Area in 1974. On his Web site, located at http://www.itsabouttimebpp.com/Our_Stories/Chapter1/BPP_and_Father_Neil.html, Neil reports that the breakfast program began in late January 1969 with 11 youngsters on the first day and with more than 135 students before the first week ended. The *San Francisco Chronicle* included an article on the breakfast program, entitled, "The Panther Breakfast Club" (San Francisco Chronicle, January 31, 1969, pg. 3, Tim Findley). Neil also worked directly with King on the Selma-to-Montgomery March in 1965 and Open Housing Drive in Chicago in 1966. The Sacred Heart Catholic Church began assisting the breakfast program in March 1969. A white middle-class Catholic priest named Father Eugene Boyle, inspired by the charge of Vatican II, supported the Panthers' outreach. See also Daniel L. Crowe, *Prophets of Rage,* 224.

82. Cecil Williams, *I'm Alive: An Autobiography* (New York: Harper and Row Publishers, 1980), 80.

83. Ibid., 188–189. Trained at the Perkins School of Theology at Southern Methodist University in his native Texas, Williams began his ministry to a predominately white congregation in the midst of the Black Power movement in an increasingly impoverished community surrounded by the poorest of the poor, drug addicts, prostitutes, and homeless people, and contained many pornography shops. Williams referred to it as "the reddest of the red light districts."

84. Ibid., 107.

85. Ibid., 109.

86. Denice Stephenson, ed., *Dear People: Remembering Jonestown* (San Francisco, CA: California Historical Society Press, 2005), 152.

87. In the aftermath of Jonestown, Williams revealed that Jones called him while at the Los Angeles Airport before fleeing for Guyana. After urging Jones to remain in the United States, Williams called him paranoid before Jones hung up on him. See *I'm Alive!*, 149.

88. Ibid., 177.

89. Jones' political allies included Democratic presidential and vice presidential candidates, Jimmy Carter and Walter Mondale; Mayoral candidate George Moscone; and Harvey Milk. Tragically, both men would be murdered by former San Francisco Supervisor, Dan White within ten days of the Jonestown catastrophe. Jones also received support from Governor Jerry Brown, and future mayor Art Agnos. It was these men for whom the Peoples Temple rallied and marched.

90. Willie Brown, *Basic Brown: My Life and Our Times* (New York: Simon and Schuster, 2008), 131–132.

91. See James Richards, *Willie Brown*, 252 and Tim Reiterman, *Raven*, 327–328.

92. James Richardson, *Willie Brown*, 251.

93. Tim Reiterman, *Raven*, 331.

94. Denice Stephenson, ed., *Dear People: Remembering Jonestown* (Berkeley, California: Heyday Books, 2005), 6. The *Sun-Reporter* editorial was entitled "The Tragedy and the Challenge," November 23, 1978.

5

Philadelphia's Opportunities Industrialization Center and the Black Church's Quest for Economic Justice

Juan M. Floyd-Thomas

On the morning of June 29, 1967, President Lyndon B. Johnson made a surprise visit to Philadelphia with an entourage that included his wife, Lady Bird Johnson, Sargent Shriver, the director of the Office of Economic Opportunity, Hugh Scott, the Republican Senator from Pennsylvania, and other close advisors. Johnson and his group arrived in the city by 9:50 a.m. that day with the express purpose of visiting the birthplace of the Opportunities Industrialization Center (OIC) and meeting its founder, Rev. Leon H. Sullivan. There were 250 trainees present to meet President Johnson and shake his hand and, while there, Johnson took full advantage of the occasion to deliver an inspired address that day. In his praise of Rev. Sullivan's experimental job training program, Johnson stated, "I have seen men and women whose self-respect is beginning to burn inside them like a flame—like a furnace that will fire them all their lives . . . That is what this center is all about. It is a place where people find the power that was always within them—but that had been obscured by self-doubt, lack of confidence, a feeling of insecurity, and trapped by the conviction of failure."

Johnson also applauded the fact this program was a community-based initiative that defied the prevailing ethos of liberalism in the 1960s. "The Federal Government [sic] did not build this center," President Johnson asserted, "Neither business, nor labor, nor philanthropy, nor city officials built it. All of us are helping now, and I am proud of the part we are playing." In a rhetorical flourish that might have rivaled that of Rev. Sullivan himself, LBJ further commented that "the spirit built this

111

center—the spirit that wants to say 'yes' to life, that wants to affirm the dignity of every man [and woman], whatever [their] origins, whatever [their] race or religion."[1]

After showing various areas of the facility to the group of dignitaries, Rev. Sullivan pointed toward Mr. Shriver and told the President "That man took a chance and gave me a million [dollars]." Without missing a beat, LBJ quickly responded, "Remember, he gave you a million of my money." This event marked an interesting turning point in Rev. Sullivan's relationship with the federal government. Even if this incident at the OIC headquarters—a simple joke exchanged during a presidential photo-op—was meant as a lighthearted moment, it also revealed the underlying tensions that have perennially confounded American society regarding the establishment of an economic order that is more equitable and humane while also struggling with deeply ingrained modes of social oppression, most chiefly racism, sexism, and classism.

This encounter between Johnson and Sullivan, and the close relationship between OIC and government that it symbolizes, raise certain questions. First in pursuing the creation of a fair economy, how is a meaningful synergy between the private and public sectors supposed to take shape? Moreover, how is the federal government supposed to interact with a faith-based initiative based on genuine partnership rather than offering either generous patronage from the Left or gross paternalism on the Right? This chapter intends to explore critical aspects of Rev. Sullivan's vision of economic justice, looking at key phases of Sullivan's robust activist ministry and their implications for economic justice in the twenty-first century.

By the time Rev. Leon H. Sullivan became pastor of North Philadelphia's Zion Baptist Church in 1950, his life's journey had already been interesting. He was born in 1922 in Charleston, West Virginia as the only child of a divorced couple. Growing up in one of the poorest sections of town, he attended Charleston's Garnet High School for Blacks. Upon graduation, he matriculated for undergraduate studies at West Virginia State College in 1939, receiving a basketball and football scholarship. After a foot injury abruptly ended his collegiate athletic career, Sullivan was forced to pay for his college education by working in a nearby steel mill. Although Sullivan had accepted his call to preach as a Baptist minister when he was eighteen years old, the direction of his life was changed immeasurably when Sullivan met Rev. Adam Clayton Powell, Jr., the legendary pastor of Abyssinian Baptist Church and the long-serving congressional representative from Harlem. During a visit to West Virginia in 1943, Powell persuaded Sullivan to relocate to New York City and hired the young preacher as his assistant. Meanwhile, from 1943 to 1947, Sullivan received his theological education at Union Theological Seminary and later completed his graduate studies in religion at Columbia University. It was at Union where he was exposed to the passionate liberal Protestant teachings and progressive commitments of the Social Gospel movement amidst the likes of Reinhold Niebuhr, Paul Tillich, and Harry Emerson Fosdick, to name a few.

It is important to note that much of Sullivan's evolution as a social reformer, civil rights advocate, and religious leader took place during his sojourn in New York. For example, Harlem offered a rich variety of examples of black faith communities confronting the ravages of unemployment and economic exploitation, including the notable example of Father Divine's Peace Mission. Father Divine's group stood out amongst a host of Great Depression-era alternative black religious movements in Harlem through its devotion to acting directly on behalf of the poor, regardless of race. Divine's Peace Mission did this through cooperatives known as "heavens" which provided food, shelter, and jobs to the downtrodden in ways that neither traditional black churches nor the government had the capacity or willingness to do at the time. Additionally, Sullivan's increasing involvement in civil rights protests and community organizing, including the successful "Don't Buy Where You Can't Work" boycotts sharpened his leadership abilities greatly. Although these efforts rarely broke the prevalence of racial discrimination in hiring during this period, this form of galvanized economic action and public protest had a direct influence on Rev. Sullivan and other activist ministers of his generation, most notably Dr. Martin Luther King, Jr. These activities led Sullivan to famed labor organizer, A. Philip Randolph during the organizing stages of the 1942 March on Washington Movement, thus beginning a long working relationship between these two civil rights leaders. The combination of Sullivan's experiences in ministry, education, and activism while he was in New York served him well as he made his way to the City of Brotherly Love.

In its efforts to confront racial as well as economic inequality in urban America, the story of the OIC actually dates back to the Second World War. The transformation of urban demographics in modern America was a result of the latter phase of the Great Migration. Much like the demand brought on by the labor shortages during the First World War sparked the bulk of the Great Migration of nearly 500,000 African Americans from the rural South to the industrial North and Midwest, the Second World War witnessed a sizable expansion of that migratory pattern. The influx of African Americans from the South into various urbanized sections of the nation seeking wartime jobs during the 1940s was an estimated 1.6 million; by comparison, the preceding three decades of the early twentieth century witnessed a combined emigration of roughly 1.5 million black men and women. According to the U.S. Census, the black populace within major American cities increased by 69.5 percent, while the general population only rose by 40 percent from 1940 to1950.

The urbanization of black America was also accompanied by an effort to gain a foothold, no matter how meager, in the industrial sector of the labor market. Due to the overwhelming labor demand arising from the government's need for war materiél, black men and women were making steady inroads into previously closed labor markets.[2] From 1940 to 1950, the most considerable gains occurred as black men across the nation found jobs as semiskilled, blue-collar workers, with the number of such workers increasing from 464,195 to 1,012,362 during that decade.[3] The rate of increase for African Americans seeking and obtaining semiskilled employment hovered around 118 percent, as the total number of blue-collar laborers increased by only 35.1 percent. Black women also made gains in accessing clerical and sales jobs during this period, increasing from 20,765 to 99,747. As for the skilled trades, black employment more than doubled from 132,110 to 281,002.

In addition to the dire economic circumstances of the war years, government policy improvements in combating racial discrimination also contributed to the increased presence of African Americans in manufacturing jobs. Faced with the threat of Randolph's March on Washington Movement, President Roosevelt signed Executive Order 8802 and subsequently created the Fair Employment Practices Commission (FEPC). Coaxing the White House to push forward plans for the FEPC during wartime, Randolph's movement guaranteed African Americans the right to employment and training in defense plants.[4] Although the FEPC might have been somewhat toothless, the federal government's role in securing wartime job opportunities for African Americans in the defense industries amounted to moderate gains.[5] In the wake of the FEPC's founding, however, black men and women in the workforce remained overwhelmingly sequestered in the low wage segment of the labor market.[6]

During the early postwar era, there were several other negative economic trends that contributed to the rise of the OIC. Faced with a gross national product (GNP) markedly lower than that of the war years, the Eisenhower administration became gravely concerned about its inability to design fiscal and monetary policies capable of constraining the nation's inflationary tendencies. GNP growth hovered at an annual rate of 2.4 percent from 1953 to 1960, down by nearly half from the average annual rate of 4 percent from 1946 to 1953. The national workforce increased by 7.1 percent from 1955 to 1960, a development that corresponded with a productivity index (estimated output per man-hour) that rose at an annual rate of 3.5 percent. In turn, unemployment was steadily on the rise across the nation during this period as a result of unabated inflation and ineffective economic strategies.

The unemployment rate, which was at 4.3 percent between 1947 and 1952, increased over the following decade from 4.4 in 1955 to as high as 6.8 percent in 1958 and, by 1960, the average unemployment rate was 5.1 percent. For African Americans, however, these unemployment figures were much more devastating. Throughout the early postwar years, the unemployment rate for African Americans soared from a level of 5.5 percent upward to 12.6 percent. By the mid-1950s, the black unemployment rate was firmly twice that for white Americans.[7] A worsening situation thereafter cut across all age groups within the black community, and was especially hard-hitting amongst the urban black populace. Furthermore, even black male workers who were employed found themselves virtually trapped in the semiskilled/blue-collar segment of the labor market without much chance of upward mobility. Ironically, with the racial demographics of many American cities shifting, black female workers made significant gains in job opportunities during this period, but also failed to experience any boost in occupational upgrade or upward mobility. In light of poor or no job prospects, a growing contingent of working-age African Americans dropped out of the American workforce altogether and were rendered occupationally invisible.

The emergence of the mid-twentieth century Civil Rights Movement with its assault on *de jure* racial segregation also helped frame thinking about the economic realities of the struggle. The southern phase of the civil rights struggle arose when African Americans across the region began to organize themselves against Jim and Jane Crow racism in collective efforts to achieve equity in education, use of public accommodations, and voting rights. Meanwhile, the quest for first-class citizenship by African Americans outside the American South was often defined by the fight against institutionalized (sometimes informal) racial discrimination in job hiring and housing patterns, among other things. By the early 1960s, however, the national civil rights agenda began focusing more and more on ensuring economic progress for black America. It was becoming plainly obvious that, even if civil rights activism ended some markers of racial prejudice in political or cultural realms, the nation's legacy of discrimination surely prohibited African Americans from the economic dimension of the "American Dream."

Bolstered by the utopian promise of Dr. King's "I Have a Dream" speech as expressed during the 1963 March on Washington for Jobs and Freedom, as well as passage of the Civil Rights Act of 1964 and Voting Rights Act of 1965, President Johnson's "Great Society" proposed a "war on poverty" that was intended to abolish human misery and economic hardship in modern America. Despite the sweeping social justice agenda advanced by Johnson's administration, Congress lagged behind greatly in its support by withholding adequate appropriations for many government programs. In turn, this legislative logjam greatly compromised the potential impact of these various programs thus rendering the president's declarations little more than lip service. As one former assistant director of the Office of Economic Opportunity commented, the average poor person in America had virtually no contact with the War on Poverty initiatives "except to hear the promises of a better life to come."[8]

In light of this looming cynicism, the federal government's inertia in fulfilling promises of ensuring human welfare inspired grassroots action. This is clearly demonstrated by the notable shift in the overall thinking amongst the acknowledged leadership of the Civil Rights Movement in the years after 1965. For instance, echoing a key insight from Michael Harrington's classic text on U.S. poverty, *The Other America*, Dr. Martin Luther King noted, "New laws are not enough. The emergency we now face is economic, and it is a desperate and worsening situation. For the 35 million poor people in America . . . there is a kind of strangulation in the air. In our society it is murder, psychologically, to deprive a [person] of a job or income. You are in substance saying to that [person] that he [or she] has no right to exist."[9] Dr. King further explicated this point by stating "many white Americans of good will have never connected bigotry with economic exploitation. They have deplored prejudice but tolerated or ignored economic injustice. But the Negro knows that these two evils have a malignant kinship."[10] By outlining his position in this manner, King sharpens the focus of the civil rights struggle toward the needs of the working poor and unemployed while also trying to muster support from wealthy and middle-class liberals who thought the struggle for justice and equality was over.

In hindsight, it seems appropriate that the culmination of the civil rights struggle in the early 1960s coincided with the passage of two of the decade's most pivotal policy initiatives: the Manpower Development and Training Act of 1962 and the Economic Opportunity Act of 1964. These policies and their subsequent programs reflected the federal government's effort to broaden the scope of job opportunities for those people who were victims of chronic unemployment and endemic poverty. One key battleground for this challenge to the status quo was Philadelphia. For instance, employment trends in the local construction industry were abundant and lucrative during the 1950s because of the push to rehabilitate the Center City region as well as the building of public housing projects and assorted other facilities in the greater metropolitan area. Yet, while those construction jobs were growing precipitously, racial discrimination in employment practices against African Americans also rose sharply, lending to the dilemma of mounting black unemployment that would plague the city in the 1950s and 1960s. It must also be noted that there was a high level of juvenile delinquency and a growing crime rate that developed during the very same period had a very telling effect on the city's black community.

Following Sullivan's arrival in Philadelphia, he soon became known as one of the city's premier black pastors and was affectionately hailed the "Lion from Zion." Beyond the walls of Zion's sanctuary, Sullivan became chiefly involved in the battle against juvenile delinquency. Sullivan was influential in the creation of the Philadelphia Citizens Committee Against Juvenile Delinquency in 1953, a role that led to his ascendancy as a local leader in police-community relations. During the remainder of the 1950s, he received many accolades for his work with troubled youth. In an effort to move beyond the work accomplished by the Citizens Committee, Rev. Sullivan established a Youth Employment Service in Zion Baptist Church in order to combat black youth unemployment through direct action. During this period, Sullivan asserted "even with citizens working to clean up and protect their neighborhood, the fact remains that the intolerable, festering population pressures are still there. Even citizens' committees do no more than 'dust off' the slums while the forces that created and maintain them remain and expand. . . . We must do more than contain bad conditions; we must eradicate them."[11]

Despite the civic goodwill and persuasive leadership at the heart of local youth rehabilitation programs, Sullivan recognized that a more aggressive campaign against job discrimination was necessary to secure any true and meaningful employment gains for Philadelphia's black youth. Given the shifting urban demographics towards a larger black populace, the Montgomery bus boycott of 1955–56 offered a model of direct action governed by three key factors: the leaders of urban black churches could work with grassroots organizers to lead a mass social movement; an effective leadership could galvanize the black community into a unified force for social change; and black purchasing power could be utilized as an economic weapon. By 1959, the pastors of 400 African American churches in Philadelphia came together to form a group commonly hailed as the "Black 400" in order to mobilize the black community into a mass boycott campaign akin to the Montgomery strategy. The merger of religion and race-based activism was quite obvious to Sullivan, as evident in his statement: "[E]very movement of significant proportions to survive in the black community has had its roots in the [black] church."[12]

Between 1959 and 1963, the Black 400 initiated a selective patronage campaign against roughly thirty firms in the greater Philadelphia area, including TastyKake Baking Company, Sunoco, Gulf Oil, Pepsi-Cola, and others in order to open the doors of job opportunity for thousands of their followers. As a result of the selective patronage campaign's success, the Black 400 garnered a great deal of publicity nationwide including a front page story in the *New York Times* and a featured article in *Fortune* magazine. In roughly four years, Sullivan and the Black 400's victory set a clear precedent for those seeking to galvanize an active and committed coalition of black church leadership by wielding black economic power wisely against the unfettered might of big business. This example became so compelling that in 1962 Dr. King and the Southern Christian Leadership Conference (SCLC) asked Sullivan to share the secrets of his group's success with them, with this exchange of information leading by 1967 to SCLC's creation of "Operation Breadbasket" under the leadership of Rev. Jesse Jackson.

The selective patronage campaign provided crucial leverage against private industry throughout the metropolitan area as well as ensured the loyalty and satisfaction of the rank-and-file members of the boycott movement. Quite simply, the more successful the 400 ministers were at bringing major companies to the negotiating table, the more jobs they secured for African Americans throughout the city. This was an essential concern for the preachers because they fully understood that forcing these companies to meet their demands translated into real and substantive job creation rather than merely dealing with quotas or set-asides for their constituency.[13] This was pressure politics in its purest and most effective form.

Nevertheless, these consumer boycotts also revealed the deceptively conservative bent of the civil rights agenda espoused by the Black 400. Like their counterparts across the spectrum of the middle-class civil rights leadership, Sullivan and other members of the Black 400 wanted to integrate African Americans into the existing capitalist system rather than radically transforming it. As Rev. Sullivan declared, "I have nothing against free enterprise. I believe that free enterprise is the best way to economic prosperity that I know of in the world today. . . . The problem is that the free enterprise system as we knew it was free enterprise for . . . White people and not for . . . Black people." While the Black 400 had devised a winning civil rights platform that opened the door to potential economic empowerment for black Philadelphians, the next test was to invalidate racist claims that there were no African Americans qualified for these newly available jobs. Therefore, the shift from a protest paradigm to a job-training program was both a foreseeable and necessary development. It was Rev. Sullivan's opinion that "certainly we needed a massive training program" because "I could see that integration without preparation was frustration."[14]

A considerable issue for Rev. Sullivan and other members of the Black 400 was creating a job-training program that would bring black job applicants up to par with industry hiring standards in order to gain the implicit trust of the private sector. In his study of the OIC's operations, industrial analyst Bernard Anderson explains "the shift in strategy from protest to job training required confidence in the willingness of employers to cooperate in a new environment of fair employment opportunity."[15] By 1964, the general consensus among Philadelphia's civil rights establishment was that the best way to improve the life chances for economically disadvantaged African Americans was to work with rather than against potential employers.

From 1964 to 1974, the OIC grew from its humble origins to eventually become the most influential community-based provider of manpower development and job training services for the urban poor and unemployed. Through Sullivan's guidance, the OIC expanded beyond its roots in Philadelphia to found more than 150 centers throughout the United States as well as Latin America, the Caribbean, and Africa. During its first decade in operation, the program enrolled roughly 200,000 trainees and spent about $150 million in providing a variety of human personnel services. OIC's organizational dynamism was so phenomenal that it quickly served as the subject of numerous external examinations, academic studies, and government evaluations investigating its nationwide operations.[16]

There were several reasons why OIC became the focal point of so much national acclaim and interest. First, the OIC achieved an extraordinary level of growth and development in a relatively short period of time. Sullivan's philosophy had put in motion a national manpower service system that vastly outpaced that of any other community-based effort of its day. Speaking in relative terms, the scope, scale, and expansion of the OIC largely surpassed the Johnson administration's Job Corps and Manpower Act programs because of its inspiring philosophy. Second, the OIC was unique because the relationship between the national office in Philadelphia and the local OIC affiliates across the nation had an extremely flexible nature that provided the local entities great degrees of autonomy in designing and implementing their own programs. Finally, even though the organization's staff and trainees were demographically diverse, the OIC was always identified as a fundamentally "black" enterprise because: its origins as the brainchild of a black Baptist preacher; its geographic location in mostly black communities within major metropolitan areas; an estimated 85 to 90 percent of the program's enrollees were black; and many of the local centers were staffed by black professionals. Furthermore, at the height of a decade punctuated by the intertwined realities of the "urban crisis,"[17] the Civil Rights Movement, and Black Power era, countless supporters from all walks of life saw the OIC movement as an efficient and even divinely inspired model for the organization, education, and management of the inner city's financial and human resources.

With respect to redirecting the guiding thought and activist spirit of his ministry toward matters of economic justice, Sullivan's OIC occupied an interesting middle ground in the political and economic landscape of the black freedom struggle during the late 1960s. On the one hand, Sullivan's OIC differed from the SCLC's Operation Breadbasket in that it was much more openly interventionist and intentional about seeking to transform the extant economic order into a full-employment economy. On the other hand, OIC was much more conciliatory and pro-capitalist in outlook than the Marxist-inspired efforts of Rev. James Forman's "Black Manifesto" or the Black Power-influenced demands by groups such as the National Council of Black Churchmen, focused as they were on reparations from America's foremost ecclesiastical institutions for the historic legacy of racism as well as on a radical restructuring of the American economy. By moving beyond either strategic protests or strident posturing, Rev. Sullivan was able to help promote systematic, structural remedies to historic patterns of unemployment as well as underemployment.

In devising the basic philosophy of the OIC, Rev. Sullivan centered on three guiding ideals in an effort to promote a sense of empowerment amongst the disadvantaged peoples being served by the centers. First, he asserted that the plight of the unemployed and underprivileged could only be addressed through the education of the whole person. The vocational education received by the OIC trainee had to encompass not only the acquisition of job skills but also the socialization of the individual into behaviors and attitudes in keeping with values acceptable to mainstream society. Second, the purpose of the OIC was to train individuals for "good" job opportunities with prospects for the future. Third, the goals of the OIC could only be accomplished with the general input and full cooperation of the local community. Without broad-based community support for their efforts to recruit new participants and guide them through successful vocational training and job placement, the OIC surely would have floundered.

Having clearly defined the organization's governing concepts, Rev. Sullivan's plan to found the OIC was underway. He solicited commitment from supporters representing professionals, organized labor, social reformers, various religious denominations, and members of the private sector for the OIC's original board of directors. In addition to the initial contributions from local churches and grassroots organizations, Rev. Sullivan received a financial gift of $50,000 from the William Penn Foundation as seed money for their efforts. This initial sum allowed Sullivan to begin OIC operations on a modest scale and draw the attention of other benefactors, both public and private. For example, the city provided Sullivan an abandoned jailhouse as the base for the organization's operations for the nominal fee of one dollar a year. Shortly after settling into its new space, the OIC came to the attention of the Philadelphia Council for Community Advancement and the Ford Foundation, a situation that served as the basis of a very advantageous relationship between these charitable organizations and Sullivan's industrial self-help movement. In addition to providing various levels of financial support for the fledgling OIC movement, the affiliation with the Ford Foundation was particularly fruitful because it brought this community-based manpower services program to the attention of officials in the Johnson administration. As Sullivan and his relatively inexperienced team implemented the OIC's three-point philosophy, their non-traditional approach to job-training and other manpower services helped them avoid the blunders most routinely committed by comparable government-sponsored efforts.

Quite unlike the efforts to promote manpower delivery services or vocational education brought forth under the aegis of LBJ's liberal "Great Society" legislative agenda, the OIC was consciously designed to respond to the specific needs of local communities rather than conform to some monolithic set of procedures. As the OIC evolved and became more stable in its mission as well as organizational structure, the program's job-training model revealed some of Sullivan's innovative thinking. The rudiments of the Philadelphia OIC's vocational education had seven components: outreach (recruiting); intake (processing); counseling (assessment); feeder (pre-vocational training); occupational skills training (instruction); job development and placement (employment opportunities); and follow-up (job retention of former trainees). This multifaceted approach not only prepared the trainees for successful introduction into the skilled portion of the labor market, it also provided them the widest array of social instruction to overcome the various forms of institutionalized oppression. Another crucial element of the OIC's early developmental success came with the notion of open entry/open exit enrollment, the belief that training should emphasize the abilities and needs of the individual rather than ascribe to a rigid prefabricated plan. Moreover, the trainees during this period participated in the OIC program without a training allowance or stipend. At the programmatic level, the OIC was unique in that it was a highly structured operation that also had an amazing degree of flexibility for its enrollees.

With OIC's visionary approach motivating cities across the nation to recreate the success of the Philadelphia center, the OIC National Institute was established in 1966 and served as a clearinghouse for operational information, general guidance, and technical assistance for new and existing centers. In this fashion, each local OIC center could maintain its autonomy and yet also function in accordance with a reasonably consistent set of educational standards and practices endorsed by the National Institute. This development was also noteworthy because both the Office of Economic Opportunity and the U.S. Department of Labor funded this endeavor, with this level of joint funding demonstrating a clear investment by the federal government in expanding the role of community-based efforts to resolve issues of high unemployment and economic privation in urban areas.

In 1967, the federal government sought to coordinate the distribution of manpower services for areas with higher concentrations of poverty and economic dislocation and created the Concentrated Employment Program (CEP). As part of its mandate, the CEP was intended to improve the management of various organizations focused on vocational education and manpower delivery services at the local level in order to help the unemployed and underemployed become ready to participate more fully in the workforce as reliable, productive members. In Pittsburgh, Birmingham, Cleveland, Baltimore, Boston and a few other cities, OIC centers received CEP support in order to maintain the feeder and occupational skills training phases of their basic operation. Within a matter of years, these centers' ability to function became totally contingent upon financial support from the CEP. This marked a considerable compromise of the localized, autonomous, grassroots spirit of the OIC movement that made it a symbol of the Great Society's liberal reforms. At the same time, the Philadelphia OIC chose to receive CEP funds only through RISE, an ancillary component of the main program, which allowed for greater autonomy by maintaining the legitimacy of local control of such efforts. This distinction illustrates an effort on the part of Sullivan and the core administration of the OIC movement to constantly adapt and compensate to new developments.

By 1973, the Nixon administration enacted the Comprehensive Employment and Training Act (CETA), a federal law geared towards training disadvantaged workers and providing them with public sector jobs. Much like Sullivan's OIC, the various programs funded by CETA also offered work to unskilled workers, the long-term unemployed, and low-income high school students seeking seasonal employment. Through CETA, full-time jobs were provided in either public agencies or private not-for-profit organizations over the course of a one to two year period. The imperative was to convey marketable skills that would allow participants to move eventually to an unsubsidized job in the private sector. Although the law was enacted as an extension of the Works Progress

Administration (WPA) program from the 1930s, CETA was intended to decentralize federal control of job training programs by giving more power to the individual state governments. With the advent of CETA, the federal government emphasized subordinating programs like the OIC to strict guidelines that mandated competition among various social service entities and that limited strict dependence on increasingly limited federal monies. Nevertheless, a growing reliance by OIC and similar community-based programs on the funding and policy direction of the federal government ultimately worked to their disadvantage during the ascendancy of conservative Republican ideology by the late 1960s and early 1970s. Therefore, despite Sullivan's attempt at a more strategic acceptance of government funding, a growing dependence upon federal funds to underwrite OIC's work chipped away at its viability as a vehicle for black empowerment in the United States.

Ultimately, the awkward joke shared between Johnson, Shriver, and Sullivan during that impromptu visit in 1967 symbolized the dynamic, albeit troubled relationship between the OIC's brand of community self-help and the Great Society's so-called "War on Poverty." Although helpful in the short term, such federal funding had so many strings attached that it eventually proved detrimental to the OIC movement in the long run. On the verge of realizing its own vast potential beyond state intervention, however, the OIC compromised its fundamental faith in its own ability to achieve the American Dream once the OIC's fate became too intertwined with governmental largesse doled out by liberal allies on one hand and bureaucratic constraints by conservative critics on the other. Consequently, such entanglements undermined burgeoning prospects of more innovative, community-based efforts such as the OIC to meet the needs of the growing ranks of the poor and dispossessed. The object lesson to be learned from Sullivan's example is that, while not wanting to reproduce the dependencies and constraints that come with governmental involvement with faith-based community development initiatives, the alternative cannot and should not be severing the relationship between Church and State altogether. In this matter, the influential theologian Reinhold Niebuhr asserts, "the sad duty of politics is to establish justice in a sinful world." Yet how will the body politic—from our leaders to ourselves—be able to fulfill this task without a Church that can work in tandem with the State to ascertain what is sinful and what is just, while doing so with a sense of courage, compassion, and confidence?

Moreover, even as much as the interconnection between black faith and politics has been widely recognized, an emphasis on economic justice has always been a glaring weak spot. In that spirit, any reflection upon Rev. Sullivan's work serves as an effort to rectify such a shortcoming.

Despite such problems, the founding of OIC can best be understood in relation to Rev. Sullivan's attempt to achieve both fair and full employment for all, regardless of background. Even in light of OIC's more recent economic woes, Rev. Sullivan's life and ministry represent a vitally important, yet overlooked phase of the civil rights struggle—a quest for economic justice—that might, in turn, promote a vision of social responsibility, economic sustainability, and human dignity.

Notes

1. "Text of President Johnson's Address," *Philadelphia Evening Bulletin*, 29 June 1967.

2. Herbert R. Northup, et al., *Negro Employment in Basic Industry*, Studies of Negro Employment, vol. 1 (Philadelphia: Industrial Research Unit, The Wharton School, University of Pennsylvania, 1970); Charles C. Killingsworth, *Jobs and Income for Negroes* (Ann Arbor: Institute of Labor and Industrial Relations, Wayne State and University of Michigan, 1968); Merl Reed, "Black Workers, Defense Industries, and Federal Agencies in Pennsylvania," *Labor History* 27 (1986): 356–84; Cheryl Lynn Greenberg, *Or Does It Explode?: Black Harlem in the Great Depression* (New York: Oxford University Press, 1991), 198–210; Earl Lewis, *In Their Own Interests: Race, Class and Power in Twentieth-Century Norfolk, Virginia* (Berkeley: University of California Press, 1991), 173–87; and Thomas J. Sugrue, *The Origins of the Urban Crisis: Race and Inequality in Postwar Detroit* (Princeton, NJ: Princeton University Press, 1996).

3. Herbert R. Northup, et al., *Negro Employment in Basic Industry*, Studies of Negro Employment, vol. 1 (Philadelphia: Industrial Research Unit, The Wharton School, University of Pennsylvania, 1970), 27–28.

4. Louis Ruchames, *Race, Jobs, and Politics: The Story of the FEPC* (New York: Columbia University Press, 1951); Herbert Garfinkle, *When Negroes March: The March on Washington Movement in the Organizational Politics for FEPC*, (Glencoe, IL: Free Press, 1959); Manning Marable, *Race, Reform, and Rebellion: The Second Reconstruction in Black America, 1945–1990,* (Jackson, MS: University Press of Mississippi, 1991), 13–15.

5. Robert C. Weaver, *Negro Labor: A National Problem* (New York: Harcourt, Brace, and World, 1946), 35–42.

6. Herbert R. Northup, et al., *Negro Employment in Basic Industry*, Studies of Negro Employment, vol. 1 (Philadelphia: Industrial Research Unit, The Wharton School, University of Pennsylvania, 1970), 28.

7. Matthew A. Kessler, "Economic Status of Nonwhite Workers, 1955–62," *Special Labor Force Report* No. 33, (Washington, DC: U.S. Bureau of Labor Statistics, 1965), 3; Bernard E. Anderson, *The Opportunities Industrialization Centers: A Decade of Community-Based Manpower Services*, Manpower and Human Resources Studies no. 6 (Philadelphia: Industrial Research Unit, The Wharton School, University of Pennsylvania, 1976), 13.

8. Joe William Trotter, Jr., *The African American Experience* (Boston: Houghton Mifflin, 2001), 561.

9. *The Words of Martin Luther King, Jr.* Selected and With an Introduction by Coretta Scott King (New York: Newmarket Press, 1996), 45.

10. Ibid.

11. Leon H. Sullivan, *Build, Brother, Build* (Philadelphia: Macrae Smith, 1969), 65.

12. Ibid., 70.

13. Leon H. Sullivan, *Alternatives to Despair* (Valley Forge: Judson Press, 1972), 52.

14. Sullivan, *Build, Brother, Build*, 86.

15. Bernard E. Anderson, *The Opportunities Industrialization Centers: A Decade of Community-Based Manpower Services*, Manpower and Human Resources Studies no. 6 (Philadelphia: Industrial Research Unit, The Wharton School, University of Pennsylvania, 1976), 31.

16. Greenleigh Associates, Inc., "A Pilot Study of the Opportunities Industrialization Center—Philadelphia, Pennsylvania," report prepared for the Office of Economic Opportunity, 1967; A. L. Nellum and Associates, "An Evaluation of the Opportunities Industrialization Center of Greater Milwaukee," report prepared for the Office of Policy, Evaluation and Research, Manpower Administration, U.S. Department of Labor, 1968; Bernard E. Anderson and H. A. Young, *An Evaluation of the Opportunities Industrialization Center, Inc.—Charleston, W. Va., Erie, Pennsylvania* (Philadelphia: Industrial Research Unit, The Wharton School, University of Pennsylvania, 1968); Greenleigh Associates, Inc., "An Overall Review Report—The Opportunities Industrialization Center for Greater Milwaukee," report prepared for the Office of Policy, Evaluation and Research, Manpower Administration, U.S. Department of Labor, 1968; M. E. Lawrence, *Training the Hard-Core in an Urban Labor Market—The Case of the Bedford-Stuyvesant Opportunities Industrialization Center* (Philadelphia: Industrial Research Unit, The Wharton School, University of Pennsylvania, 1970); Noah Robinson, *The Opportunities Industrialization Center—Jacksonville, Florida* (Philadelphia: Industrial Research Unit, The Wharton School, University of Pennsylvania, 1970); F. D. Barry, "The Roxbury Opportunities Industrialization Center—An Economic Case Study of Self-Help Job Training in the Ghetto," (MA thesis, Cornell University, 1973); R. B. Peterson, "An Evaluation of the Seattle Opportunities Industrialization Center" (MA thesis, University of Washington, 1968); Bernard E. Anderson, *The Opportunities Industrialization Centers: A Decade of Community-Based Manpower Services*, Manpower and Human Resources Studies no. 6 (Philadelphia: Industrial Research Unit, The Wharton School, University of Pennsylvania, 1976).

17. An exceptional introduction to the negative race relations, economic upheaval, and urban decline of the era is Thomas J. Sugrue, *The Origins of the Urban Crisis: Race and Inequality in Postwar Detroit* (Princeton, NJ: Princeton University Press, 1996). Also see Jon C. Teaford, *The Rough Road to Renaissance: Urban Revitalization in America, 1940–1985* (Baltimore and London: The Johns Hopkins University Press, 1990) and Vincent J. Cannato, *The Ungovernable City: John Lindsay and His Struggle to Save New York* (New York: Basic Books, 2001).

6

The Black Panther Party
and the Black Church

Steve McCutcheon
Judson L. Jeffries
Omari L. Dyson

The Black church was born over 350 years ago, engaged in a survival program. The Black Church was born out of an effort to deal with the concrete conditions and needs of Black people. It was born in an attempt to enable and empower Black people to survive the racist and exploitative system of slavery in America. Its mission and purpose today is the same as it was 350 years ago, although at a higher level. That mission and purpose is to see to its utmost that Black people and other oppressed people's survive, with dignity and humanity, American racism and capitalism.

—Father Earl Neil
The Black Panther

Black churches have always played an integral role in black people's fight against racial injustice and oppression. Many a freedom fighter has emerged from the black church. Henry Highland Garnett, a dynamic Presbyterian pastor, is one such example. Garnett gave a spellbinding oration at the 1843 National Negro Convention in Buffalo, New York, that came to be known as the "Call to Rebellion" speech. Garnett exclaimed:

Neither god, nor angels, or just men, command you to suffer for a single moment. Therefore, it is your solemn and imperative duty to use every means, both moral, intellectual, and physical that promises success . . . Brethren, arise, arise! Strike for your lives and liberties. Now is the day and the hour.

> Let every slave throughout the land do this, and the days of
> slavery are numbered. You cannot be more oppressed than you
> have been—you cannot suffer greater cruelties than you have
> already. Rather die freeman than live to be slaves. Remember
> that you are Four Millions!

Garnett's words were no less poignant 100 years later, as black churches were featured prominently during the modern Civil Rights Movement, arguably the most transformative period in twentieth-century America. In 1984, Aldon Morris wrote in *The Origins of the Civil Rights Movement* that, "the Black Church functioned as the institutional center of the Modern Civil Rights Movement."[1] Elaborating further, Morris maintains that in regard to the movement, the black church served as an organized mass base for the modern Civil Rights Movement; provided a cadre of clergymen largely economically independent of white patronage and adept at managing people and resources; institutionalized finances through which protests were financed; and provided meeting space for the masses to strategize for the hundreds of demonstrations, marches, and sit-ins that occurred during the 1950s and 1960s.[2] Many black preachers and their congregations were active in the fight for civil rights; and as a result, some churches were bombed. Many black preachers were threatened, beaten, jailed, exiled, and murdered because of their civil rights activities. Hence, it is not hyperbole to submit that without the black church, there may not have been a modern Civil Rights Movement.

An argument put forward in *Black Power in the Belly of the Beast* by Judson L. Jeffries is that the black church was not featured prominently in the Black Power Movement.[3] This is not to say that the black church did not have its place. A cursory look at several of the major, and less prominent organizations that comprised the Black Power Movement reveals a relationship that varied across organization. An examination of Us, the Congress of African People, Republic of New Afrika, the League of Revolutionary Black Workers, the Defenders, the Black Liberators, and the Sons of Watts has uncovered little evidence that suggests these groups had strong ties with the black church. Some of these organizations may have held events and activities at a black church from time to time; and some of its members may have worshipped at black churches, including William Smith (the Defenders) and Rev. Charles Koen (the Black Liberators). But on the whole, the black church was not central to the Black Power Movement in ways comparable to its role within the mid-twentieth-century Civil Rights Movement.

Of the Black Power groups, the Deacons for Defense and Justice had perhaps one of the strongest relationships with the church. Founded in 1964, the Deacons arose in response to Ku Klux Klan activity in Jonesboro, Louisiana. The group's membership was comprised mostly of churchgoing men who agreed on the name "Deacons" as a reflection of their background in the church. The name also represented their perception of themselves as servants of the community and defenders of their faith. It is no accident that some of the men who held leadership positions in the Deacons for Defense and Justice were actual deacons in the church. Another group, the Black Panther Party (BPP), perhaps the most ballyhooed of the Black Power organizations, had a mixed relationship with the black church. For reasons that are unclear, this fact has at best been underexplored, and at worst, unacknowledged altogether by students of history. In turn, this chapter seeks to fill that gap by examining the role that black churches played in the philosophy and development of the Black Panther Party.

The role of religion and spirituality was a nebulous part of the Black Panther Party, as the organization was born amidst sweltering racism and oppressive social, economic, and political conditions. Such forces became the foci of the Party's work. While many ministers spoke of these insufferable conditions from the pulpit, the sermons that told of the salvation of the body and spirit could only be actualized and achieved (as far as the church was concerned) by those who accepted a supreme omnipotent savior in an intangible kingdom. Such an ideology was perceived by some Panthers, especially those in leadership, as disconnected from the harsh realities that beset poor blacks in the United States. As students of Malcolm X, some Party members (especially during their Black Nationalist phase, 1966–1968) accepted Malcolm's position that blacks were living in hell, as their oppressor was enjoying the fruits of heaven. As the self-proclaimed heirs to Malcolm X, the Panthers set out to alleviate the conditions that consigned blacks to an inferior position within both the national and international community. Though many Panthers had been involved in the activities of black churches (i.e., as choir members, young deacons, Bible study groups, and in other capacities), the immediacy or relevancy of those experiences and contributions did not figure prominently in the BPP's 10 Point Program/Platform or day-to-day community work. Regardless of this fact, at times the Panthers enjoyed a positive working relationship with some black churches throughout the country.

In 1969, the organization's National Headquarters forged a relationship with St. Augustine's Episcopal Church in West Oakland. Father Earl Neil presided over the church, and developed a rapport with Party members following the death of BPP member James "Lil'" Bobby Hutton on April 8, 1968. Father Neil eulogized Hutton, the first party member killed by police, and later eulogized Alprentice "Bunchy" Carter, George Jackson, and his brother, Jonathan Jackson. As the relationship grew, Neil agreed to let the Panthers set up their Free Breakfast Program at the Church. As Father Neil said, "the free breakfast program was the first of its kind, either in the public or private sector."[4]

Shortly after the Free Breakfast Program got underway at St. Augustine's Episcopal Church, the Panthers started conducting weekly political education classes at the church. In addition to the Free Breakfast Program and political education classes, Panther leaders routinely gave speeches at the church to large audiences, which were comprised of Panthers and community residents. These classes not only served to raise people's consciousness, but proved to be an effective recruiting tool for the BPP. One Panther joined the Party in 1968 after hearing speeches by Bobby Seale and Eldridge Cleaver at the church. To believe that any church would have accommodated Cleaver given his penchant for delivering invective lectures, might seem incongruous with the typical tone and decorum of most churches.[5] However, Father Neil saw past the inflammatory diatribes of some Panthers and judged Panthers based upon their works rather than their histrionics. Moreover, Father Neil had a long history working with groups of varying ideologies and tactics, including years residing in McComb, Mississippi where he put his life on the line for the civil rights struggle, and was not put-off easily then by the Panthers' strident posture.

Reverend Cecil Williams of Glide Memorial Church in San Francisco was another Panther sympathizer who opened his doors to accommodate the Panthers' Free Breakfast Program. Chairman Bobby Seale and Chief of Staff, David Hilliard, understood that the black church was the oldest institution in the black community and that it played a major role in the day-to-day lives of African Americans. After all, churches were where many African Americans engaged in networking, joined reading groups, and participated in clubs of various types, which made them potentially important as places where the BPP in Oakland could anchor their community survival programs. By reaching out to the black churches, the BPP demonstrated its willingness and ability to work with an established institution whose goals and mission may have, in some ways, differed widely from those of the BPP. A closer examination reveals, however, that the BPP and the church had at least one major commonality—both were concerned with enhancing people's life chances. Although there were many potential points of divergence, the assistance of black churches enabled the BPP to demonstrate how a partnership between a grassroots organization and an established faith-based institution could provide sorely needed services to thousands of poor and working-class people—populations that were practically neglected by the U.S. government in many areas of the country.

With the establishment of the initial Free Breakfast Program in 1969 at St. Augustine Episcopal Church, Party members throughout the country began approaching churches in their respective cities. Many of those outposts developed their first breakfast programs and other community survival programs in neighborhood churches. In Seattle, Chicago, and Philadelphia, political education classes and liberation schools for children were also held in black churches. Quite naturally, the level of cooperation between the branches and chapters of the BPP and black churches varied from city to city.

In Philadelphia, BPP member Sultan Ahmed remembers that Father John Gracy of Miller Memorial Church in the Germantown area was supportive of the breakfast program as early as 1969, allowing the Panthers to use its facilities for a time.[6] Father Paul Washington of the Church of the Advocate in North Philadelphia also supported the Panthers' Breakfast Program by opening its doors to it and the BPP's political education classes. Additionally, the Church of the Advocate served as a site for the BPP-led Plenary Session for the Revolutionary People's Constitutional Convention on September 4–6, 1970. This meeting, held in Philadelphia nearly two centuries after the signing of the Declaration of Independence, provided a space for activist groups and individuals from all walks of life to unite and rewrite what originally had been written by the country's "founding" fathers in 1787—a new constitution "providing authentic liberty and justice for all."[7]

When the Party decided on Philadelphia as the host city, it recognized it would need the assistance of all who had any sympathies for its objectives. Finding a venue was the first order of business, and the Panthers wasted no time in asking the well-known and highly regarded Father Washington for the use of his church—a request to which he agreed. This church alone would not suffice, however, because a much larger public space was needed to accommodate the thousands expected to attend the convention. Consequently, the Panthers decided to approach Temple University and request that it make its large new gymnasium available. Father Washington joined a group of citizens that included Philadelphia Bar Association President Robert Landis in meeting with Temple officials to win their cooperation. Temple agreed, and the site was set.[8]

Aside from using the Church of the Advocate as a venue for the People's Revolutionary Constitutional Convention, the church also permitted the Panthers to hold workshops on gang violence prevention. Because the proliferation of gangs was eroding the inner fabric of Black Philadelphia, the Panthers and Father Washington teamed up to mitigate the problem. In August 1970, the Panthers summoned rival gangs to the church to broker a truce. The combined efforts of the Panthers and Father

Washington provided residents with a sense of security and an added assurance that gang violence would not be tolerated.[9] It is also important to note that Father Washington felt a special kinship with the Panthers. His fondness for the young militants was exemplified when he joined with the Panthers and held a memorial service for Mark Clark and Fred Hampton—two Panthers who were slain by police officers attached to the State Attorney's office in Chicago on December 4, 1969.[10]

Ahmed points out that although the Philadelphia branch worked very closely with the Church of the Advocate, Father Washington was not their spiritual advisor.[11] Oakland's Father Neil was viewed as spiritual advisor for the entire Panther organization—BPP's unofficial Minister of Religion—although there were no formal arrangements between clergy and Party branches and chapters elsewhere in the country.

Despite the absence of formal partnerships across the country between black churches and local BPP branches, Bobby Seale readily acknowledges that most of the Panthers' Free Breakfast Programs were held in neighborhood churches. In Houston, Texas Charles "Boko" Freeman a member of the local branch, recalls soliciting the cooperation of black churches as a site for its breakfast program. Mt. Horeb Baptist Church was chosen because of Reverend Samuel Smith, its progressive pastor. Smith was receptive to the Panthers' Breakfast Program from the outset; and believed that the breakfast program was an activity that would surely benefit the community.[12]

In Sacramento, former BPP member James Mott explains that "black churches there were more than willing to support BPP programs, [which lent] to increased interaction between the BPP and members of the various churches in that city."[13] One church in Sacramento's Oakpark area, the First Baptist Tabernacle Church, supported Dr. Martin Luther King, Jr., during one of his visits to the city in 1967. Also, Mott remembers that BPP member and early Defense Captain, Charles Bronson, was a choir member at the Shiloh Baptist Church and used his position to muster support for the branch's early community survival programs. In 1969, the Church of Christ, under Reverend Childers, also welcomed the branch's breakfast program—which was the first breakfast program created outside of the Oakland-Bay area. Mott adds that churches "welcomed BPP-sponsored literacy classes and other programs too."[14] During that same period in June, 1969, when the BPP came under attack from local police departments and from government agencies nationwide, black clergy in Sacramento spoke out, condemning police raids and the vilification of party members and their programs. Mott maintains that not only did black churches offer to host and support BPP programs, these churches actively proclaimed their solidarity with the BPP.

In the view of former Panther, Jimmy Slater, it was the Cleveland Panthers that "had the best relationship with the churches of any Panthers that I have been around, anyplace."[15] Attempting to mobilize churches to assist in their various programs, the Panthers contacted Father Gene Wilson, pastor of the St. Adalbert Church, only a few blocks west of the Panther office. From the start, Father Wilson supported the Free Breakfast Program and assisted in the development of the Panthers' programs by providing space and support. In addition, the Panthers utilized the Church to distribute clothes and shoes to those who requested them.[16] Panther member Tommie Carr often did the "church circuit," speaking at various locations to garner support for the branch. For example, teenage members of the Woodland Hills Community Presbyterian Church organized a Youth Sunday service that featured Carr and several other Panthers. Carr took the opportunity to elaborate on the local branch's offerings and stressed the need for black churches to open their facilities "to respond to the needs of the poor."[17]

Frank Stitts, a member of St. Adalbert, reaffirmed the necessity of the Panthers' program: "When I looked around our community where [the Panthers] were feeding kids . . . there was a great need, and they met the need."[18] In fact, they encouraged and recruited members of the community to become involved in the maintenance and development of their alternative institutions. These interactions between community residents and the "super-militants," as Stitts called the Panthers, helped counter the demonic image of Panthers as portrayed by the media and agents of the social order. The sharing of resources between the Panthers and institutions such as the church, not only ensured the success of the Party's community survival programs, but provided poor residents with services they may not have received otherwise.

In Harlem, Henry Mitchell recalls that there were a plethora of black churches that were willing to host the breakfast program and it's Liberation School for children. The BPP worked with black churches of various denominations.[19] In some cities, branches and chapters held programs and activities at Baptist, Methodist, and Episcopalian churches simultaneously. The denomination of the church did not seem to matter, as the BPP did not consider religious denomination in its efforts to forge community ties and build and expand its community survival programs. By the end of 1969, many churches in major cities were flooded with requests from Panthers to collaborate. The Panthers realized that the church afforded them the type of anchor needed to become a stabilizing force within black communities across the country.

In Los Angeles, the Panthers intended to make inroads into every major black community in the city. Consequently, they set out to establish breakfast programs throughout L.A., realizing that to be successful they needed to allay concerns that congregations might have about allowing them to use their churches. After much deliberation, a small group of Panthers led by Gwen Goodloe went before the Los Angeles Conference of Baptist Ministers with a presentation of the goals and objectives of their community survival programs. Impressed, the ministers voted unanimously to give the Panthers their endorsement and commendation. This vote of confidence gave the Panthers a sense of legitimacy in the eyes of the black bourgeoisie.

While the BPP enjoyed a degree of support from the faith community, sometimes church officials and their congregations were split over whether to work with the Panthers. For example, in one Los Angeles case, the initial breakfast program (called the John Huggins Breakfast Program for Children in honor of the slain deputy chairman) was established in early 1969 at the University Seventh Day Adventist Church to the chagrin of the congregation. Despite the parishioners' uneasiness about the Panthers, Associate Pastor Reverend Lorenzo Payte gave the Panthers permission to use the church's facilities with one stipulation: that meat not be served. Despite the fact that between forty and fifty children, aged three to fourteen, were served daily, some church members were opposed to having any association with the Panthers. The Panthers claimed that once the congregation saw how successful the program was, support grew exponentially.[20] Interestingly, shortly after the program began, Reverend Payte was informed that he was being transferred to another church, casting doubt on the claim about the congregation's change of heart. If Payte's transfer was related to his work with the Panthers, it would not have been the first time a man of the cloth was reassigned after he appeared receptive to the Panthers' message. Weeks earlier, in October 1969, the bishop of the San Diego Catholic diocese abruptly transferred Father Frank Curran to New Mexico after it was discovered that he allowed the Panthers to use a local church to feed indigent children in the San Diego area. The reception on the part of some black churches was equally inhospitable in Houston, Texas. Charles E. Jones says "due to a lack of support from area churches, the Houston Panthers sponsored their first Free Breakfast program at the Dew Drop Inn," a local watering hole.[21] Houston Panthers were unable to make any inroads into the black ecclesiastical community as they were shunned by nearly every black minister to whom they reached out. Reverend Samuel Smith of Mt. Horeb Baptist Church came to their rescue in Spring 1973, but his benevolence did not go unpunished. John "Bunchy" Crear of the Houston branch of the BPP incredulously remarked that the "other ministers accused Reverend Smith of working with the devil for allowing us to use his church for the free breakfast program."[22] Leon Valentine Hobbs says that the Seattle chapter had similar encounters with black churches. "We had to hold our free breakfast programs in locations like the Atlantic Street Youth Community Center and the Highpoint housing project, because we received zero support from the black church."[23] Conversations with Panthers in other parts of the country such as Baltimore, Indianapolis, and Detroit reveal a similar theme. Says Gwen Robinson of Detroit: "I don't remember any black church being receptive to us [the Panthers].[24]

Despite such setbacks, the Panther brass encouraged local branches to utilize churches as a venue for their breakfast program. Its decision was based on the following reasons: 1) churches could accommodate large groups of people; 2) holding the breakfast program in a house of God would make it less likely that the police would barge in and harass its occupants, or so the Panthers thought; 3) association with churches gave the Panthers a degree of legitimacy among those who may have been leery about allowing their children to frequent a program put together by black militants; 4) most church facilities were of sufficient standards as to free Panthers from concerns about their program locations conforming to building codes; and 5) churches did not require Panthers to pay rent, which allowed them to expand existing survival programs or create new ones.

There were several reasons various black churches were neither interested in working with the Panthers nor receptive to their message. First, some churches were fearful that any association with the Panthers would bring unwanted attention and/or harassment from law enforcement agencies. History had shown that churches and other places of worship were not entirely off limits when it came to the repression of black groups, radical or otherwise. Nation of Islam's Temple #27 had been fired upon by members of the Los Angeles Police Department in the early 1960s. In the late 1960s, New Bethel Baptist Church in Detroit was riddled with bullets when police officers and members of the Republic of New Africa clashed.

Second, some believed that the Panthers were impractical, if not completely unrealistic in their belief that a revolution could take place in the United States. Third, churches received misinformation about the Panthers from media, local police, and the Federal Bureau of Investigation, which hindered any healthy relationship between the Panthers and many black churches.[25] Fourth, some black church leaders had tired of the constant criticism and ridicule they received from Panthers. For example when David Hilliard spoke before the National Committee of Black Churchmen that met in Berkeley in the early 1970s, he called the preachers "a bunch of bootlicking pimps" and "motherfuckers"—comments that by any reasonable standard were disrespectful, unwarranted, and divisive. During the same meeting Hilliard inexplicably threatened that if the preachers did not align more closely with the Black Power movement, the Panthers would "off" (i.e., kill) some of them. [26]Such comments only served to alienate the Party from churches and by extension a large sector of the black community. Little wonder then that when Huey Newton demanded in the summer of 1971 that CAL-PAK (an organization consisting of twenty-two black businesses) provide the Party with a weekly cash donation or face a boycott, the Reverend Charles Belcher, president of Oakland's Interdenominational Ministerial Alliance charged the Panthers with extortion. Said Belcher, "Let us emphatically state that under no circumstances does Huey P. Newton, the Black Panther Party . . . have the support . . . of our congregations."[27]

Incidents like these strained relations between the Panthers and black churches and haunted the Panthers in a number of ways, including during Bobby Seale's run for mayor in 1973. According to Newton "the black preachers did not support us in the mayoral election, but the members of their congregations did."[28] It is true that many black ministers were not supportive of Seale's campaign for mayor, but the idea that their congregations were supportive deserves closer scrutiny. For example, Newton spoke of the Party's alienation from the Church in a 1971 address at the Center for Urban Black Studies at UC–Berkeley in which he admitted that the Party's public criticism of the church did irreparable damage to the BPP's relationship with the church and drove a wedge between the BPP and the black community in general. Partly as a result of this, the Panthers found it necessary at times to reach out to white churches, simply because they had worn out their welcome with black churches in some communities.

Fortunately for the Panthers, the justness of their cause made their entry into white religious communities less difficult than might have been imagined and yielded numerous examples of support from white churches. In Baltimore for example, the Panthers received $8,000 from the Catholic Archdiocese earmarked specifically for the breakfast program.[29] Also, in 1970 when scores of Panthers were swept up in a slew of dragnet-like raids by the Baltimore Police Department, the Interdenominational Ministers Alliance issued statements condemning the city's police commissioner.[30] In 1973, the National Episcopal Church gave the Winston-Salem branch of the BPP $37,000 to support their emergency ambulance service. Pennsylvania Quakers also assisted the Panthers during times of need. First, local Quakers in tandem with doctors in the community donated a facility and medical equipment to institute the Mark Clark People's Free Medical Clinic.[31] "By opening a Clinic, the Panthers were able to address one of the most pressing needs among communities of color—the lack of adequate healthcare."[32] Second, after a planned incursion by police officers on three Panther offices on August 31, 1970, a total of fourteen people (two non-Panthers) were arrested with bail set at $100,000 each. In response, the Religious Society of Friends (Quakers) expressed outrage and posted bail for Defense Captain Reggie Schell after Common Pleas Judge Thomas M. Reed reduced the initial amount to $2,500. The Quakers raised the bail by putting up the deed to the building that housed the Mark Clark Memorial Clinic.[33]

In Milwaukee, Panthers held rallies in May and June of 1969 at St. Boniface Church and at Cross Lutheran Church's Youth Center (aka the "Soul Hole") to advertise their Free Breakfast Program. After the June rally at Cross Lutheran Church, Panthers inquired whether they could operate their breakfast program at the church—which had 400 members, 40 percent of which were black. Rev. Joseph Ellwanger hesitantly approved, and stated that he would consult with the church's council. Prematurely, however, the Panthers took Ellwanger's approval and ran with it. When the council received word on the proposal, they disapproved stating they "would not allow this controversial black militant group to use its facilities, regardless of their good intentions."[34] Incredibly, Paul Crayton, lieutenant of religion of the Milwaukee Panthers and former intern pastor at Cross Lutheran, decided he would therefore host the breakfast program at his home.[35]

Although the Panthers suffered a degree of humiliation from this public mishap, their breakfast program figured prominently in discussions regarding the state of childhood hunger in the city of Milwaukee. With the efforts of Rev. Ellwanger, among others, the Citizens for Central City School Breakfast (CCCSBP) was created on July 21, 1969 with the express purpose of implementing breakfast programs in Milwaukee's public schools. Although the battle was rocky, by 1972 the organization was instrumental in establishing programs in numerous schools and facilities and fed more than 2,000 children.[36] Again, the combined efforts of the Panthers and church officials led to much-needed resources for inner-city youth.

Oddly, active religious involvements or pursuits were not openly encouraged by the BPP. If members chose to pray or worship in some way, they did so of their own accord. One possible reason for this may be found in the teachings of Malcolm X, the Panthers' ideological mentor. In his *Ballot or Bullet* speech, Malcolm X articulated that religion functioned as a medium to reinforce differences, and essentially, disallows any opportunity for people to come together against a common enemy. His solution was to keep religion at home, in the closet. Carter G. Woodson echoed a similar sentiment decades earlier. He wrote:

While serving as the avenue of the oppressor's propaganda, the Negro church, although doing some good, has prevented the union of diverse elements and has kept the race too weak to overcome foes who have purposely taught Negroes how to quarrel and fight about trifles until their enemies can overcome them. This is the keynote to the control of the so-called inferior races by the self-styled superior. The one thinks and plans while the other in excited fashion seizes upon and destroys his brother with whom he should cooperate.[37]

The BPP did not disavow religion, but as dialectical materialists, some found it difficult to relate to matters of the world that could not put be under scientific examination. The Panthers were interested in testable hypotheses related to the physical world and its tangible conditions and in examining and seeking remedies to matters plaguing the oppressed here on earth. Religion, as far as many Panthers were concerned, was a realm that did not lend itself to rigorous empirical study. And, because Karl Marx was required reading for members of the BPP, it is likely that many Panthers, including Huey P. Newton, the BPP's chief theorist, believed religion was an ideology that served as an opiate for the People rather than as a stimulant for independent thinking and action. In the minds of many Panthers, Christianity (as projected by many black churches) was synonymous with whiteness since a caucasian "god" was the pervasive image of the deity within this realm.[38] These religious representations, prevalent throughout history, limited the consciousness of people and consciously or unconsciously reinforced the system of white supremacy and black inferiority.[39] Christianity, as an imposed religion on African people, ran counter to the BPP's goal of self-determination, self-reclamation, and self-governance (i.e., Black Nationalism). Hence, to be a Panther and a Christian was an oxymoron of sorts.

After his release from prison in 1970, Huey P. Newton began rethinking some of his previous statements and positions regarding the black community and its institutions. In May 1971, Newton spoke at the Black Odyssey Festival at the University of California in Berkeley where he explained the BPP's position on black churches and on the philosophical interconnectedness of religion and the BPP. Newton stated:

We say [religion] is only a ritual; it's irrelevant, and therefore we have nothing to do with it . . . that is one way of defecting from the community, and that is exactly what we did. Once we stepped outside of the church with that criticism we stepped outside of the thing that the community was involved in and we said, "You follow our example; your reality is not true and you don't need it."[40]

Newton argued that both the BPP and the church were in a stage of development. The BPP was in search of concrete and practical answers and solutions to matters related to oppression, poverty, healthcare, among others, while the church attempted to look for answers through a belief in God. Although Newton was concerned about the fact that in churches such as the Antioch Baptist Church that he and his family attended, persons were "encouraged to see prayer as the only way to salvation,"[41] Newton also recognized a positive benefit of church attendance on people's mental well-being. He wrote:

> Everybody in the church prayed with you, sharing a common purpose that relieved tension and had a cathartic effect. No other outlet provided such an outlet . . . for me the church offered a countermeasure against the fear and humiliation I experienced in school. Even though I did not want to spend my life there, I enjoyed a good sermon and shouting session. I even experienced sensations of holiness, of security, and of deliverance. They were strange feelings, hard to describe, but involving a tremendous emotional release. Though I never shouted, the emotion of others was contagious. One person stimulated another, and together we shared an ecstasy that can fill a church during the service. There is no music, like that music, no drama like that drama of the saints rejoicing, the sinners moaning, the tambourines racing, and all those voices coming together crying holy unto the Lord . . . Their pain and their joy were mine, and mine were theirs—they surrendered their pain and joy to me, I surrendered mine to them. Once you experience this feeling, it never leaves you.[42]

For a short time Newton even wanted to become a minister like his father, but over time he began to question the concept of religion and the very existence of God. In fact, at one point Newton felt no need for religion and downplayed the importance of culture, which for many are inextricably linked. As C. Eric Lincoln and Lawrence Mamiya asserted, religion was perhaps the best prism to cultural understanding, that culture was a form of religion, and religion was the heart of culture.[43] Newton understood and acknowledged that churches were a necessary part of life, but he admits eventually finding it necessary to question and examine every idea that touched his life and, as a result, he reached an impasse with the church. Newton states the following conclusion:

> I think that [the church] is a thing that man needs at this time, and he needs it because of what? Because we [social] scientists cannot answer all of the questions. . . . In the Black community we have the church as an institution that we created . . . You cannot fight an organized machine [i.e., the white power structure] individually, so we would work with the church in order to establish a community which will satisfy most of our needs so that we can live and operate as a group.[44]

Newton's statement reflected the new, yet original ideology of the BPP relative to the church and other community organizations, and in the process sought to mitigate damage done to the BPP-black church relationship by some Panthers who castigated black churches for their various failings. Newton's respect for churches stemmed from the fact that religion was "one of the most long-lasting influences" on his life[45] and that both of his parents were God-fearing people. His father's ministry encompassed serving as pastor of Bethel Baptist Church in Monroe, Louisiana, and after moving to Oakland, ministering in several churches there. Newton's entire family was involved in church life, holding offices, singing in the choir, and serving on the usher board and on other committees. During his youth, Newton himself regularly attended Sunday school, attended worship services weekly, and served as a junior Deacon. The Church was integral to Newton's life as he makes clear in a 1973 *Christian Century* magazine interview wherein the interviewer points out Newton "quoted liberally from Ecclesiastes, his favorite book of the Bible."[46]

It is not surprising that in the early 1970s the BPP gained a foothold among persons who, like Newton, were favorably disposed at some level to black churches based upon their upbringing. After the BPP relocated its Central (National) Headquarters from West Oakland to East Oakland in 1973, the BPP created a nondenominational Sunday service called the Son of Man Temple. "Originally housed in one of the Panthers small campaign district offices, the Party soon acquired a 500-seat church sanctuary that gave the services more of a church feel to it."[47] Through a combination of sermons, stories, and political education, Bobby Seale, the brain-trust behind Son of Man Temple, provided some members with the spiritual nourishment they were seeking. The Son of Man Temple was initially limited to Party members and community workers but soon after opened its doors to the general public. Six months after Seale created the Son of Man

Temple he turned the reigns over to James Mott. From 4:00 to 5:00 p.m. attendees were treated to the spell-binding oratory of Mott and the sweet sounds of the Son of Man Temple Singers, the temple's choir. According to Steve McCutchen, the Sunday events grew into quite a large enterprise that included a number of activities, especially after it transitioned into the Oakland Community Learning Center in 1974/75.[48]

By connecting the spiritual with the practical, the BPP developed within the black community another level of awareness/consciousness. The Son of Man Temple and its community-based nature offered the BPP a place for worship and spiritual uplift, and a forum that brought people together in the name of God (not unlike the Nation of Islam or the Shrine of the Black Madonna). Though the Son of Man Temple was not religiously-based or spiritually-based in the traditional sense, it offered a Sunday settings with qualities many people found familiar. As McCutchen recollects:

> The program began with a presentation by a Panther spokes-person, usually James Mott, and focused on community issues and the relationship of Black and poor people to the social, economic, political, and human conflicts of the world and in Black communities everywhere. The discussions were intended to inform, to prod people to think, and then to search for concrete ways to address their day-to-day lives, their dreams, and their hopes. The Son of Man Temple choir added to the church-like feeling, yet the music was drawn from popular songs that had been revised by members of "The Lumpen," the BPP song group, with additional songs from BPP leading member Elaine Brown, a polished vocalist in her own right. Again, the Son of Man Temple program presented a church atmosphere that many people could identify with.[49]

With the departure of Bobby Seale from the BPP in 1974, the Son of Man Temple (which was renamed the Oakland Community Learning Center), lost some of its religious character.[50]

The Black Panther Party was rooted in the black community, and as the organization attempted to address issues such as police brutality, poverty, inadequate healthcare, crime, and miseducation of black youth, the BPP placed greater focus on its community survival programs. And although the church was a logical venue for some of the Panthers' programs, the church's impact on the BPP was not an integral part of the organization's quest to liberate black and oppressed people throughout the world. Black churches were part of a larger front the BPP hoped would help lead oppressed people to higher levels of revolutionary ideas and action.

In sum, the Black Panther Party's affiliations with black churches appear to have been based largely on pragmatism and political expediency rather than deep spiritual kinship or connection (with a few notable exceptions, as stated above). Nonetheless, the BPP reached out to black churches in a way that enabled the Panthers to make significant inroads into black communities across America. Moreover, while the relationship the Panthers cultivated with black churches may have been politically motivated, there was a common commitment to liberation between the Panthers and many churches. Despite broader ideological and strategic differences between the BPP and black churches, the Panthers appear to have a more meaningful relationship with black churches than any of the other groups that comprised the Black Power Movement, with the possible exception of the Deacons for Defense and Justice.

Notes

1. Aldon Morris, *The Origins of the Civil Rights Movement* (New York: The Free Press, 1984) 4.

2. Ibid.

3. Judson L. Jeffries (ed.), *Black Power in the Belly of the Beast* (Urbana, IL: Illinois University Press, 200s).

4. Itsabouttime website.

5. Hugh Pearson, *The Shadow of the Panther* (Reading, Mass: Addison-Wesley, 1995).

6. Sultan Ahmed, telephone interview with Steve McCutchen, October 2009.

7. George Katsiaficas, Organization and Movement: The case of the Black Panther Party and the

Revolutionary People's Constitutional Convention of 1970. In Kathleen Cleaver and George Katsiaficas, *Liberation, Imagination, and the Black Panther Party* (New York: Routledge, 2001), 142.

8. Paul Washington and David Gracie, *"Other Sheep I have": The Autobiography of Father Paul M. Washington* (Pennsylvania: Temple University Press, 1994; Omari L. Dyson, The life and work of the Philadelphia Black Panthers: The curricular and pedagogical implications of their social transformation efforts (unpublished dissertation, 2008).

9. Omari L. Dyson, The life and work of the Philadelphia Black Panthers: The curricular and pedagogical implications of their social transformation efforts (unpublished dissertation, 2008).

10. Ibid.

11. Sultan Ahmed, telephone interview with Steve McCutchen, October 2009.

12. Charles "Boko" Freeman, telephone interview with Steve McCutchen, September 2009.

13. James Mott, telephone interview with Steve McCutchen, August 2009.

14. Ibid.

15. Jimmy Slater, telephone interview with Ryan Nissam-Sabat, August 31, 1998.

16. Ryan Nissim-Sabat, "Panthers Set Up Shop in Cleveland." In Judson L. Jeffries, *Comrades: A Local History of the Black Panther Party* (ed.), (Indiana: Indiana University Press, 2007).

17. Woodland Hills Church: " 'The Misery of Blackness' is Theme of Youth Sunday," *Call and Post*, March 6, 1971, 8A.

18. Frank Stitts, telephone interview by Ryan Nissim-Sabat, August 1998.

19. Henry Mitchell, telephone interview with Steve McCutchen, April 2009

20. "LA Open First Community Center," *The Black Panther*, November 11, 1969, 2.

21. Charles E. Jones, "Arm Yourself or Harm Yourself." In Judson L. Jeffries, *On the Ground: The Black Panther Party in Communities Across America* (ed.), (Jackson, Miss: University Press of Mississippi, 2010), 31.

22. Ibid.

23. Leon Valentine Hobbs, telephone interview with Judson L. Jeffries, October 10, 2010.

24. Gwen Robinson, telephone interview with Judson L. Jeffries, March 23, 2010.

25. Andrew Witt, "Picking up the Hammer: The Milwaukee Branch of the Black Panther Party." In Judson L. Jeffries, *Comrades: A Local History of the Black Panther Party* (ed.), (Indiana: Indiana University Press, 2007).

26. Huey P. Newton, *To Die for the People* (New York: Random House, 1972), 74.

27. Hugh Pearson, *The Shadow of the Panther* (Reading, Mass: Addison-Wesley, 1995), 245.

28. Cornish Rogers, "Demythologizing Huey Newton," *Christian Century* 90 (1973), 795–6.

29. John Robinson, "Black Panthers: Revolution and Social Change," *The News American*, September 6, 1970, 1.

30. "The Community Talks About the Panthers Arrests," *Afro-American*, May 5, 1970, 27.

31. Geller, Laurence H. (1970d, December 8), "Police restraining case here rested by complainants," *The Philadelphia Tribune*, 1, 3; Omari L. Dyson, The life and work of the Philadelphia Black Panthers: The curricular and pedagogical implications of their social transformation efforts (unpublished dissertation, 2008).

32. Omari L. Dyson, The life and work of the Philadelphia Black Panthers: The curricular and pedagogical of their social transformation efforts (unpublished dissertation, 2008), 106.

33. Anthony Lame and Ken Shuttleworth (1970, September 5), "Panther captain released after bail is cut to $2500," *The Philadelphia Inquirer*, 9; Omari L. Dyson, The life and work of the Philadelphia Black Panthers: The curricular

and pedagogical implications of their social transformation efforts (unpublished dissertation, 2008).

34. Andrew Witt, "Picking up the Hammer: The Milwaukee Branch of the Black Panther Party." In Judson L. Jeffries, *Comrades: A Local History of the Black Panther Party* (ed.), (Indiana: Indiana University Press, 2007), 201.

35. Ibid.

36. Ibid.

37. Carter G. Woodson, *The Mis-Education of the Negro* (New Jersey: African World Press, Inc, 1933/1990), 61.

38. Akbar, Na'im. *Breaking the Chains of Psychological Slavery* (Florida: Mind Productions & Associates, Inc., 1996).

39. Ibid; Wilson, Amos. *Blueprint for Black Power: A Moral, Political, and Economic Imperative for the Twenty-First Century* (New York: African World Info-Systems, 1998).

40. Huey P. Newton, *To Die for the People* (New York: Random House, 1972), 63–64.

41. Huey P. Newton, *Revolutionary Suicide* (New York: Harcourt Brace Jovanovich, 1973), 36.

42. Ibid, 38.

43. C. Eric Lincoln and Lawrence Mamiya, *The Black Church in the African American Experience* (Durham, NC: Duke University Press, 1990).

44. Huey P. Newton, *To Die for the People* (New York: Random House, 1972) 64, 66.

45. Ibid, 36.

46. Cornish Rogers, "Demythologizing Huey Newton," *Christian Century* 90 (1973): 795–6.

47. Steve McCutchen. Telephone interview with Judson L. Jeffries, October 2009.

48. Ibid.

49. Ibid.

50. Ibid.

7

Racial Discrimination and the Radical Politics of New York Clergyman, Milton A. Galamison

Clarence Taylor

One of the most controversial figures in New York City during the 1950s and 1960s was the Reverend Milton Arthur Galamison. Born on March 25, 1923 in Philadelphia, Pennsylvania, Galamison became the leader of the school integration movement in New York, conducting a number of demonstrations and boycotts to force the Board of Education to integrate the largest school system in the nation. Unlike most of the prominent black clergy in New York, who were closely associated with the Republican and Democratic Parties, Galamison was a political radical who worked with Communists and other leftists.

By the early 1950s he became the recognized leader of the more militant wing of the school integration campaign in New York. While some in the school integration campaign advocated a more moderate path to school integration involving litigation, negotiation, and compromise with school officials, Galamison argued that it was essential that ordinary people be empowered to force the status quo to make changes. Galamison, who by 1964 became an ally of the Black Nationalist leader Malcolm X, was accused of being a Communist, a political opportunist, and even a racial arsonist fanning the flames of racial hatred. This chapter argues, however, that Galamison's radicalism was rooted in his religious worldview, especially the left wing of American Presbyterianism, and in his experience with poverty and racial discrimination.

Milton Galamison and the School Integration Movement

Although New York was the most diverse city in the United States, its school system was racially segregated. Speaking at an Urban League symposium, Kenneth Clark, a professor of psychology at City College declared that the school system was segregated and that black children received an inferior education. According to Clark, the "best available estimates" showed that in thirty-five schools in districts 10 through 14, there were 103 classes with retarded mental ability (CRMD), and students who scored a 75 on an I.Q. test could be placed in these classes. On the other hand, only three schools in Harlem had programs for intellectually gifted children (IGC), with no more than six classes. Clark referenced a "small preliminary study of a number of schools in New York City" that revealed teachers in schools located in black and Puerto Rican neighborhoods had lower expectations for their students and believed that the curriculum had to be adjusted to accommodate their lower ability. The high school dropout rate was higher for black and Puerto Rican children than for white.[1]

Clark's criticisms of unequal treatment of minority group students embarrassed the Board of Education. While attention to separate and unequal school systems was generally focused on the South, the psychologist pointed his finger at the largest school system in the country, accusing it of segregating its student body. In response to Clark's criticism, Board of Education President, Arthur Levitt, requested that the Parent Education Association (PEA), an organization created in the late nineteenth century to improve the public school system, conduct an investigation of blacks and Puerto Ricans in the school system. In the fall of 1955, the PEA released its report detailing widespread segregation in the school system. There were forty-two de facto segregated elementary schools (a student body that was 90 percent or more black and Puerto Rican) and nine junior high schools (85 percent or more) in the city.[2]

In spite of the PEA's findings and the Board's promise to make changes, the school system did not take steps that satisfied New York City's civil rights community. Instead, the board argued that there was little it could do about segregation because neighborhood segregation led to segregated schools. In 1960, Galamison created the Parents Workshop for Equality in New York City Schools, an organization made up of parents who fought for school integration. The Parents Workshop challenged the Board's defense that housing discrimination was responsible for school segregation. Even when black and white children lived in close proximity, the Board zoned them to different schools.

The New York City Board of Education did little in the way of school integration. In response to nine Harlem parents protesting school segregation by keeping their children out of school in the fall of 1958, the Board of Education introduced a "permissive zoning" plan. The plan allowed junior high school children who attended segregated overcrowded schools to transfer to another school. However, very few children transferred under permissive zoning. When Galamison and his Parents Workshop announced that they would initiate a sit-out, the Board of Education responded by announcing its "Open Enrollment" plan. Open enrollment allowed parents the opportunity to voluntarily transfer their children from black and Puerto Rican segregated schools to predominantly white schools. Nevertheless, since the plan required that parents take the initiative, and since the school agency did little to inform parents of the program, few students were transferred.

Due to the Board's intransigence, civil rights groups, including all the city chapters of the NAACP, the Urban League of Greater New York, branches of the Congress of Racial Equality (CORE), the Parents Workshop, and other grassroots organizations formed the Coordinated Committee for Integrated Schools to plan strategies to force the board to act on school integration. The Coordinated Committee selected Galamison as its president and planned a one-day boycott to force the board to come up with a plan and timetable for integration. Even though board officials attempted to stop the boycott by promising to take action, New York CORE chapters issued a statement accusing the Board of Education of defaulting on its promise to submit a plan for integration. Fred Jones, state education chair of the NAACP, asserted, "we have a series of bad-faith experiences with the Board of Education and there is absolutely nothing at present which would make us call off the boycott. On February 3, 1964, the largest civil rights demonstration in the nation's history took place when close to 500,000 students stayed out of the New York City public schools in order to force the Board to come up with a plan and timetable to integrate the schools.

Despite the success of the boycott, the coalition that made up the Coordinated Committee soon fell apart. A few days after the first boycott, all of the branches of the New York City NAACP, the Urban League, and most of the branches of CORE pulled out of the organization, accusing Galamison of acting in an undemocratic manner after he publicly announced that he was planning a second boycott. The organizations that left the Coordinated Committee claimed that they had never discussed a second boycott and that Galamison acted arbitrarily.

Hurt by the withdrawal of the organizations but still determined to force the Board to come up with a timetable and plan to integrate the public school system, Galamison announced that he planned to carry out a second boycott. Unlike the first boycott that had backing from organizations and individuals from a broad political perspective, support for the second demonstration was mostly from individuals and groups who were left of center. Although the national organization of CORE refused to lend its support to the second demonstration, both the Brooklyn and Bronx chapters, two of the most militant branches of the organization, supported the second boycott. Also, the Community Council on Housing, a militant housing group that conducted rent strikes, threw its support to Galamison.[3] Moreover, Adam Clayton Powell Jr., the pastor of Abyssinian Baptist Church in Harlem and a liberal Democratic U.S. Congressman, announced he would support the boycott. In the 1940s, Powell had worked with left-wing organizations, including the American Communist Party, in order to improve conditions in Harlem. Through his Congressional leadership as Chairman of the House Education and Labor Committee during the mid-1960s, he guided much of the "Great Society" and "War on Poverty" legislation through to successful passage.

Malcolm X, the fiery young Muslim leader who called on black Americans to work for self-determination and to defend themselves against racist attacks, publicly announced his support for the school boycott. By November of 1963, Malcolm's political situation had drastically changed. Elijah Muhammad, the leader of the Nation of Islam (NOI), a group that had recruited Malcolm in the early 1950s, had suspended him for ninety days because (responding to a news reporter on the assassination of President John F. Kennedy) he had said that the "chickens had come home to roost." The comment touched off a firestorm, with the media reporting that Malcolm was glad that the President had been assassinated. Although Malcolm attempted to clarify his statement, Elijah Muhammad and those close to him had seen Malcolm as a growing threat to their leadership. Thus, at the conclusion of the ninety day suspension, Muhammad made the suspension indefinite. Malcolm left the NOI and formed the Organization of African American Unity, while also seeking to work with others, including Civil Rights Movement leaders, in challenging racial inequality and discrimination.

Finding himself in a vulnerable situation, Malcolm looked for allies. Attracted to Galamison's militancy and independence, Malcolm noted in an interview with Timothy Lee of the New York Post that religious leaders such as Dr. Martin Luther King, Rep. Adam Clayton Powell, and Rev. Milton Galamison" understood that "religion is not enough [because] the problems of the Negro go beyond religion."

In a personal telegram to Galamison on April 3, 1964, Malcolm expressed his alliance with the pastor:

Dear Brother

Saw you on news last night. Pleased to see you are not allowing a wedge to be driven between us. I promise you the same.
You have my whole-hearted support in your school project.
Just let me know how I can help. We will be at Audubon 166th
and B'way Sunday April 5 at 8:00 p.m. subject civil rights vs.
human rights. Would you like to speak, RSVP

Your Brother Malcolm X[4]

Although Galamison claimed he was not close to Malcolm, the telegram
strongly suggests that the two had formed a political bond. Malcolm's
telegram expressed trust in the Presbyterian pastor and his pledge to support the boycott revealed that he thought that they were political allies.

Another indication of their allegiance was the fact that Galamison
joined with Malcolm to form a new political party called the Federation
for Independent Political Action. The goal of the Federation was to gain
enough votes to become a political force in the city. One strategy was
to have Galamison run for mayor. The group organized a "State of the
Negro People Conference" and invited Martin Luther King, Jr., to speak
on connecting the civil rights struggle to the labor movement. The Federation for Independent Political Action's interim action committee included
historian John Henrik Clark, housing activist Jesse Gray, Malcolm X, and
Galamison.[5] In addition, the day that Malcolm was assassinated at the
Audubon Ballroom, Galamison was listed on the program of the Organization of African American Unity as the co-speaker.[6]

After the school integration movement had ended, Galamison continued to support left of center causes. In addition to what seemed to be
a growing relationship with Malcolm X, Galamison had connections with
other radicals. In the winter of 1967 he participated in a conference on
Black Power at New York University where, according to an FBI informer,
Galamison told the audience that blacks should make use of black power
by voting, by buying from black businesses, and by assuring that teachers
who would work with children living in the ghetto have the knowledge of
the problems that those children face. By the early 1970s Galamison was
supporting the Black Panther Party (BBP), a group of young black revolu-
tionaries who advocated socialism and solidarity with liberation movements
in Africa, Asia, and Latin America and argued that black ghettos were colo-
nies and that the police were occupying armies of black neighborhoods.[7]

Although the Rev. Adam Clayton Powell supported the second
school boycott, Galamison had a lukewarm relationship with fellow black

ministers within New York City. Galamison did work with members of the black clergy in Brooklyn on behalf of the city's black working class. In 1962, for example, he joined with other Brooklyn black ministers to form the Ministers Movement. The Ministers Movement fought on behalf of jobs for black residents by boycotting and picketing stores on Fulton Street. The clergy insisted that local merchants financially contribute to black organizations in the black community and that businesses adopt a "fair employment" program by hiring and promoting black and Latino workers.

In addition to Galamison, the Ministers' Movement was made up of Rev. Sandy Ray, pastor of Cornerstone Baptist Church, Rev. Simpson V. Turner, pastor of Mount Carmel Baptist Church, Rev. Frank Clemmons, pastor of the First Church of God in Christ, and Rev. Fredrick D. Washington, pastor of Washington Temple Church of God and Christ. The group used their churches as information centers to keep the black community informed of their activities and to recruit demonstrators for campaigns. Borrowing form tactics of the "Don't Buy Where You Can't Work" campaigns of the 1930s, hundreds of demonstrators picketed seven stores on Nostrand Avenue and Fulton Street, the business district of Bedford-Stuyvesant on March 31, 1962. Carrying signs that read "This is a Community and not a Plantation," "Don't Buy Where You Can't Work," and "Upgrade Negro and Puerto Rican Workers," the demonstrators marched from 10:00 a.m. to 4:00 p.m., scaring many of the merchants. Eventually the merchants decided to sit down with the ministers and negotiate a settlement, specifically agreeing to hire more blacks and to contribute financially to black civic organizations.[8]

Galamison also teamed up with his fellow clergy in 1963 when the Brooklyn Congress of Racial Equality requested the assistance of black pastors in their attempt to force the state of New York and the construction trades to hire blacks and Latinos in the building of the Downstate Medical Center in Brooklyn. These clergy formed the Ministers' Committee for Job Opportunities for Brooklyn and organized demonstrations at the construction site. Among the clergy who made up the Ministers' Committee for Job Opportunity were Gardner C. Taylor, Sandy Ray, William A. Jones of Bethany Baptist Church, Walter G. Henson Jacobs of St. Augustine Episcopal Church, Richard Saunders of Stuyvesant Heights Christian Church, Benjamin Lowery of Zion Baptist Church, and Galamison. The Committee attracted thousands of people who carried picket signs, and many blocked construction efforts by chaining themselves to the fence of the site or by sitting in front of trucks and bulldozers. Despite their actions, state officials refused to negotiate. In the end, the ministers worked out a settlement that called for the enforcement of antidiscrimination laws and the creation of hiring centers where blacks and Latinos were given a chance to gain employment in the construction trades. Brooklyn CORE denounced the settlement between the ministers and the Governor. Although he first supported the settlement, Galamison was taken off guard by community anger at the agreement and decided to join in the chorus of those opposed to the settlement—accusing one of the pastors of making a personal deal with the Governor. [9]

Black churches throughout the city also were involved in the school integration campaign. On the eve of the February 3, 1964 boycott, a rally was held at Concord Baptist Church, attracting one thousand people. The Rev. Gardner Taylor spoke of the importance of the fight for school integration. Dozens of churches, especially in Harlem and Brooklyn formed "freedom schools." During the February 3 boycott, parents who kept their children out of school sent them to the freedom schools located in dozens of churches throughout the city. Modeling themselves after the freedom schools in Mississippi during the Mississippi Freedom Summer Campaign of 1964, the freedom schools in New York were staffed by volunteers who taught the children a variety of subjects. There were at least thirty-five churches in Brooklyn that housed freedom schools, including Concord Baptist, which agreed to house 1,000 children, and Newman Memorial Methodist that pledged to house 500 children.[10]

Despite the collaboration with clergy in Harlem and Brooklyn, Galamison's left-leaning views and his willingness to work with Communists at times alienated him from his fellow black clergy. A case in point was the fight for a hospital in Bedford-Stuyvesant. The major group leading the fight for a hospital in Bedford Stuyvesant was the Bedford Health Congress, which the Congress' opponents accused of being a Communist front. According to Galamison, the redbaiting of the Bedford Health Congress was nothing more than diversion. In a sermon he contended:

> This thing came to me in a real sense during the recent campaign to establish a hospital in the Bedford-Stuyvesant area. A number of people advised me: "you can't work with that Bedford Health Congress group, there are some communists in it." But, in any case, would the fact that communists were working for the building of a hospital in this area lessen the need for one?[11]

Unlike his fellow clergy in Bedford-Stuyvesant and elsewhere in New York who kept their distance from the Bedford Health Congress, Galamison openly worked with the Congress. He even allowed the group to use Siloam for a two-day conference.[12] Moreover, Galamison also

praised the leaders of the New York City Teachers Union for their effort
to improve education for black and Latino children, despite their having
been labeled by the New York City Board of Education as a Communist
front.[13]

By the 1950s no black minister in Brooklyn openly embraced
activists in the Communist Party as much as Milton Galamison. In fact,
Galamison's affiliation with the left made him unique among his Brooklyn
ministers during the cold war years. Most of Brooklyn's black ministers
identified themselves with either the Republican or Democratic Parties.
Sandy Ray of Cornerstone Baptist Church, for instance, was a close ally
of Republican Governor Nelson Rockefeller and was so supportive of the
Party he was called "Mr. Republican." The *Amsterdam News*, New York's
black weekly, called Gardner Taylor the "unofficial Democratic chieftain in
Bedford-Stuyvesant. Among Taylor's allies was Democratic Brooklyn borough president John Cashmere who in 1952 appointed Taylor to School
Board No. 27 in Bedford-Stuyvesant. Conversely, Galamison refused to
be tied to the two major parties. As Gardner Taylor notes, Galamison
was "an independent."[14]

Scholars on the cold war note that not only conservatives but liberal
groups supported the anti-Communist effort to rid the country of "Reds"
and Communist sympathizers. Historian Ellen Schrecker contends that
civil rights, labor unions, and liberal political organizations became part of
the "anti-communist network" attempting to root out Communists from
American society. This was also true of Brooklyn's clergy. For example the
Rev. Boise Dent pastor of Tabernacle Baptist Church in Brooklyn, New
York and a prominent figure in the Brooklyn Republican Party leadership,
blamed the Communist-led New York Teachers Union for corrupting the
minds of African American school children. Testifying before the New
York Board of Education, Dent claimed that blacks were preyed upon
by those who pretended to fight on their behalf. The Teachers Union,
Dent declared, was disloyal to America because it served a foreign master,
while blacks had a long tradition of loyalty to the United States. Insisting
that Communists were particularly a menace to African Americans, Dent
stated, "I am of the opinion that Communism has made an inroad into
our public schools to the extent that I blame Communism for 98 percent of the delinquency among Negro children in the Borough of Brooklyn today." Dent went as far to assert that "We as a race are suffering
today in Brooklyn because of inroads of Communism . . . You don't find
them [Communists] doing anything that would help the underprivileged
children."[15]

While prominent Brooklyn black clergy joined the anti-Communist
crusade, Galamison made it abundantly clear through his sermons and

actions that he was willing to work with Communists to improve the plight of black people. Brooklyn's black ministers' decision not to work with the far left prompted Galamison on occasion to criticize them. He labeled the black clergy as "Uncle Toms" that redbaited Annie Stein (who was a member of the Brooklyn branch of the NAACP and a member of the Communist Party)."[16] Galamison remained a political independent, and although he worked off and on with his fellow black clergy, his stronger political ties were with those who were left of center and affiliated with grassroots organizations.

Galamison's Radicalism

In accounting for Galamison's radicalism, the Federal Bureau of Investigation (FBI) put forth as an explanation Galamison's association with the Communist Party. According to the FBI, as early as 1949 the young pastor filed an amicus brief on behalf of John Gates, editor of the Communist Party USA's *Daily Worker*. Gates was one of eleven high ranking officials of the Communist Party who had been arrested for violating the Smith Act. Passed by the United States Congress and signed into law by FDR, the Smith Act made it a crime to advocate or belong to an organization calling for the overthrow of the United States government. The FBI also claimed that Galamison endorsed the World Peace Appeal (calling for a ban on nuclear weapons), which was listed in the House Un-American Activities Committee's "Guide to Subversive Organizations and Publications" as a Communist front. An assertion was also made by *Counter Attack*, a publication that wanted to provide Americans "facts" about American Communism and Communists, that Galamison was an executive board member of the National Emergency Civil Liberties Committee (NECLC). The NECLC was created in 1951 to defend the rights of citizens placed on the House Un-American Activities Committee's list, and persons associated with the Citizens Committee for Henry Wallace (who was the former vice president of the United States and ran for president as the candidate of the left-leaning Progressive Party). Other of Galamison's left-wing activities noted by the FBI included his support of amnesty for Henry Winston, the national chairman of the American Communist Party who had been convicted for violating the Smith Act and for addressing a rally of the Fair Play for Cuba Committee. The group contested the United States' portrayal of Cuba, calling for a more objective coverage of the revolution by the media.

Top leadership of the FBI were convinced of Galamison's subversiveness, as evident when an FBI agent arguing that Galamison did not warrant a full investigation was overridden by the director of the bureau, J. Edgar Hoover, who thought Galamison was dangerous. With Galamison's civil rights activities increasing, and Gus Hall, head of the Communist Party USA, urging the Soviet Communist party to invite the Presbyterian pastor to the Soviet Union,[17] the national office of the FBI claimed an investigation of the Presbyterian pastor was needed:

> He has a history of association with subversive organizations and the Bureau has learned through information supplied by the [the name blacked out] that the subject is highly thought of by officials of the Communist Party, USA. This and his obvious influence among the Negro population of Brooklyn qualifies him for inclusion in the Reserve Index, Section A.[18]

Although Hoover had no evidence that the pastor was a member of the Communist party, anyone close to the party was considered to be as dangerous as any card-carrying member. Hoover testified before the House Un-American Activities Commission that "for every party member there are 100 others ready, willing and able to do the party's work." One important obligation of the bureau, Hoover claimed, was "indentifying undercover Communist, fellow travelers, and sympathizers" because "fellow travelers and sympathizers can deny party membership but they can never escape the undeniable fact that they have played into the Communist hands, furthering the Communist cause by playing the role of innocent, gullible, of willful allies."[19]

When Galamison invited Bayard Rustin to help organize the boycott of the New York City public schools, the FBI concluded that this was proof that Galamison was carrying out the work of the Communist Party and decided to launch a "counterintelligence move" against the pastor. Believing that Rustin was a Communist, the bureau had trailed him since the early 1940s when he was a field representative for the Fellowship of Reconciliation. Two days after the February 3, 1964 citywide school boycott, FBI agent J. A. Sizoo sent a memo to William C. Sullivan, a high ranking official in the bureau, informing him that Rustin had visited the Soviet Mission to the United Nations. The bureau recommended that a reporter from the *New York Daily News* contact Galamison, asking him if he were being used as a front and explain his relationship with the Communist Party.[20] The objective was to get the *Daily News* to print an article that would be embarrassing to Galamison, thereby undermining his credibility.

According to FBI documents, the Communist Party's campaign to recruit Galamison was quite vigorous in 1964, including the effort by Gus Hall to have the Soviet Union invite Galamison to head a delegation of six prominent black leaders to the Communist country. Such a trip, Hall felt would make it easier to persuade the pastor to join the Communist Party, although party members recognized that Galamison was not a person who would "adjust" easily to party discipline. Nevertheless, according to one FBI source, "Galamison's recruitment was close."[21]

Hoover's depiction of Galamison as a fellow traveler, doing the work of the Communist Party, and *Counterattack's* description of the pastor as a Communist sympathizer are unsubstantiated. The evidence is overwhelming that Galamison worked with organizations that the Federal government classified as subversive. He also supported amnesty for a leader of the Communist Party who was convicted of violating the Smith Act. He even went as far to defend the Soviet Union. In one sermon the Siloam pastor claimed that Marxism was an important historical force. The "ideas of human dignity and justice are the basis of Marx's writings and these ideas created modern socialism and Russian Communism." Galamison argued that the power that defined the Russian Revolution was a "concept of man: Faith in oneself, faith in the common man, in his ideas, his power, in his rights. It is this idea of man which has dominated Russia and made her one of the great nations of the world today."[22]

Despite the Party's attempt to recruit Galamison, the evidence is that Galamison apparently was not influenced by Communist ideology or the Party. Even the FBI concluded that the Party's attempt to recruit Galamison was a failure. Informers who were familiar with "certain phases of the Communist Party activity in New York City area," were contacted in January 1964 but they could not provide any information "concerning the subject and the Party."[23] Following the February 3, 1964 boycott, one informer reported that Galamison was "power happy" and liked the spotlight but that he was no Communist. The FBI also reported that Galamison asserted: "I have no political alliance [with the Communist Party]. I don't give a damn for Socialism-Communism." According to the FBI's report, Galamison was only interested in helping young people and rejected political labels. An FBI "confidential source" confirmed that there was no evidence that the Communist Party was in control of the school boycotts. At a Communist Party New York Commission on Schools meeting, party members noted, that "Milton Galamison made his own policy." In fact, the Communist Party USA attacked the pastor because of his tactics and his "refusal to support and cooperate" with it.[24]

Others explanations of Galamison's radicalism included that he was a political opportunist or an out-of-control Black Nationalist willing to stirring up racial discontent. Author Miriam Wasserman claimed that Galamison was a person "who probably had some political ambitions."[25] Tamar Jacoby paints Galamison as an extremist who fought for unrealistic goals and was more than willing to fan the flames of racial discontent in the city. He aligned himself with militants such as Malcolm X.[26] Historian Fred Siegel also describes Galamison as a loose cannon and even hypocritical. "Galamison, who sent his son to private school, insisted that rather than back off from his vaguely stated demands for total integration, he would rather see it (the public school system) destroyed."[27]

One of the best explanations of what historian Jerald Podiar called Galamison's "radical egalitarianism,"[28] is given by historian Lisa Yvette Waller, who contends that "social Christianity" was at the center of Galamison's political thought. It was his understanding of the gospel that provided his "radical approach toward the advancement of African American and Puerto Rican people, who were economically marginalized during the middle and late twentieth century."[29] Galamison was influenced by a wing of Christianity referred to as the "social gospel." This brand of Christianity emerged in the late nineteenth century and focused on the salvation of individuals and society. Jesus' message was not only to heal the sin of the individual but also of society. The social gospel contended that Christians must be concerned about Kingdom on earth as much as the Kingdom in Heaven. The most prominent proponent of the social gospel was Walter Rauschenbusch.[30]

By the early twentieth century, the northern wing of American Presbyterianism, in particular the Presbyterian Church of the United States of America (PCUSA) had moved away from a Calvinistic theology that stresses believers address individual transgression to one that embraced a politically left agenda that addressed the sins of societies. This transformation was due, in large part, to modernist thinking and ideas that spread through universities and seminaries. Higher criticism, which emphasized a textual analysis of the scripture, was adopted by theologians at seminaries, thus rejecting literal interpretation of the Bible. Science, including the theory of evolution, also influenced some religious scholars who rejected miraculous Creationism. As the century progressed, pro-modernist theologians gained important positions in seminaries and church councils.[31]

Galamison was educated in what was considered liberal Presbyterian institutions. His undergraduate studies took place at Lincoln University in Pennsylvania, the first historically black institution of higher learning. The school, founded by a Presbyterian minister in 1854, contended that its objective was to bring a "liberal Christian education" to African American men. Although Lincoln's annual catalogue offered a conventional education to its students, the list of guest speakers invited to the university suggested that the institution possessed a quite liberal mindset. During the 1940–41 academic year, speakers with liberal and left-leaning tendencies included Professor Brand Blanshard of Swarthmore College who spoke on "The Present Conflict in Ideas." Howard Kester, an organizer of the Southern Tenant Farmers Union who embraced a radical form of Christianity and held a Marxist interpretation of the American economy, spoke about the "The Organization of Tenant Farmers in the South." Donald Smucker of the Fellowship of Reconciliation, a pacifist organization, spoke on a "Pacifist's Critique of the Second World War." Walter White, Executive Secretary of the NAACP, addressed the issue of the "NAACP Program for the Education of Negroes in the United States." Professor Doxey Wilkerson of Howard University and later a member of the American Communist Party spoke about the "Future Vocational Opportunities for the Negro College Graduate."[32] In the 1942–43 academic year, the college organized a conference entitled "The Conference on the Negro in a Fighting Democracy." Among its speakers were anthropologist Margaret Mead, Congressman Adam Clayton Powell, Jr., Krishnalal Shridharani of India, and Walter White.[33] Galamison did extremely well at Lincoln, receiving the "Thomas W. Conway Award in English and the Class of 1900 Prize" when he graduated in 1945. [34]

Galamison received a Master's degree at Princeton Theological Seminary, a PCUSA institution that stressed piety in the learning approach but also emphasized "solid learning" and its Reformed tradition's commitment to the intellectual integrity of the faith. Galamison's Master's thesis, entitled "The Theme of Salvation in the World's Great Religions," was a comparative study of Hinduism, Buddhism, Confucianism, Islam, and Christianity that attempts to provide a better understanding of how the most celebrated religions addressed salvation. [35]

Another indicator of the influence of Presbyterianism's new agenda on Galamison's thinking was his sermons. Like the new agenda of American Presbyterianism which condemned racial oppression, militarism, and class exploitation, Galamison's sermons hammered away at these social injustices and stressed that the duty of Christians was to fight to eliminate address these social transgressions. In one sermon entitled "A Study in First John Continued," the Presbyterian pastor contended:

> It's all so unreasonable, isn't it? It's hate that's stupid and blind and without reason—like the way we suffer from the hate of some white people, who simply hate us without bothering to know us. And this hatred results in war and domestic strife and unrest and suffering, hate because as John says, they are blind. They have no power to see that hate and prejudice are getting us no place but into more and more trouble, wars and social unrest.

Reflecting American Presbyterianism's "new agenda," Galamison
advocated an ecumenical approach and tolerance toward other faiths:

> We boast that we worship the true God who came down from
> heaven in the form of man and we are loud in our condemna-
> tion of the Jewish people who through centuries have rejected
> Christ and refused to believe in him as Lord. We would say
> that for the Jewish people God has never become a Christian.
> But one needs only to hear a Rabbi preach today to know that
> the Jewish people under the name of Judaism have discovered
> that beautiful way of life that we like to call Christian and
> which is Christian in everything but name. The equality of all
> under God, the priesthood of lay as well as clerical believers,
> the life-giving balance of multiple forms witness and worship,
> and the necessity of verbal proclamation with active demonstra-
> tion of divine grace have all acquired a deeper a new meaning
> in this situation.[36]

For Galamison, Christianity was a revolutionary ideology; Jesus,
Paul, and other biblical figures were social radicals who fought for the
oppressed. They were the examples that Christians should follow and by
following Christian principles as embodied by these figures and as outlined in Christian scriptures, humanity could gain social and economic
justice.[37] Galamison's stress on moral and religious solutions demonstrated
that he wanted to appeal to people's sense of fair play. The Bible and those
modeling its principles pointed the way, but the Presbyterian pastor also
urged his congregation to heed those who offered political solutions to
militarism, racism, and class exploitation. In a sermon titled "Speaking
Your Mind," Galamison argued that presidential candidate Henry Wallace
was "the greatest prophet on the international scene today" because he
stood up to the "international thugs in an effort to achieve peace." Wallace,
unlike other politicians, had the fortitude to criticize his country because
it was using its power and wealth for strategic military purposes. Despite
the fact that Wallace had been vice president in Franklin Roosevelt's third
term and had run as a left-wing third-party candidate for president in
1948, Galamison did not see him just as a progressive politician. Instead,
he compared him to the prophet Micah because both condemned war.[38]

Galamison's view of the state was also grounded in biblical principles. In one sermon, entitled, "The Political Significance of the Cru-
cifixion," the pastor told his congregation that Jesus had opposed the
corruption and decadence of the Roman Empire. Jesus, the revolutionary,
came to destroy the corrupted state. Comparing the Roman Empire and

the contemporary United States, he noted that the state "has guarded not the highest, but the lowest, aspect for property rights and the office-holding classes of human life." Claiming that Jesus had little respect for property rights and the office-holding classes of his day, Galamison argued that contemporary politicians only manipulated people for their own selfish needs. Like the Roman politicians, contemporary office holders were parasites. Jesus wanted a society "in which no military forces drained the substance and life of the people." He declared that it was militarism that had crucified Christ and advised Christians to give allegiance not to governments and armies but to God. [39]

In a sermon delivered at Siloam Presbyterian Church, Galamison did not shy away from focusing on the class divide. He noted the existence of individual sin but turned his attention to sins of a society. While an individual could and does transgress against God, a "few sinful individuals can create an evil social order." This collective sin corrupts society and stops people from "hearing God." He declared that the greatest social sins people faced were racial discrimination, class inequality, and war—evils that stemmed from the greed of the rich and powerful. Galamison declared that class exploitation was a major reason for the development of inequality. According to the pastor, there have always been people willing to destroy liberty and social justice to further their own privileges, people willing to "prostitute public decency for private gain." Using Karl Marx's notion of superstructure, i.e., the realm of ideas and culture that reinforce the capitalist political-economic order, Galamison argued that individuals, culture, the state, and the Protestant churches within America, had all perpetuated class and race inequality and warfare."[40]

While Galamison was influenced by the liberal wing of Presbyterianism, his experience of growing up in poverty also shaped his radical views. By 1935, Galamison's mother had separated from her husband and she and her two sons, Joseph and Milton were living with her mother. Galamison's mother worked as a maid in a clothing store and his grandmother became a domestic worker in an attempt to make ends meet. Galamison remarked in his autobiography that the family was so poor it had to move from place to place to avoid paying rent.[41] Poverty and racism also determined Galamison's high school education. He notes that despite the fact that he desired to take an academic program in college that would prepare him for college, he, like countless black children in the Philadelphia school system were assigned the vocational training program.[42] Despite his later success in life, Galamison did not adopt a rags-to-riches philosophy, emphasizing individual responsibility as the avenue to success.

Galamison's embrace of liberal Presbyterianism and his personal experiences were at the core of his radicalism. His sermons strongly indicated how the "new agenda" of Presbyterianism shaped his theology and political views. His personal experience with racism reinforced his determination to actively fight against racial injustice. In particular, he targeted schools because he argued that education shaped children's perception. Appealing to Brown v. Board of Education, Galamison argued that racially segregating children instilled in them at an early age sense of inferiority. "In an integrated school your child will receive the benefits of a democratic education that will enable him to live, play, and work with children of all backgrounds. Your child will develop a better appreciation of himself as a human being—born free and equal in dignity and rights with other children. . . . When all children have the opportunity to know children of other backgrounds as equals, they lose any feelings they may have of inferiority or superiority."

In her assessment of Milton Galamison, Tamar Jacoby claims that he was a black militant making an unrealistic demand of immediate racial balancing of the New York City public school student body. She described his actions as vindictive and nihilistic. In fact, he had replaced the "southern-style church rallies and hopeful odes to racial harmony" of the first boycott with "ultimatums and threats of violence" in the second boycott. [43] Fred Siegel contends that Galamison's demand for "total integration" had no precedent. According to Siegel, New York was not "Upsouth" as Galamison and other black militants claimed. "There was no one white community to integrate with. In any case, even if you added up all the whites in the public schools, there simply weren't enough to make for integrated schools without the sort of massive bussing that was as disruptive as it was unpopular among both whites and blacks." [44]

The blame for the failure of integration, even on a small scale, does not lie with Galamison but with the growing white resistance. White parents organized a campaign of resistance when the Board of Education transferred just 400 children from schools in Bedford-Stuyvesant, Brooklyn's largest black community, to predominantly white schools in Glendale and Ridgewood, Queens. White parents held demonstrations outside of the Board of Education's office. In order to relieve white parents' fears of racial mixing, Board of Education Superintendent John Theobald, told a crowd of white parents that the transfers were not an attempt at integrating the school system but just to relieve overcrowding. White parents in East Flatbush in Brooklyn successfully stopped the transfer of their children to a junior high school in the predominantly black community of Brownsville, Brooklyn by suing the Board for racial discrimination. When the Board tried to implement an integration plan entitled "Blueprint for Further Action toward Quality Integrated Education," two white parents' organizations, Parents and Taxpayers Coordinating Council and the Brooklyn Joint Council for Better Education, claimed that they had a "full-scale battle plan" to stop the integration plan. In September 1964, 275,638 white children were kept out of the school to stop the implementation of the Board's integration plan.

Despite the resistance to Galamison and those who fought for school integration in New York City, his fight to remove all racial barriers and to create a society where all children were granted the same opportunity to succeed was morally correct. There is no doubt Galamison was not willing to compromise when it came to his objective of creating a fully integrated public school system. Galamison saw the possibility that racial barriers to an equal education could be eradicated from the largest school system in the country. Unlike others who would be willing to make deals for partial victory, Milton Galamison was not willing to tolerate a school system that provided some children with a good education while robbing other children of that same opportunity. For Galamison, it was simply immoral for the school system and city officials to maintain inequality or to take just small steps that had little or no impact. Galamison displayed tremendous courage in taking on a system that had for decades denied thousands of children a full day of instruction, assigned the least experienced teachers to schools with predominantly black and Latino student populations, and did little to address the fact that black and Latino neighborhoods had the most dilapidated and oldest school buildings in the city. Instead of making deals with those in power for remedies that offered no real solution, Galamison decided to stand with parents, community activists, and civil rights groups in their fight to erase racial inequality and promote greater democracy in the school system and city of New York.

Notes

1. Clarence Taylor, *Knocking At Our Own Door: Milton A. Galamison and the Struggle to Integrate New York City Schools* (Columbia University Press, 1997), 52–53.

2. Ibid., 54.

3. Ibid., 157–58.

4. Ibid., 158–59.

5. Ibid., xxxv–xxxvi.

6. David Bradley, "The Ever Evolving Malcolm X," *Orbit Magazine*, May 19, 2009, orbit-mag.com/articles/the-everevolving-malcolm-x.

7. Clarence Taylor, *Knocking At Our Own Door*, xxxvi.

8. Author's interview with Rev. Milton A. Galamison, Brooklyn, October 21, 1988; Amsterdam News, April 14 and April 21, 1962.

9. Clarence Taylor, *The Black Churches of Brooklyn*, 142–160.

10. City-Wide List of Freedom Schools, Bayard Rustin Papers, Reel 12.

11. Sermon, "How Cheap is Salvation," November 5, 1950, Galamison Papers, Box 2, Folder 9, Schomburg Center for the Study of Black Culture.

12. Ibid.; Health Press, newsletter of the Bedford-Stuyvesant Health Congress (1958). Copies of the newsletter are located at the Brooklyn Historical Society.

13. Rose Russell to Milton Galamison, The Galamison Papers. State Historical Society of Wisconsin, Folder 33.

14. Author's interview with the Rev. Gardner Taylor, August 1, 1988.

15. Ellen Schrecker, *The Age of McCarthysim: A Brief History with Documents* (Boston: Bedford Books, St. Martin's Press, 1994), 9–15; "Teachers Union Gives Support to Red Charge," *Tablet*, April 1, 1950.

16. Author's interview with Milton A. Galamison, October 21, 1987, Brooklyn.

17. Ibid., xxv.

18. Memorandum, Director, Federal Bureau of Investigation to SAC, New York, "Milton Arthur Galamison," February 27, 1964, Bureau File 100-440326.

19. Ellen Schrecker, *The Age of McCarthyism: A Brief History with Documents* (Boston: Bedford Books, St. Martin Press, 1994), 114–15.

20. Memorandum, J. A Sizoo to W. C. Sullivan, "Milton Galamison and Bayard Rustin," February 5, 1964.

21. Ibid., xxx.

22. Sermon, "What Are We Any How," delivered on March 12, 1950, Milton Galamison Papers, Schomberg Center for the Study of Black Culture.

23. Communist Influence in Racial Matters, Internal Security, "Proposed Boycott on New York City Schools by City-Wide Integrated Schools," March 1965, Galamison File.

24. Clarence Taylor, *Knocking At Our Own Door*, xxxv.

25. Miriam Wasserman, *The School Fix, NYC, USA* (New York: Clarion Books, 1970), 314.

26. Tamar Jacoby, *Someone Else's House: America's Unfinished Struggle for Integration* (New York: Basic Books, 2000), 166.

27. Fred Sigel essay review of Joshua Freeman's *Working Class New York*, Public Interest Summer 2000, www.cooper.edu/humanities/humanitiescities.htm.

28. Jerald Podair, *The Strike that Changed New York: Blacks, Whites and the Ocean Hill-Brownsville Crisis* (Yale University Press, 2004), 24.

29. Lisa Yvette Waller, "Holding Back the Dawn: Milton A. Galamison and the Fight for School Integration in New York City, A Northern Civil Rights Struggle, 1948–1968," PhD dissertation, Duke University, 1998.

30. Lisa Yvette Waller, "Holding Back the Dawn: Milton A. Galamison and the Fight for School Integration in New York City, a Northern Civil Rights Struggle, 1948–1968" PhD dissertation, Department of History, Duke University, 1998, 35–39; Walter Rauschenbusch, *A Theology for the Social Gospel*, (New York: Macmillan Co., 1922).

31. John A. Battle, "Presbyterianism in America: The 20th Century" *WRS Journal* 13:2 (August 2006), 26–43.

32. Lincoln University College and Theological Seminary Catalogue, 1908–1909 at www.lincoln.edu/library/specialcollections/.../1908-09.pdf.

33. Ibid., 1942–43.

34. Ibid., 1945–46.

35. Clarence Taylor, *Knocking At Our Own Door*, 32–33.

36. Milton J. Coalter, John M. Mulder, and Louis B. Weeks, eds. *The Confessional Mosaic Presbyterians and Twentieth Century Theology* (Louisville, KY: Westminster John Knox Press, 1991), 33–34.

37. Ibid., 29.

38. Ibid. 30–31.

39. Ibid.,30.

40. Clarence Taylor, *Knocking At Our Own Door*, 34–35.

41. Ibid.,21.

42. Ibid. 19.

43. Tamar Jacoby, *Someone Else's House: American Unfinished Struggle for Integration*, (New York: Basic Books, 1998), 165–166.

44. Fred Siegel, *The Future Once Happened Here: New York, D.D., L.A, and the Fate of America's Big Cities*, (Jackson, TN: Encounter Books, 1997), 64–65.

PUBLIC SPHERE CAPITAL AND CONTEMPORARY RIGHTS EXPECTATIONS

8

Black Clergy, Educational Fairness, and Pursuit of the Common Good

R. Drew Smith

The debate over school funding adequacy versus school choice has become a central battlefield for black clergy in the fight to lay claim to the Civil Rights Movement legacy—with both sides connecting their cause to the Movement. Americans on either side of this *educational fairness* debate cite America's continued acceptance of underperforming and primarily black- and Latino-serving public schools as a de facto sanctioning of a separate educational system for urban minorities that is inferior to that of suburban whites. Whether advocating more adequate school funding or a greater ability by low-income students to transfer from underperforming schools to higher-performing schools, a core social conviction among contemporary activists of school funding equality has been that the diminishing social prospects of poorly educated minority youth are an unacceptable and contradictory feature of an advanced democracy.

In a political context characterized by a diversity of publics with competing social interests, interpretations of governmental priorities, and claims on public resources, activists for school funding adequacy are situated directly within tensions and conflicts over stewardship of public purpose. Although there is clearly no singular public, no *e pluribus unum*, some conceptions of public as embraced by persons, groups, and institutions within the United States are broader and more inclusive than others. Does a given conception of the public good, for example, view quality education as a right or a privilege? If it is viewed as a right, is it a right in the sense of a claim or entitlement that legally applies (or should legally apply) to every citizen within a state or within the nation? Do Americans, do activist black clergy, view public access-by-all to quality education as a binding, indivisible citizen entitlement and public good?

While many Americans may be sympathetic to the principle of quality education as the right of every citizen, the way this is approached in
practice seems an entirely different matter. For example, while the Illinois
state constitution says that "The state shall provide for an efficient system
of high quality public educational institutions and services,"[1] (with "high
quality" assigned a minimum dollar amount by the state), Illinois' per
pupil spending ranges from less than $5,000 in poorer districts to more
than $18,000 in wealthier districts (with the minimum funding level for
a "high quality" education set in 2006 at $5,334 per pupil). Are activists
for funding adequacy who employ civil rights language really committed
to quality education as a binding, indivisible claim applying to all citizens in the same sort of way that Civil Rights Movement activists were
committed to equal protection under the law from racial oppression and
discrimination?

Black clergy activists from several ideological directions have
appealed to civil rights symbolism in an attempt to infuse educational
fairness with the urgency and ideological clarity of the mid-twentieth
century movement. But unlike that movement, and its central spokesman Martin Luther King, Jr. (who depicted social interrelatedness as "an
inescapable network of mutuality" and argued for the "indivisibility of justice"),[2] contemporary black clergy have been less convincing (and perhaps
less convinced) that core national interests are at stake in the urban school
crisis. Some feel, perhaps, that while many low-income racial minority
students may be failing, unprecedented numbers of working-class and
middle-class minority students are excelling and joining a growing proces-
sion of upwardly mobile minorities. Moreover, confidence by some in the
public sector's ability to solve big problems has greatly diminished, and
persons feel less need to worry about public spaces when so much capacity
exists for creating alternative spaces less burdened by public considerations (and constituencies). Against this contemporary backdrop, the right
to a quality education for all as something fundamental to our national
interest and common public purpose is a difficult case to make. But it is
precisely this conceptualization that black clergy must re-appropriate and
reapply to this modern "civil rights" movement.

Unfortunately, black clergy activists (and other educational fairness activists) have lacked the kind of systematic theoretical framework
operative within the mid-twentieth century Civil Rights Movement and,
consequently, have found it difficult to mobilize educational fairness into
a broad-based, coherent movement. Where black clergy have engaged the
educational fairness issue, they have been split between those insisting on
increased school funding for low-income districts (especially where dis-

parities exist between suburban public schools and low-income urban and rural schools),[3] and those advocating greater school choice for low-income students so that they not be forced to wait on system-wide reforms. And while activists on both sides of the debate (the funding adequacy and school choice sides) have drawn connections between their educational fairness position and the earlier Civil Rights Movement, unlike the earlier movement, the positions of contemporary educational fairness activists are identified more with divisible rights applying to sub-publics than with indivisible rights applying to the American public as a whole. In the current context, educational fairness is made to appear as an urban problem (read: minority problem), affecting shrinking populations of urban public school students (i.e., those who have not exited to the suburbs), or the even smaller subset of urban public school students targeted by advocates of public and private alternatives to underperforming public schools (e.g., public charter schools or public voucher-supported private schools).[4] But if a genuine connection is to be made between educational fairness and the earlier Civil Rights Movement, than educational fairness must be framed as a binding, indivisible right by all to quality education—a right central to America's common good.

However, as this chapter points out, a number of factors reduce the odds of black clergy activists bringing to educational fairness activism the kind of moral clarity and influence that Dr. King and cadres of activist clergy brought to the movement of his day. First of all, the chapter argues that the clarity and mobilizing power of civil rights symbolism has been weakened by its appropriations (including by Civil Rights Movement icons) on more than one side of debates about applications of educational fairness. Second, since school funding formulas and operational policies are determined mostly at state and local rather than federal levels, and since these formulas and policies may vary from one state or locality to the next, educational fairness initiatives tend to be localized and focused on matters specific to that context. A third factor impacting the expansiveness and coherence of educational fairness activism has been the ability of resourceful national organizations (including foundations) to mobilize local activists on both sides of the educational fairness battle, with the effect of entrenching the prevailing arguments and the conflicts and divisions stemming from those arguments.

The chapter explores these factors within the context of a few highly publicized local battles over educational fairness and then looks closely at three prominent black clergy who have been at the forefront of competing positions on educational fairness: Jesse Jackson, Floyd Flake, and Al Sharpton. The chapter begins, however, with an outline of school resource and performance disparities at the national level.

Indicators of Contemporary School Inequality

The 1954 U.S. Supreme Court ruling determining that separate school systems for blacks and whites were inherently unequal was made within a context where the average spending in the South for white students was roughly $40 per pupil and for black students was only $16 per pupil.[5] The actual dollar amounts for per pupil spending are currently dramatically higher now than they were in the 1940s and 1950s, but the gap between per pupil spending in suburban districts versus heavily minority districts has remained unacceptably wide. In 2005, average spending on primary and secondary education in the United States was $8,701 per student. Eastern states were at the top of the spending list, including New York at $14,119 per student, New Jersey at $13,800 per student, and the District of Columbia) at $12,979 per student, while western and southern states, which serve a disproportionate number of the nation's poor children, were at the bottom of the spending list, including Arizona at $6,261, and Mississippi at $6,575 per student.[6] Not only do richer states spend more per student than poorer states, but richer states also have some of the widest gaps between per pupil spending within the wealthier school districts versus the poorer and more minority-serving districts. For example, as analysis in 2006 by the Education Trust shows, the highest spending school district outspent the lowest spending district by $2,927 per student in New York state and by $2,355 per student in Illinois. Even in poorer states, the highest spending school district outspent the lowest spending district by $736 per student in Arizona, $656 per student in Alabama, and $191 per student in Mississippi. Nationally, wealthier school districts outspent poorer school districts by an average of $1,307 per student.[7]

Correlations have been made between funding levels and quality of the educational experience provided to students at a number of levels, including the comprehensiveness of the curriculum, the availability of instructional tools and technologies, the ability to attract and keep the best teachers, the extent of supplemental curricular and extracurricular programming, and the safety and desirability of the facility. Unfortunately, as a report from the Education Trust points out:

> . . . we've rigged the system against the success of some of our most vulnerable children . . . [b]y taking the children who arrive at school with the greatest needs and giving them less in school. Our low-income and minority students, in particular, get less of what matters most; these students get the fewest experienced and well-educated teachers, the least rigorous curriculum, and the lowest quality facilities.[8]

There is considerable debate, however, about the extent to which spending rates account for student performance. It has been argued, for example, that school districts with comparatively high per-pupil spending have sometimes ranked poorly in their on-time graduation rates and standardized test scores, while districts with comparatively low per-pupil spending have sometimes ranked well in their on-time graduation rates and standardized test scores.[9] Nevertheless, studies have shown that less funding has contributed in some cases to lower student performance in a number of ways, including lower standardized test scores,[10] larger class sizes that contribute to lower student performance,[11] and lower student motivation to enroll in additional years of schooling.[12]

Whether one places the emphasis primarily on funding inadequacies or on other systemic or social factors, it is clear that many public school students, especially in low-income and minority communities, are falling farther and farther behind. Black clergy, among others, have spoken of the urban school crisis in civil rights terms. U.S. Congressman John Lewis (D-GA), a Baptist clergyman, comments on the historical urgency of educational fairness, when he remarks:

> What is happening right now in the poorest communities of America—which are largely black communities—is the worst situation black America has faced since slavery. . . . (There is) a mistaken assumption among many that the struggle for civil rights is finished. . . . This is preposterous. . . . We need look no further than our schools. . . .[13]

Al Sharpton and Joel Klein build on this theme in a *Wall Street Journal* editorial: "Americans today run the risk of forgetting that the nation still faces one last great civil-rights battle: closing the insidious achievement gap between minority and white students."[14] Lewis, Sharpton, and Klein capture the urgency many feel about educational fairness, while suggesting its movement proportions. But as the following discussion shows, these sentiments have led in competing strategic directions.

The Scope of Recent Clergy Activism on Educational Fairness

Educational inequalities within America are readily apparent, and so is the lack of consensus about how to respond to these inequalities. The term, "equality" (a term central to the historic civil rights struggle) has itself been drawn on widely and in fairly contested ways by educational fairness advocates representing various strategic orientations. Rod Paige, who served in George W. Bush's first presidential term as Secretary of Education, has recently written a book that refers to the achievement gap between black and white students as the "greatest civil rights challenge of our time." For Paige, the great inequality he tracks throughout his analysis is an inequality in black and white student academic performance and it is an inequality about which he speaks passionately. He states: "closing the black-white achievement gap would do more to advance African Americans toward our long-sought-after goals of racial equality than any civil rights strategy available to us today."[15] Although Paige acknowledges school resource inequalities as one possible factor in this achievement gap, the factors he emphasizes more are the cultural backdrop of underperforming students as well as attitudes by these students and teachers that seem to predispose their academic situation toward failure. The movement Paige seeks to mobilize is a cultural and attitudinal transformation among low-income school populations, along with attitudinal and pedagogical shifts within the schools serving these populations.

When the problem is seen as having mainly to do with factors internal to underperforming schools and the familial and cultural milieu of their students, the primary strategic focus is generally on getting more out of teachers and administrators within these schools[16] and, short of that, getting students out of underperforming schools and into schools that can put taxes allocated for those students' education to better use. With respect to the latter, significant disagreement exists over whether tax dollars allocated to public school systems should be reassigned to families as vouchers that can be used in purchasing private school alternatives for their children. Support for the idea of school vouchers in the United States began at least as early as the 1950s when southern governments proposed tuition grants as a means of circumventing mandated school desegregation. These southern strategies proved largely unsuccessful, but by the 1960s, the school voucher concept caught the attention of parochial school advocates who recognized the potential vouchers possessed as a buttress for parochial schools (mainly Catholic ones).

Nevertheless, apart from a few limited examples, there was not much progress in implementing voucher programs prior to the 1990s.[17] Voucher programs of notable size and scope were implemented in Milwaukee in 1990, in Cleveland in 1995, and on a statewide basis in Florida in 1999. By 2007, twelve states and the District of Columbia provided publicly funded tuition scholarships to approximately 150,000 primary and secondary school students across the United States.[18] Also, at least eleven states have submitted voucher programs for voter approval as part of statewide referenda, although in all eleven cases voters rejected these voucher initiatives. Moreover, with the exception of the District of Columbia's program (a five-year program providing tuition grants for 1,700 students as of Spring 2009), federal backing for voucher programs has been blocked by forces opposed to vouchers. Even the "No Child Left Behind" legislation, widely viewed as a rejoinder to public schools, gained Congressional approval in 2001 only after all voucher proposals had been removed from the bill. It would appear, at least for now, that Congress, and the majority of American voters, remain largely unconvinced that voucher strategies represent the best way to respond to the educational crisis.

While voucher supporters may not constitute a majority in Congress or among voters in many states, polling data suggests strong support for vouchers among African Americans. In surveys conducted by the Joint Center for Political and Economic Studies, 57 percent of African American respondents from their 1997 and their 2002 surveys favored voucher programs. In a 1998 Gallop poll, 62 percent of African Americans supported vouchers. These data would seem to indicate solid black support for vouchers among African Americans. But, as some scholars have argued, the reality may be far more complicated than the data suggest. For example, BlackCommentator.com points out that surveys attempting to measure support for vouchers have operated largely in a hypothetical realm, given the paucity of existing voucher programs on which respondents can base their opinions. Instead, the argument continues, black support for vouchers is more accurately measured by how blacks have voted on voucher issues when put to a referendum—and consistently blacks have voted against voucher programs in these instances.[19] While polling data have not reliably predicted how blacks ultimately responded to concrete voucher propositions, these data may however suggest authentic theoretical support for vouchers that could translate into actual support under certain conditions or circumstances. Therefore, black opinion data potentially yields important insights into aspects of black positioning on voucher issues.

One particular benefit of these data is the ability to analyze demographic categories of black respondents tending to favor vouchers and those tending to oppose them. Specifically, among black survey respondents, it has been shown that support for vouchers has been strongest among younger, lower-income black respondents, and opposition to vouchers strongest among black elites, including clergy and elected officials. For example, a 2000 Joint Center poll showed 76 percent of African American respondents ages 26 to 35 favored vouchers. When asked in a 1992 California survey whether they would use a proposed $2,600 voucher to send their children to private school, 69 percent of African Americans with school age children, and 62 percent of respondents with household incomes of $25,000 or less said they would.[20] Similarly, analysis

of a 2000 and a 2004 National Annenberg Election Survey showed that
support for vouchers was strongest at lower income levels among black
respondents, (which was just the opposite of white respondents, whose
support was strongest at higher income levels).[21] Although black elite
opposition to vouchers may constitute a minority viewpoint within the
black population in general, black elite opposition to vouchers is fairly
systematic, especially among black elected officials—69 percent of which
were opposed to vouchers within a 2001 Joint Center poll.

Black clergy, however, appear to be a bit more evenly divided on
vouchers, according to data from Morehouse College's 1999–2000 Black
Churches and Politics Survey (BCAP). When asked whether educational
tax dollars could be put to better use in the form of vouchers, 44 percent of the largely clergy respondents agreed, while 54 percent disagreed.
That black clergy are a bit more supportive of vouchers than other black
elites may derive both from their agreement with the principle of expanding educational alternatives for black students and with their interest in
increasing black enrollment in faith-based schools, including a growing
number operated by black churches.[22]

While both factors may play a part in black clergy voucher support, what comes through clearly in black clergy statements of support
for vouchers is that there is an educational crisis with respect to African
American and other low-income youth. Alveda C. King, a niece of Dr.
Martin Luther King, Jr., and a senior fellow at the Alexis de Tocqueville
Institution in Washington, DC, invokes the legacy of her famous activist
family on behalf of vouchers. She comments:

> I believe that if Martin Luther King and A. D. King were here
> they would say 'Do what's best for the children.' . . . U.S. citi-
> zenship guarantees all parents an education for their children.
> This is a true civil right. Yet some children receive a better
> education than others due to their parents' abilities to pay for
> benefits that are often missing in public schools.[23]

Although proponents and opponents of vouchers have tied their
respective causes to national symbolism and discourse relating to civil
rights, the outcomes of contemporary educational fairness battles rely
more on factors operative at local and state levels. The point gains illustration from two of the pioneering voucher programs, Cleveland and Milwaukee, where the outcomes in those instances were determined largely
by the role foundation and corporate funding played in securing state
legislative approval and continuation of voucher programs within those
contexts. An important study of the Cleveland case details the role of

elite businesspersons and politicians in configuring a pro-voucher political framework in Cleveland, including mobilizing the finances necessary to secure Republican majorities in both chambers of the state legislature, resulting in legislative approval of Cleveland's voucher initiative in 1995. Local opposition to the voucher initiative from blacks and many others within Cleveland was simply bypassed by the legislative process.[24] Black clergy remained on the periphery of the battle, for the most part, surfacing publicly on the issue only for occasional informational meetings, including a 1995 meeting of twenty black clergy hosted by Rev. E. Theophilus Caviness, a prominent Cleveland pastor and former executive assistant to George Voinovich during his tenure as Cleveland's mayor. The invited speaker was millionaire industrialist, David Brennan, the leading local funder of the voucher initiative and close protégé of, then, Governor George Voinovich. Brennan outlined his, and others' support for vouchers in an effort to gain black clergy backing for the cause.[25]

When the Supreme Court deliberated over the constitutionality of Cleveland's voucher program, (where 95 percent of voucher students used their vouchers to attend religious schools), foundations and corporations donated more than $19 million during 1999 to organizations that filed pro-voucher friend of the court briefs (which was almost twice the amount contributed that year to organizations filing anti-voucher briefs). During 2000–01, foundations and corporations contributed more than $79 million to organizations that filed pro-voucher briefs, while more than $68 million was given to organizations that filed anti-voucher briefs. The Walton Family Foundation, alone, accounted for over $44 million during 2000–01 to organizations on the pro-voucher side of the court battle, while the largest donor during that year on the anti-voucher side was the Bill and Melinda Gates Foundation at roughly $18 million.[26]

At least two important insights can be gained from the Cleveland case about the impact of foundation and corporate monies on the educational fairness battle. First, the sums of money spent on the two sides of the Cleveland voucher battle did not appear to significantly tip black clergy support one direction or the other, primarily because black clergy on neither side of the voucher debate in Cleveland were regarded as especially pivotal to an outcome decided largely by political and financial elites. The introduction of large sums of money, though, has not necessarily had the same moot impact on black alignments in educational fairness battles in other contexts, as will be shown below. Second, donor monies in the Cleveland case were in the form of larger grants from fewer donors on the pro-voucher side of the battle (an average 1999 grant of $116,382) and smaller grants from a greater number of donors on the anti-voucher side of the battle (an average 1999 grant of $55,244).[27] A pattern of pro-voucher donors outspending their opposition in leveraging educational fairness outcomes is repeated in other educational fairness battleground situations discussed below.

As in the Cleveland case, elites were pivotal to the success of Milwaukee's voucher program as well, although black clergy and other grassroots activists played more instrumental roles within this context. Milwaukee's voucher program, initiated in 1990, was among the first in the United States. The program originally provided vouchers to 341 low-income students from public schools but grew incrementally, receiving legislative approval in 2006 to extend vouchers to approximately 22,500 of Milwaukee's public and private school students. A local leader who played a principal role in voucher advocacy and in generating support for vouchers among local black clergy was Bishop Sedgwick Daniels, who pastors the 8,000 member Holy Redeemer Institutional Church of God in Christ in Milwaukee. Daniels, a former Democrat, developed strong ties to the Republican Party during George W. Bush's tenure, receiving both a $1.5 million federal grant as part of Bush's initiative to fund faith-based social services and a visit to his congregation from Bush himself.[28] Daniels also became closely identified with an influential Milwaukee foundation, the Bradley Foundation, which provided major funding in support of the Milwaukee voucher campaign—not to mention that it also awarded $1 million in grant money to Daniels' congregation for community programming.[29] Nevertheless, Daniels argues that it was not monetary incentives but, rather, his commitment to a politics emphasizing faith and values that led him to support policies such as vouchers and to endorse Bush in 2004.[30] Another black minister prominently involved in school choice advocacy in Milwaukee has been Archie Ivy, pastor of Milwaukee's New Hope Missionary Baptist Church, a former school principle and an alternate delegate to the 2000 Democratic National Convention. Ivy has contributed to school choice causes by serving as a board member of Milwaukee's Alliance for Choices in Education, a board member of the Milwaukee branch of Black Alliance for Educational Options (BAEO), and as co-chair of a Milwaukee group called Clergy for Educational Options. Unlike Daniels, there are no conspicuous benefits that have accrued to Ivy's congregation as a result of his connection to school choice causes, but the school choice organizations he is involved with are themselves connected to major funding streams such as the Bradley Foundation and the Walton Family Foundation.

The Milwaukee version of Clergy for Educational Options is a less extensive version of South Carolina's Clergy for Educational Options (CEO). The South Carolina organization was founded in 2004 by a small number of South Carolina ministers, at least two of which were black—

Maurice Revell, who pastors Agape International Ministries, and Richard Davis, a former military chaplain, school teacher, and CEO's current executive minister. According to its mission statement, CEO is concerned with "equity and quality in education," but its overarching objective, as alluded to in its organizational name, is to promote educational alternatives and choice for students. As Davis points out, South Carolina has one of the highest dropout rates in the nation, so CEO has responded by encouraging churches "to start schools . . . (and) do things to make sure these children are not left on the side of the road."[31] According to Davis, three hundred South Carolina congregations are members of CEO and account for a good deal of the organization's funding. But it has also been reported that the pro-voucher Walton Family Foundation has been an important CEO funder as well.[32]

Milwaukee has given rise to considerable pro-voucher momentum locally and nationally (especially through the far-reaching influences of its Bradley Foundation), but it has been a context where both local and national opposition to vouchers has been galvanized as well. During the mid-1990s, Milwaukee was often the site or the focus of anti-voucher advocacy by national leaders. In his early years in Congress, Jesse Jackson, Jr., directed a great deal of his criticisms of vouchers toward the Milwaukee program, even traveling to Milwaukee for anti-voucher rallies. At a 1998 citywide rally held at an African American church, Jackson shared speaking duties with two prominent leaders of People for the American Way (PFAW), an organization that has mobilized national opposition to vouchers and which brought in approximately $2 million a year in charitable funding during the early 2000s (mostly in five-figure sums).[33] PFAW's national president spoke, as did Rev. Timothy McDonald, who chairs PFAW's African American Ministers Leadership Council (AAMLC). McDonald, an Atlanta pastor and former president of Atlanta's Concerned Black Clergy, has been an outspoken critic of vouchers, as displayed in the following quote: "Dangling the conservatives' voucher agenda in front of the nation's most disenfranchised Americans under the guise of helping them is both immoral and hypocritical. Inner city parents whose schools are not performing well are desperate for solutions and the Religious Right is exploiting that frustration."[34] McDonald has fought voucher initiatives in his home context of Atlanta and has travelled the country speaking against vouchers. McDonald also testified before Congress on vouchers in 1997 and 2002.

Days before the 2002 Supreme Court ruling on the Cleveland voucher case, McDonald headlined an anti-voucher rally held at an African Methodist Episcopal church in Cleveland that was attended by anti-voucher activists from across Ohio. The Supreme Court ended up ruling in favor of Cleveland's voucher program, and on the day the ruling was handed-down, Congressman Richard Armey (R-TX) introduced a bill in Congress to make vouchers available to public students in Washington, DC. In 2004 a bill was successfully passed after being put to a surprise vote while a number of Congressional opponents (including many Congressional Black Caucus members) were out of Washington on other business and therefore absent from the vote.[35] So despite being opposed at the time by 85 percent of DC's black residents, a voucher program was launched that served approximately 1,900 of the District's students—making it the first federally funded voucher program in the United States. The program required but did not receive Congressional reauthorization in 2008, largely due to high levels of opposition to the program; opposition that gained additional traction with the release of a 2007 federal study indicating that DC voucher students performed no better than the general population of DC public school students. Nevertheless, President Obama has proposed that all students currently participating in the program be funded through their graduation dates, but that no new students be admitted to the program.

Political support for the program's continuation actually appears widespread, with a recent poll indicating that nearly 75 percent of DC residents support continuation of the program, and a majority of DC's city council members conveying support for the program in a recently released letter.[36] The large-scale reversal of opinion on the DC voucher program, at least from the perspective of BlackCommentator.com (which has engaged in extensive analysis of school choice battles in recent years), can be attributed partly at least to significant funding of pro-voucher interests by the Bradley Foundation and other pro-voucher foundations.[37] One of the leaders of the DC voucher campaign from the outset has been Virginia Walden Ford, president of the DC branch of Black Alliance for Educational Options and executive director of DC Parents for School Choice. Ford recently remarked, "Those of us who grew up during the civil-rights era can appreciate the importance of courage and persistence in facing the biggest challenges. . . . In 2009, few wrongs are greater than the inequality that endures in American education."[38] The July survey's confirmation of widespread support for the voucher program, and the relative public silence of DC's black clergy within the current battle (with a few exceptions), suggests that Ford may speak here for an increasing number of black Washingtonians, including black church persons.

Black clergy in DC have not been supportive of vouchers straight down the line, however. Black clergy were primary opponents of a 1998 DC voucher initiative by a Walton-funded group called American Education Reform Foundation (AERF). Many of these clergy opponents had endorsed AERF a year earlier, but stated later that they were misled into thinking they were endorsing educational scholarships and not a voucher proposal.[39] One of the few black clergy voicing clear and consistent opposition to DC's voucher program has been Rev. Graylan Hagler, pastor of Plymouth Congregational Church in Washington and president of Ministers for Racial, Social, and Economic Justice. Hagler's perspective on vouchers is, "The [civil rights] battle has always been around public schools, not around private academies." After desegregation, says Hagler, there was "an immediate drain of white participation from public education, going into parochial and private schools. And ever since, they have attempted to redirect public dollars out of public education and into private schools."[40] Hagler was a highly visible protester at rallies outside the Supreme Court during its deliberations over the Cleveland case. Hagler indicates that support for vouchers and charter schools among black clergy in DC has come mainly from a small number of clergy whose congregations operate private schools. "We didn't have a groundswell of support for vouchers and charters," says Hagler, "because there weren't many clergy operating private schools. Folks understood that the common denominator was the ability to get educated in a public environment." Hagler shares the belief that the battle over vouchers in DC was fueled by outside influences, stating that "vouchers were pushed on us from the outside," largely in an effort by whites to "spin-off public dollars" for their children's rising private school costs.[41]

Vouchers have been contested at local levels but also at statewide levels, including at least twenty states where lawsuits are being pursued in support of vouchers. New Jersey is one such state, and black clergy have been noticeably visible at points within this battle. The Black Ministers Council of New Jersey, and especially its executive director, the Rev. Reginald T. Jackson, has been quite supportive in recent years of various statewide school choice campaigns and initiatives. Jackson, who pastors an African Methodist Episcopal church in Orange, NJ, has long advocated increased funding for urban schools. In May 2004, however, he and a number of black clergy held a press conference to announce their support for vouchers. The New Jersey NAACP chapter attempted to counter this development by convening more than two hundred local black clergy to discuss reasons vouchers should be opposed.[42] Nevertheless, in the weeks leading up to the November 2004 elections, Black Clergy Council pastors and ministers committed to delivering sermons within their congregations on the need for school choice and encouraged involvement by their parishioners in the advocacy efforts of the New Jersey School Choice Alliance. In an indication of the urgency Black Clergy Council members attached to choice initiatives, Jackson stated that the fight for school choice was "by far the most important, the most vital civil rights issue facing us, and our children."[43] Many black New Jersey residents apparently agree, if 2004 polling data indicating 72 percent support for vouchers among African Americans living in New Jersey's poorest districts is close to accurate.[44] Moreover, Jackson serves on the board of a recently created organization called Excellent Education for Everyone (E-3) which has promoted legislation to implement voucher programs within New Jersey. E-3, a fairly diverse, multiracial organization, receives significant financial backing from the Walton Family Foundation ($400,000 per year in the early 2000s).[45]

Black clergy groups in Texas, Florida, and Michigan have also backed school choice and voucher initiatives in their respective states. The Texas Black Clergy Network in Houston has been closely allied with a school choice initiative called African American Texans for Choice. The African American Council of Christian Clergy in Miami provided support for Governor Jeb Bush's successful effort in 1999 to pass legislation implementing a statewide voucher program.[46] Also, a group of black ministers in Detroit formed a group in the late-1990s called Partnership for Parental Choice, which promoted placing a state constitutional amendment on the ballot that would allow school choice.[47] Timothy McDonald notes, however, that his national African American Ministers Leadership Council (AAMLC) group became systematically involved in efforts to defeat the statewide voucher initiatives in Michigan and in California (which were ballot issues in both states in 2000). AAMLC focused specifically on educating black parents and black clergy about schooling costs not covered by vouchers, including books, uniforms, and transportation. McDonald suggests that raising parent and clergy awareness to these gaps in voucher coverage changed the minds of many black clergy and parents in the two states who initially supported vouchers and contributed to the defeat of the voucher initiatives in both states.[48]

Despite interventions by resourceful external groups in key voucher battleground contexts such as Cleveland, Milwaukee, Washington, DC, and the states of Michigan and California, there have been visible cadres of black clergy on either side of the issue, but no especially pronounced black clergy momentum in either direction overall. This seems consistent with the national polling data showing black clergy fairly evenly split on the voucher issue and also suggests a fairly limited impact by external groups in *ideologizing* educational fairness among local black clergy or shifting black clergy momentum sharply one way or the other on the issue.

Although the voucher issue (along with the linkage between student and teacher performance) have been issues with significant traction within educational fairness debates, mobilizations around the idea of equality have not been limited to persons emphasizing internal contextual barriers to achievement gaps between black and white students. There have also been persons (including black clergy) systematically pursuing resource equality between black and white schools—in similar fashion to the earlier Civil Rights Movement. Interestingly in this regard, Arne Duncan, who serves in President Barack Obama's cabinet as Secretary of Education, announced at the March 8, 2010 Selma, Alabama commemoration of the 1965 clash between protesters and police referred to as "Bloody Sunday" that the U.S. Department of Education will be launching thirty-eight investigations into possible civil rights violations by schools and colleges across the nation. Although no specifics of these cases were divulged, presumably these cases have something to do with inequalities of resources and opportunities. Moreover, lawsuits challenging school funding have been brought in forty-five of the fifty U.S. states.[49] Black clergy have been party to some of these lawsuits, as in the case of a 2008 lawsuit against the state of Illinois brought by the Chicago Urban League, clergy, and community leaders concerned with addressing unequal school funding within the state. This action was followed up by much higher-profile protest activities by Chicago clergy related to the school funding issue, as seen below. But also as seen below, black clergy protest credentials and credibility have been put to use on more than one strategic side of the educational fairness battle.

Mixed Messages from Civil Rights Movement Standard Bearers

Assigning Civil Rights Movement significance to either side of educational fairness activism has been complicated by the fact that activists from both sides have occasionally attempted to confer such significance to their side of the debate, but also by the fact that prominent standard bearers of the Civil Rights Movement legacy have landed on opposite sides of the issue. A lack of consensus, for example, between prominent clergy with significant civil rights and Democratic Party leadership bona fides has blunted moral legacy claims by either side, while contributing no doubt to the lack of a broad-based black clergy mobilization on educational fairness.

Jesse Jackson and Al Sharpton, have actively promoted fair funding of urban public schools while opposing vouchers and choice strategies that draw resources away from these schools. Jackson, as one of the stronger post-Civil Rights Movement advocates of school funding adequacy, has often argued that voucher programs cannot address the problem of inadequate educational opportunities for millions of at-risk public school children. Says Jackson, "Vouchers are no substitute for a quality program for all. It is a rope for a few rather than a net for all."[50] This succinctly summarizes the concerns many have expressed about vouchers, but it also points to broader concerns about school funding adequacy Jackson has expressed dating back to the early-1970s formation of his Operation PUSH organization (later renamed Rainbow/PUSH Coalition).

Jackson ally and Rainbow/PUSH board member, James Meeks, has also brought significant profile to the school funding adequacy issue. Meeks, a Chicago-area megachurch pastor and State Senator, called for a student boycott of Chicago public schools during the first week of class in September 2008. Approximately 1,000 student boycotters, accompanied by Meeks and numerous chaperones, boarded buses on the first day of school and headed to a suburban school north of Chicago to symbolically attempt to enroll the students in that school. The following day the students and chaperones, including Meeks, held sit-ins in the lobbies of several downtown Chicago corporations and Mayor Richard Daley's office. Meeks ended the boycott after the second day to attempt negotiations with Illinois Governor Rod Blagojevich. The point being made by Meeks, the parents, and approximately fifty clergy that supported the boycott was that funding urban public schools via property taxes inevitably leads to urban-suburban disparities of the sort found in metropolitan Chicago, where the 2008 Chicago Public school allocation per-student was $9,600 compared with more than $19,000 per-student in the northern suburb of Evanston. Both Jackson and Sharpton were active supporters of the boycott.

Where Rev. Sharpton has attracted far more attention on educational fairness matters, however, has been in his recently emerging leadership of an organization called Education Equality Project (EEP). The EEP, founded in 2008 by Sharpton and New York City Schools Chancellor Joel Klein, states its mission to be ". . . leading a civil rights movement to eliminate the racial and ethnic achievement gap in public education by working to create an effective school for every child." It pursues this through, among other things, promoting the formation of charter schools and performance-based funding of public schools (which are concepts that some believe draw resources away from existing public schools).[51] The organization has been endorsed by prominent Democrats and Republicans, including Senator Michael Bennett (D-CO), Congressmen John Conyers (D-MI), and Harold E. Ford, Jr. (D-TN), Democratic Mayors Richard Daley (Chicago), Adrian Fenty (DC), and Antonio Villaraigosa (Los Angeles), as well as Senator John McCain (R-AZ), Jeb Bush (former Republican governor of Florida), former Congressmen Newt Gingrich (R-GA), and J. C. Watts (R-OK). Rev. Meeks is also a signatory of EEP.

High profile activist clergy have also lent their support to voucher programs, including former Congressmen Andrew Young (D-GA) and

Floyd Flake (D-NY). Young made the following remarks about the 1.25 million low-income families that applied in 1999 for 40,000 scholarships of $4,000 offered by the nonprofit Children's Scholarship Fund:

> Certain flash points in America's civil rights struggle represent moments of moral awakening: Rosa Parks' refusal to give up her bus seat; John Lewis' beating at the Edmund Pettus Bridge; Martin Luther King Jr.'s letter from Birmingham jail. . . . This month witnessed another such moment: 1.25 million cries for help voiced by poor, largely minority families, seeking something most Americans take for granted—a decent education for their children. . . . I predict that we will one day look back on the 1.25 million who applied for educational emancipation—for the chance to seek the light and oxygen of a nourishing education—not as victims, but as unwitting heroes with whom a great awakening was begun.[52]

In a similarly strong and straightforward endorsement, Flake states:

> I've been a strong supporter of school vouchers, though I don't think that they are the ultimate answer for the solution of the problems of public education. My thesis is, in any situation where you put billions of dollars . . . into a system that is not educating your children, you don't sit there and say, "We're not going to move dollars around because we are afraid that it's going to make things worse." You move dollars around and say, "Let's try and invest in some things that are different and see if maybe there are some other solutions to the kind of problems we're having." . . . [T]here's more than enough money to educate all children, but you have to have enough competition within the system to make the system feel that it's going to lose those students if it does not do what it ought to be doing properly.[53]

Rev. Flake also accepted an offer in 2000 to head the charter school division of Edison Schools, a for-profit national initiative offering both private management of public schools and various curricular inputs into public schools. Founded in 1992 as the Edison Project (and currently known as EdisonLearning), the company was serving 350,000 students in twenty-four U.S. states and in the United Kingdom by 2008–2009. Although it went through a period where the "U.S. Securities and Exchange Commission was scrutinizing its financials and regulators were challenging its test

scores and school performance," for-profit "education management organizations" such as EdisonLearning remain a viable part of the educational
fairness strategic mix.[54] Flake, who also served on Edison Schools' Board
of Directors, is no longer closely identified with Edison.

Clearly these prominent black clergy activists have embraced a
diversity of viewpoints and involvements within the educational fairness
debate. While it may be easier to see educational fairness in polarities
when contrasting the positions of large collectivities such as the (conservative) Bradley Foundation and (liberal) People for the American Way,
the various educational fairness positions may seem more proximate and
somewhat overlapping when viewed through the positioning and sometimes re-positioning of these closely related clergy activists. Nonetheless,
the ambiguities of prominent black clergy on educational fairness serve
as one more factor contributing to what has been a stalemate relative to
black clergy impact on the issue.

Conclusion

Although black clergy activists have made their presence felt within educational fairness activism, they have rarely been a driving force at conceptual
or organizing levels. To the extent that black clergy have engaged educational fairness matters, they have often followed rather than led, attaching their
advocacy to organizations with significant financial resources and weak
ties to black communities more than to civil rights, community-based, or
ecclesiastical structures rooted in black communities. The absence of black
clergy collaborations on these issues with organizations strongly associated
with black church civil rights traditions at the national level, (organizations such as the NAACP or national denominational structures of the
African Methodist Episcopal Church or the Progressive National Baptist
Convention) has limited the ability of black clergy activists to broaden their
educational fairness activism beyond its current geographic and conceptual
boundaries. What this needs to suggest to black clergy advocates of educational fairness is that the battlefronts on this issue include not only local
and national public policy fronts but also the national denominations and
advocacy organizations with which they are involved that are themselves
insufficiently engaged on educational fairness issues.

It is reasonable that black clergy activists would align with foundations and other well-financed organizations that have the resources to
effectively contend in the highly charged, hotly contested educational fairness debate. It is also understandable that black clergy may find themselves on opposite sides of such a complex policy debate. The fact that

these differences of black clergy opinion seem more pragmatic than deeply ideological, though, may bode well for prospects for achieving a more unified and unifying approach to educational fairness that focuses on the principle of quality education by all as a core American commitment. Black clergy activism centered around principles of equal opportunity in the earlier movement and provides them with a strong legacy on which to build. By keeping that principle out in front of the educational fairness debate, the chances are greater that there will be agreement among black clergy and others on strategies that will contribute to the greatest improvements in educational quality for the greatest number of public school students.

Notes

1. Illinois State Constitution, (Section 1 of Article 10).

2. Martin Luther King, Jr., *Letter From Birmingham Jail* (Stamford, CT: Overbrook Press, 1968).

3. In states where the funding available to school districts is based largely upon property taxes within those districts, significant disparities in school funding can exist between poorer urban districts and wealthier suburban districts—as is the case in Illinois, for example. Since property taxes are not the only mechanism through which public schools are funded in some states, such as Indiana, there may be greater per-pupil spending in low-income urban districts than in wealthier suburban districts.

4. This "shrinking" public clientele phenomenon is poignantly illustrated in Detroit, which announced in March 2010 that it will close 44 schools due to an enrollment that has shrunk from 16,000 in 1994 to 6,000 in 2010, and in Kansas City, MO where the school board approved a plan in March 2010 to close 28 of the 61 public schools in the district due to an enrollment that has shrunk from 75,000 in the late 1960s to less than 18,000 currently.

5. Figures represent the situation as of 1940. See National Education Association, *Horizons of Opportunities: Celebrating 50 Years of Brown v. Board of Education, May 17, 1954–2004,* https://hems.nea.org/brownvboard/index2.html.

6. U.S. Census Bureau News, "National per Student Public School Spending Nears $9,000" (May 24, 2007); http://www.census.gov/Press-Release/www/releases/archives/education/010125.html.

7. All of the spending amounts are adjusted (rather than actual) figures that reflect cost burdens in poorer school districts for higher numbers of special needs students, school security, and other costs with which wealthier districts are less burdened. All figures are from the report, *The Education Trust Funding Gaps 2006.*

8. Education Trust, *Funding Gaps 2006,* Washington, DC, 2006, 1, http://www.eric.ed.gov/ERICDocs/data/ericdocs2sql/content_storage_01/0000019b/80/28/0c/92.pdf

9. Dan Lips, Shanea Watkins, and Jon Fleming, "Does Spending More on Education Improve Academic Achievement?" Heritage Foundation, Washington, DC, September 8, 2008; Christina Settima, "Best and Worst School Districts for the Buck," *Forbes Magazine*, August 5, 2007.

10. David Card and Abigail Payne, "School Finance Reform, the Distribution of School Spending, and the Distribution of SAT Scores," Working Paper 6766, (Cambridge, MA: National Bureau of Economic Research, 1998).

11. Harold Wenglinski, "How Money Matters: The Effect of School District Spending on Academic Achievement," *Sociology of Education* 70, July 1997, 221–237.

12. David Card and Alan Krueger, "Does School Quality Matter? Returns to Education and the Characteristics of Public Schools in the United States," *Journal of Political Economy* 100/1, February 1992, 1–40.

13. John Lewis, *Walking With the Wind* (San Diego: Harcourt Press, 1999), 448.

14. Joel Klein and Al Sharpton, "Charter schools can close the education gap," *Wall Street Journal*, (January 12, 2009).

15. Rod Paige and Elaine Witty, *The Black-White Achievement Gap: Why Closing it is the Greatest Civil Rights Issue of Our Time* (New York: American Management Association, 2010) 3.

16. President George W. Bush's major educational initiative, "No Child Left Behind," placed significant emphasis on rewarding and punishing teachers based upon student performance. Ironically, President Barack Obama's educational initiative announced in March 2010 is being criticized for maintaining some of the same emphasis.

17. There were small, short-lived pilot programs in California and in New York during the 1970s.

18. Dan Lips and Evan Feinberg, "Utah's Revolutionary New School Voucher Program," Heritage Foundation, WebMemo #1362, (February 16, 2007), http://www.heritage.org/Research/Education/wm1362.cfm#_ftn2.

19. BlackCommentator.com, "Poll Shows Black Political Consensus Strong," Issue 17, Nov. 21, 2002, 7.

20. Janet Beales, "Survey of Education Vouchers and Their Budgetary Impact on California," Reason Foundation Working Paper, Number 144, August 1992, http://reason.org/files/09e700faf23a677e337560724f675840.pdf.

21. Andrew Gelman, "Who wants school vouchers? Rich whites and poor non-whites," Columbia University Department of Statistics online, (June 15, 2009), http://www.stat.columbia.edu/~cook/movabletype/archives/2009/06/who_wants_schoo.html.

22. As of 2000, there were reported to be 400 historically black independent schools in the United States serving 52,000 students, with many of these schools operated by black churches. Gail Foster, "Historically Black Independent School" in *City Schools: Lessons From New York* edited by Diane Ravitch and Joseph Viteritti (Baltimore: Johns Hopkins University Press, 2002), 299.

23. Alveda C. King, "Fighting for School Choice; It's a Civil Right," *Wall Street Journal*, September 11, 1997.

24. Gregory Bodewell, "Grassroots Inc.: A Sociopolitical History of the Cleveland School Voucher Battle, 1992–2002," Dissertation, Case Western Reserve University, Cleveland, 2006, 38–9

25. Rev. Marvin McMickle telephone interview with author, August 4, 2009.

26. Bodewell, 214–218.

27. Ibid, 214.

28. Peter Wallsten, et al., "Bush Rewarded by Black Pastor's Faith," *Los Angeles Times*, January 18, 2005.

29. Black Commentator.com, "Voucher Tricksters: The Hard Right Enters Through the Schoolhouse Door," Issue 7, (July 11, 2002).

30. Wallsten, op cit.

31. Thomas Hanson, "Black groups advocate parental choice in education," http://thomashanson.com/voucherblack.htm.

32. Gervais S. Bridges, More on Clergy for Educational Options, Barbecue and Politics blogosphere, Thursday, July 26, 2007, http://scbarbecue.blogspot.com/2007_07_01_archive.html.

33. Bodewell, 342.

34. "False Choices: Vouchers, Public Schools, and Our Children's Future," *Rethinking Schools Online*, Spring 1999, http://www.rethinkingschools.org/special_reports/voucher_report/v_quotes.shtml.

35. Black Commentator, "D.C. Voucher Passage is Huge Defeat," September 11, 2003.

36. "Poll: D.C. Residents Strongly Support School Voucher Program," *Business Wire*, July 28, 2009.

37. "D.C. Voucher Passage . . .", op cit.

38. Virginia Walden Ford, "Why We Must Fight For School Choice," *National Review*, March 28, 2009.

39. People for the American Way Foundation, "Privatization of Public Education: A Joint Venture of Charity and Power," April 20, 1999, http://67.192.238.59/multimedia/pdf/Reports/privatizationofpubliceducation.pdf.

40. Barbara Minor, "Distorting the Civil Rights Legacy," *Rethinking Schools Online*, Spring 2004, http://www.rethinkingschools.org/special_reports/voucher_report/v_kpsp183.shtml.

41. Rev. Graylan Hagler interview with author, Washington, DC, October 21, 2010.

42. Keith Jones, "New Jersey NAACP Opposes Publicly Funded Voucher Programs," *Nubian News*, July 11, 2004.

43. *Black Commentator*, "Briber + Vouchers = Black Bush Supporters," Issue 124, February 3, 2005.

44. "Black Clergy Group Endorses Vouchers for New Jersey," *Trenton Star-Ledger*, May 25, 2004.

45. *Black Commentator*, "Bribes + Vouchers = Black Cush Supporters," Issue 124, February 3, 2005.

46. Peter Schrag, "The Voucher Seduction," *American Prospect*, (November 30, 2002).

47. David Kirkpatrick, "Voices for School Choice," *New York Times,* (January 5, 1998).

48. Rev.Timothy McDonald telephone interview with author, November 2, 2010.

49. See, http://www.schoolfunding.info/states/state_by_state.php3.

50. Paul Magnusson, "The Split Over School Vouchers," *Business Week,* (October 13, 2003).

51. Charter schools, which are public programs funded by public school dollars on a per student basis (and by other federal and private grants), have been opposed by some public school advocates because they compete with and draw resources away from existing public schools.

52. Andrew Young, "Let Parents Choose Their Kids' Schools: Scholarships, or Vouchers, Will Allow Them the Option of Finding a Decent Education," *Los Angeles Times,* (April 29, 1999).

53. Floyd Flake, "Religion & Ethics Newsweekly," Episode 804, (September 24, 2004), http://www.pbs.org/wnet/religionandethics/week804/interview.html.

54. Sharon McCloskey, "Is Profit Dead?" News21, (July 30, 2009), http://columbia.news21.com/?p=752.

9

Black Churches and Black Voter Suppression in Florida and Ohio

Maurice Mangum

Introduction

Preserving and protecting black voting rights has been a constant struggle, dating back to the 1870s. One of the great beacons within the black community in countering vote suppression has been the black church, which is interpreted in this analysis as any congregation with a predominantly black membership. Black churches were integral to countering the Jim Crow laws in the South and the machine politics of the North and to ensuring that black votes counted. Through intimidation tactics, Jim Crow laws, and manipulation, black voters have repeatedly had their votes suppressed, or in some cases nullified entirely. Black churches and black clergy are needed now as much as they were after Reconstruction and during the mid-twentieth century.

Since blacks vote primarily for the Democratic Party, a method of guaranteeing victory for the Republican Party in presidential elections has been to suppress the black vote.[1] In predominantly black Florida communities in 2000 and predominantly black Ohio communities in 2004, many black voters were prevented from voting at their precincts due to various ploys including "caging," roadblocks, manipulation, long lines, faulty voting machines, misinformation about polling locations, and intimidation and harassment. Also, many ballots were reportedly discarded, disqualified, or lost. In both elections, the Bush Administration created problems in the voting precincts where large turnouts of black voters were anticipated. In Florida in 2000, more than 90 percent of its black citizens cast their votes only to learn that thousands of those votes were discarded.

Approximately 357,000 black voters were disenfranchised in Ohio in 2004. They were either prevented from voting or had their votes discarded. Suppressing black votes is viewed by some as necessary for the Republican Party to win elections.[2]

This chapter details responses by black churches and black clergy to widespread allegations of a suppression of black votes that may have influenced the outcomes in both the 2000 and 2004 presidential elections. The chapter examines myriad voting irregularities and methods to disenfranchise voters in the 2000 presidential election in Florida and the 2004 presidential election in Ohio and addresses ways black churches and black clergy combat new forms of voter suppression.

This investigation finds that although black churches and black clergy have been strongly supportive of their communities and strongly motivated to ensuring the rights of their parishioners, their impact has been modest in countering black voter suppression. While many black churches and black clergy within Florida and Ohio adhered to longstanding black church commitments to improving the community and ensuring equal social and political rights, black churches within these contexts were notably silent or reactive toward problems facing black voters, including voter suppression and disenfranchisement.

Two sections are provided to discuss in detail black voter suppression during the presidential elections of 2000 and 2004 in Florida and Ohio, respectively. While voter suppression may be employed as a general political tactic (irrespective of any racial connotation) to diminish the chances of the opponent winning, the chapter makes clear that in the Florida and Ohio cases efforts to subvert voting targeted blacks, not Democratic voters as a whole, and clearly affected black Democrats more negatively than white Democrats. Another section summarizes responses by black churches and clergy to presumed suppression of the black vote in Florida in 2000 and in Ohio in 2004. Differences are noted in black religious responses to the two contexts, with black churches and black clergy more active in Florida in 2000 than they were in Ohio in 2004. The final section concludes with a discussion of the similarities and differences in the level of black religious responses to black voter suppression since the 1960s, and also describes what black churches and clergy did differently for the 2008 presidential elections to ensure that voter suppression and disenfranchisement were not repeated in Florida and Ohio.

A Brief History of Black Voter Suppression

Voter suppression is electoral fraud that refers to using campaign strategies, governmental power, or private resources to reduce votes from a segment of voters (as opposed to simply changing voting preferences by influencing opinions of potential voters). Voter suppression has come in various forms. Procedures and practices that amounted to restrictions included poll taxes, literacy tests, grandfather clauses, black codes, gerrymandering, and white-only primaries.[3] Poll taxes refer to fees that had to be paid in order to vote and, with the fees often too high to pay, the effect was to limit voting participation. Literacy tests required a voter to demonstrate reading and learning proficiency. These tests were made harder and longer for blacks and most were unable to succeed because of high illiteracy rates. The grandfather clause restricted voters from voting if their grandfather was not eligible to vote before the ratification of the 15th Amendment, which extended the vote to black males. Black codes and Jim Crow laws prevented black social and economic freedom and created racial segregation. Fraud was used to prevent black votes from being counted, as in the case of post-Reconstruction districts in the South where black votes were often ignored and ballots were reported as misplaced or accidentally destroyed. Gerrymandering made it nearly impossible for blacks to be elected, and white-only primaries barred black participation in Democratic primaries.

Although voting rights for blacks had been granted by constitutional amendments (15th and 19th Amendments), federal statutes (Civil Rights Act of 1964 and Voting Rights Act of 1965) would be needed for them to be realized. Movements for black voting rights in the South were spearheaded by black ministers, including Dr. Martin Luther King, Jr., in Georgia. Individually, black clergy helped in the empowerment of black voters, and collectively they formed the Southern Christian Leadership Conference, which stood as the vanguard of the Civil Rights movement of the 1960s.

Emphasizing black rights, the long-standing efforts of many religious leaders influenced the Voting Rights Act of 1965, regarded as one of the strongest efforts to eliminating black voter suppression. The Voting Rights Act of 1965 banned discriminatory voting procedures and practices that caused widespread disenfranchisement of blacks. As an immediate response, a quarter-million black voters had been registered by the end of 1965. With this Act, Jim Crow laws were abolished, states were forced to stop infringing on black voter rights, and activities of terrorist organizations like the Ku Klux Klan were to be prosecuted. Furthermore, the Act included protections against future attempts to suppress black votes by requiring state and local election officials to announce all voting requirements, rules, regulations, and polling places well in advance of elections.

Nevertheless, black voter suppression persisted, though in less obvious ways. One form of contemporary black voter suppression has been the purging of voter rolls. Purging was originally meant to remove the deceased, duplicate names, and ineligible voters from the voting rolls. This can become a form of voter suppression when the names of eligible voters are removed from the lists. Part of the injustice is that these purges have been done secretly with no warning to voters. Too often, those being erroneously purged from voter lists have been blacks. In a related manner, another attempt to suppress the black vote has been the disenfranchisement of ex-felons. This has a disproportionate effect on the black electorate given that blacks constitute 14 percent of the United States' prison population.[4]

Michael Fauntroy voices a perspective shared by many when he states that the Republican Party has spent millions of dollars in support of "electoral integrity" schemes with the only real purpose being to reduce the number of blacks who vote.[5] Reflecting primarily on the last two to three decades, Republican Departments of Justice administered vote integrity and vote security initiatives aimed at purging blacks from voter rolls and intimidating blacks in ways that discourage them from coming out to the polls.[6] Recently, the Bush 2000 and 2004 presidential campaigns have worked with Republican secretaries of state, most notably Florida in 2000 and Ohio in 2004, to create conditions where large numbers of black voters and votes were suppressed. The Civil Rights Division of the U.S. Justice Department was also implicated in these ongoing Bush Administration efforts.

Florida in 2000

The 2000 presidential election was one of the most controversial elections in American history. For only the second time in the nation's history, the winner of the popular vote did not win the election, which was due to the role the Electoral College system plays in deciding U.S. presidential elections. Presidents are elected directly by the Electoral College. They are elected indirectly by the popular vote, for the popular vote in each state translates into electoral votes for the candidates winning the popular vote in that state. The candidate who wins the most votes in all states gets all of that state's Electoral College votes, except for Maine and Nebraska where the candidates receive Electoral College votes in proportion to the popular votes received. Also, for the first time since the Civil Rights era, voter suppression became a major issue. Arguments contesting the validity and legality of the election were not based solely on the votes counted, but on the votes that were not counted and the tactics used to omit those votes.[7]

Numerous reports have been submitted concerning the difficulties blacks had in registering to vote and with being denied the right to vote.

Also, upon being allowed to vote, black ballots were frequently disqualified, discarded, or lost.[8] Casting the ballot also presented problems, with voting machines outdated or confusing, and polling places incapable of accommodating the large numbers of voters in the poorer areas. Black voters encountered numerous difficulties at their assigned precincts on Election Day, including being falsely told that the precinct to which they had come was not the precinct where they had been designated to cast their vote.

Large number of black voters were kept away from the polls by various means, (examples below), while others were forced to stand in line for hours and were unable to vote when polls closed prematurely. Some were given misinformation, including that their names were not on the list, or that they needed two pieces of government-issued identification in order to vote. There were also allegations that black voters were harassed by police and poll workers, and that voters requesting translators were ignored or given translators incapable of assisting them. Black churches were also harassed during the election, as in the case of the Internal Revenue Service sending out letters to black churches indicating that they could not hold political forums at their churches.[9] In one such instance, First Baptist Church of College Hill in Tampa, Florida was told that their political forum could not take place during their Sunday service and would have to be moved to a nearby public library.

Continuous allegations of voter suppression in Florida prompted the need for independent, and federally funded investigations into the practices of polling stations, party leaders, and law enforcement during and prior to the election.[10] In the 2001 U.S. Commission on Civil Rights report titled, "Voting Irregularities in Florida During the 2000 Presidential Election," investigators concluded that voter disenfranchisement was the largest contributing factor to the outcome in Florida. Investigators conducted polls and gathered statistical information to reveal that black voters faced both greater difficulties at polling locations, and were blatantly denied the opportunity to cast ballots in their respective precincts.

Perhaps the most controversial method of suppressing the black vote was to purge the voter roll of persons presumed to be ex-felons. Before the election, Katherine Harris, Florida's secretary of state, and Jeb Bush, Florida's Governor, hired a firm (which became known as ChoicePoint) to remove the names of voters which were similar to those of former felons.[11] This purging resulted in 82,389 names being removed from the voting lists. After a thorough investigation of the voting rolls and the name purges, it was shown that 95 percent of the names removed from the voting rolls were individuals in the county who were legally eligible to vote. More than half of the 82,389 names purged were black, with many of the persons who were purged residing in areas where overwhelming numbers of blacks vote Democratic.[12] According to a report by Choice-Point, the firm connected to the list construction of the Florida voters whose registration status was challenged, over 400,000 voters (in addition to the above-mentioned 82,389) were labeled ineligible, and over half of these voters were black. ChoicePoint's board of directors, dominated by major Republican funders, was accused of collaborating with Florida and national Republican officials in intentionally suppressing the black vote in order to deliver Florida, and ultimately the presidential election, to George W. Bush.

Ohio in 2004

Evidence concerning the 2004 presidential election suggests that the election was stolen in Ohio. Nevertheless, not a single major American news outlet has published a serious investigation in the year subsequent to the election of whether the victory was properly awarded to George W. Bush.[13] Troubling to many because of an apparent conflict of interest was that Ohio's Secretary of State Ken Blackwell, was chairperson for the Republican election committee and was elections commissioner for the state of Ohio. In 2002, the Help Americans Vote Act created a provisional ballot for people who experienced problems related to their names being included on the roll. Blackwell, however, eliminated provisional ballots before the elections started.

Ohio had a significant black population that experienced many of the same registration and election-day difficulties that occurred in Florida in 2000 (problems with registration statuses, poorly trained election officials, unlawful identification requirements and, most importantly, disregarded absentee and provisional ballots). Also, as in Florida, the Republican Party in Ohio purged eligible black voters from the voting rolls. This was carried out through vote integrity and vote security initiatives, spearheaded by the secretary of state in Ohio in 2004 (in a direct parallel to what occurred in Florida in 2000). Many of the purged names were those of eligible black voters in the Cleveland area. Although this was characterized as an attempt to ensure that only registered voters were allowed to vote, the initiatives actually caused the numbers of new black voters to be greatly underestimated, leading to more voting day difficulties as the polling places were understaffed and lacked sufficient resources to deal with the turnout.[14] Officials also failed to process thousands of voter registration cards in several predominantly black precincts.[15]

The election-day problems were more apparent in heavily diverse cities in Ohio, including Cincinnati, Toledo, Columbus, and Cleveland.[16] In the Ohio presidential election of 2004, people complained of voter intimidation and some people were even pulled over by state troopers and held for countless hours. Upon arrival at the polling booths, blacks stood in long lines, sometimes waiting four to seven hours due to a paucity of voting booths. Many of these presumably Democratic voters received information via telephone or at their polling place that their voting location had changed or that voting would be continued Wednesday. It was discovered that 125 voting booths that were accounted for during the Ohio primary went missing in the general election. Broken voting machines were also a problem, including in one Cleveland-area precinct where only two voting machines were working out of fourteen.

Moreover, some ballots from black areas were not counted or they were spoiled. Most of the spoiled ballots (whose votes went uncounted) occurred in Ohio's big cities. In Cleveland, where nearly13,000 votes were ruined, a *New York Times* analysis found that black precincts suffered more than twice the rate of spoiled ballots as white districts.[17] In Dayton, precincts leaning toward Democratic candidate, John Kerry, had nearly twice the number of spoiled ballots as Bush-leaning precincts. In April 2006, a federal court ruled that Ohio's use of punch-card balloting violated the equal-protection rights of the citizens who used them for voting.[18]

While many of these activities have been explained away as normal voting day headaches experienced potentially by anyone living in a heavily populated district, the pre-election voter suppression has been a major target of concern. A *New York Times* report regarding the use of Florida state police officers attempting to influence elderly volunteers in retirement communities during the 2000 election was seconded by reports in Cincinnati.[19] Many black voters in Ohio were sent completely false, but official-looking letters that stated if they were registered to vote by an organization such as the NAACP, they would not be able to cast a ballot in the November 2 elections because they were registered to vote illegally.[20]

Another widely used form of voter suppression in 2004 was "caging," a practice instituted to verify voter residency and registration status.[21] First-class mail is sent to voters and, if the mail is returned to the sender, the voter's name and address are placed into a caging list, indicating the need to register anew and making challenges to voting eligibility possible. A report claimed that in caging lists found in both Ohio and Florida in 2004, all of the names were predominantly those of black voters. This maneuver is legal only if used to ensure registration status, but it was very apparent that this was an attempt to delay rightfully registered voters in their ability to vote, as the effort was conducted only a week before the election. As a result of these various tactics, estimates are that at least 357,000 Ohio voters were prevented from casting their ballots, or from having their votes counted in the 2004 presidential election.[22]

Black Churches and Black Clergy Fight Back

Black churches have been very effective in highlighting issues of importance to the black community, and have long been involved in the struggle to eliminate laws that circumvent the voting rights of blacks. During the 1960s, black churches and clergy helped pass the Civil Rights Act of 1964 and the Voting Rights Acts of 1965 and subsequently worked with other civil rights groups in ongoing voter reform initiatives. This included the "Help America Vote Act," which made many improvements in the voting process and aimed to replace punch-card voting systems.[23] The Help America Vote Act requires each polling location to have at least one voting system for those with disabilities and allowed voters who were declared ineligible, but believed themselves to be eligible, to cast provisional ballots. More recently, black church efforts to resolve black voter suppression have included assisting black voters with registration prerequisites such as ensuring residency details in order to avoid problems on Election Day.[24]

Black churches and clergy sometimes mobilize their congregation in ways that other groups cannot. Prior to the 2000 election in Florida, for example, black churches placed an emphasis on pre-Election Day voter mobilization, to counter the fact that much of their resources had been geared typically toward turnout and transport on Election Day.[25] Spurred partly by anger over an executive order written by Florida Governor Jeb Bush to end affirmative action programs in Florida education,[26] black and Democratic voters formed an opposition strategy called "Arrive with Five" that asked black voters to arrive at the voting polls with at least five or more other voters. "Arrive with Five" is credited with a 6 percent higher black turnout in 2000 than in 1996. Bishop Victor Curry, pastor of New Birth Baptist Church and former head of the Miami NAACP traveled the state, meeting with black clergy and recruiting them to participate in a new voter mobilization program he calls the "Sanctified Seven," a pledge to bring six others to vote with you.[27] The importance placed on black churches and black clergy helping to assist with black voter mobilization was shared by Pastor Gregory Alexander of New Hope Baptist Church, Miami, Florida. He stated:

The voting programs headed by our black leaders are much overdue for the state of Florida. African Americans have a voice and it needs to be heard. We gave bus rides to the people of the church using our church vans and even picked up the sick and shut in if they had the strength to go. The struggle of our people did not die with the death of the civil rights movement, but is rather alive and relevant today. I support the programs that are being implemented and plan to have the support of my congregation.[28]

After the 2000 election controversy, black churches began focusing on encouraging voters to vote early in order to avoid the problems and complications that arose on Election Day in 2000. Pastor Timothy Price of Greater Faith Methodist Church Hawthorne, Florida addresses the continued relevance of black churches and black clergy in combating black voter suppression:

The black voters of today are dealing with an old enemy that some are fooled into thinking has gone. As a church, my followers and I were at the polls watching and monitoring activities to make sure no one's rights were infringed on. Any sight of unacceptable behavior would be reported. Voter suppression is affecting the community as a whole, and should be dealt with as a community. Arriving at the polls early will help deter some of the tactics implemented by those who wish to silence the black voice.[29]

In Florida, black churches along with civil rights activists, held rallies and forums to spotlight the issue of voter suppression. Jesse Jackson held rallies to draw attention to the issue in Ohio. Congressional hearings were held in Washington, DC with participating clergy from the states where issues of voter suppression arose. Nevertheless, while black churches have strong legacies of involvement in civil rights activism, and while churches have come to wield significant human and financial capital, some feel black churches could have done more to prevent voter suppression, especially in the Ohio case. Pastor William Gunn of 46th St. Baptist Church, Columbus, Ohio, discusses his disappointment and his and his church's efforts:

We as a church in the body of Christ have an obligation to the people. We must perform our duties as Christians but also as citizens of this country. Speaking from the pulpit about the effects of voter suppression is not enough; we must truly support efforts [to oppose voter suppression], financially and socially if we expect to see any change in the environment and voter turnout. My church made sure these things were done by going to the polls and documenting anything that may have occurred using camera phones and video phones so that when we report these acts, there will be proof that cannot be denied.[30]

Although black churches in Ohio were not completely acquiescent to voter suppression, their responses left much to be desired. There is no real evidence that black churches launched any large scale protest in Ohio or even across the nation as it relates to the allegations of disenfranchisement in Ohio. There could have been several factors which led to the low levels of activity, including wedge issues dividing the black community and its clergy, IRS audits and audit threats, John Kerry's hasty concession to George Bush after the polls closed in the 2004 election, and the cooptation of the black church and clergy by city and state governments (including placing black clergy on task forces and allowing them to participate in decision-making bodies). Reverend Marcus C Wright of True Love Community Church, Cincinnati, Ohio, points out the lack of fire among black churches and black clergy:

> The issues facing voting in the African American community are vast and important. There was a true lack of excitement for Mr. Kerry and that really affected the outcome of voter turnout. Due to the lack of excitement, many were not inclined to go the distance necessary to see this process through. My faith is that we will be able to come together as a church and do something about these issues. Factors are present that prevent some actions that would normally have taken place. Nevertheless, the voter suppression will continue to be fought, next time with even more momentum.[31]

Another factor limiting black church challenges to these recent voter suppression tactics has been the skillful use of wedge issues to divide black church opposition. The matter of wedge issues is expounded upon by New York Congressman Major Owens in discussing the growing rift between black politicians and black churches. He contends that Republican countermeasures are now aimed at courting black churches because of their influential position within black communities.[32] Randal Archibald believes this rift is regional, noting differences in atmosphere between the North and the South. He argues that the South, although a hotbed for continued voter suppression, values the civic and political leadership frequently provided by black churches, but suggests that activism by black churches in the North is not as well received within that context.[33]

While there may be some regional differences in the acceptability of black church political activism, there is substantial opposition in general to black church political activism (both internal and external to black churches) that may account for political hesitancy on the part of these churches in responding to election violations in 2000 and 2004. A 2008 Pew study showed that 55 percent of black Protestants oppose church endorsements of political candidates, while 52 percent of the general public believes churches have no place at all in politics.[34] It is also important to note the gag order, in effect, placed on churches by Internal Revenue Service (IRS) requirements that churches remain independent of partisan political endorsements and advocacy if they want to retain their 501 (c) (3) tax-exempt status. In 2004, churches received letters from the IRS threatening to revoke their tax-exempt status for failure to desist from endorsing political candidates. The aggressive stance taken by the IRS seems to have had a chilling effect upon black churches.

Al Gore, Democratic challenger in 2000, fought within the courts to ensure that every vote was counted and every error corrected. This gave black churches a springboard for taking actions that would minimize the chances that the election violations in 2000 could be repeated. In the Florida case, black clergy, along with many other enraged citizens around the country, demanded that action be taken and a recount be initiated and completed. Kerry's early concession in 2004 hindered similar black clergy efforts to correct wrongdoings within that election context.

Moreover, both black churches and clergy were less active compared with black churches and clergy in the 1960s. Some might argue that black churches and clergy were frightened of becoming involved in such a controversial issue as the disenfranchisement of the black vote, given the national magnitude of such an issue. Black churches in the 1960s were not afraid to go-it-alone because they had been doing so for so long; however, black churches in the twenty-first century may fear losing monetary or other forms of support from their diversified memberships or undermining their stature and support bases within the governmental sector and society-at-large.

Conclusion

Since the early 1980s, the Republican Party implemented a strategy of suppressing the black vote in competitive states to win statewide offices.[35] The rationale behind the strategy was that since blacks vote overwhelmingly Democratic, a way to ensure that Republicans win is to suppress the black vote. Therefore, for the last thirty years, Republican Party officials and Republican Departments of Justice have engaged in "vote integrity" and "vote security" efforts to purge blacks from the voter rolls and intimidate those who appear at the polls. The Republican Party and the Bush campaigns in 2000 and 2004 worked with Republican secretaries of state (Florida in 2000 and Ohio in 2004) to create voting obstacles where blacks were predicted to vote in high numbers. With inadequate numbers of voting machines and understaffing of polling places in these areas, the hope was that long lines would create disincentives to vote, while disqualifying black voters and understaffing election phone lines would undermine confidence among black voters that they were eligible to vote at all.

The history of voter suppression in the United States has been long and damaging. The prime target of voter suppression has been black voters. Although black churches have been influential in encouraging the participation of blacks in the voting process, it was not churches but, rather, the National Association for the Advancement of Colored People (NAACP) and members of the Congressional Black Caucus (CBC) that were most vocal in the events surrounding the 2000 presidential election in Florida and 2004 presidential in Ohio.

Black churches and clergy have become more than just religious institutions and figures. They are integral to political and economic structures and processes. As such, they have established relationships with sectors of political and economic power. Federal, state, and local government officials have seated them on task forces and cabinets and channeled resources into church programs. Black churches and clergy therefore have vested interests in working within the political system rather than outside of it. While this may lead some to feel there is less need to engage in unconventional behavior, the 2000 and 2004 elections make clear that such behaviors may remain necessary in contexts where black interests are ignored or suppressed.

Notes

1. G. Derek Musgrove, "The GOP's Black Voter Suppression Strategy," *The Black Commentator*, Issue 168, January 26, 2006; M. Fauntroy, "Conservatives and Black Voter Disenfranchisement," 2007, www.michaelfauntroy.com/2007/09/conservatives-a.html.

2. Musgrove, 2006.

3. Michael J. Klaman, *From Jim Crow to Civil Rights: The Supreme Court and the Struggle for Racial Inequality* (New York: Oxford University Press, 2004); Mark Miller, *Loser Take All: Election Fraud and The Subversion of Democracy, 2000–2008* (New York: Ig Publishing, 2008).

4. CBC News Online, "Courting Black Concerns," October 22, 2004, http://www.cbc.ca/news/background/uselection2004/blackconcerns.html.

5. Fauntroy, 2007.

6. Ronnie Dugger, "How They Could Steal the Election This Time," *The Nation*, August 16, 2004.

7. Musgrove, 2006.

8. Mike Glover, "In Florida, Gore Urges Blacks to Turn Anger Into Votes," *Washington Post*, October 25, 2005, A07; Robert Kuttner, "The Lynching of the Black Vote," *Boston Globe*, December 10, 2000.

9. Kuttner, Robert. 2000, December 10, "The Lynching of the Black Vote," *Boston Globe*. http://www.commondreams.org/views/121000-101.htm.

10. Shelden Rampton, *Banana Republicans: How the Right Wing is Turning into A One-Party State* (New York: Tarcher/Penguin, 2004).

11. Spencer Overton, *Stealing Democracy: The New Politics of Voter Suppression* (New York: W. W. Norton Company, Inc., 2006).

12. Jack N. Rakove, *The Unfinished Election of 2000* (New York: Basic Books, 2001). While the numbers differ, another source points out that Governor Jeb Bush and Secretary of State Katherine Harris took the additional step of hiring a private company to "scrub" the list of Floridians who could be deleted from the rolls due to felonies. See, Jeffrey Toobin, *Too Close To Call: The Thirty-Six-Day Battle to Decide the 2000 Election* (New York: Random House Publishers, 2001).

13. Mark Hertsgaard, "Was Ohio Stolen in 2004 or Wasn't It?" *Mother Jones*, Vol. 30, Issue 6, November 1, 2005, 75–84.

14. Musgrove, 2006.

15. Overton, 2006.

16. Richard Hayes Phillips, "Voter Suppression: Stealing Votes in Ohio Urban Areas," *The Free Press*, December 3, 2004.

17. James Dao, Ford Fessenden, and Tom Zeller, Jr., "Voting Problems in Ohio Spur Call for Overhaul," *New York Times*, December 24, 2004.

18. Lisa A. Abraham, "Punch-Card Voting is Illegal." *Akron Beacon Journal*, April 22, 2006.

19. Bob Herbert, "Suppress the Vote?" *New York Times*, August 16, 2004.

20. Karen Juanita Carillo "Voter Suppression Efforts Evident, As Expected, During Election '04," *New York Amsterdam News*, Vol. 95, Issue 45, November 4, 2004, 3–33.

21. Mark E. Johnston, "Voter Suppression," June 26, 2007, http://www.epluribusmedia.org/features/2007/20070621_supressing_the_vote_2004.html.

22. Overton, 2006.

23. Ibid.

24. Kate Zernike and William Yardley, "Charges of Fraud and Voter Suppression Already Flying," *New York Times*, November 1, 2004.

25. Adam C. Smith and Tamara Lush, "Kerry Sounds Clarion Call To Florida's Black Voters," *St. Petersburg Times Online*, October 25, 2004.

26. Marc Cooper, "Florida Again?" *The Nation*, Vol. 278, March 22, 2004.

27. Smith and Lush, 2004.

28. Gregory Alexander, telephone interview with author, February 15, 2011.

29. Timothy Price, telephone interview with author, February11. 2011.

30. William Gunn, telephone interview with author, February 8, 2011.

31. Marcus C. Wright, telephone interview with author, February 15, 2011.

32. Tom Hamburger and Peter Wallsten, "GOP Sees a Future in Black Churches," *Los Angeles Times*, February 1, 2005.

33. Randal C. Archibald, "The 2004 Election: The Black Vote; In This Campaign, South Carolina's the Belle of the Ball," *New York Times*, December 21, 2003.

34. Brooklyne Gipson, "Black Churches Have a Changed Role in Election 2008," *The Loop*, October 27, 2008, http://www.theloop21.com/news/black-churches-have-changed-role-election-2008.

35. Musgrove, 2006.

10

African American Churches, Health Care, and the Health Reform Debate

Larry G. Murphy

The mission statement of the African Methodist Episcopal (A.M.E.) Church, which asserts its intention to "minister to the spiritual, intellectual, physical, emotional, and environmental needs of all people," provides a window into black churches and their posture on the currently contested issue of health care within the U.S.[1] This mission statement, which also speaks of "caring for the sick, shut-in, (and) the mentally and socially disturbed," reveals that A.M.E.s, similar to other historically-black denominations,[2] have from the outset seen the holistic care of their constituents as fundamental to their mandate. Beyond the primary focus on evangelism for spiritual transformation, the well-being of the socially-impacted and denigrated bodies of black people has been a perennial aim. This is reflected in the early emergence of "sickness and burial" societies (also called "mutual aid" societies) through which participating individuals and families received assistance in confronting the inevitable crises of physical ailments and material losses—crises for which the larger society offered no provision or safety net for persons of color. Some of the earliest black congregations developed from these social ministry associations, as did the A.M.E. congregation that originated in the late eighteenth century from Philadelphia's Free African (sickness and burial) Society.

As public provision for the health and physical welfare of the citizenry advanced and increasingly widened the options for care and support for whites, black people continued to be excluded and denied access, leaving them to their own devices. Barred by racial discrimination from educational institutions for training in the medical sciences, they drew upon the traditions of healers that were the residual heritage of their African past, including root doctors, conjurers, and folk repositories of healing arts. As blacks successively embraced Christianity, they indigenized its tenets into their resident theological notions that sickness has both spiritual and biological causes and requires cures grounded in both. They appealed to the Christian God, whom they experienced directly or via the scriptures, and to the spiritual powers of their clergy leaders for the healing that they sought but did not receive from public health care providers. For many African Americans (up through the twentieth century), when the limits of folk medicinal knowledge were reached, the preacher and "Dr. Jesus" were the only health providers they accessed. The latter, of course, brought a surfeit of existential assurance, since Jesus was "the doctor in the sickroom," "the doctor who never lost a patient."

Even as racial barriers lowered, allowing a trickling of blacks into medical training, and as blacks initiated their own hospitals and schools for producing nurses and doctors, churches continued to see their role as standing in the enduring gaps. This was reflected, for instance, in the cooperation of black churches as key operating venues for the National Negro Health Movement, active from its inception by Booker T. Washington in 1915 until 1950. This partnership with the United States Public Health Service aimed at promoting the health and well-being of African Americans, particularly in light of the their higher morbidity and mortality rates than the general population and the obvious disparities in health resources available to them.[3]

A classic study of black churches in the early twentieth century found that health programs in some form were common among the 794 urban and rural congregations studied, including free health clinics, child care, and recreational activities.[4] Further, "nurses guilds" became common features of local congregations. These auxiliaries, still common today, draw upon the nursing skills of their volunteer participants to minister to the health crises of members that emerge during Sunday worship time, and to provide care and safety for persons overcome with spiritual fervor during those worship services.

A 2006 publication, "Key Attributes of Health Ministries in African American Churches: An Exploratory Survey," reported on the outcomes of a study designed "to explore the perceived importance and existence of [twenty] health ministry-related attributes in predominantly African American churches." Attributes included such things as displaying health information in churches, hosting health fairs for church members, and incorporating health messages in Sunday bulletins. The researchers reported that 65 to 73 percent of their survey respondents affirmed five of the listed attributes as "very important" (top rating category). There was a gap, however, between the number rating the attributes "very important" and the number who actually implemented these in their congregations (range diff. in %: -8.3 to -22.2).[5] This outcome is similar to that of a 1986 case study of African American churches in Chicago, co-led by the present author, in which pastors were asked about the importance they placed on certain health-related interventions for their congregants and communities. There was a high valuation accorded to a variety of possible interventions and an expressed desirability for those interventions in their churches. However, a lack of resources for implementation and lack of knowledge of how to interface with public agencies toward collaborative implementation meant that few of such measures were actually present in any of the congregations.[6] Although neither of these studies had survey samples representative enough for generalization, one thing they suggested is that black clergy affirm health-related social services as within the purview of ministry and thus black churches could offer a prime venue for health-related programs.[7]

This historic and on-going attention to health concerns on the part of black churches would seem to have positioned them as advocates in the recent U.S. health care reform debate in Congress and among the general populace. One of the key concerns in that debate had to do with coverage for the 47 million U.S. citizens not protected by health insurance, a significant portion of whom were African Americans and persons of color. Another concern was the skyrocketing costs of insurance and of health services that were increasingly placing these beyond the means of large segments of the population, especially the more economically challenged, (again, highlighting African Americans). Because employers have, since the mid-nineteenth century, been the chief funders of health coverage through employee benefit provisions, the burgeoning costs challenge the productivity and viability of businesses, thus impacting negatively the health of the overall economy, and, in turn, the ability of the nation to compete in the international economy.

The health care system existing at the time of the debate, with its burgeoning costs, service provider inefficiencies, and lack of attention to preventive care, combined with the numbers of uninsured (the costs for whose inevitable needs for care are shifted onto the public treasury) was universally acknowledged to be unsustainable. Further, there was the underlying issue of whether health care is a privilege or a national right of citizenship and a moral/ethical responsibility of the nation, as other nations consider it to be. Again, then, an emphasis by black churches on living out a mandated theological concern for the plight of the dispossessed would seem to have positioned them for aggressive entry into the health care debate. The anomaly is that, in addressing health care issues, black churches have focused upon delivery of services to those in need but not upon challenging and holding accountable systems whereby these issues might be fully and equitably managed.

African American Health Disparities
and the Traditional Concern for Health

As African American churches have moved through the twentieth century and into the twenty-first, the dual foci of evangelism and the social/
physical support of their marginalized communities have retained their
prominence—in that order of priority. Due to their traditional concern for
the holistic care of their members, in tandem with the prophetic vectors
of black church history, one might expect black churches to be impelled
to action by the persisting disparity between African Americans and the
larger national populace in health status, health care access, and related
morbidity and mortality.

In fact, the missional response of black congregations to these realities has taken on a rich array of programmatic forms. A 2007 survey
conducted by the National Council of Churches USA found that African
American churches, along with suburban and urban downtown churches,
ran disproportionately more health education programs and were more
likely to engage in health care advocacy than other congregations in the
study.[8] Research by Tammy Williams of Duke Divinity School concluded
that black churches across denominations were becoming more proactive
relative to the health of their members. "Churches today," she says, "are
asking important questions about illness and health. They are beginning
to see sickness as a group issue, as a phenomenon, which requires the
church to think about healing the entire body." She adds, "The practice
of healing takes a different shape in contemporary churches than it did
20 years ago. Churches are trying to reflect on the large social context."[9]

This proactive approach on black health matters has extended
beyond the congregational level into ecumenical and cooperative ministry ventures. For example, Faith & Health Ministries, operating under the
Centers for African American Health in both Denver and Phoenix, works
with faith-based institutions "to promote healthy lifestyles and disease
prevention." This is carried out through clergy-appointed volunteer health
liaisons who, with Center staff, coordinate health education and health
screenings and promote physical activity and healthy eating habits.[10] In
Denver, the liaisons work with eighty participating congregations. Along
with education initiatives, they offer blood pressure and breast cancer
screenings, workshops on nutrition, healthy cooking, and senior wellness, plus workshops on such subjects as living well with diabetes and
other chronic diseases. The Arizona organization does prostate screenings, HIV/AIDS education and referral services, and, through the Tiny
Miracle Baby Project, fosters resources for pre- and post-delivery maternal
and child health.[11] California's Black Infant Health Program, under the

Public Health Department, collaborates with the black church community through the Creative Health Ministries Project to address issues of nutrition, diabetes, and overall health improvement.[12]

In the online community, BCNN1.com [blackchristiannews.com] focuses on news deemed pertinent to the black faith community, with one of its twelve sub-pages dedicated to health. The health page contains numerous articles on various aspects of black health issues, including promotion of healthy diet, African American health disparities, the latest research on health conditions in the African American community, and news on health advocacy that is of particular relevance to African Americans. It currently posts an announcement from the Conference of National Black Churches (CNBC), comprised of the national leadership of the historically black church denominations, that the CNBC plans to support an upcoming Prostate Health Education Network's Father's Day Rally Against Prostate Cancer. Similarly, the African American Reach and Teach Health Ministry (AARTH) is a web-supported health education and wellness initiative that has as its mission: "To build the capacity of churches and faith-based institutions that serve people of African descent through education, access to resources and self-advocacy for better health care services." Headquartered in Seattle, AARTH publishes and reprints on its site articles on various aspects of health and wellness, including the conjunction of spirituality and physical healing. It also conducts workshops and symposia, administers a speakers' bureau, and provides congregational training on nutrition and healthy eating choices through its *Body and Soul* program.[13]

In addition to the many denomination-specific programs that are active, there are major ecumenical initiatives in operation. In 2009, a video message on HIV/AIDS was recorded by bishops and religious leaders from several black communions and church-related agencies and uploaded on YouTube. This was done in support of the Ninth Annual "Our Church Lights the Way! HIV Testing Campaign," sponsored by Balm in Gilead, an organization created to stem the tide of HIV/AIDS infection in the black community through the cooperation of black churches. Concern over the epidemic of HIV/AIDS in the African American community prompted the inauguration of "The Black Church Week of Prayer for the Healing of AIDS" by Pernessa C. Seele, leading to her 1989 founding of Balm in Gilead (where she continues to serve as CEO).[14] The organization's Mission Statement conveys its expansive agenda and its grounding in the African American faith community: "The Balm In Gilead, Inc.,™ is a not-for-profit, non-governmental organization whose mission is to improve the health status of people of the African Diaspora by building the capacity of faith communities to address life-threatening diseases, especially HIV/AIDS."[15] Balm in Gilead subsequently partnered with the ISIS Project (Intimate Sessions for Informed Sexuality), a new national coalition that aims to educate and empower black women about cervical cancer and Human Papillomavirus. Moreover, Balm in Gilead has partnered with the Women's Missionary Societies of the African Methodist Episcopal (A.M.E.), African Methodist Episcopal Zion (A.M.E.Z.), and Christian Methodist Episcopal (C.M.E.) denominations to foster the "African American Denominational Leadership Health Initiative," which sponsors a network of disease prevention and health promotion activities in the United States, the Caribbean, and Africa.[16]

Another significant national ecumenical effort is the National Black Church Initiative (NBCI), which has as its insignia: "The Church as Health Educator." The NBCI is a coalition of 16,000 African American and Latino churches and 18,000 sister churches of other racial/ethnic identities that provides wellness information and health pre-screening services to its members. Its purpose is "to partner with national health officials to provide health education, reduce racial health disparities, and increase access to quality healthcare." NBCI sponsors a number of programs, some focused on healthy teen sexuality, such as "Keeping It Real"; the Health Disparities Initiative, a 24-church model created by religious leaders and health care professionals to collect critical data on health issues in targeted underserved minority rural and urban communities; the Baby Initiative Fund, designed to address abuse, neglect, and death among infants and young children; the Health and Wellness Initiative childhood and adult divisions, aimed at reversing the tide of obesity that has become a national concern; and other programs focusing on nutrition and on women's health and wellness matters.[17]

Rationale for African American Church Health Ministries

The energizing force behind the health care activism of the black church may be said to have a socio-theological base. That is, a primal concern for the existential well-being of one's cognate identity group combines with a biblical affirmation of the sanctity of human physicality and a corresponding mandate for the faithful to care for the least and the dispossessed. Further, there appears to be a growing recognition that there is no practical effect to appeals to live active, faithful Christian lives if persons are not free from infirmities and disabling conditions. Hence, spiritual health and physical health are asserted to be intimately interrelated, and the ultimate success of evangelism, which continues as the central mission of the churches, cannot be achieved without also addressing issues of preventive and corrective physical care.

The Health Ministry page of the Zion Baptist Church, cited earlier, quotes from the New Testament writer of 3 John, Chap. 1, verse 2: "Beloved, I wish above all things that thou may prosper and be in health, even as thy soul prospers." In the Spring, 2003, edition of the Clinton AME Zion church's "Health Matters," Pastor William M. White, Jr., presents an article on "Biblical Foundations for Holistic Health and Healing," in which he asserts:

> God has demonstrated throughout the Scriptures that God desires the wholeness of individuals. The body is the temple of God, and the very act of creation has made the human body sacred . . . Jesus' ministry was concerned with the wholeness and well-being of the complete person, spirit, body and mind. Jesus healed the person's physical body, restored their emotional and mental health, and restored them to fellowship with God and their community. The Scriptures are replete with stories of God's concern for the health and condition of God's creation, and also of stories of Jesus' ministry to those broken in body and spirit.[18]

And as the Full Gospel Baptist Church Fellowship says in Web literature describing its extensive health ministry: "Our mission is to lead the way in empowering members to achieve *the health God desires for service to Him* (emphasis added)."[19]

These ministries and health initiatives occur in recognition of and in response to historic and ongoing disparities in health care provisions for black and other minority populations, even in the face of recent national legislation moving the nation's health delivery system toward greater inclusivity in quality care. In composing its "Health Emergency Declaration," the NBCI expressed its despair over prospects for a timely implementation of such reform and opted, instead, to address black health care needs directly. The Executive Summary of the Declaration says:

> The Black Community . . . can ill afford to wait for health reform that would not truly take hold for another ten years . . . The National Black Church Initiative, having grown morally frustrated on the pace of achieving equality in health in any area, is moving with immense speed to reveal its Health Emergency Declaration (HED). The NBCI, through its HED,

will institute throughout its 34,000 churches proven health prevention strategies and modes that will begin to alter, transform
and eliminate the negative health statistics between whites and
blacks in this country.[20]

Service and Policy Advocacy:
Complementary or Alternative Missional Paths?

This NBCI statement brings to the fore the issue of direct service vs. public
policy advocacy. Up to this point, the present essay has outlined broad
involvements by the African American church community in health services delivery. Black churches have been shown to be advocates for health
and wellness in their communities, with that advocacy mostly taking the
form of educating black religious constituencies about health maladies
besetting black people, providing for them health support services, and
urging them to take preventative measures and to seek proper medical interventions when issues occur. Furthermore, advocacy has entailed
soliciting public and private resources for African American health care
initiatives and effecting collaborations and partnerships with institutions
in implementing these initiatives.

Black churches have been much less visible, though not absent, in
forms of advocacy that directly confront the systemic causes of health
disparities. The National Baptist Convention of America (NBCA) has
one such program, called S.T.O.P.P. (Strategies to Oppose Public Policies), which, among other things, monitors "Deficiencies in the Healthcare
System." The Full Gospel Baptist Church Fellowship's Health Ministry's
Web page includes an "Advocacy" link with the caption, "Cover the Uninsured," that links to a Web site for a Robert Wood Johnson Foundation
project by the same name that advances the cause of universal health
care coverage in the United States. The Social Action Commission of
the A.M.E. Church, in collaboration with its Health Commission, issued
an appeal to the denomination's membership and friends to join in an
August, 2009, national telephone conference with President Obama on
health care reform.

BCNN1.com., the online black Christian news magazine, featured in
its September 9, 2009, edition a story entitled "Religious Leaders Focus on
Ethics of Health Overhaul." It offered an overview of discussions among
various U.S. religious communities on health care reform, though the balance of the article made no reference to where, how, or whether *African
American* religious leaders were weighing in on the subject. NBCI issued
at least two health-related press releases in September, 2009, including one

calling for U.S. businesses to offer health insurance to all of their full- and part-time employees. The press release declared health care "a moral obligation for any free society," as well as "a critical factor in improving America's competitiveness around the world (given that a) healthy employee is able to produce more goods and services."[21] The second release called for a boycott of sodas and other sugary drinks as a response to the crisis of obesity, diabetes, and other chronic ailments in the nation, particularly within the African American community. Likewise, it pledged support of its 34,000 member churches for a proposal some groups were to circulate within Congress for a soda tax to be included in health care legislation.[22] These kinds of information-sharing and consciousness-raising activities are demonstrative of an emphasis by NBCI and by other black religious collectivities on impacting public policy through the mobilization of large ecumenical coalitions.

In July 2009, the Partnership of African American Churches held a press conference at the West Virginia state capitol to speak out on health care reform. The Rev. James Patterson, executive director of the organization, cited data on the disparities in such matters as black/white life expectancy, infant mortality rates, and access to affordable care. He stressed the urgency of engaging what was then the raging national debate so that, in his words, "as we put some kind of healthcare reform in place that we do so thinking about and taking into consideration the disparities that exist."[23] Then, in September 2009, the six-million member Church of God in Christ (COGIC), weighed in specifically on the health care reform debate. A statement issued by its presiding prelate, Bishop Charles Blake stated firmly:

> The Church of God in Christ calls upon the other major Black denominations, and our brothers and sisters of all races in their major denominations and the rest of the faith community to set a moral example which moves our country beyond the noise of racial division and partisanship by supporting President Obama's courageous initiative to address this vital issue. People of faith all over this country have a responsibility to stand for the millions who suffer from a lack of adequate heath insurance by pleading the cause of the needy, and raising their voices in support of the President's health care reform agenda.[24]

In something of a "null" address to the debate, a group of black pro-life clergy reacted to this statement by urging its retraction until such time as the health care reform bill as finally presented for consideration clearly prohibited funding for abortion.[25]

Case Study: The African Methodist Episcopal Church

The Mission Statement of the AME denomination, quoted in the opening lines of this chapter, speaks to its concern for physical and emotional
health. In fact, the denomination claims a deep, historical heritage of concern for health care. In 1793, the Rev. Richard Allen, who would become
the founding bishop of the denomination, mobilized Philadelphia's black
community to provide critical medical assistance to the general citizenry
of that town as they were in the midst of a deadly yellow fever epidemic.
The sacrificial service which they rendered became iconic of a faith-based
commitment to social action for community well-being that still informs
A.M.E. identity. Further, the Free African Society, out of which the first
A.M.E. congregation emerged, had as one of its chief member benefits
insurance-type support for members who incurred illness.

Against this backdrop, select A.M.E. bishops and clergy interviewed
for the present chapter stated that A.M.E. theology places Jesus' concern in the gospels with access to life in its abundance as central to its
denominational mission, with life being understood to include both material prosperity and physical vitality.[26] Moreover, interviewees noted that
the ability of Christians to actively, effectively partner with God in God's
work in the world depends on their being in a sufficient state of physical
well-being to do so. Thus, since God desires of Christians this co-creative
relationship, it is incumbent upon them to be intentional about wellness.
And while A.M.E. theology attests to the salutary power of prayer, it
fully embraces medical professionals and medical procedures as normative channels whereby divine healing may occur.

The interviewees affirmed the A.M.E. Church's ongoing, active
concern with issues of health. For instance, some twenty years ago, the
General Conference, the central legislative and administrative body of
the church, established a denominational Commission on Health. The
commission is headed by medical doctors and collaborates with health
associations to facilitate health education and programming for local congregations. The commission maintains an active, informative Web site
(amechealth.org) replete with links related to faith-based health programs,
physical activity, healthy eating, health conditions, and health resources.
The Health Commission coordinates with the church's Christian Education Department to extend the reach of its health education initiatives.
The General Conference further authorized that in each of the Episcopal
Districts there would be a health director, a medical professional to function in coordination with the denominational commission.

At its June 2007, biennial meeting, the A.M.E. Council of Bishops issued a statement that included the announcement that the A.M.E.

Church should take leadership in HIV/AIDS testing and education, given the widespread, deleterious impact of the HIV/AIDS crisis in the black community. The bishops of the Council opted to lead by example and were first in line to receive the testing that was sponsored at that connectional gathering. The A.M.E. Church thus became the first major denomination in which top leadership modeled such leadership on HIV/AIDS. At the most recent quadrennial meeting of the General Conference, health and wellness were addressed as central issues of concern. A position paper on the matter was issued and the conference challenged the connectional membership to pursue healthier lifestyles. For instance, members were encouraged to drop the smoking habit.

Also, realizing the need to attend to the physical well-being of clergy, particularly in light of an alarming number of health problems among them, several Episcopal Districts in the denomination have arranged with insurance carriers to offer comprehensive health coverage for their clergy and staff, many of whom are uninsured or underinsured. Moreover, across the denomination, many local congregations regularly host health fairs, preventative screenings, physical fitness programs, and informational workshops. And there are some innovative approaches to encouraging health, such as the Bryant Temple A.M.E. congregation of Los Angeles that promotes among its members the "Cookie Diet," centered on a nutritionally formulated confection that is part of a weight loss regimen. They even post the record of weight loss progress among the members in the Sunday worship service bulletin. The connection noted by the A.M.E. General Conference between wellness and lifestyle is being acknowledged by local congregations as they adjust their meal menus to include healthier choices for main courses and desserts. Some have even declared their mealtimes to be "no fry zones."

A growing number of individual congregations are partnering with public agencies around health concerns. For instance, the Trinity A.M.E. congregation in Waukegan, IL, secured a grant from the American Heart Association to do health screenings and to offer Zumba exercise classes. The pastor of the congregation leads by example, scheduling Tuesdays as "Zumba with the Pastor" day. Trinity also sponsors a farmers market to allow its members access to fresh produce as one means of counteracting the fact that its community is a "food desert."

On a broader cooperative scale, there are instances such as the Women's Missionary Society (WMS) in the Fourth Episcopal District, which received a $150,000 grant through the Illinois Public Health Department to work on issues of childhood obesity. The initiative was inspired by President Obama's motto of "Winning the Future," as well as by U.S. First Lady Michelle Obama's campaign to address childhood obesity. Desiring to avoid the potentially off-putting reference to "obesity," the WMS chose to title their effort "Fit to Lead." To bolster the participation of youth, parents and other adults were also recruited for participation so that it would become a family matter. And "fitness" was projected to include the well-being of the body, but also emotional and spiritual fitness.

The grant charged its recipient to work for "systems change," a shifting of the paradigm of self care. Programs have been set up in thirteen congregations in Cook County as "target" sites, even while implementation of program goals proceeds in other congregations, with the aim of expanding the program across the Episcopal District. To illustrate aspects of the implementation, Sunday School superintendants are to structure twenty minutes of exercise for each sixty minutes of sedentary instructional time. That exercise might be aerobics, or liturgical dance, or any other activity that ensures that the students are involved in physical movement. In those cases where Sunday School students frequent the pastor's office to enjoy his/her hospitality bowl of candy, pastors are encouraged to replace the candy bowl with a bowl of fruit or other healthy snacks. Church vending machines are to replace or supplement the typical sugary soft drinks, chips, and candy with water and healthy treats. At the scheduled meetings of the WMS, sessions are interleaved with seasons of physical activity. There are morning stretch exercises and morning "prayer walks" for which each meeting attendee is given a pedometer. Rather than sitting and socializing between sessions, there are fitness alternatives, such as Tai Chi and liturgical dance, or for those physically challenged, there are certain "Sit to Be Fit" exercises.

At the upcoming Fourth District Christian Education Congress, again each attendee will receive a pedometer and be encouraged to accomplish a quota of daily steps—10,000 for adults, 12,000 for girls, and 15,000 for boys. Each noonday worship service will be preceded at 11 o'clock with an hour of physical activity, whether Zumba, or Sit to Be Fit, or working out on the rented Gymboree equipment, or participating in the "Liturgical Dance Goes Hip Hop" session. Medical professionals have been contracted to lead the pastors in workshops on how to include health and wellness into their ministries. That training is to continue at periodic times in the coming years. Fourth District Episcopal Supervisor Rev. Cecelia Bryant says "systemic change is hard for pastors and congregations," but she and her husband, the Rt. Rev. John Bryant, the bishop of the District, intend to forge ahead with this initiative because they perceive its critical need in the congregations and because it is essential to a vibrant living out of the Christian faith.

Further health supportive activity is noted in the several A.M.E. annual conferences and Christian Education Congresses that host health classes, workshops, and screenings for high blood pressure. In the Eighth Episcopal District, under Bishop Carolyn Tyler Guidry, connectional head for Social Action, all district meetings include a "weigh in," again in keeping with U.S. First Lady Michelle Obama's campaign to address obesity.

Moreover, some interviewees noted that increasingly one can hear sermons that reference concern for health and wellness and God's desire for human wholeness, including physical wholeness.

During the lead up to the congressional vote on Pres. Barack Obama's health care reform initiative, the A.M.E. Council of Bishops issued a letter to the president firmly supporting passage of the reform legislation. The reform legislation was discussed at various church conference gatherings and said by some to be essential to Christian witness. Communications were sent to A.M.E. membership encouraging their support of the proposed reforms. One bishop had members at his annual conferences use their cellphones, during the conference session, to call their congresspersons to urge their support for the reform legislation. Since its passage, several A.M.E. clergy have participated in the monthly conference call with Health and Human Services officials on health issues, including calls related to "Medicare and Medicaid 101." Also, the Social Action Commission has repeatedly encouraged members to request their congressional representatives' support retention of the reforms that were passed, in face of the concerted efforts from some quarters to overturn them.

These representations of the A.M.E. Church's implementation of its missional commitment to health and wellness may be only a partial dimension of the story. One interviewee suggested that while the existence of a denominational Commission on Health is an important component of what the church should be about, the funding for the commission may be less than adequate for significant programmatic work. Others offered their perception that the General Conference position paper on health care reform might not have filtered down to the congregational level, and its endorsement of health care reform had not been followed up at the annual conference and congregational levels with informational discussions of the components of the legislation so that members might fully understand its positive implications for their situations.

What emerges from the interviews is the sense that episcopal and pastoral leadership, as well as congregational membership, increasingly rank issues of health prevention and care as of critical importance, and a number of institutional and programmatic measures have been initiated in response—at all levels within the denomination. Nevertheless, the response has not necessarily been uniform or consistent. Much has been conditioned upon the financial resources available to fund this or other aspects of church mission, and the African American community continues to be challenged in regard to financial resources.

To achieve broader and deeper congregational participation, much will depend on the ability to effect changes in endemic cultural lifestyle patterns, including dietary choices and the prevalent reactive rather than proactive approach to health and healing—i.e., addressing maladies after they have presented, rather than through adequate preventative care. For this there needs to be both increased educational and awareness activities, as well as more systemic remedies to extend to African Americans greater access to insurance coverage and to health programs and resources available in the larger society. Much also will depend on the ability to handle the challenges of pastoral appointments. A good percentage of congregations in the denomination are small, many with very senior membership. And many small congregations have only part-time pastors. Often these pastors are reluctant or unable to expend the amount of time, finances, and energy needed to implement the kind of ministry programming, including health ministry, they might affirm as important. As they struggle to maintain the viability of their parishes, their attention may be consumed in finding ways to sustain the physical facilities and the basic pastoral services. But much may also depend upon the priorities and vision of church leadership. In terms of a progressive, prophetic construct of one's ministerial calling, as one episcopal interviewee phrased it, "Not everyone is there yet." So, while some pastors may ostensibly evaluate health as an issue of importance, it is not evidenced in the generality of their sermons and bible studies, or in the other leadership activities that claim the focus of their energies.

Concluding Comment

Since its beginnings in the days of slavery, up through the Civil Rights Movement and subsequent civic involvements, the black church has sustained a commitment to the well-being of both the souls and the bodies of its constituencies. Taken as a whole, it has fostered organizational and institutional initiatives in education, the arts, political activism, and health care, among other things. As the work of sociologist Mary Pattillo has shown, its collective ethos and its theology of a God who is active in worldly matters supports this communal engagement.[27] The black church, therefore, could be expected to involve itself in concerns of health promotion. The actual picture of that involvement has been a gradient, ranging from a quietist non-engagement, to varying levels of programmatic service delivery, to active public policy advocacy.

As the foregoing discussion has suggested, when black churches address the matter of health and wellness, this has typically taken the form of direct health services delivery, either individually, per congregation, or in collaboration with external agencies. Policy advocacy relative to health care, including the redress of the disparity between the resources available to black versus white communities, is present but is not pervasively nor systematically pursued. Each of these areas has been informed and/or moderated by a commitment to evangelism, i.e., "winning souls for Christ" and nurturing the relationship of the believer to the divine, as the presumed core charge of ministry.

Even the performance of this evangelistic commitment is impacted by the complex of challenges inherent in administering the life of congregations and sustaining their viability. Pastors are often consumed, or allow themselves to be consumed, by meeting these challenges, leaving few personal or visional resources for ministries more widely cast into areas of social witness and application of the gospel to the needs and cares of the larger world.

In regard to the priority of evangelistic and devotional matters over social witness, black churches are not dissimilar to the larger U.S. church community. As reviewers of a major study of U.S. congregations recently stated:

> . . . despite the media focus on the political and social activities of religious groups, the arts are actually far more central to the workings of congregations. Here [in this study] we see how, far from emphasizing the pursuit of charity or justice through social services or politics, congregations mainly traffic in ritual, knowledge, and beauty through the cultural activities of worship, religious education, and the arts.[28]

This contextualizing of the operational agenda of the black church within that of the larger church domain illuminates, in part, a lower level of advocacy than might be expected on social concerns such as health care (despite the fact, as cited earlier, that black churches may demonstrate a higher likelihood of advocacy activity than the general church population).[29]

There is ample evidence in the church-based social intervention activities cited in this chapter that large numbers of black church bodies and religious leaders resonate with the missional balance articulated by Bishop Blake in his statement supporting health care reform: "Based on our understanding of the Holy Scriptures it is not only our mandate to encourage men and women to come into right relationship with their Creator, but also to proclaim and advocate justice and compassion throughout all creation."[30]

However, although past and current black church missional commitments to black health and wellness suggest the likelihood of continued black church energies and resources devoted toward health services, there is no clear indication of a concerted, lively, prophetic engagement of the current national battle over the retention and implementation of the 2010 health care reform legislation, the Affordable Health Care for America Act.

Notes

1. The Mission of the African Methodist Episcopal Church is to minister to the spiritual, intellectual, physical, emotional, and environmental needs of all people by spreading Christ's liberating gospel through word and deed. At every level of the Connection and in every local church, the African Methodist Episcopal Church shall engage in carrying out the spirit of the original Free African Society, out of which the A.M.E. Church evolved: that is, to seek out and save the lost, and serve the needy through a continuing program of (1) preaching the gospel, (2) feeding the hungry, (3) clothing the naked, (4) housing the homeless, (5) cheering the fallen, (6) providing jobs for the jobless, (7) administering to the needs of those in prisons, hospitals, nursing homes, asylums and mental institutions, senior citizens' homes; caring for the sick, the shut-in, the mentally and socially disturbed, and (8) encouraging thrift and economic advancement.

2. Currently numbered as eight ecclesial institutions: the African Methodist Episcopal Church, the African Methodist Episcopal Zion Church, the Christian Methodist Episcopal Church, the National Baptist Convention, USA, Inc., the National Baptist Convention of America, the National Missionary Baptist Convention, the Progressive National Baptist Convention, and the Church of God in Christ. The Full Gospel Baptist Church Fellowship, a national body with episcopal leadership, opts against the designation of "denomination."

3. Stephen B. Thomas et al., "The Characteristics of Northern Black Churches with Community Health Outreach Programs," *American Journal of Public Health*, 84/4, April 1994, 576; http://health-equity.pitt.edu/index.html.

4. See the 1933 study by Benjamin E. Mays and Joseph H. Nicholson, *The Negro's Church*, (New York: Institute of Social and Religious Research, 1933).

5. See http://www.ncbi.nlm.nih.gov/pubmed/17203634. (The survey had obvious limitations, however, in that it was administered to 72 respondents out of 98 religious leaders attending a conference on health and spirituality).

6. See "Involving the Religious Community as Partner with Health Providers," with Lynn Olson et al. in *American Journal of Preventive Medicine*, 1987.

7. The "Key Attributes" study, conducted by the Institute for Health, Social and Community Research at Shaw University, drew upon 98 clergy who were attending health and spirituality conference in Raleigh, NC; the Chicago study sampled 176 churches in six low-income, predominantly black neighborhoods on the South Side of the city. They were drawn from public directory listings.

8. www.ncccusa.org/pdfs/healthsurveyfinal.pdf, pp. 6, 8.

9. http:/news.duke.edu/11/williams.

10. www.thecaahaz.org/Programs/Default.aspx#Faith.

11. See www.caahealth.org/page.cfm/ID/30/Faith-and-Health-Ministries/; www.thecaahaz.org/Programs/Default.aspx#Faith.

12. www.sccgov.org/portal/site/phd/agencychp?path=%2Fv7%2FPublic Health Department (DEP)%2FMaternal%2C Child %26 Youth Health Programs%2FBlack Infant Health%2FCreative Health Ministries.

13. See www.aarth.org/index.htm.

14. See http://www.highbeam.com/doc/1P1-93040964.html; http://health. usf.edu/nocms/nursing/newsannounce/07/newsannounce_Jan07-Aug07.html; balmingilead.org.

15. http://balmingilead.org/about/mission.asp.

16. http://balmingilead.org/index.html.

17. See http://www.naltblackchurch.com/.

18. http://clintonamezion.org/pdf/healthmatters03.pdf.

19. http://www.fullgospelhealth.org/Plan.html.

20. http://www.naltblackchurch.com/health/pdf/health-emergency-declaration.pdf, p. 5.

21. See http://www.naltblackchurch.com/pdf/employer-coverage.pdf; http://www.blackpressusa.com/news/Article_NatNews.asp?NewsID=19441

22. See http://www.naltblackchurch.com/pdf/soda-tax.pdf.

23. http://www.wvpubcast.org/newsarticle.aspx?id=10630.

24. file:///F:/AA%20Church%20and%20Health%20Care/Black%20Church%20Leaders%20Speak%20Out%20in%20Support%20of%20Obama%E2%80%99s%20Health%20Care%20Reform%C2%A0_%C2%A0CHURCH%20OF%20GOD%20IN%20CHRIST.htm.

25. See http://www.christianpost.com/article/20090929/black-pastors-criticized-for-endorsing-obama-healthcare-plan/index.html.

26. Telephone interviews were conducted with Bishop John H. Bryant, Fourth Episcopal District, April 26, 2011; Rev. Cecelia Bryant, Episcopal Supervisor, Fourth Episcopal District, April 29, 2011; Bishop Carolyn Tyler Guidry, Eighth Episcopal District, May 2, 2011; Bishop Gregory G.M. Ingram, Tenth Episcopal District, April 26, 2011; Presiding Elder Walter R. Bauldrick, North District, Chicago Annual Conference, April 18, 2011; Rev. Basil A. Foley, retired, Houston, TX, April 25, 2011. An in-person interview was conducted with the Rev. Dr. Reginald Blount at Garrett-Evangelical Theological Seminary, Evanston, IL, March 23, 2011.

27. Susan Markens, Sarah A. Fox, et al., "Role of Black Churches in Health Promotion Programs: Lessons from the Los Angeles Mammography Promotion in Churches Program," http://www.ajph.org/cgi/content/full/92/5/805.

28. Publisher comments on *Congregations in America*, by Mark Chaves (Cambridge: Harvard University Press, 2004), http://nucat.library.northwestern. edu/cgi-bin/Pwebrecon.cgi?v1=1&ti=1,1&Search_Arg=chaves&Search_Code=NAME&CNT=50&PID=C5a6Upy2D4FxqjCuJaGeyjCEhsiY&SEQ=20091030100115&SID=1

29. *Supra*, 5.

11

The Obama Administration, Faith-Based Policy, and Religious Groups' Hiring Rights

David Ryden, Hope College

If you get a federal grant, you can't use that grant money to proselytize to the people you help and you can't discriminate against them—*or against the people you hire*—on the basis of their religion.

—Barack Obama, July 1, 2008 campaign appearance at the East Side Community Ministry, Zanesville, Ohio

"On the hiring issue . . . [w]hat the president has decided to do . . . [a]s issues arise out in agencies, whether it's on co-religion in hiring, hiring discrimination or any other difficult legal issue, we will consider them. We will work with the White House counsel and with the Department of Justice, the attorney general, to fully explore that individual case and make a recommendation to the president . . . on a case by case basis.

—Joshua DuBois, executive director of the White House Office of Faith-Based and Neighborhood Partnerships, February 5, 2009

Introduction

On February 5, 2009, less than a month into his presidency, Barack Obama formally announced the creation of his Office of Faith-Based and Neighborhood Partnerships. Drowned out by the swell of major events and crises occurring in the early months of the Obama administration, the announcement revealed Obama's intention to follow through on a campaign pledge, and to continue what was unarguably one of the most controversial and contested domestic policy initiatives of his predecessor, George W. Bush. Almost exactly eight years earlier, President Bush had launched with great fanfare his White House Office of Faith-Based and Community Initiatives—what would commonly come to be known as the Faith-Based Initiative (FBI). The Obama announcement surely disappointed some opponents of the Bush-backed faith-based initiative, who had hoped it would quietly fade away with Bush's departure from office.

To the surprise of some observers, President Obama retreated from a campaign pledge he had made to address the most disputed facet of Bush's faith-based policy—the right of publicly funded religious nonprofits to make hiring decisions based on the religious commitments of the applicant. Rather than reversing the Bush policy and definitively rejecting hiring rights for publicly funded groups, Obama proposed an ad hoc approach in which the Department of Justice would weigh the validity of faith-based organizations' hiring policies on a case-by-case basis.

The decision by Obama to continue the faith-based initiative is of special significance to black churches and their leaders, who initially were among the most positively disposed toward the idea of partnering with the government to better serve their neighbors. For a variety of reasons, however, the Bush FBI failed to generate a discernible increase in the numbers of black churches seeking government assistance to help finance their social service outreach. The time may be ripe, then, for black clergy and congregations to revisit the possibility of availing themselves of federal funding to support and expand their social programs. As they do, however, they should be mindful of the unsettled nature of their rights in the personnel department.

Background

At the heart of the Bush faith-based policy was a desire to counter a perceived bias against religious organizations that might wish to access public monies to assist in their provision of a variety of social services. The essence of the proposal that was introduced in Congress in the spring of 2001 was a leveling of the playing field between religious nonprofits and their secular counterparts in pursuing government grants and contracts to support their social programs. Thus it required the federal government to give equal consideration to religious service providers when it looked to the private sector for assistance in delivering services. Moreover, for those religious groups that successfully garnered public funds, the initiative aimed to preserve their religious identity and character from federal regulations that would strip them of their essential mission. In other words, they were not to be required to secularize as a price for doing business with the government. Finally, the faith-based initiative—like the charitable choice provision after which it was modeled[1]—explicitly concluded that those faith-based organizations who provided social services financed by the government preserved their exemption from the nondiscrimination laws under Title VII of the Civil Rights Act of 1964. In other words, they maintained the right to make personnel decisions along religious lines, notwithstanding the fact that they took federal funding.[2]

Viewed inside and out of the Bush administration as a signature plank of Bush's domestic policy agenda, the faith-based initiative appeared to have a popular appeal that would draw broad-based support from a variety of constituencies across the usual partisan and ideological divide. Instead, that appeal quickly faded once the initiative became ensnared in the legislative process. Within eighteen months of taking office, Bush's faith-based legislative proposal in Congress had provoked a contentious high profile debate and was left for dead before it reached the floor of either chamber.

Stymied on the Congressional front, the Bush administration opted for an aggressive parallel executive strategy, by which the president strove to achieve through administrative fiat what he was unable to accomplish legislatively. With a December 2002 executive order, President Bush significantly expanded the faith-based initiative beyond the White House Office. It created a handful of faith-based satellite offices in specified federal agencies, with the aim of extending faith-based social service delivery in such areas as housing, hunger relief, employment training, ex-offender rehabilitation, and youth mentoring.[3] The order commanded a review of federal administrative contracting rules to eliminate those which might present obstacles to faith-affiliated groups' pursuit of public dollars. It earmarked funds for religious applicants, instituted greater protections for the religious autonomy and identity of religious recipients of grants, and in particular sought to secure the hiring rights of those religious recipients. In short the executive order aimed to create a more favorable bureaucratic environment and regulatory regime for religious groups desirous of partnering with the government.[4]

The December 2002 executive order was only the beginning of what was to be a full court press by the White House in its effort to administratively transform the relationship between the federal bureaucracy and the faith-based community. By the end of the Bush administration's second term in office, faith-based partnerships with the government had acquired a genuine momentum of their own. Whether for better or for worse, the Bush White House ultimately succeeded quite dramatically in altering the nature and reality of the relationship between religious nonprofits and government at the national, state, and local levels. By Bush's final year in office, spending on the federal level flowing to faith-based groups was estimated to exceed $10.6 billion.[5] Perhaps more significantly, the federal faith-based policy had a huge trickle-down effect to lower levels of government. Within a few years, a broad majority of states, and even many cities, had followed suit by creating faith-based offices and enacting faith-friendly legislation easing the path to government-faith sector partnerships. Faith-based programs existed across the country, addressing virtually every kind of social service need imaginable—substance abuse, after school mentoring, housing for the homeless, parenting skill training, food pantries, medical clinics, and much more. By 2008, faith-based governmental collaboration was occurring on an unprecedented scale.

Despite such signs of broad support for the policy, the Bush faith-based initiative continued to generate a fair amount of controversy and opposition. Many viewed the policy as pushing the envelope on church-state relations too far and harshly criticized the legal and constitutional status of the initiative. Given the anemic popular standing of Republicans in the final years of the Bush administration, the secular wing of the Democratic Party anticipated that a Democratic administration would use its executive authority to undo the faith-based politics of the Bush White House. Much to their chagrin, candidate Obama made it clear in the summer of 2008 that he had no such intention. Instead, he gave a high-profile speech touting the positive aspects of collaborations between government and religious organizations, while announcing his intention if elected president to continue a Faith-Based Office in an altered form. The Obama campaign also published a policy paper confirming the candidate's desire to continue to look to faith-based groups to advance government policy objectives and offering details of the plan.

Candidate Obama did reassure opponents of the Bush faith-based policy on one key aspect—the question of the legality of publicly funded religious groups hiring only those with religious commitments compatible with those of the organization. That a religious organization could use public funds to create positions, which it then filled based upon explicit religious criteria, was first asserted in the context of the 1996 debate around the proposed welfare reform legislation. That right found its way into the charitable choice provision that was part of the final bill enacted into law. Charitable choice explicitly gave religious groups the right to base employment decisions on religious compatibility, even when filling government-funded jobs.

However, the hiring policy did not attract widespread attention or opposition until faith-based policies were spotlighted as part of the Bush administration's emerging agenda. When the legislative efforts in

2001–2002 sought to include employment language that mirrored chari- table choice, opponents were prepared. They employed highly effective rhetoric implying that the faith-based initiative required the government to support "religious discrimination" with taxpayer funds. The language of government funded religious discrimination proved to be much more successful than more abstract church-state objections leveled at the initia- tive. Portrayals of zealous religious groups practicing intolerance through discriminatory hiring—with the aid of public dollars—captured public attention as no other issue had. This quickly eroded the short-lived politi- cal popularity of faith-based initiatives. In the end, the public debate over the rights of faith-based groups to exercise "religious discrimination" in their hiring practices was a primary factor in slowing and eventually derailing the legislative proposals.

Even as the Bush initiative progressed administratively, it remained hotly contested whether religious groups who took public money retained the right to hire along the lines of religious affiliation. The hiring issue was a hot potato, surfacing repeatedly in congressional debates over reauthori- zation of various social service funding streams where this right was the major stumbling block.[6] Clear battle lines, reinforced by highly energized and attentive advocates on both sides of the issue, ensured that Congress would remain stalemated on the issue. It was significant, therefore, when candidate Obama assured his backers that, as president, he would demand that religious groups receiving federal funds not discriminate in their hir- ing practices based on religion.

The Obama Office of Faith-Based and Neighborhood Partnerships

Once elected, President Obama didn't delay on the faith-based front, announcing on February 5, 2009 the creation of the Office of Faith-Based and Neighborhood Partnerships (OFBNP). Most of the executive order was unsurprising and noncontroversial. The administration left in place the existing legal structure, including the eleven faith-based satellite offices across the executive branch bureaucracy created during the Bush years. The order established a 25-member advisory council comprised of secular and religious leaders representing a wide variety of faiths and denomina- tions. The president named as director Joshua DuBois, a 26-year-old Pen- tecostal minister who was the head of religious outreach during Obama's campaign.[7]

Most of the policy details reflected Obama's campaign stance. For example, no federal funds were to be used to proselytize or to provide religious instruction; there was to be no discrimination against potential beneficiaries or clients on the basis of their religion or lack thereof; and taxpayer dollars were only to be applied to secular dimensions of funded programs. Each of these criteria had been generally accepted as legally required under the Bush faith-based initiative as well.

Nevertheless, there were discernible differences, at least on paper, between the Obama and Bush faith-based models.

- The Obama order called for greater accountability, oversight, and transparency in the spending of federal funds. The Bush initiative was viewed by many as too lax in the area of oversight and giving religious groups freedom from intrusive regulations.

- The Bush initiative was conceived originally as an effort to ease church-state constraints in order to level the playing field between religious and secular providers in their pursuit of federal grants and contracts. The Obama plan seems to assume that this problem has been adequately addressed and is focused instead on mobilizing government-faith sector partnerships toward articulated policy goals (reducing poverty, encouraging summer learning programs, etc.).

- Obama signaled that his faith-based office would more carefully scrutinize expenditures of public funds to ensure that they were not used for religious purposes. The Bush faith-based regulations had been criticized as intentionally ambiguous so as to put as few actual constraints on faith-based groups as possible.

- The Obama program was less singularly focused on religious groups, aiming instead at enlisting all forms of small neighborhood organizations, whether religious or not.

- The Obama plan suggested a possible expansion of the faith-based policy, by increasing government staffing and program funds. A central criticism of the Bush initiative was that its failure to make significant financial investment through added spending indicated a lack of genuine commitment to responding to poverty and other social ills.

On the central point of opposition to the Bush program, however, Obama backpedaled from his earlier campaign statements. His order backed away from his campaign promise to end Bush administration regulations protecting the right of publicly funded religious nonprofits to hire based upon the religious bearings of the individual. Instead, the newly appointed executive director of the OFBNP indicated that the rules on hiring practices would be reviewed on a case-by-case basis as complaints arise (and subject to legal findings of the Justice Department).

At first glance, the president's decision to backtrack on the hiring issue seems inexplicable. Public opinion seemed to be on his side, with broad public opposition to hiring decisions based on religion when a group is publicly funded. Seventy-three percent of respondents to a 2008 Pew Forum on Religion & Public Life survey thought religious groups taking public money should not be allowed to hire only people who share their religious beliefs.[8] Public opinion notwithstanding, Obama's decision was likely a concession to the murky status of faith-based hiring rights, both as a policy issue with far reaching ramifications and with regard to the legal arguments involved.

The Confusing Legal Status of Religion-Based Hiring

The attempts under the charitable choice provisions of the 1996 welfare reform bill and the subsequent Bush faith-based initiative to protect funded religious nonprofits' hiring prerogatives were much debated from the start. No other element of the Bush plan generated more acrimony and emotion. Unfortunately the fervor of the participants' arguments was rarely matched by substantive clarity or accuracy. While the employment issue is one of the most often mentioned aspects of the faith-based policy, it is almost surely the least understood.[9] While the claims on each side typically have been proffered with great confidence and assurance, the state of the law is far more difficult to discern. Indeed, most fair-minded observers who have weighed in on the question reach the conclusion that no definite answer exists.[10]

The unsettled nature of the legal issues at hand is attributable to the fact that controversy over hiring did not arise as a matter of practice until 1996 and after. Hence the issues are indeed novel, with little prior judicial interpretation to suggest how courts might decide the matter today. Before 1996, the thrust of establishment clause doctrine essentially worked to keep funded faith-based organizations from making hiring decisions based on religion. This was due to the Court's reliance in its establishment clause jurisprudence on the principle of "pervasive sectarianism." Organizations whose social services were so intertwined with their religious identity and practice as to be inseparable were considered "pervasively sectarian," and were disqualified from public funding. It was thought that public financial support of those groups could not occur without furthering their religious activities, thus running afoul of the establishment clause prohibition against government advancement of religion.

Indeed, the Supreme Court had even explicitly identified a group's policy of making employment decisions based on faith requirements as indicative of a pervasive sectarianism (*Bowen v. Kendrick* 1988). Thus the pervasive sectarian standard, as commonly understood, essentially precluded public funds from flowing to groups that made hiring choices on the basis of religion. The kinds of groups that later might be inclined to pursue funds under the charitable choice provision enacted in 1996 were unlikely to do so prior to then. As a result, the employment question rarely found its way into court, thus explaining the lack of precedent on the point.[11]

The movement to encourage government/religious sector partnerships in the late 1990s altered the legal landscape significantly. Beginning with the Welfare Reform Act of 1996 and again in subsequent legislation enacted in 1998 and 2000, Congress authorized government agencies to treat faith-based groups on a par with their secular counterparts as potential program partners when the government turned to the private sector for assistance. The original charitable choice provision explicitly protected religious hiring rights for those religious groups that accepted public funds as part of programs funded through Temporary Assistance for Needy Families. The later acts did likewise. What was not clear, however, was whether the legislation required that the federal government extend grants to otherwise qualified religious groups without regard to their policies on faith-based hiring.

Questions surrounding the hiring issue remained largely moot during the second term of the Clinton administration. It was only with the incoming Bush administration's emphasis on faith-based collaborations with government that greater numbers of religious nonprofits began more aggressively pursuing and receiving government funding. This quickly brought into focus the question of whether public funding compromised a group's right to hire based on religion.[12]

Any current analysis of the issue is complicated by the fact that President Bush was relegated to using an executive order to advance his policy. Because he was unable to persuade Congress to formally enact his policy through legislation, his executive orders did not override specific statutes governing particular funding streams. A number of those expressly prohibit religious groups from hiring based upon religious preferences. Hence there now are varying treatments of the hiring practices of publicly funded religious groups. Charitable choice provisions protecting the religious freedom of the nonprofit are embedded in some federal statutes. Other federal laws take the opposite approach, and bar religiously motivated hiring. Finally, some statutes are silent on the issue, in which case regulatory or executive orders tend to fill the gaps in divergent ways.

The debate over the legal status of the Bush employment policy implicates both statutory and constitutional considerations. At the heart of the debate is the viability of the exempt status that churches and religious groups have enjoyed under the Civil Rights Act. Title VII of the Civil Rights Act of 1964 (the equal employment opportunity section of the Act) prohibits employers from discriminating in employment on the basis of religion, among other things. But exemptions to that prohibition are granted to certain religious entities. Those have been understood as allowing religious nonprofits to take religious affiliation or conviction into account in their hiring and personnel decisions, a position that was unanimously upheld by the Supreme Court in *Corporation of the Presiding Bishop v. Amos* (1987).[13]

The application of the exemption from Title VII prohibitions is clouded by the fact that it makes no specific provision in situations where the religious entity is acting as a recipient of federal funding. Opponents of faith-based hiring contend that *Amos* is inapt, and that the receipt of public monies disqualifies religious groups from the exempt status that otherwise would exist under civil rights laws. They argue that to extend the exemption to situations involving federal contracts or grants is tantamount to governmental endorsement of discriminatory hiring.[14] In short, they assert that a faith-based provider's acceptance of federal money should cause it to lose its Title VII exemption.[15]

Faith-based backers counter that to adopt such an analysis would constitute unacceptable (and unconstitutional) bias against religious freedom and activity. They argue that publicly funded secular organizations would never be compelled to hire applicants who were at odds with the organization's ideological or policy aims. To strip publicly funded religious charities of the right to hire as they please would offend evenhandedness by imposing a constraint on religious nonprofits not felt by secular charities.[16] The unavoidable message would be one of government bias against religious providers.[17]

In a carefully measured analysis of the issue, Melissa Rogers concedes that religious organizations do not generally forfeit their Title VII exemption from federal civil rights restrictions when taking public funds. Most courts have found that the organizations cannot waive the exemption through their conduct,[18] and at least one federal appellate court has held that the receipt of government funding does not strip the organization of the exemption (*Hall v. Baptist Memorial Health Care Corporation,* 2000).[19]

An additional question is whether the Title VII exemption affirmatively compels Congress to grant that same protection to faith-based groups in any subsequent legislation. In other words, even if the Title VII exemption is found to exist for religious groups that accept public funds, it may not necessarily preclude Congress or state legislatures in grant programs that include religious recipients from explicitly requiring publicly funded religious providers to comply with any relevant nondiscrimination clauses in their hiring practices. A number of federal statutes prohibit grant recipients from taking religion into account when hiring employees (e.g., the Workforce Investment Act). Because Congress had enacted these prohibitions by statute, the Bush White House could not simply override them via executive order, as it had implemented other aspects of its faith-based agenda.

Conflicting opinions exist on this question. In Rogers' opinion, federal programs that explicitly require funded religious organizations to forego discriminatory hiring practices should trump the exemptions of Title VII. Unsurprisingly, the Bush White House reached the opposite conclusion, questioning the legality of congressionally imposed prohibitions on faith-based hiring practices. In 2007, Bush's Office of Legal Council within the Department of Justice concluded that federal statutes prohibiting faith-based hiring were inapplicable to religious groups. The OLC relied upon the Religious Freedom Restoration Act of 1993, which prohibited the government from imposing "substantial burdens" on religious groups and their practices. The memo determined that making funding contingent on hiring restrictions constituted a "substantial burden" upon religious providers, for which government lacked any compelling interest. It resulted in a *Catch-22*—if religious groups could engage in faith-based hiring only by foregoing federal funding, it would hinder their ability to provide needed services. Conversely, if groups could solicit funds only by ceasing faith-based hiring, it would undermine their ability to maintain their religious character and mission.[20]

These are admittedly novel arguments, which have yet to be tested or challenged in court. In addition to the arguments related to the statutory exemption from nondiscrimination laws, there are also potential constitutional objections to religiously based hiring. Indeed, the debate raises profound and complex questions that go directly to the faith-based initiative and the legality of its general intent.

As with the Title VII question, existing case law seems to leave open whether faith-based groups are free under the U.S. Constitution to make religiously-based hiring decisions, since the U.S. Supreme Court has yet to engage the issue directly. This has not stopped commentators from asserting that the religious exemption to nondiscrimination requirements should constitute a violation of the first amendment. Rogers, for example, marshals an impressive argument based upon policy considerations, historical and legal precedent, and overarching constitutional values in concluding that the Title VII hiring clause for religious groups receiving public funds should be a violation of the establishment clause.[21] The argument is straightforward; public funding of religious groups who in turn engage in religiously based hiring inevitably have the effect of advancing the particular faith of that group. Moreover, a reasonable observer would likely view the fact that only religious groups have an exemption from nondiscrimination in hiring as a general government endorsement of religion. Hence an allowance for religiously based hiring fails the constitutional standard of neutral, equal-handed treatment of religious and nonreligious actors alike.

But other aspects of the first amendment also are implicated by the debate over hiring rights, such as the *free exercise of religion*. The matter of hiring rights undoubtedly opens up unanswered questions regarding what constitutes a collective exercise of religion. In short, does the provision of social services by a religious nonprofit qualify as a religious exercise, so as to trigger the protective umbrella of the free exercise side of the first amendment religion clauses? Does free exercise include collective social action that is not religious per se, even when those engaging in it believe it to be biblically mandated? And if collective social action is in fact a form of religious exercise, does it merit constitutional protection even when it occurs with the support of public money?

Defenders of the hiring rights of religious social service providers contend that collective action in the form of social service is at the center of the faith for many. Without tangible social activism as evidence of their belief, their faith seems empty to them. And to deny them the benefits of public dollars to assist in their social outreach is to undercut their ability to maximize this form of religious exercise. While this is a convincing argument, it does run counter to the overwhelmingly individualistic nature of rights-based jurisprudence that has dominated in the United States.

A second underlying question is the extent to which the first amendment *freedom of association* is implicated by attempts to strip religious groups of their freedom to choose who they ultimately hire as employees. The first amendment offers some constitutional protection to those who wish to associate with others of shared commitment or interest, whether a political party, social group, private civic organization, or religious denomination. The fundamental question is whether the right of association applies to a religious group—acting with the aid of public funding—who uses the hiring policy to shape its association in ways that may affect its delivery of service.

In sum, the constitutionality of the hiring policy generates a swirl of first amendment arguments, most of which are largely untested. How the Court as currently constituted would decide the issue and on what grounds is a matter of significant uncertainly. In the end, very few firm conclusions can be drawn about either the statutory or constitutional viability of the hiring right.

Devolving Faith-Based Policy, Devolving Law

Finally, considerations of *federalism* further complicate the debate over the legality of religious nonprofits' personnel decisions based upon the applicant's religion. In addition to the U.S. Constitution and federal legislation, most states have their own legal and constitutional frameworks for addressing religion and faith-based practices. An open question is the degree to which these may also impact the validity of programs that receive benefits from funding at the state and lower levels of government. Consequently, Obama's policy decisions in the faith-based realm, while important, are by no means definitive for the universe of faith-based social service delivery.

Indeed, much of the recent contentiousness over the hiring issue has involved debates at the state rather than federal level. In 2008, a highly public battle was waged in Colorado over a proposed bill to prevent faith-based groups that receive public money from basing their hiring decisions on applicants' beliefs. The previous year Colorado had passed a law outlawing discrimination in hiring based upon sexual orientation or religion, but that law exempted religious and nonprofit organizations. The more recent legislative proposal—which sought to eliminate that exemption—eventually stalled when an array of religious leaders complained that, if passed, it would force them to end their participation in government-funded social service delivery.[22] A similar battle was waged in California after it passed a law in 2007 mandating that all groups receiving government aid—including religious ones—must abide by the state's nondiscrimination policies, without exemption.[23] An attempt the following year to reverse that law led to spirited debate before eventually going down in defeat.

These local battles suggest that the controversy over faith-based hiring is alive and well, even outside the federal arena. This is due in no small part to the extent to which faith-based social delivery has devolved to the lower levels of government in the past nine years. Indeed, this is one of the biggest untold stories of the faith-based movement. While first conceived primarily as a federal policy, the faith-based initiative succeeded in leading a striking expansion of church-state collaboration at the state and local levels. The extent to which faith-based policies have seeped down to, and been absorbed by, states and localities is nothing short of remarkable, as the following show:

- *State legislation*: Between 2003 and 2005, twenty-seven states passed legislation encouraging greater partnerships between states and faith-based organizations.

- *Administrative action*: In that same time frame, twenty-eight states significantly altered state rules and regulations to encourage greater faith-based governmental partnerships. This included creating faith-based offices, hosting summits with a faith-based focus, easing regulatory burdens on faith-based actors, and more.

- *State liaisons*. By 2005 thirty-two states had a designated person or office with official responsibility for connecting state social services to faith-based groups.

In addition to this, many mid-sized and large cities also have created similar offices and launched similar efforts in the faith-based social service area. In sum, the train of faith-based services clearly has already left the station. Obama may be wise to hop on board, although it is not likely that he will easily control many aspects of this train's journey.

The laws governing these lower-level collaborations are as diverse as the programs themselves. A crazy-quilt patchwork of legal, regulatory, and constitutional provisions at the state level are likely to impact those programs that are funded in whole or part by states and localities. Most states have their own state constitutions with clauses regulating the interplay between state government and religious institutions. Many of these clauses—known as Blaine amendments—take a strict approach in prohibiting any public funds to religious groups. Some explicitly include the social services arena. Others are more permissive of financial support for religious entities, while still others simply mirror the religion clauses of the U.S. Constitution.[24]

In addition, virtually every state has its own civil rights laws, with many of these placing restrictions on hiring on the basis of religion. Likewise, a substantial number of cities have their own civil rights and non-discrimination ordinances. Virtually every state has legislatively created employment discrimination norms. Also, the vast majority of those states have carved out exemptions for faith-based organizations from state laws prohibiting religious discrimination in employment decisions. Of those states, eighteen explicitly provide that faith-based groups entering into contracts with the state do not retain that exemption. In other words, the legal picture is complicated by state laws, which are as varied as the states in which they originate.

The point here is that too much emphasis can be placed on the president's policy edicts on the FBI and the hiring issue at the federal level. Ultimately, the mushrooming of faith-based policy at the state and local level may end up determining the legal status of church-state partnerships. Indeed this may be a desirable development, given the significant differences in implementation that exist in faith-based policy across, and even within, states.[25] Not everyone agrees with this analysis. Dr. DeForest Soaries, pastor of First Baptist Church of Lincoln Gardens (Somerset, New Jersey) and former New Jersey Secretary of State, contends that the signals from the White House continue to set the tone for real faith-based policy progress. He sees little or no evidence of genuine faith-based policy implementation during the Obama administration's first two years. At the same time, Soaries attributed this in no small part to the host of pressing policy crises that dominated the administration's efforts and attention. [26]

The Hiring Issue from the Perspective of Black Churches

What the unsettled status of the hiring issue means for black churches and religious leaders otherwise inclined to enter into partnerships with the government is unclear. Undoubtedly, the portrayal of religiously-based hiring as discriminatory resonates with blacks, particularly among government elites and the traditional black civil rights leadership. The Congressional Black Caucus (CBC) was an early and persistent opponent of charitable choice and of Bush's faith-based initiative. The CBC even hosted conferences on the subject, one entitled "Charitable Choice: A New Threat to Civil Rights." Likewise the NAACP actively opposed the hiring provisions of charitable choice.[27]

How widely those views have been shared by average black citizens is much less clear. Historically there has been a close relationship between black churches and leading civil rights organizations, so black clergy might be expected to respond to cues from the NAACP on the hiring issue. Virtually no empirical work exists that measures the extent to which antidiscrimination sentiments of black elites are shared by average citizens, particularly within black religious communities. A potentially significant factor for black public opinion on the hiring issue is that much of the opposition to religiously based hiring targets the employment rights of gays and lesbians. A strong undercurrent in the entire debate over religiously based hiring is the contention that it is essentially cover for discrimination against gays and lesbians. Admittedly, conservative and orthodox faiths and denominations may well have a strong doctrinal aversion to hiring gays even within the social service arms of their denomination. Moreover, many blacks balk at equating discrimination based upon skin color with that based upon sexual practices or orientation. Furthermore, blacks tend to be quite conservative on the issue of gay rights. Finally, one would expect that the degree of conservative resistance to gay hiring rights would be even greater among those blacks who are deeply religious or are regular church goers.

Several high-profile black clergy interviewed for this essay tended to take a pragmatic approach to the issue of faith-based hiring rights. To Dr. Soaries of First Baptist Church of Lincoln Gardens, the question is a simple one—"where public funds are used, public standards have to be applied."[28] That is, publicly subsidized churches and religious nonprofits ought to abide by applicable nondiscrimination laws. Bishop Harold Ray of Redeemer Life Fellowship Church in Florida and a pioneer of the faith-based movement, sees the issue mostly as a distraction. He takes what he calls a corporate approach. Rather than obsess about religious compatibility, he looks for those potential employees who acknowledge the vision of the organization and are able to buy into it. In short, "do they believe in the product?"[29]

Obama's Faith-Based Initiative and Black Churches

Notwithstanding the legal uncertainties surrounding the hiring autonomy of publicly-funded religious organizations, faith-based social service collaborations under the Obama administration are likely to receive a close look from black congregations. Since the enactment of charitable choice, the reactions of black religious and political leaders to faith-based services delivery have been ambivalent, ranging from skepticism to guarded enthusiasm. For a variety of reasons, black churches have had a complicated relationship with contemporary advocates of government-faith sector partnerships.

To the extent they were aware of the charitable choice in 1996, black clergy were deeply skeptical of it. Even though the law sought to ease the legal path to government-faith sector partnerships, any benefits those provisions might have held out for black congregations were largely obscured by the fact that they were embedded in welfare reforms seen as punitive toward poor blacks. Many saw in welfare reform legislation a culmination of two decades of devolutionary politics that had shrunk governmental support for a broad range of social service programs of particular importance to lower-income minorities. The charitable choice law was protested as a thinly veiled effort to diminish the government's financial obligation to the poor, while shifting the onus for responding to poverty onto already overburdened churches and religious nonprofits.

When President Bush expanded and enlarged faith-based social services in 2001, one hope was that it would mobilize conservative black clergy support for the initiative and for a broader conservative agenda. He held high-profile meetings with black leaders, including a faith summit on Capitol Hill featuring a number of black conservative and megachurch leaders. Throughout his presidency, Bush continued to tout faith-based social service delivery as a way of empowering black churches to bring badly needed social services to their communities.[30]

Bush's outreach to black churches and clergy seemed logical as a matter of substantive policy. First, blacks have exhibited levels of religiosity unmatched by other demographic or ethnic groups.[31] Black churches have remained relatively strong even in neighborhoods where other social and economic institutions have eroded or fled. Moreover, the work of black churches often extends well beyond the spiritual to include many social ministries. Surveys confirm a strong orientation among black churches toward social services and community outreach;[32] they are more likely than their white counterparts to provide tangible aid to the poor.[33] Also, as a relatively stable institution in poorer urban communities, black churches have a demonstrated capacity for reinforcing community within these contexts in ways exceeding the ability of state and secular providers.[34] For the same reason, hard-to-reach populations, which may harbor deep distrust of the state or other outside organizations, may be more accepting and likely to avail themselves of services from the church down the street.[35] As Bishop Ray put it, "no one [besides black churches and their pastors] has a bigger day to day connection to the populations that are in dire need" of the programs government has to offer.[36]

Lastly, black clergy and churches have evidenced a relatively strong inclination toward working in collaboration with government to serve the poor. A National Congregational Study in 1999 found black churches far more open than white churches to seeking public support for their social service activities. In sum, these factors suggested a confluence of potential, opportunity, and interest between the Bush proposal and the orientation of many black churches.[37]

Bush administration collaborations with black churches failed to materialize for a host of political reasons. One simply had to do with the way in which Bush took office, and the questions surrounding the presidential election of 2000. The combination of record African American voter turnout in Florida, questions involving widespread ballot disqualification, and the narrowness of the result led many blacks to harbor serious reservations about the legitimacy of Bush's victory. Widespread resentment toward Bush persisted among many African Americans long after the conclusion of the election.

The rollout of the Bush plan also prompted many to suspect that the true objective was to use the program for political and partisan purposes, in hopes of attracting greater support among black voters from whom Bush received less than 10 percent support in 2000.[38] Bush's efforts to gain black support undoubtedly suffered from his close association with conservative Republicanism, and by perceptions of the faith-based initiative as a ploy to shrink governmental commitment to the poor while increasing the faith sector's responsibility for poverty issues. The Bush plan did little to bolster federal spending on social services to the poor, leading many to conclude that the faith-based plan was more about cutting these social services than enhancing them.

There also were philosophical differences among black religious leaders over the wisdom of aligning churches too closely with the state. That churches had so often served as a political catalyst on issues of concerns to blacks raised a genuine concern that partnering with the state would undermine their ability to speak boldly and clearly to condemn ongoing injustices impacting black people.[39] There was a very real fear that faith-based programs would prove to be the modern form of political patronage, with funds dispensed to individual religious leaders in exchange for their political support, acquiescence, or silence.[40]

There is evidence, however, that the above factors may present fewer obstacles to black church participation in government-funded programs than was earlier believed. Consider the following findings in a study on black churches and the faith-based initiative conducted by the Joint Center for Political and Economic Studies in 2006:

- As of 2006 (the midpoint of Bush's second term), most of the 750 black pastors surveyed expressed a positive view of the faith-based initiative (59 percent had a positive view compared to only 20 percent with a negative view). Most ministers who discussed the faith-based initiative with their parishioners concluded that the congregations favored the initiative (72 percent generally supportive versus only 14 percent voicing opposition).

- Only small percentages of clergy respondents expressed suspicions of political motives underlying the faith-based initiative.

- A majority of pastors indicated their churches were interested in taking part in the faith-based initiative. Interest was strongest among large urban churches, those with progressive theology, and socially liberal congregations.

Notwithstanding these favorable indicators, the primary reasons given by clergy respondents for hesitancy toward the faith-based initiative were concerns that the government was shifting its responsibilities onto the religious sector, that government would become overly intrusive in their work, and the potential for church-state conflicts. A significant concern for 44 percent of clergy respondents was that involvement with the government would compromise their independence or prophetic voice.[41]

Overall, then, these findings suggest real potential for President Obama to tap black churches as potential partners in the domestic social service arena. Given the largely positive perceptions of, and interest in, the faith-based initiative among black clergy and their congregants, depictions of black clergy wariness of the faith-based initiative as a political ploy appear exaggerated. As the Joint Center study concluded, "[t]here was surprisingly little cynicism about who was receiving FBCI grants. . . ." Surely that cynicism would be even less involving programs at the behest of a friendlier political figure. To put it concisely, ". . . most black churches have an interest in participating [in the FBCI], have a variety of social service programs in place, and would seem capable of participating in the program."[42]

The modest results in attracting black church participation in the initiative appear to be largely due to lack of information and outreach. Only one in three pastors had a familiarity with the details of the faith-based initiative, which suggests that the lack of participation by black churches could be overcome with aggressive outreach and information-sharing efforts. Presumably, a black president with training as a community organizer and a personal faith experience shaped largely in a black church is well positioned to improve upon the outreach and information efforts of his predecessor.

The one clear note of foreboding in the Joint Center survey was the level of anxiety among churches that partnering with government might impinge on their freedom to pursue their own moral, social, and political agendas. Almost half the clergy respondents expressed fears that having the government as collaborator would come at the expense of their prophetic voice and their ability to address injustices that impact their congregants. Such concerns may be eased with the Obama administration by virtue of his popularity among African Americans. But threats to the prophetic role of the church will not necessarily evaporate with an Obama administration; if anything, the potential for political co-optation may be greater from a president whose standing is so strong among African Americans. Obama's popularity with fellow blacks may prevent them from holding him accountable on issues of central importance to black communities. Too cozy a relationship with government, even under this president, may result in the loss of the prophetic capacity of the black church.

Tempering Expectations

Several interviews conducted for this article indicate the need for some tempering of expectations of a new era of collaboration between black churches and the Obama administration's faith-based office. While hardly a cross section of black religious leadership, the interviews raise real challenges to the notion that black church support for the president's faith-based policy is somehow inevitable.

   Dr. Soaries, a person with extensive involvements in politics as New Jersey secretary of state and in faith-based policy, drafted a white paper upon which New Jersey's faith-based statute was based. Nevertheless, Dr. Soaries' views on faith-based programs under Obama are hardly bullish. Despite once being an enthusiastic backer of faith-based collaboration, Soaries is deeply skeptical of such partnerships. Characterizing the faith-based initiative as completely politicized under both Bush and Obama, Soaries has concluded that publicly funded faith-based social services are sure to suffer a "perversion of politics."

   Soaries identifies several key contributors to the downfall of government-religious sector partnerships. One is the inevitability of church-state challenges, regardless of the actual state of the law or the details of the particular program. This makes it difficult to realize the actual benefits or genuine potential that Soaries sees in such partnerships. Soaries also is critical of black churches generally, which he sees as emulating one of two models in their pursuit of government funds. Some exhibit an *entitlement* mindset, in which they seem simply to want a check and to be free to do with it as they please. Others are of the *protest* variety, intent on confronting government or taking on an antagonistic relationship to it. They would rather castigate public education than sponsor a charter alternative; they prefer to decry a racist correctional system than come up with a plan for going in and improving prison life. Whether they are of the entitlement

or protest variety, Soaries sees little evidence of pastors or churches genu-
inely seeking to address deep social problems as effectively as possible.
As a result, Soaries has essentially given up on faith-based partnerships,
preferring instead an entrepreneurial model with an emphasis wholly on
the private sector and free of church/state constraints or considerations.[43]

Bishop Ray of Redeemer Life Fellowship is hardly more optimis-
tic, albeit for different reasons. Ray ran a faith-based center even before
the policy became a central plank of the Bush administration. He sees
the faith-based office under Obama to date as primarily one of missed
opportunity. To Ray, the key to successful collaboration between government and the religious sector is reaching out and connecting to faith-
based leadership. Thus far, he sees little evidence of such outreach by the
administration. For example, Ray was on Obama's e-mail and text list
for campaign updates and mobilization efforts; he continues to receive
regular text messages exhorting the list to support the president on various legislative issues. Yet, Ray views it almost as "a form of malpractice"
that the same data base has not been used by the administration to make
connections and conduct outreach for the faith-based office.

Ray is surprised that, with his faith-based background, he hasn't
been contacted by the administration. He has not seen, or at least not been
privy to, any "national action plan that will really engage the communities
of faith that can be monitored and assessed with targeted outcomes." He is
quick to acknowledge that the administration has had a full plate since it
took office, and that its inattention to faith-based policy is understandable
politically. Nevertheless, he characterizes the faith-based efforts to date,
or rather the lack thereof, as a failed realization of opportunity bordering on tragedy. While not quite ready to concede defeat, Ray asserts that
"without a more transcendent leadership and a commitment in priorities,"
the faith-based office is unlikely to make much of a difference.[44]

Final Reflections

Obama's decision to move forward with a faith-based program, while
leaving the hiring decision unresolved, seems like a deeply pragmatic, and
ultimately wise, decision. From a legal standpoint, his moderate position is
most reflective of the ambiguous state of the law on the question. Obama
deserves much credit for refusing simply to opt for the easy choice of
constricting hiring rights, as desired by most of his political supporters.

The decision also reflects political savvy by making the best of a peril-
ous conundrum in which the sides are clearly drawn and starkly polarized.
Obama runs a risk of alienating many of his supports who were wary of the

faith-based initiative from the outset and who would rather see no initiative whatsoever. The heavily pluralistic slant of the policy, in terms of both its substance and the makeup of its advisory council, should ease much of the animus that many among the left held toward Bush's faith-based initiative. While civil rights organizations such as the ACLU, Americans United for the Separation of Church and State, or People for the American Way are surely disappointed with Obama's stance on the hiring issue, the policy takes pains to offer appropriate assurances that the plan will not exist merely to serve religious ends or the Democrats' electoral aims.

Meanwhile, the policy serves as tangible evidence of Obama's efforts to demonstrate his genuine sympathy for the public dimension of faith and his respect for adherents of faith across the spectrum. While on the campaign trail, Obama was intent on shattering the stereotype of Democrats as hostile to faith, and the initiative reflects his easy comfort with the language of faith and with religious cultures and constituencies. Also, Obama assiduously courted evangelical voters during the campaign, and while he garnered relatively small electoral support from them, he clearly has not abandoned hopes of making inroads with them. The middle ground he has staked out attempts to avoid unnecessarily alienating evangelicals.

The conflict over hiring rights may be one that exists mainly in theory because it is unclear that religiously-based hiring is widespread or that there have been many actual situations where there was a refusal to hire the most qualified person because of religion. Where social services are most needed—in poor, largely minority, urban neighborhoods—it may be that black churches and social service providers have been less interested in hiring along religious lines than in taking whoever can do heavy lifting in serving these badly impoverished neighborhoods. But it appears there might be significant fallout if Obama were to impose a rigid, absolutist ban on faith-based hiring. For many religious organizations, it is imperative to preserve their religious identity and character, an important piece of which is their ability to hire people whose beliefs align with the organization's religious mission. They fully believe that their religious core will be compromised if they cannot hire people who share their faith, who understand and are committed to their mission, and whose desire to serve grows out of that common religious commitment.[45] The possible impact on the fight against poverty and other social ills might be substantial if religious organizations receiving public funds were to lose their right to make personnel decisions that ensure compatibility with their religious mission and identity.[46] One need only look at the reach of the Catholic Church's social services, hospitals, schools, and other enterprises to sense the trouble that could arise if faith-based providers were forced to choose between taking government funding and retaining their religious intentionality.[47]

The provision of social services to populations in need is likely to be achieved most effectively by utilizing community institutions best situated to access difficult to reach constituencies. Channeling social services through black churches is simply an acknowledgment that they are uniquely situated to get government benefits into the hands of socially distressed persons who need these benefits. Participating in the faith-based initiative would be a means of expanding the important social service contributions black churches are already making. Of 750 black churches surveyed nationwide in 2006, 93 percent of them reported having a social outreach ministry—youth and senior programs, food and clothing banks, prison ministries, health care, after school and mentoring programs, substance abuse treatment, housing, and more.[48] Meanwhile the litany of social ills that plague inner-city blacks are well known: sky high prison incarceration rates, depressingly low high school graduation rates, nearly two-thirds of children born out-of-wedlock, and unemployment rates significantly higher and median income levels significantly lower than other demographic groups. In sum, faith-based partnerships between black churches and the state may be a policy collaboration borne out of necessity. Their presence and existing social service structure means urban black churches are likely the last best hope for serving persons struggling against some of society's most debilitating social conditions.

At the same time, the dangers of church/state collaboration are most acute in the case of black churches. Long a prophetic voice pricking the conscience of the state on behalf of a dispossessed minority, the political activism and moral authority of the black church will be challenged by too close a relationship with the government. Public funding of black congregations increases the risk that the state will limit the ability of black churches to protest and object to government action or inaction.[49] A classic justification of the need for an intermediate civil society sector is that it acts as a buffer between citizens and government where citizen concerns can be pursued with a degree of independence from the overbearing state.

In the final analysis, black churches perhaps have the most to gain and to lose from partnering with the state. Therefore, it is important to enter into such collaborative arrangements with eyes wide open to the political and legal realities. An effective balance is difficult to strike between legislative or political advocacy and the pursuit of social change through services made possible by government. Black church appeals for justice must be combined with proactive cooperation with government in implementing policy. Only then will black congregations be able to reconcile the social services and prophetic dimensions of their identity.

Notes

1. The controversial 1996 welfare reform legislation signed into law by President Bill Clinton contained a "charitable choice" provision which was the precursor to the FBI. It specified that religious groups deserved equal consideration for federal grants and contracts, without having to purge themselves of their religious character to receive such consideration.

2. David A. Bositis, *Black Churches and the Faith-Based Initiative: Findings from a National Survey* (Washington DC: Joint Center for Political and Economic Studies, 2006), 1.

3. Frank A. Pryor III and David K. Ryden, "Serving the Inner City: Social Programs in Black Churches" in *Sanctioning Religion? Politics, Law, and Faith-Based Public Services.* David K. Ryden and Jeffrey Polet, eds. (Boulder, CO: Lynne Rienner Publishers, 2005), 130. Eventually Bush's efforts to infuse the federal government with faith-friendly grant making policies and procedures would result in there being a total of twelve such faith-based satellite offices spread throughout the federal bureaucracy.

4. David K. Ryden and Jeffry Polet, "Faith-Based Initiatives in the Limelight" in *Sanctioning Religion? Politics, Law, and Faith-Based Public Services*, David K. Ryden and Jeffrey Polet, eds. (Boulder, CO: Lynne Rienner Publishers, 2005), 3–4.

5. *Innovations* in Compassion: The Faith-Based and Community Initiative: A Final Report to the Armies of Compassion. The White House, December 2008.

6. See e.g., the congressional debate in 2008 over the reauthorization of the Workplace Investment Act.

7. The appointment of DuBois as director of the faith-based office was criticized by some as a politically motivated effort to reach out to those evangelical Christians whom the president spent some time wooing during the campaign. More recently, the president's naming of several high-profile evangelicals to his Faith-Based Advisory Council again drew protestations of ulterior political motives. One of the selections was Leith Anderson, president of the National Association of Evangelicals, the other Lynn Hybels, the spouse of Bill Hybels of the highly influential Chicago area megachurch, Willow Creek. Jim Towey, the second director of the Faith-Based Office under President Bush, has also charged President Obama with politicizing his faith-based initiative by urging religious and clergy supporters for such political purposes as hawking the health care legislation. See, Jim Towey, "Pastors for ObamaCare?" *Wall Street Journal*, September 25, 2010. http://online.wsj.com/article/SB100014240527487045236045 75511920142932674.html. Accessed February 27, 2011.

8. The Pew Forum on Religion & Public Life, "More Americans Question Religion's Role in Politics," 21 August 2008. http://perforum.org/docs/?DocID=340. Accessed February 9, 2010.

9. Melissa Rogers, "Federal Funding and Religion-Based Employment Decisions," in *Sanctioning Religion? Politics, Law, and Faith-Based Public Services.* David K. Ryden and Jeffrey Polet, eds. (Boulder, CO: Lynne Rienner Publishers, 2005), 105.

10. See generally Ira C. Lupu and Robert W. Tuttle, *The State of the Law 2008: A Cumulative Report on Legal Developments Affecting Government Partnerships with Faith-Based Organizations*. http://religionandsocialpolicy.org/docs/legal/state_of_the_law_2008.pdf. Accessed February 9, 2010; see also Rogers, 2005.

11. Rogers, 2005: 119.

12. The Pew Forum on Religion & Public Life, "Hiring Law for Groups Following a Higher Law: Faith-Based Hiring and the Obama Administration," 30 January, 2009. http://pewforum.org/events/?EventID211. Accessed February 9, 2010.

13. The original exemption applied only to "religiously significant" jobs. Congress expanded the exemption in 1972 for religious groups engaging in faith-based hiring for any job ("Hiring Law for Groups").

14. Jeffrey Polet and David K. Ryden, "Religion, the Constitution, and Charitable Choice" in *Sanctioning Religion? Politics, Law, and Faith-Based Public Services*, (Boulder, CO: Lynne Rienner Publishers, 2005), 192.

15. Rogers, 2005: 110–111.

16. Polet and Ryden, 2005: 193.

17. An array of policy arguments have been invoked for both sides. For a representative statement of those views in opposition to the exemption, see Rogers. Esbeck, Carlson-Thies, and Sider (2004) do a thorough job of articulating the policy arguments on the other side.

18. Rogers, 2005: 110.

19. See also the statements of John Dilulio, the first director of George W. Bush's WHOFCI who also is an enthusiastic supporter of Obama's faith-based plan. He reaches a definitive conclusion that the Title VII exemption for religious nonprofits is absolute. That is, it protects faith-identified groups who take religion into account in hiring even for social service operations funded with tax dollars. He does add the caveat that "[a]ll tax-funded work must be and be deemed purely secular in nature" (Dilulio).

20. The Pew Forum on Religion & Public Life, "30 January 2009.

21. Polet and Ryden, 2005: 193.

22. Anne Farris, "Colorado Leaders Join Religious Hiring Rights Debate," *The Roundtable on Religion and Social Welfare Policy*, February 19, 2008. http://www.religionandsocialpolicy.org/news/article_print.cfm?id=7772. Accessed February 20, 2008.

23. Farris, 2008.

24. David K. Ryden, "The Relevance of State Constitutions to Issues of Government and Religion" in *Church-State Issues in America Today: Religion and Government*, eds. Ann W. Duncan and Steven L. Jones, (Westport, CT: Praeger Perspectives, 2008), 229.

25. Ibid.

26. DeForest Soaries telephone interview with author, February 4, 2011.

27. Ryden, 2008: 259–260.

28. Soaries interview.

29. Harold Calvin Ray (senior pastor, Redemptive Life Fellowship Church). Telephone interview with David K. Ryden, February 2, 2011.

30. Pryor and Ryden, 2005: 131.

31. George Gallup, Jr., and D. Michael Lindsay, *Surveying the Religious Landscape: Trends in U.S. Beliefs* (Harrisburg, PA: Morehouse Group, 2000), 53.

32. C. Eric Lincoln, and Lawrence H. Mamiya, *The Black Church in the African American Experience*, (Durham: Duke University Press, 1990); Michael Leo Owens, *Sectarian Institutions in State Welfare Reforms: An Analysis of Charitable Choice* (New York: Rockefeller Institute of Government, 2000); Bositis, 2006.

33. Mark Chaves, "Religious Congregations and Welfare Reform: Who Will Take Advantage of 'Charitable Choice,'" *American Sociological Review*, 64 (1999), 836–846.

34. Sheila Kennedy has done extensive empirical research on this question, and should be consulted for a fuller and sometimes contrary view. See generally Sheila Suess Kennedy and Wolfgang Bielefeld. *Charitable Choice at Work: Faith-Based Job Programs in the State* (Washington, DC: Georgetown University Press, 2006). See also Sheila Suess Kennedy, "Government Shekels and Government Shackles Revisited: Questions for Church and State," in *Exploring Black Philanthropy: New Directions for Philanthropic Fundraising*, No. 48, Patrick Rooney, and Lois Sherman, eds. (Jossey-Bass, 2005).

35. Pryor and Ryden, 2005: 132.

36. Ray interview.

37. Barbara Williams-Skinner, "Will President Obama's New Faith-based Initiative Support or Silence the Black Church?" *Los Angeles Wave*, March 27, 2009. http://www.wavenewspapers.com/opinion/op-ed/41986752.html. Accessed February 27, 2011.

38. Bishop Harold Calvin Ray hosted a faith-based summit early in the Bush administration's first term, an event that some opponents of faith-based legislative proposals pointed to as evidence of the ulterior motives of the administration. When interviewed for this article, Ray denied that the Bush administration was politically motivated by the goal of greater black support, and stated that he saw absolutely no evidence of such ulterior motives. Ray likewise defends the Obama administration from some charges that the objectives underlying its extension of the faith-based initiative are driven by politics. (Harold Calvin Ray telephone interview with author, February 2, 2011).

39. Pryor and Ryden, 2005: 133. That prophetic voice of opposition had been on display during the debate surrounding charitable choice provisions back in 1996. The Congressional Black Caucus, the NAACP, and black religious leaders vociferously opposed charitable choice on grounds that it was attached to an inherently unjust welfare bill.

40. Pryor and Ryden, 2005: 134.

41. Bositis, 2006: 6, 8–9, 16

42. Bositis, op cit. Bositis concludes that this potential needs to be harnessed through technical information on grant application training, legal advice, program evaluation, and better access to public policy information. Page 6.

43. Soaries interview.
44. Ray interview.
45. Ryden and Polet, 2005: 86.
46. There still are a range of moves that the Obama administration could pursue on the statutory handling of religiously based hiring. Those include (1) pursing the status quo by adopting the Bush OLC's memorandum supporting the religious hiring exemption, (2) lobbying Congress to repeal all charitable choice provisions, and (3) issuing its own executive orders where the statute is silent on the question of funding religiously-based hiring. Each of these carries its own political pitfalls, whether it's causing serious heartburn to many congressional Democrats and among the liberal blocs in his corner, alienating religious conservatives who Obama hopes to woo, or putting the outcome in the hands of a Congress stuck in a stalemate for years over the hiring issue. Moreover, the peril of litigation exists around more than one corner depending on what option the administration pursues.
47. Ryden and Polet, 2005: 87–88.
48. Bositis, 7
49. Ryden and Polet, 2005: 126

Prevailing Boundaries of
Social Difference

12

Black Church Burnings in the 1990s and Faith-Based Responses

Katie Day

Four decades after the beginnings of the mid-twentieth-century Civil Rights Movement, there were echoes both of oppression and activism as the United States again had to confront manifestations of racism—specifically racial hatred against faith communities—and public challenges to this hatred. In the spring and summer of 1996, African American churches were headlining the news as they fell victim to a new wave of arsons and bombings. Television news reports carried dramatic images of churches engulfed in flames. Morning papers carried stories of devastated church members standing around the smoldering remains of their beloved sacred spaces. Heartbroken, they remembered how they had been nurtured in these, often small, houses of worship by the faithful members who were their extended families. They would recount how their grandparents had been married there, their parents baptized there, and their loved ones "funeralized" at what was now a pyre of smoking ashes.

As these witnesses were also painfully aware, the burning of black churches was not a new phenomenon. Historically serving as the heart of African American communities, churches had long been targeted by those motivated by racial hatred. During both Reconstruction and the later Civil Rights Movement, the betterment of African Americans had prompted well-intentioned white Northerners to journey South to aid in that struggle. It had also triggered white backlash, one expression of which was torching black churches. This was not the first time burned churches had been the subject of shocking national news. In 1963, the bombing of the 16th Street Baptist Church in Birmingham, Alabama, by white racists had left four little girls dead. The following year, three northern college students were kidnapped and murdered on their way to investigate a recent church burning in Neshoba County, Mississippi. Over forty black churches had been burned or bombed during that period.

For many African Americans—particularly those in the South— this third wave of violence seemed eerily familiar. What was surprising, however, was the sudden public attention. While victimized by arson for generations, this time, it seemed, the whole world was watching. Had the media just discovered a troubling undercurrent of hate crimes that had always been part of the fabric of race relations, or was something else going on here? It was difficult to discern whether the spike in incidents being reported so widely in the media could be attributed to a fresh wave of violence or to better accounting. Documenting the church fires in the last decade of the century was not only a challenge but became a contested process. There was no reliable baseline of data on attacks on black churches prior to 1995, when the federal government began monitoring church arsons in earnest. According to their statistics[1] there was a noticeable up-tick in 1996. They documented 52 incidents of attempted arson or bombings against houses of worship in 1995. The following year the number of cases they investigated jumped to 297. Of these, a disproportionate number were African American (120, or 40.4 percent). Black churches in the South accounted for 30 percent of all church attack incidents that year. Given that African American congregations comprise only 18 percent of all congregations in the country, they were more than twice as likely to be targeted for attack.

It should be noted that these numbers were considered unreliably low by other organizations monitoring the trends (particularly the National Coalition of Burned Churches based in Charleston, SC).[2] The federal data had also been criticized internally, mainly because the mechanism for reporting attacks against houses of worship is not reliable across the board. Some locales were connected to the central reporting system; others were not. There were a number of known burned churches that do not show up on the annual report of the National Church Arson Task Force, for example. Despite the problems with statistics, it was widely assumed that the official numbers did reflect the general geography of the trends, albeit lower. In 2000, after six years of interventions (which will be described later), attacks on houses of worship under federal investigation had fallen to 130, well above the 52 first documented. Although acts of hatred against black churches persist, the reporters have long since left and public attention shifted.

In the case of church arsons in the 1990s, three sectors worked in parallel and interactive ways to create (and eventually to "uncreate") burning black churches as a public issue. The media, government, and various voluntary organizations (including religious, philanthropic, and independent "watchdog" groups) moved into "perfect storm" positions, putting the problem on the public's agenda so effectively that it spawned an enormous public response. Houses of worship had long been targets, but in the mid-1990's there was a distinctly *racial dimension* to the problem, which tapped into deep historical themes in the culture, fueling its drama and sense of urgency. However, the very racialization of the problem also provided the context in which the problem was finally deconstructed and disappeared from public attention altogether. In other words, race became an ambivalent, but powerful, variable, driving both the construction and the deconstruction of the social problem of burned black churches.

Coalition Building and Policy Action

The story begins with the National Council of Churches (NCC)—not because it was the first player in the drama, but because it was, arguably, the most influential. The ecumenical body is comprised of thirty-five Protestant communions, including seven of the historic African American denominations[3] and several Orthodox bodies. Founded in 1950, its roots run back to the Social Gospel Movement of the nineteenth century. Its predecessor body, the Federal Council of Churches (FCC), was founded in 1908. Throughout the twentieth century the FCC, then-NCC, had the dual function of reflecting and solidifying the centrality of Protestantism in American culture. Mainline Protestant denominations were strong in their public presence, especially around issues of racial justice. They represented the single largest religious group, with over a third of the country affiliated with Protestant churches. With growing membership in their constituent bodies, the NCC could afford to devote significant resources to the effort. Further, they had political capital they could spend, which they did in joining the moral crusade of the Civil Rights Movement

Riding the momentum created by the passage of the Civil Rights Act of 1964, the NCC threw their weight behind Freedom Summer. This project was organized by the Student Nonviolent Coordinating Committee (SNCC) and led by Robert Moses. Students were recruited from northern colleges for a summer in Mississippi to register voters and establish Freedom Schools.[4] Over 1,000 idealistic and overwhelmingly white students participated. The NCC coordinated the orientation for the Freedom Summer volunteers at the Western College for Women in Oxford, Ohio. In addition, they recruited 275 "minister-counselors," who supported the volunteers and provided much-needed pastoral care in what became a stressful summer. By the end of the orientation, the enthusiastic volunteers confronted the sobering realities of Southern racism—three of their number disappeared and were found dead later in the summer. The murders of James Chaney, Andrew Goodman, and Mickey Schwerner served to crystallize the moral vision and resolve of the volunteers, the NCC minister-counselors, and all those who supported their effort.

Riding the momentum into the fall, the NCC kept their focus on Mississippi and instituted the Delta Project. This statewide effort took a more systemic and longer-term approach to civil rights. Having researched the extent of poverty, they developed a strategy to address its causes. Their activities varied from direct relief to community development projects such as organizing Headstart programs and later, economic development projects. They continued with voter registration and education, and also contributed to communications within the civil rights community by starting a news service. Delta even launched an experimental utopian community called Freedom City.[5] Falling short of its vision, as most utopian communities do, they nevertheless built thirty houses for displaced poor farmers before funding dried up. This multifaceted ministry lasted for ten years, reflecting again a theological commitment to letting the world set the agenda for the church. In this phase of their civil rights involvement, the NCC deepened its understanding of their role in social change. Drawing on the writings of martyred theologian Dietrich Bonhoeffer, the Christian organization identified its efforts as "servant ministry."[6] In so doing, they continued to take direction from local African American leaders about where support was most needed in the larger project of bringing justice and equality to people of color in Mississippi.

It was in this time of organizational servanthood that the NCC experienced, in many ways, what became their glory days. To be in the fray, risking life and limb for a moral cause close to their understanding of the Christian faith, was a defining moment for the organization. Mainline Protestantism was experimenting with a new understanding of what it meant to be a church. In moving from the comfort of their armchairs and pulpits to the frontlines of social change, a different ecclesiastical identity was taking shape. These church leaders, mainly of European descent, risked social status in their often-unpopular advocacy for racial justice, and power, as they took direction from leaders in the Civil Rights Movement. Social and cultural capital was spent for the cause, as well as considerable financial capital. Over time, however, there was a decline in its involvement in issues of racial justice. By the time the Delta Ministry folded in 1974, the NCC had largely moved out of its civil rights involvement. A number of factors had contributed to the demise of their involvement:

- Mainline Protestant denominations were no longer enjoying ever-increasing memberships and treasuries. With the declines came cutbacks and a refocusing on denominational survival;

- The Vietnam War had drawn federal resources away from the War on Poverty programs; and

- The struggle for racial justice had lost Martin Luther King, Jr., as its leader, and nonviolence as its strategy for change. Frustrated hopes exploded in the cities and Black Nationalist identity movements pursued separatist goals. The dominant culture grew ambivalent at best toward the cause—and reactionary at the worst; many whites who had supported the Civil Rights Movement grew weary, if not alienated and hostile.

By the mid-1990s, the NCC's racial justice activism had become increasingly distant, and anxieties about the organization's future more pronounced as it approached its 50th anniversary. Then along came the issue of burned black churches. The issue immediately struck a chord with the NCC, resonating with core values and commitments forged during their Civil Rights Movement involvements. The NCC Board had decided to make racial justice its top priority in 1985, committing itself and calling on member communions to "eliminate racism from church structures and to initiate and support efforts to eliminate it from society" for the coming decade.[7] This was an important link between the NCC's focus in the early 1960s and the 1990s.

The NCC, however, was not the only national organization that mobilized in response to the church burnings. In the early-1990s, the liberal watchdog agency Center for Democratic Renewal (formerly the Anti-Klan Network) was among the first to notice an increase in the number of church arsons, particularly African American houses of worship in the South.[8] In 1990 they were aware of four black churches which had been burned around Louisville, Kentucky and in Mississippi. In 1991 and 1992, the number crept up to five per year and the geographical net had widened to include Arkansas and South Carolina as well as continued arsons in the original states. By 1993 there were seven reported arsons in black churches. That number doubled the next year and by 1995 the Center for Democratic Renewal had confirmed that thirty-one African American or integrated congregations around the South had been victims of arson.[9] This is slightly more than the government later confirmed for 1995 (25), their first year of collecting data on church burnings.[10] The

CDR began to connect the dots and sensed that a racist conspiracy might be at work. They contacted the NCC among others, which took on the issue and made it a central organizational focus for the next three years.

The NCC mobilized quickly, through the moral and organizational leadership of Rev. Dr. Mac Charles Jones, a prominent leader in the National Baptist Convention of America and pastor of St. Stephen's Baptist Church in Kansas City, Missouri. He was also on the board of the CDR when he was appointed to be the General Secretary's Associate for Racial Justice in 1995. He was eventually promoted to become the deputy general secretary and director of National Ministries. Rev. Jones was, by all accounts, a compelling leader.

> He was a wonderful motivator; he had a presence that motivated and inspired you . . . He came through as having no self-serving motives of any kind. It was, "This is real. This needs to happen and we need to do something. Now."[11]

Through his participation in the CDR, "Mac" was well aware of the increasing numbers of church arsons, especially among African American churches in the South. He pulled together a meeting in September of 1995 in Birmingham, Alabama which included Sara Coppler (Habitat for Humanity), Joe Hamilton (United Methodist Volunteers in Mission), Rose Johnson (CDR), Rev. Terrence Mackey (Pastor, Mt. Zion Church of Greeleyville, South Carolina which had been burned in June of 1995) and a young African American reporter for USA Today, Gary Fields. Participants at that meeting left feeling that there was something insidious about the rise in burning churches—"This was a major problem, not just an isolated problem."[12]

The issue of burned churches first got national (and even international) media exposure during the Super Bowl of 1996. The late Green Bay Packers player Reggie White, also a minister, spoke in an interview about the arson and bombing of the church he pastored the week before, the Inner City Church, in Knoxville, Tennessee. Local businesses had received leaflets reading, "1996 shall be the year of white triumph and justice for the master supreme race."[13] There was an implication that this was a racially-motivated hate crime and the specter of a conspiracy was raised publicly for the first time. Six other African American churches had been torched in his state in 1995 and three black churches had just been razed in Boligee, Alabama, during the previous three-week period. But it had taken the Packers' defensive lineman to get the attention of the media, and more importantly, the public.

Rev. Jones immediately contacted Reggie White, and a wave began to build. In March, Jones led a delegation to visit White's church, then called on federal law officials to more aggressively investigate that and other attacks on churches. During the spring of 1996 he led a delegation of representatives from the NCC, the Center for Democratic Renewal, and the Center for Constitutional Rights (NY) to several dozen other churches throughout the South which had been victims of arson. They concluded:

> most of these church arsons were the work of hate groups with racist ideologies. . . . Far more churches had been torched than had originally been estimated. Indeed, a veritable epidemic of domestic terrorism was prevalent throughout the South and the Nation as a whole was unaware of this crisis[14]

In the meantime, the NAACP had sent a letter to the Justice Department in February of 1996 asking that they investigate the emerging wave of church arsons. They had copied the letter to *USA Today*, which ended up on the desk of Gary Fields. He immediately contacted the Justice Department and realized that the civil rights organization had more information than the federal government about the phenomenon. So began an aggressive investigation into the phenomenon by a newspaper not known for its investigative reporting. Boosted by journalistic passion, Gary Fields advocated for the story within the paper; he finally received a *carte blanche* and "unlimited resources" were deployed to the story.[15] By the spring of 1996, Fields was heading a group of twenty reporters who combed the South covering the issue. In June of 1996, there was a special four-page report which presented the findings of more than 500 interviews. By October of that year, *USA Today* had run sixty stories on the burned churches, including eleven on the front page. Stories were running in other major papers as well during 1996. However, what was unique about *USA Today*'s coverage is not only the extent of it, but that through their database searches and methodically contacting local fire departments, they were able to provide data to the departments of Justice and Treasury (Alcohol, Tobacco and Firearms, ATF).

The information provided in the print media created *public interest*, but it was the dramatic images of churches engulfed in flames on the nightly televised news that fanned *public outrage*. By June it was the lead story on network news. In just the first two weeks of that month, the major news shows (ABC, CBS, CNN, and NBC) had devoted nearly 45 minutes of evening coverage to the story.[16] All-too-familiar images conjured up painful national memories. Mississippi was burning again. It was difficult not to see in the rash of attacks on black churches an effective, if insidious, conspiracy at work.

Evidence of racist motives was not uncommon at the crime scenes. Racist threats and symbols had been found spray-painted on church walls.

Although arson is a difficult crime to prove (since the evidence is often destroyed) and racial hatred even more difficult to substantiate, there were several well-publicized arrests and convictions of members of hate groups in cases related to attacks on African American churches. Morris Dees of the Southern Poverty Law Center (SPLC) was prosecuting two members of the Christian Knights of the KKK in South Carolina, accused in the burning of Macedonia Baptist Church in Manning, SC. The SPLC prevailed, sending two Klansmen to prison and landing the largest settlement they had had to date in a case—$37.8 million, almost $13 million more than they had requested![17]

Rev. Jones was convinced a racist conspiracy was at work. In his Senate testimony in June of 1996 he stated:

> We in the NCCC are convinced that both the overall climate of racism and the organized hate groups spawned by this climate are primarily responsible for this wave of domestic terrorism. These are not random, disconnected acts carried out by "disturbed" or "deranged" youngsters but rather a systematic campaign of intimidation directed and orchestrated by organized white supremacist groups. These groups are in contact with each other in a national and international network. They are armed, violent and more sophisticated in their tactics than the old-style Ku Klux Klan. Their common denominator is an ideology akin to Hitler's Nazism.[18]

Rev. Jones was not alone in his analysis. The Center for Democratic Renewal had just published a book entitled *The Fourth Wave: A Continuing Conspiracy to Burn Black Churches*[19] in which it had argued that white supremacist groups were striking black churches in an effort to ignite a race war. Rev. Terrance Mackey, an A.M.E. pastor of a burned church in South Carolina and founder of the National Coalition for Burned Churches reported hearing a KKK leader predict the coming race war and the targeting of black churches as their central strategy.[20] African American writer Manning Marable observed the racist logic of such a strategy:

> Being black in America had long since taught us that violence against black folk was "as normal as cherry pie," to paraphrase H. Rap Brown. . . . The African American church has been, since slavery, the central social institution of the black community. It has been the spiritual heart of the black experience, through our long sojourn through this nation. To destroy the black church is to cut out the heart of the black community.[21]

Also, Reggie White was clear in his interviews that he sensed a well-organized campaign of terror was behind the fires. "Until this country starts dealing with *organizations* that do things like this, then we're still going to have problems . . ." he said in an interview published in the *Boston Globe*.[22] In a *New York Times* article appearing on the same day he further explicated his belief that black churches were burning because of an organized effort. "When is America going to stop tolerating these *groups*?"[23] Reggie White was not being paranoid: a few days after the fire, local businesses received menacing leaflets stating, "1996 shall be the year of white triumph and justice for the master supreme race." It went on to say that integrated communities and institutions, as was White's congregation, would not be tolerated.[24]

Others were not so convinced that the church burnings represented such an orchestrated effort, as investigations by media and public officials did not unearth anything like a national map filled with pushpins in a Klavern hall, or even a central database. The *USA Today* stories were dramatic, yet balanced. Despite a sense that evil was afoot, Fields did not find evidence of an organized racist conspiracy and was careful not to give that impression in his articles. (*USA Today* did find evidence of four regional "pockets" of arson, however). Fields wasn't even clear whether there was, in fact, an upsurge in attacks on black churches or whether it had just been discovered by the media and was now being better reported. He had no organizing theory about what was going on—just that churches were burning and, if he could do something that could bring about an end to that, he would.

The specter of a racist conspiracy sparked a national debate. However, lack of evidence did not make the burning of black churches any less insidious. Most social commentators were careful to keep a focused critique on the racism in American society which would allow and even cultivate church burnings without making such statements dependent on criminal evidence of a centralized conspiracy. "Conspiracy" itself was rhetorically enlarged. For example, Noah Chandler of the Center for Democratic Renewal said flatly, "The conspiracy is racism itself."[25] Even so, public statements which even subtly suggested an organized conspiracy by hate groups provoked a backlash which would ultimately contribute to dimming the public spotlight on the issue.

In June of 1996 media coverage was at its peak and the public response was overwhelming. Clearly this issue had hit a nerve with Americans. Financial contributions poured into the NCC—during one two-month period in 1996 they received $7.7 million in financial and in-kind donations.[26] The financial contributions which flowed to address the problem of burned churches were diverse in their sources and the collection was dramatic in its proportion, although the final sum received by the NCC may never be known. Large donations were made not only by their member denominations but by unlikely contributors as well, including: the Olympic Dream Team ($150,000); the American Jewish Committee ($200,000); "New York Undercover," a FOX television series ($13,000); gospel singer Kirk Franklin ($250,000); and the "Queen of Mean," Leona Helmsley ($1.5 million). In addition, major foundations such as Ford, Annenberg, Kellogg, MacArthur, Mott, Andreas, Rockefeller, Robert Wood Johnson, and Pew all sent money to the NCC to support the rebuilding effort and to underwrite their anti-racism community education programs. Thousands of individual contributions poured in, from young and old, religious and secular donors who were moved by the problem. Churches held bake sales, youth groups sponsored walk-a-thons, bikers rode for sponsorship—this rare display of public compassion was spontaneous and creative. Other agencies received money as well. The Lilly Endowment sent $6 million to the Congress for National Black Churches (CNBC) for their oversight in rebuilding fifty churches.

Conservative Christian groups who did not sit at the NCC Board table also pitched in. The Evangelical men's group Promise Keepers raised over $1 million. The predominantly white Christian Coalition also committed itself to raising $1 million. Leader Ralph Reed acknowledged, "the white evangelical church was not only on the sidelines but on the wrong side," of the Civil Rights Movement. In announcing his organization's decision he added, "We come with broken hearts, a repentant spirit and ready hands to fight this senseless violence."[27] Earlier they had offered a $25,000 reward for information leading to the cause of the crimes.[28]

The public not only opened their checkbooks but their datebooks as well. The NCC was swamped with individuals, congregations, and even corporations offering to volunteer to rebuild the burned churches. Despite the fact that they had hired veteran staff from Habitat for Humanity to get volunteer rebuilders to arson sites throughout the rural South (Sara Coppler), the NCC could not accommodate all the volunteers who offered to help. Nevertheless, they did assert by 1997 that they had mobilized over 15,000 volunteers—an amazing number given the devolution of grassroots involvement they had seen in the preceding two decades. Firm numbers are hard to nail down, not only in terms of the money raised but also the number of volunteers who helped rebuild and the number of churches rebuilt. Some of the churches were built with out-of-town volunteers and grants from the NCC or CNBC. Others used local volunteers and had insurance to aid in their rebuilding. The best estimate of churches rebuilt through some use of volunteer labor coordinated through the NCC is 125.

Although the number of new structures was impressive, the total fell short of the number of documented attacks on houses of worship between 1995 and 2000 investigated by the Justice Department.[29]

These were again heady days for the National Council of Churches, bringing a fresh surge of life to the beleaguered organization which had been struggling with its fiscal health, corporate identity, and future. Reversing trends of diminishing resources and downsizing, energetic staff positions were being added and the coffers were flooded. Internally, the NCC created a division to receive donations, research reports of church arson, distribute financial aid, provide technical assistance to victimized churches, and mobilize volunteers for the rebuilding. At the peak, there were seventeen staff members working on the project. In addition, the NCC helped with the organization of ecumenical intermediary agencies which coordinated the rebuilding effort on site and with which they worked closely (including Quaker Workcamps and Interfaith Rebuilding Partnership). They brokered relationships with an expanding number of partners not only within the religious sector, but in the corporate, philanthropic, media, and government sectors as well. Once again the NCC had moved from the sidelines to the limelight, echoing the energy, passion, and relevance they had demonstrated during Freedom Summer.

It was through the efforts of the NCC—especially Mac Jones and General Secretary Joan Brown Campbell—that burned churches moved to the top of the Clinton Administration's agenda. It should also be noted that President Bill Clinton was in the midst of his re-election campaign and there were reasons for making sure the African American vote should not be taken for granted. In May of 1996, there had been a gathering of white police officers in Tennessee called a "Good Ol' Boys Roundup" with blatantly racist overtones. A number of ATF agents had been in attendance, resulting in sharp criticism from black leaders and contributing to the distance and distrust felt by African Americans toward federal law enforcement agencies.

Also in May (and again in June) of 1996, Rev. Jones testified before the House Judiciary Committee about the recent wave of church fires, including how offended many of the pastors felt by their treatment at the hands of federal investigators. In early June, the NCC convened a meeting in Washington of thirty-eight pastors of victimized churches. President Clinton, Attorney General Janet Reno and members of Congress heard from the clergy about their painful experiences in often being regarded as suspects in the ATF's investigation into their churches' fires, adding insult to injury for these victims of hate crimes.[30]

Knowing that welfare reform was imminent[31] and could cost him support in the African American community, Clinton could not afford to further alienate black voters—a key component of his base. He needed to weigh in strongly on the issue of church arson. On June 8, 1996 he dedicated his weekly radio show to the topic and continued to speak out strongly on the subject in several venues, displaying his understanding of Southern racism and empathy for its victims. On June 12, President Clinton appeared in South Carolina with Rev. Terrance Mackey, pastor of a burned church and an emerging leader in the movement responding to burned churches. His words were unequivocal:

> You think about what happened—90 years ago when the other church was built, people might have expected things like a church bombing. That was the time of Jim Crow and there were even lynchings in the South. It was a time of abject poverty, worse than anything we call poverty today. It was 90 years ago an expression of faith and courage for people to get together and build a church. But it was the church that saved the people until the civil rights revolution came along. And it is, therefore, I think doubly troubling to see our native South engulfed in a rash of church burnings over the last year and a half. We have to say to all of you who've been afflicted by this we know that we're not going back to those dark days, but we are now reminded that our job is not done. Dr. King once said, "What self-centered men have torn down, other-centered men can build up." The men and women of Mt. Zion have shown us the meaning of these words by refusing to be defeated and by building up this new church.[32]

Clinton's outreach to the African American community around this issue was palpable. Earlier in the spring he and Vice President Gore had worked on a rebuilding a church in Tennessee—an event widely covered by the media. Later in June he again met with NCC General Secretary Joan Brown Campbell, church leaders and pastors of burned churches for breakfast at the White House. This event coincided with the successful passage of the Church Arson Prevention Act. The day the president appointed Jim Johnson from the Treasury Department to co-chair the Task Force, he instructed him, "Let them know we *care.*"[33]

The message got through. An overwhelming majority of black voters supported the president in November. In January, a choir composed of members of burned churches ("the Resurrection Choir") sang at his inauguration. At the State of the Union address Clinton again called the country into moral battle with the evil of racism:

We still see evidence of biting bigotry and intolerance, in ugly words and awful violence, in burned churches and bombed buildings. We must fight against this, in our country and in our hearts.[34]

Even as the issue of burned churches became a rallying point across the theological spectrum within the religious community, so too was it initially a "no brainer" in the political realm. The Church Arson Prevention Act had passed unanimously at the end of June and was signed into law July 3. With even the religious right supporting it, there was a national consensus as well as a political one that the burning of black churches was a social problem, a phenomenon which would not be tolerated by the American public or their elected government.

The Church Arson Prevention Act accomplished a number of things including:

- Church arson was upgraded in its severity as a crime;

- The troubling trend among insurance companies to cancel church policies was designated a crime;

- Federal guaranteed loan monies were designated ($10 million) to enable victimized churches to be rebuilt;

- Ongoing strategies for arson prevention and community building were stipulated.

But the most significant provision of the Act was the establishment of the Church Arson Task Force—an uncharacteristically collaborative effort among a number of federal agencies, including the FBI, the Department of Justice (Civil Rights and Community Relations Divisions), Department of the Treasury (especially Alcohol, Tobacco, and Firearms), Federal Emergency Management Agency, and Department of Housing and Urban Development. The Task Force was to be co-chaired by Jim Johnson, the assistant secretary of the Treasury, and Deval Patrick, director of the Civil Rights Division, Department of Justice. The Task Force met weekly beginning in June of 1996. Johnson reported that he and Patrick were "joined at the hip," and came to be referred to as "the bookends . . . I felt strongly that the best investigations were when prosecutors and investigators are working together from the beginning, side by side."[35] In January of 1997, Bill Lann Lee replaced Patrick as co-chair. Through the unusual collaboration and allocation of resources, over 200 agents from both ATF and the FBI (normally perceived as having "chilly relations") were deployed to investigate church arsons. They each had their own set of numbers, as did the Justice Department, so developing a common reporting mechanism and data base became a priority. In addition, ATF, stinging from the Good Ol' Boys scandal, was still perceived with suspicion in minority communities. Their traditional approach to investigating arson—assuming the owners of buildings to be potential suspects—only exacerbated the tension. So there were public relations issues, which were addressed through their collaboration with the Civil Rights Division of the Justice Department as a new investigative protocol was put into place. Eventually, Johnson recalled, "the public perception of the ATF had really turned around, so much so that by November, Deval and I were given an award by the NCC for our efforts."[36]

The Task Force issued its first annual report of findings in June of 1997. They reported that in the two-and-a-half-year period when their database began, 429 houses of worship had been destroyed by arson or bombing. African American churches were more than twice as likely to be destroyed as others. Of all houses of worship victimized in the nation during that period, in fact, nearly one-third were black churches in the South. But the Task Force found no evidence of a centrally organized conspiracy, although there was plenty of support for racial hatred as a motivation. Two-thirds of those arrested in the burnings and bombings of African American churches had been white (as opposed to the 7 percent of those arrested in attacks on white churches that had been black). Further, they had been able to demonstrate racial motives in a number of cases and successfully won criminal civil rights convictions in three-fifths of the cases in five Southern states and Nevada.

The Task Force produced a report annually; the last statistical report was issued in September of 2001 at the beginning of the Bush Administration. As can be seen, the spike in numbers of church arsons during 1996 gradually declined to earlier levels, a change the Task Force attributed to the results of their aggressive investigation and prosecution strategy. The coordinated effort of the Task Force had consistently been *twice as successful* in the arrest and conviction rate for church arsons as compared to other types of arson. But the decline in church arsons could be the result of a number of factors besides effective investigative and prosecution efforts, including:

- A decrease in copycat crimes (following its disappearance from the media)

- Better prevention strategies (including efforts by the insurance industry to install security and sprinkler systems)

- High profile rebuilding efforts in communities.

The Task Force was rightfully proud of its record; while acknowledging other factors were at work, they took a share of the credit for
the decline in church arsons. Beyond that, they considered their other
two important accomplishments to be the arrest of Jay Ballinger (a one-
man burning machine who was convicted of 29 of the arsons) and the
establishment of a model of interagency collaboration within the federal
bureaucracy.[37] To outsiders such collaboration seems to be an obvious
strategic response. However, given the Weberian trajectories of specializa-
tion within the federal bureaucracy, their coordination of effort became
exemplary.

There were personal rewards for those involved in this issue as well.
Many of the players who held public roles that necessitated a high level
of "professionalism" found that confronting the attacks on African American churches touched them deeply. Bill Lann Lee, the embattled Clinton
appointee who spent three years as "*Acting* Director of the Civil Rights
Division" before finally being confirmed, had co-chaired the Task Force.
Looking back, he cast his involvement with burned churches as doing battle with "the ancient curse of racism" which was a manifestation of "evil in
society."[38] Donnie Carter, deputy assistant director of ATF and a member
of the Task Force, welcomed the opportunity, as an African American, to
"finally" work on a civil rights issue.[39] Jim Johnson, also African American
and an active Methodist layperson, found this assignment drawing him
into behavior uncharacteristic of a federal bureaucrat—worshipping in
black churches ("and I knew all the words to the hymns!"), speaking at
religious gatherings, and studying the biblical book of Ruth to convince
a white pastor to support the administration's policy. "Personally, this
brought together all of who I was—as a Christian, a lawyer, an Assistant
Secretary and a human being. . . . Political considerations aside, it was
just the right thing to do."[40] Similar sentiments were echoed by Gary
Fields, the *USA Today* reporter who played a critical role in getting the
issue on the country's radar screen. Fields, who went on to work for the
Wall Street Journal, is open about his Christian beliefs and that he felt a
sense of "call" to this story.[41] "When I heard about (the burnings), it was
like the Lord called me on the phone and said, 'Hey, you work for a major
national paper. Do something.'" Looking back, he felt a sense of pride in
his work that year, concluding, that "It was the closest I ever came to the
purity of journalism." By exposing what he saw as a sickness in society,
his work had inspired positive social change, not without taking a lot
of criticism. Across the sectors of religion, media, government and even
the corporate sector, actors spoke of their personal investment. Volunteer
rebuilders, who were largely white, reflected in interviews both before
and after their service, a moral outrage and commitment to addressing
racial hatred. For most, this was their first volunteer effort which involved

traveling to a different region of the country as well as representing a significant contribution of time and personal resources.[42] Clearly this was a public issue which had tapped moral passion.

Given the passion generated by the issue of church burnings, it is surprising that public attention was not sustained and social transformation was not more lasting. As 1996 was ending, the issue of burned churches was fading from the public spotlight. By 1999 the issue was dead and the activities it had spawned had almost completely dried up even as many churches were still smoldering. In the same way the issue had been constructed through a complex interplay of public actors, institutions and social forces, the deconstruction resulted from the interaction of numerous variables. The very same sectors now moved wildly out of alignment, leaving those who very victimized by the church arsons and those organizing the volunteer response feeling confused and betrayed.

The media was among the first to lose interest in burned churches as a social problem. Beginning in the summer of 1996, the decline in coverage was dramatic. Although *USA Today* emerged as an unlikely leader of the journalistic charge on the burned churches issue, deploying twenty reporters who produced sixty articles on the subject by October of 1996, only five articles in that paper were published about church burnings in 1997 and only one in 1998. Other papers, while not having the quantity of articles mirrored the same trend. The *New York Times* had thirty-nine articles dedicated to the phenomenon by August of 1996 and it was referenced in almost one hundred other articles, letters, and op-ed pieces. But in the next fifteen months, there were only six articles about burned churches. By the time the Church Arson Prevention Task Force released their second report in the fall of 1998, only six newspapers picked up the Associated Press story. In December of that year, when seventy representatives of burned black churches gathered in Atlanta to meet with officials from the Task Force, the National Council of Churches and representatives from HUD, only the *Atlanta Journal and Constitution* ran a story—on page two of the local news section.

As the coverage plummeted, churches continued to be targets of arson. There were 209 arsons in 1997 and 166 the following year according to the federal report. Of these 375 fires, 97 were in black churches. Granted, the incidence of documented arsons in houses of worship was on the decline, but the decline in news coverage of the issue was far more dramatic than the decline in actual church burnings. By the time of the November 1996 presidential election, the story disappeared almost entirely from the press. This was largely due to several well-placed and well-timed articles which questioned any interpretation of a racist conspiracy.[43]

As reporters left the story, and the klieg lights were turned off, public interest waned. Contributions and volunteers trickled to a halt.

Still, church arsons have continued, if not at the levels seen in 1996. For example, a decade later, three white college males torched ten churches in an explosion of religious, if not overtly racist hatred (five of the churches were black).[44] On November 5, 2008, the Macedonia Church of God in Christ in Springfield, Massachusetts, was burned to the ground. In the indictment of three white men in January 2009, it is alleged that they had "conspired to burn the church in retaliation for the election of the country's first African-American president."[45]

What has not continued, however, is the public outrage, or even public conversation, which had been prompted by the phenomenon. Public interest had been dependent on media, government, and religious institutional attention. But the social conditions which allowed the wave of church arsons to crest in 1996 have not been eradicated. They are still smoldering.

Conclusion

In the summer of 1996, the burning of black churches had moved from an ongoing collection of local incidents, to a nationally recognized public issue. As has been seen, this outcome had resulted from the rare alignment of disparate institutional orbits. More significantly, not only had each sector elevated the issue in its internal priority structure, it had done so in relationship with the others—that is, institutional sectors became interactive and mutually reinforcing. Fueled to varying degrees by institutional, commercial, and political self-interest, the NCC, the media, and the federal administration were in close communication regarding this issue, encouraging and reinforcing each other's involvement.

During this time, the NCC was able to participate in, and influence, public policy formulation. Staff members testified before Congress, brokered meetings with the president and cabinet members with representatives of burned churches, and advocated on behalf of the victims for federal support. They had not enjoyed such access to the Oval Office and Halls of Congress since the 1950s and early 1960s. Furthermore, the NCC interacted effectively with the media, issuing press releases, staying in communication with the press, and even producing a book and a documentary as well. In parallel ways, other unlikely partners joined together in coalition. The federal government relied on the media and independent watchdog organizations (Center for Constitutional Rights, National Coalition of Burned Churches) for updated information. They, in kind, could offer a patina of legitimacy to the issue. Almost concurrent with media coverage, advocacy from the religious community, and the formulation of policy, was the public response. Americans perhaps reacted so strongly because it was an easy problem to get a handle on. The images of burning steeples were dramatic and the problem was simple to understand—torching houses of worship, particularly those of African Americans in the South, is wrong and must be stopped. The racism manifested here was extreme, far away (to non-Southerners) and it was "fixable," a compelling combination.

The emotive response was channeled into activism, expressed in both financial and volunteer contributions. The well-publicized contributions by celebrities, corporations, foundations, and just regular folks not only provided the needed bricks and mortar but fueled the sense of viability of real change as well. Volunteer rebuilders were motivated not only by moral outrage at the attacks on innocent churches, but by a belief that this outbreak of racial hatred could be undone. This time, we will not let Mississippi burn.

Clearly, during the attention on black church arson in the late 1990s there were echoes of earlier days. Images of the burning black churches tapped a primal shame in this country and prompted a desire to return to the moment when America reflected its collective better self, the Civil Rights Movement. But finally this mobilization was not sustained. Certainly the abandonment of the issue by the institutional players had a major impact. Perhaps Americans confronted the complexity and intransigence of racism that could not be so easily fixed. Perhaps we could not sustain confronting our national shame any longer. Maybe religious communities were pulled back into a private, rather than public faith. But the burned church chapter served as an epilogue to the narrative of the struggle for civil rights and demonstrates that the story continues to be written in our history.

Notes

1. National Arson Task Force Annual Report to the President (1997, 1998, 1999, 2000).

2. Established in October, 1997, the NCBC is "a non profit, multiracial, interdenominational coalition of burned church victims whose places of worship have been burned or firebombed" through initial grants from the Center for Democratic Renewal, the W. K. Kellogg Foundation, and the Mary Reynolds Babcock Foundation.

3. The seven are the African Methodist Episcopal Church (A.M.E.), African Methodist Episcopal Zion Church (A.M.E.Z.), Christian Methodist Episcopal Church (C.M.E.), National Baptist Convention, USA Inc., National Baptist Convention of America, National Missionary Baptist Convention, and Progressive National Baptist Convention.

4. Mississippi at that time was only one of two states without mandatory public education. Expenditures per student were minimal—$81.66 for whites and $21.77 for African Americans. The Freedom Schools provided remedial education for over 3,000 students that summer. See Doug McAdam, *Freedom Summer* (New York: Oxford University Press, 1988), 83–86.

5. Findlay, op cit., 129–30.

6. Ibid., 121–122.

7. Policy Statement on Racial Justice, adopted by the Governing Board of the NCC, 11/10/84, amended 11/6/85.

8. The Center for Democratic Renewal was founded in 1979 as the Anti-Klan Network. They are a multiracial organization which has focused specifically on racism, particularly as expressed in hate crimes. They work closely and collaboratively with religious groups, including the NCC, often providing research on racial violence. They first exposed the skinhead movement and Christian Identity Church, with its attendant white supremacist theology.

9. "Black and Multi-Racial Church Burnings, January 1990–September 1996," Center for Democratic Renewal.

10. National Church Arson Task Force, 2001.

11. Joe Hamilton interview by author, Atlanta, March 2001.

12. Joe Hamilton interview.

13. "Arson at black churches revives old fears," Brian Cabell, *Washington Post*, January 19, 1996.

14. "Out of the Ashes," report of the NCCC Burned Churches Project, Vol. 2, No. 1.

15. Telephone interview with Gary Fields, 10/20/01.

16. Laura Olson, "The Making of an Issue: Elite Responses to Southern Church Burnings." Unpublished paper presented at Southern Political Science Association meeting, 1997, Norfolk, VA.

17. Katie Day, "The Southern Poverty Law Center," *Journal of Religious and Theological Information*, Vol. 4(2), 2001, 52.

18. Rev. Dr. Mac Charles Jones, testimony before the Senate Judiciary Committee, 6/27/96.

19. The Fourth Wave: A Continuing Conspiracy to Burn Black Churches, Center for Democratic Renewal, March, 1997.

20. Linda Bloom, "Pastors of Burned Churches Find Support," United Methodist News Service, 4/5/99, (http://gbgm-umc.org/advance/Church-Burnings/support.html).

21. Manning Marable, "Why the Churches Are Still Burning," *The Black World Today* 7/4/99, (http://www.tbwt.com/views/manning/manning_07-04-99.asp).

22. Michael Madden, "White Says Church Attack was Racially Motivated," *Boston Globe*, 1/12/96.

23. Thomas George, "For Reggie White, Racism is the Hardest Foe," *New York Times*, 1/1/2/96.

24. Brian Cabell, "Arson at Black Churches Revives Old Fears," *Washington Post*, 1/19/96.

268 Katie Day

25. William Booth, "In Church Fires, a Pattern but No Conspiracy," Washington Post.com (http://washingtonpost.com/wp-srv/national/longterm/churches.

26. Carol J. Fouke, "Contributions to NCCCUSA Burned Churches Fund $7.7 Million to Date," NCCC Press Release, 7/17/96.

27. Kevin Sack, "A Penitent Christian Coalition Offers Aid to Burned Churches," New York Times, 6/19/96.

28. "Black Ministers Ask for Arson Inquiry," Reuters, New York Times, 4/23/96.

29. National Church Arson Task Force: Current Statistics, 9/18/01.

30. Associated Press, "Inquiry is Harassing Parishioners, Pastors of Burned Churches Say," New York Times, 6/10/96.

31. The Welfare Reform Act, also known as the Personal Responsibility and Work Opportunity Reconciliation Act, was in fact passed in August of 1996.

32. Elizabeth Farnsworth, "Resurrection," NewsHour Online: Church Burning in Greeleyville, South Carolina, 6/12/1996.

33. Jim Johnson interview by author, Washington, DC, 11/05/01.

34. President Clinton's Message to Congress on the State of the Union, 2/5/97.

35. Jim Johnson interview.

36. Jim Johnson interview.

37. Bill Lann Lee (Church Arson Task Force) interviews by author, Atlanta, 6/8/00 and 10/16/01.

38. Bill Lann Lee, Interview, 10/16/01.

39. Church Arson Task Force interview, Atlanta, 6/8/00.

40. Jim Johnson interview.

41. Gary Fields interview.

42. Over 200 interviews with volunteers were conducted by the author between 1998 and 2001, made possible through a research grant by the Lilly Endowment.

43. Michael Fumento, "A Church Arson Epidemic? It's Smoke and Mirrors," Wall Street Journal, 7/9/96; Michael Kelly, "Playing with Fire," New Yorker Magazine, 7/15/96;

"Who was Burning the Black Churches?" Joe Holley, Columbia Journalism Review, September/October, 1996.

44. C. Strain, Burning Faith (University of FLA Press, 2008), 145–152.

45. Department of Justice press release, "Three Men Indicted for Racially-Motivated Church Arson in Springfield, Mass.," 1/27/09.

13

Civil Rights Rhetoric in Media Coverage of Marriage Equality Debates

Massachusetts and Georgia

Traci C. West

The civil rights movement[1] of the 1950s and 1960s was characterized by tactics and rhetoric that demanded justice and equality in the laws and everyday public practices of the United States. During this period of history, certain extraordinary black Christians (and others) created activist strategies that highlighted the moral costs to American society of tolerating institutionally sanctioned inequalities. Committed white Christians and Jews joined with black Christians in a struggle for social change that included protest marches, rallies, and nonviolent demonstrations in a variety of local communities. The movement in Mississippi, for instance, focused on the political and economic disenfranchisement of poor blacks. The Chicago-based movement focused on racially segregated housing and inadequate city services in poor neighborhoods. As many of these campaigns received mass media attention, both nationally and internationally, the moral authority of black Christian leaders grew, as did their capacity for exerting public pressure in pursuit of specific policy demands.

Through protracted, costly struggle the movement successfully lobbied for policy changes that dismantled longstanding practices of discrimination in the nation. The hard-won 1964 Civil Rights Act, for example, included prohibitions against employer discrimination on the basis of race, color, religion, sex, and national origin. The expansions of freedom and equality produced by the movement have been widely embraced, however public debates about broadening legal access to marriage at the beginning of the twenty-first century have sown confusion about the kind of equality and justice the 1950s and 1960s civil rights movement stood for and to whom that kind of justice should be applied in its aftermath. Media coverage of the marriage equality debates displayed moral and religious rhetoric by community leaders that helped to create this confusion with simplistic language, but conflicting interpretations of equality and justice.

Although the goals and methods of the 1950s and 1960s civil rights movement profoundly influenced many subsequent activists who struggled on behalf of full equality for socially marginalized groups,[2] attempts to link that civil rights movement legacy to the struggle for equal and just treatment of gay and lesbian citizens have been strongly criticized. Some of that criticism has come from contemporary black Christian leaders who have invoked their particular racial link to the 1950s and 1960s movement and utilized the currency of their moral influence as religious leaders to try to ensure that gay men and lesbians are denied equal treatment under the law. In 2004, claims about that earlier civil rights movement were at the heart of particularly contentious public debates over marriage rights in Georgia and Massachusetts.

In both states, cadres of black clergy utilized the public stage of the news media to express opposition to gay rights through legislative (Georgia) or court mandated as well as legislative (Massachusetts) public policies. Certain anti-gay-rights black clergy leaders issued statements explicitly denouncing the legitimacy of any analogies between the current gay-rights struggle and the earlier civil rights movement of the 1950s and 1960s (while other, pro-gay-rights black leaders affirmed the connection between the two movements). In the end, the political battles in Georgia and Massachusetts over equal access to state-licensed marriage for gay and heterosexual couples produced completely opposite outcomes.

In one instance during the Georgia state Constitutional amendment debate, a group of black clergy supporters issued a public statement claiming, that "to equate a lifestyle choice to racism demeans the work of the entire civil rights movement."[3] After approval by the Georgia state legislature, a constitutional ban limiting marriage rights exclusively to heterosexuals was placed on the ballot. It was overwhelmingly passed by Georgia voters and added to the Georgia state Constitution in 2004. In the wake of the legislature's approval of the amendment, a press report suggested that "public opposition by black clergy to same-sex marriage helped" to make the ban's success possible in Georgia because "black lawmakers, some of whom initially opposed the amendment, voted to approve it after hearing from their largely religious constituents."[4]

Throughout the 2004 public debates in Massachusetts similar anti-gay-rights claims by black clergy were reported in the media. A state constitutional amendment, comparable to the one in Georgia, was proposed in Massachusetts in 2004. One article in the *Boston Globe* described how "the three major associations of Greater Boston's black clergy, exercising their considerable influence within the minority community and asserting moral authority on civil rights matters, have shaken up the debate over same-sex marriage with their insistence that the quest by gays and lesbians for marriage licenses is not a civil rights issue."[5] In a nationally televised network news program, Bishop Gilbert Thompson, a part of that effort in Boston, decried: "I resent the fact that homosexuals are trying to piggyback on the civil rights struggle of the '60s."[6] Eugene Rivers, another black Boston minister who worked against legalizing equal marriage rights and benefits, was quoted by the *New York Times* as saying that this was another instance, similar to "the women's movement," where the struggle of black people was being "opportunistically appropriated."[7]

Despite these widely publicized articulations of opposition to gay rights by black clergy as well as organized opposition by several other religious and political factions, the Massachusetts constitutional amendment restricting marriage rights to heterosexuals was defeated in the state legislature in 2005. Consequently, the 2003 ruling of the state Supreme Court requiring equal treatment without regard for sexual orientation for couples applying for marriage licenses was allowed to stand. Massachusetts became the first state in the United States where gay and lesbian couples were able to legally marry and truly have equal access to the social and financial benefits and obligations of marriage regulated by the state.

The public reports of statements by anti-gay-rights black ministers present a complex web of multiple moral claims where truthfulness can appear indistinguishable from opportunism at the expense of truth. The rhetoric of the public debates about marriage rights in Massachusetts and Georgia raise questions about the authentic legacy of the 1950s and 1960s civil rights movement and about who can be considered its most legitimate interpreters. The Massachusetts and Georgia cases also raise questions about when and how clergy appropriately wield their moral authority in order to apply public pressure on issues of justice and equality.

The mass media forum for these public debates further complicates the task of distinguishing between authenticity and opportunism. It may not be possible to determine if or to what extent some clergy were using the media to create a spectacle that would give them status and influence (and perhaps new church members),[8] or whether the media used certain black clergy voices to create a spectacle that would draw the most public attention and thus increase their profits. Unfortunately, the emotional, economic, and social well-being of lesbians and gay men and their children at stake in these public battles seemed, at times, to be occluded by rhetorical jousting over the appropriate circumstances for legitimately invoking the civil rights movement. While sorting through this rhetoric, it is imperative to remember that the Massachusetts and Georgia debates on marriage rights in which black religious leaders and many others engaged, were not merely about *issues* of race, sexuality, religion, and U.S. social movement history, but about gay and lesbian people's *lives* and how those lives would be valued or devalued.

Nevertheless, how these issues are morally framed for public consumption matters. Any evaluation of the moral claims of community leaders quoted in the media requires acknowledgment of the role of the media and, in some cases, of orchestrated strategies by activist groups in framing those claims. As political scientists, Thomas E. Nelson and Donald R. Kinder explain,

> frames are more than simply positions or arguments about an issue. Frames are *constructions* of the issue: they spell out the essence of the problem, suggest how it should be thought about . . . Because frames permeate public discussions of politics, they in effect teach ordinary citizens how to think about and understand complex social policy problems.[9]

In the debates over marriage equality, for example, the media helped to teach the public that there were (only?) two opposing sides interpreting how the moral legacy of the twentieth-century civil rights movement for racial equality relates to the current struggle over marriage equality. The media representations of facts also taught the public that certain conservative black Christian ministers were sufficiently informed about the history of that earlier movement to credibly interpret it. I am not concerned, however, with providing a comprehensive schematic of the media frames utilized to influence public opinion.[10] Rather, I explore the particular dynamics of how race-based and religious claims infused these debates creating moral confusion about the meaning of justice, equality, and an entitlement to civil rights for certain groups of United States citizens.

Finally, the moral courage of black Christian civil rights activists, bravely protesting publicly sanctioned racial and economic discrimination has, admittedly, been a major source of inspiration to many, including myself. I strongly believe in continuing to teach their heroic acts within as many diverse contemporary communities as possible, in hopes of inspiring new generations to emulate them. When I analyze rhetoric about what demeans and what honors the 1950s and 1960s civil rights movement in the current debates about marriage rights, I eschew any quest for a static preservation of movement history, as if safeguarding an old, cherished relic for viewing in a museum. Instead, I am interested in what it means to authentically learn from the commitment to creating social change and building communities that support the well-being of every member on the part of 1950s and 1960s civil rights movement activists (including black leaders, though not exclusively) and to apply those lessons to contemporary struggles for social justice.

The Broader Political Context of the Debates

The political battles over state constitutional amendments restricting marriage rights in Georgia and Massachusetts were set within a broader context of related political and legal challenges during the preceding decade. Arguments over marriage rights took place in numerous forums, including town council chambers, mayor's offices, religious assemblies, corporate employee benefits divisions, and national governments elsewhere in the world. The moral issues in the heated, polarized debates showcased in mass media news coverage and discussed below centered on communal entitlements to respect, equal treatment, and just public practices. What kind of public respect are the covenantal, intimate relationships of gay and lesbian couples entitled to? Should societal respect for human equality be conditionally allocated, in this case, for heterosexuals only? Based upon its obligation to uphold a consistent standard for citizen rights and responsibilities, what constitutes a just policy for government regulation of marriage? These intense public conversations frequently included direct references and comparisons to racial discrimination historically experienced by blacks in the United States and the activist efforts that have been needed to minimize it. The 2004 debates in Massachusetts and Georgia and the voices of black clergy quoted in the *Boston Globe* and *Atlanta Journal–Constitution* emerged within this broader, decade-long, fractious climate that included significant, popular opposition to "gay marriage" at both federal and state levels.

One of the most influential state battles of the 1990s took place in Hawaii. A 1993 Hawaii State Supreme Court decision invalidated a law prohibiting same-sex couples from marrying.[11] The Hawaii legislature then passed a state constitutional amendment, ratified by voters in 1998, reserving the rights of marriage to "opposite-sex couples."[12] At the time, white gay-rights activists such as Evan Wolfson who was marriage project director for Lambda Legal Defense and Education Fund, publicly argued for equal marriage rights, drawing comparisons to legal victories ending racial discrimination against African Americans in the 1960s. In 1996, during the court battles in Hawaii, for example, Wolfson was quoted in the Honolulu press explaining: "Thirty years ago it took courts with cour-age to tear down racial discrimination in marriage."[13]

Following the 1993 Hawaii Supreme Court decision, conserva-tive political activists became concerned about the possibility of equal marriage rights and benefits for all adult couples becoming the law in Hawaii and "spreading" to other states around the nation. In response to those concerns, the federal "Defense of Marriage Act" (DOMA) was quickly drafted and passed by Congress with overwhelming support in both chambers. Signed into law by President Bill Clinton in 1996, DOMA restricted marriage rights exclusively to heterosexuals within the frame-work of federal laws, programs, and policies. DOMA also stipulated that "no state, territory, or possession of the United States, or Indian tribe, shall be required to give effect to any public act, record, or judicial proceed-ing of any other State, territory, possession, or tribe *respecting a relation-ship* (emphasis added) between persons of the same sex that is treated as marriage under the laws of such other State, territory, possession, or tribe, or a right or claim arising from such relationship."[14] Moral issues pertaining to respect and basic rights are clearly articulated here. When DOMA became law, it ensured disrespect for the consensual intimate relationships of a specific group of adult citizens: same-gender couples. It guaranteed federal protection for the denial of any civil rights they may have attained elsewhere (abroad or within a particular U.S. municipality) or claim to have as a family unit.

By the end of 1996, fifteen states created and passed laws restrict-ing marriage rights to heterosexuals.[15] Georgia was among them, adding restrictions in 1996 to its state codes governing domestic relations, as follows:

> Marriages between persons of the same sex are prohibited in this state. No marriage between persons of the same sex shall be recognized as entitled to the benefits of marriage. Any mar-riage entered into by persons of the same sex pursuant to a marriage license issued by another state or foreign jurisdiction or otherwise shall be void in this state.[16]

Despite the fact that DOMA and Georgia's 1996 "mini-DOMA" restricted marriage to heterosexuals and prohibited any state from being compelled by any other state to have equal access to marriage rights, Georgians still felt a need for a state constitutional amendment reiterating this prohibition. As previously noted, the Georgia state legislature passed this amendment, placed it on the state's ballot in 2004, and Georgian vot-ers overwhelmingly approved it. Similar ballot measures were approved in twelve other states in 2004.[17]

One black Georgia lawmaker, Sharon Beasley-Teague, who did not vote the first time the amendment narrowly failed in the House, but voted to support it when the Georgia legislature approved the measure, argued against the idea that the "gay marriage" ban was a civil rights issue or in any way discriminatory. Noting that she had come to her decision on her vote after "a lot of prayer and bible study" Beasley-Teague asserted: "This will not keep them from doing what they want to do as far as voting, as far as going to school or as far as where they eat."[18] It seems that, for this elected leader, if none of the rights historically denied blacks in the segregated south were currently being withheld from gay and lesbian Georgians (across racial/ethnic groups) then their civil rights were not being violated. Furthermore, the news consumer is not informed of the rights Beasley-Teague omits related to discrimination in employment or access to health care that African Americans experienced under southern segregation and might be comparable to contemporary discrimination on the basis of sexual orientation and gender identity.

On the day that the Georgia legislature passed the amendment, reactions by activists who had opposed the anti-gay-marriage legislation were described in the news: "many cried and gasped. Some started singing the civil rights anthem, 'We Shall Overcome.'"[19] The singing of this "civil rights anthem" seems to have brought comfort in the midst of their defeat. Yet it also served as a public reminder of Georgia's long history of support for racially discriminatory laws, and by implication, linked the contemporary white and black Georgia legislators celebrating their enactment of discriminatory marriage law to that racist legacy. The newspaper's report of the sound of anguish followed by an "anthem" in that chamber depicts an almost liturgical moment of communal mourning as they watched the literal de-moralization of gay citizens enacted. This *Atlanta Journal–Constitution* article concludes with a comment by Sadie Fields, a white woman who headed the Georgia Christian Coalition, the primary lobbying group behind the passage of the amendment. Celebrating her victory with a supporter, Fields says: "To God be the Glory."[20] In the newspaper's representation, there are two dueling religious perspectives attached to the two sides of the vote, and the article gives the last word to the winner.

In contrast to Georgia, in the late 1990s there was a successful struggle in Vermont for state legislation granting all of the rights and responsibilities commensurate with marriage to same-gender couples who enter into civil unions. When the law was signed in 2000 by their governor, Howard Dean, Vermont became the first state in the nation to allow civil unions for same-gender couples. Because of Vermont's close geographical proximity to Massachusetts and the extensive coverage given to the Vermont case by the *Boston Globe,* the political battles over civil unions in Vermont had a significant impact on subsequent marriage debates in Massachusetts. As was true of public discussions on same-gender couples' rights in other states, reports of Vermont's legislative debates included Christian references to the bible, especially in arguments opposing civil unions.[21] One opponent of civil unions, Vermont State Representative, Nancy Sheltra, was quoted in the *Washington Post* utilizing the terminology of the King James translation of *Leviticus* (18.22, 20.13). According to the *Post*, Sheltra asserted on the first day that civil union licenses were issued: "As a Christian woman, I believe this is really an abomination to God . . . I never thought this would happen in my state."[22]

In Massachusetts, a state constitutional amendment on marriage was proposed after a 2003 state Supreme Court ruling, *Goodridge v. Department of Public Health*, granted marriage rights to all couples seeking them. In *Goodridge*, the court decided:

> [T]he question before us is whether, consistent with the Massachusetts Constitution, the Commonwealth may deny the protections, benefits, obligations conferred by civil marriage to two individuals of the same sex who wish to marry. We conclude that it may not. The Massachusetts Constitution affirms the dignity and equality of all individuals. It forbids the creation of second-class citizens.[23]

A comparison with past restrictions on marriage eligibility prohibiting interracial marriage because of prevailing racial prejudice against blacks was at the heart of both the legal strategy of the plaintiff's attorneys and of the court's decision.[24] In a February 2004 Massachusetts Supreme Court ruling, a compromise bill, drafted after the *Goodridge* decision, proposed civil unions instead of marriage, but the Court dismissed it as a viable option. The Court concluded: "the history of our country has demonstrated that separate is seldom, if ever, equal."[25] In their rejection of unequal marriage rights in Massachusetts, the justices used language that directly referenced white supremacist segregationist law.

In June 2003, a landmark case striking down Texas sodomy laws, *Lawrence v. Texas*, was decided by the U.S. Supreme Court.[26] In this decision, hailed by marriage equality activists around the country, the court ruled that the private sexual conduct of the two consenting adult males who had been arrested for "deviate sexual intercourse" could not be criminalized. Celebrating this victory, Evan Wolfson, as founder and director of Freedom to Marry, proclaimed in a *New York Times* article: "we are in a *Brown v. Board of Education* moment right now." [27] Wolfson reflexively used a pinnacle event in the campaign for racial equality as a metaphor for this significant moment in the movement for gay rights. Furthermore, he pointed to other lessons from civil rights movement history when he stated, "it is important to remember what came after *Brown*: major legal challenges and acts of courage but also fierce resistance."[28]

Wolfson attempted to demonstrate the significance of the *Lawrence* decision by associating it with racial justice milestones that might be familiar to the general public. Apparently, he intended this reference to *Brown* to positively reinforce an understanding among the public that extending equality to disenfranchised minority groups is something that serves the interests of the common good. But Wolfson could easily be read as problematically *equating* the history of racial subjugation with the history of heterosexism, rather than *comparing* them. He also used the analogy to *Brown* to send a signal to existing gay-rights supporters, warning them about the likelihood of a backlash response to the *Lawrence* decision. More clarification should have been added by Wolfson to avoid the troubling impression that he thought that the same kind of "fierce resistance" awaited marriage equality supporters as blacks encountered after *Brown*. Surely he did not mean to imply that resistance by the state might occur akin to state officials across the south closing down schools for all white children to avoid integrated schooling with black children. Additionally, at least in the quotations included in this *New York Times* piece, Wolfson does not appear to have expressed any sense of gratitude for the specific work of combating anti-black racism that occupied the legal strategists and community activists whose legacy he was rhetorically building upon.

Less than a year after the *Lawrence* decision, President George W. Bush lent support to the fervor for state constitutional ballot initiatives restricting marriage, like the one making its way through the legislature in Georgia at that very moment. Although sweeping federal DOMA regulations had been in place since 1996, President George W. Bush in February 2004 called for an amendment to the federal Constitution that would "protect marriage" for heterosexuals. In his presentation to the press, President Bush provided a moral framework for creating this change claiming: "our government should respect every person, and protect the institution of marriage. There is no contradiction between these responsibilities. We should also conduct this difficult debate in a manner worthy of our country, without bitterness or anger."[29]

President Bush's press statement cleverly denies any moral contradiction while creating one. In his justification, Bush's message of respect for all citizens is tethered to an attempt to change the Constitution of the United States with a provision for withholding the rights and freedoms of one class of citizens and securing them for another. Using deceptive political rhetoric, his presentation to the national press created the false impression that legalizing discrimination against certain citizens, same-gender couples, constituted respectful treatment of them. There was also an element of performance in his presentation at the press conference that enhanced the hypocrisy and deceptiveness of his message. In a seeming display of respectfulness President Bush claimed to be concerned about the tenor of future debates. Such displays teach the public to hypocritically separate the form (respectful tone) from the substance (constitutionally mandated disrespect for equal rights) in their expression of communal moral values.

Following this announcement by President Bush, black Baptist ministers in Chicago held a press conference to articulate their support for the enactment of a federal constitutional amendment. Rev. Gregory Daniels, one of the organizers of the event, supported the President's initiative but did so in a particularly abrasive manner.[30] According to the *New York Times* report, Daniels declared: "if the KKK opposes gay marriage, I would ride with them."[31] Daniels' extreme position does not reflect the sentiments expressed in the majority of the anti-gay-rights rhetoric publicly aired by conservative black ministers. Granted, there is an irresistible attention-grabbing quality to a news story about a black male minister (surrounded by other black ministers) flippantly remarking that he would ride with the Ku Klux Klan to serve the interests of denying gay and lesbian couples the legal right to marry one another. But the actual horror of Ku Klux Klan terror against blacks, including the lynching of black men, is thoroughly trivialized by Daniels' matter-of-fact presentation.

National political organizations also influenced the moral tone and political strategy of anti-gay-rights activism in Georgia and Massachusetts. For example, the conservative Family Research Council urged black pastors to include objections to analogies between the movement for gay rights and the 1950s and 1960s civil rights movement in their anti-equality arguments. A few weeks after President Bush announced his support for amending the U.S. Constitution, the *New York Times* reported that Genevieve Wood, a white leader of the Family Research Council told a national gathering of black evangelical ministers gathered in Washington, DC: "They are wrapping themselves in the flag of civil rights . . . I can make arguments against that. But not nearly like you can."[32] As the article points out, the moral influence of black pastors was utilized in a deliberate public relations strategy. In the tactics of the Family Research Council, anti-gay-rights black pastors were apparently seen as useful for disseminating misleading public rhetoric reinforcing the idea that an authentic understanding of "civil rights under the law" refers to a conceptual bedrock of the 1950s and 1960s protest movement and was intended to be an exclusive remedy for racism experienced by black (heterosexual?) community members. The article maintains the dualistic, competitive frame found in most news media coverage, indicating that "advocates on both sides are busily seeking support from the same source: black clergy members."[33] Black leaders "on the left" are cited alongside of conservative ones.

Besides contests over black spokespersons and who can authentically invoke "the mantle of civil rights,"[34] what were the actual legal protections and specific moral values at stake?

Civil Rights Protections and Morality Claims

Marriage is a personal, covenantal decision, usually based on a combined romantic, emotional, and physical attraction that evolves through willful, mutual, and private interactions between two people. Therefore, for some, the amount of time, energy, and resources elected officials and religious leaders have dedicated to restricting access to it might be baffling. Simply put, what's the problem? As long as marriage involves a consensual agreement between two adults, dissolvable at the discretion of either/both of them, why don't all citizens have the civil right to legally marry whomever they choose? Any attempt to understand the intensity of the political opposition to equal access to marriage must take into account the particular legal rights and material benefits of marriage granted to couples by the state. Attention to details of the debate about the appropriateness of comparisons between the 1950s and 1960s civil rights movement and the marriage equality movement reveals more complexity. Scrutiny of the claims highlighted by the media allows for a better grasp of what is truly at stake for broad-based communal morality related to just public practices and the moral capitol of societal respectability desired by historically oppressed groups.

So many of the political debates about amending the state constitutions in Georgia and court rulings in Massachusetts drew attention to the relevance of the 1950s and 1960s civil rights movementt, to God's will and Christian scripture, or competition between the uniqueness of black (heterosexual?) political suffering and the political struggles of homosexuals, that one could almost forget that these arguments were generated by legislation (or court rulings) determining government regulatory power over citizen rights and obligations. Which legal rights, privileges, and obligations of marriage were in fact at issue? State governments require that every citizen and public institution recognize that the marital bond of two partnered, adult citizens includes legal agreements such as:

- the right to make medical decisions for an incapacitated spouse;

- sharing of property, wages, and debts;

- shared employment benefits including health and pension benefits for state workers;

- shared responsibility for and benefits of state and local taxes

- the right to make funeral arrangements for and determine the disposition of the remains of a deceased spouse;

- the right to family medical and bereavement leave; and

- the rights and responsibilities related to custody, visitation, support, and adoption of children.

Marriage, of course, consists of much more than contractual rights. Ideally, marriage is an intimate relationship grounded in mutual, trustworthy, loving, and joyful emotional attachment and commitment. Nevertheless, denial of the legal benefits of marriage enacts considerable disadvantages for the financial stability, emotional well-being, and physical health of the families of same-gender couples. The role of the state in enforcing this discriminatory policy reflects the popular prejudices of a heterosexual majority that privileges their own heterosexuality as innately morally superior and therefore deserving of laws biased in their favor.

Although the definition of civil rights law was a repeated theme in the arguments against marriage equality reported by the media, unfortunately, most of that reporting failed to even mention any of the rights and obligations listed above that the contested law would regulate, instead racial and Christian religion infused morality claims prevailed. For example, as part of a national news broadcast on ABC television, a segment called "A Closer Look at Same-Sex Marriage" began with the reporter stating: "civil rights protection, many argue, is meant for people, not behavior."[35] A black, Atlanta, Georgia Pastor, Garland Hunt, is then introduced and reiterates this confusing view of civil rights in the reporter's introduction. "It doesn't protect behavior patterns,"[36] Hunt declares. The reporter, Steve Osunsami, goes on to assert that for "many African Americans, who began the civil rights movement in the churches of the conservative South, gay and lesbian Americans are people of poor behavior."[37] Then, Pastor Hunt concludes: "Same-sex marriage has nothing to do with civil rights; this is an issue of morality."[38]

There are multiple inaccuracies and distorted messages in this ABC news report. "People" are spuriously contrasted with "behavior." Contrary to the information in this news story, civil rights law certainly does protect "behavior patterns," such as an individual's practice of any religion she or he chooses, or the choice not to practice any religion at all. At the same time, civil rights law is intended to protect "people," such as gay men and lesbians, *from* discriminatory and bigoted "behavior patterns" that can occur in employment, housing, health care, and other areas that are directly related to the rights and obligations of marriage (as the list above attests). Also, neither the ABC news narrator nor the black pastor, explains why the choice by gay and lesbian couples to marry constitutes poor behavior. In this report, "gay and lesbian Americans" are juxtaposed with African Americans, erroneously portraying two mutually exclusive groups, as if there are no African American gay men and lesbians.[39]

Furthermore, in Pastor Hunt's final point stating that "same-sex marriage has nothing to do with civil rights; this is an issue of morality," he disconnects "morality" from "civil rights," while attaching "morality" to same-sex marriage and creates yet another distortion. Without a doubt, an individual's decision to marry constitutes a moral decision insofar as it involves moral issues like promise-keeping, trust, and material, physical, and emotional commitments to another individual. But the equal right by all citizens to governmental recognition of their marriage covenant is a community-wide moral issue too. Remember that whether concerned with voting rights or public education, a quintessential moral demand of the 1950s and 1960s civil rights movement focused on the state living up to its obligation to regard all citizens as equal before the law. Civil rights are inseparable from moral concerns because civil rights are a measure of society's moral accountability to each of its citizens through the laws of the state. Whether they are expansive or restrictive, the laws of society reflect moral relations between the state and its citizens.

In the ABC news report, "morality" is used as a code word for sexuality. Presumably the morality problem, the so-called "poor behavior" associated with same-gender couples entering into marriage, but not with heterosexuals entering into marriage, is their *sexual desire* for one another. This core moral concern remained largely unexplored in most of the media coverage of the debates over access to marriage. Anti-gay-rights black religious leaders and many others often implied or suggested through code language about preserving "morality" and Christian "family values" that the overriding ingredient in the legal definition of marriage is the couple's capacity for heterosexual sexual desire, sexual intercourse, and procreation through heterosexual sexual intercourse. Comments reflecting the same assumption certainly surfaced in the rhetoric of others too. Phil Travis, a white Massachusetts state representative and active opponent of marriage equality, explained that: "The union of two women and two men can never consummate a marriage. It's physically impossible."[40] A heterosexual couple's capacity for procreative sex or any kind of sexual intercourse is not, however, a requirement for a marriage license in any state. Impotent male, post-menopausal female, and infertile heterosexuals are allowed to marry. The skewed focus by some religious and political leaders on heterosexual sexual desire and procreation as the defining moral ingredients of a state-endorsed marital covenant demands much more interrogation in news media coverage.

Confusion about the definition of civil rights was often perpetuated in black clergy statements invoking God. One Georgia pastor quoted in the *Atlanta Journal–Constitution* argued that "Gay marriage has nothing to do with civil rights . . . Marriage has already been defined by God as being between one woman and one man. How can you take that and try to make it a civil rights issue?"[41] This pastor seems oblivious to any conception of separation between church and state that prohibits governance guided by particular religious beliefs or that inhibits the free exercise of citizens' belief systems.[42] But even if one were confined to a Christian-centered worldview for guiding state regulations, this pastor's definition of civil rights does not allow for an alternative Christian emphasis on God having created in God's own image all humankind with equal worth and dignity. This alternative Christian view morally overlaps with civil rights laws ensuring equal treatment of all citizens.

An acceptance of universal moral values where equal human worth and dignity are recognized is at the crux of this dispute over society's regulation of marriage, especially in the religious arguments. In religion, when it comes to allocating access to power, hierarchy based upon particularity often trumps equality based upon universality. Many Christians, for instance, have long held the belief that the particular male identity of Jesus together with specific prohibitions "by God" in the Christian bible bar women from ordained leadership in the church, and for some, from political leadership in government.[43] In the case of access to marriage rights, black clergy anti-gay-rights activists are following standard religious and social traditions of exclusivity. Invoking God has traditionally proven to be an effective way to narrow rights and privileges to a select group of people who are deemed innately superior.

There were black Christian leaders who spoke out against a state constitutional amendment on marriage precisely on the basis of a universal understanding of equality and civil rights. In Massachusetts, Rev. William Sinkford, an African American, served as president of the Unitarian Universalist Association in Boston. He presided at the religious marriage ceremony of the first same-gender couple to receive a marriage license. Referring to his religious tradition, Sinkford told reporters: "we have supported civil unions as a civil right for decades, and we are strongly in favor of civil marriage as a civil right."[44] In the *Boston Globe* coverage, Rev. Sinkford is identified as part of a small group of pro-gay-rights "black clergy" in their report on "black clergy rejection"[45] of marriage equality in a statement issued by an alliance of local clergy but not racially identified in another *Globe* story featuring his participation in an overwhelmingly white "clergy coalition"[46] of gay-rights supporters countering an anti-marriage-equality letter issued by Catholic bishops.[47]

Black clergy are consistently racially identified in press reports of these debates, while white clergy are consistently identified by their religious affiliations. Black clergy are repeatedly portrayed as motivated by racial group interests, while whites are rarely depicted as motivated by their racial-group interests. It is as if their whiteness does not matter to them, to their constituencies, to the news consumer, or in the moral influence they exert in the society. Unlike the references to him in the story about black clergy activism, when surrounded by white clergy activists Sinkford receives this privilege usually reserved for whites and is only religiously identified as a Unitarian leader who stands beside Rabbi Devon Lerner and other clergy whose views contrast with Catholic Bishop Christopher Coyne of the Boston Archdiocese.[48] In addition, does Sinkford's leadership in a predominantly white denomination prevent someone with his direct involvement in the historic Massachusetts marriage rights struggle from being included in the kind of prime time ABC evening news story referred to earlier, alongside of a Pastor Hunt? Or perhaps Sinkford was excluded from such mainstream venues because his perspective that "the struggle for gay civil rights is this generation's great challenge, just as equality for blacks was the last generation's"[49] so drastically differed from representations of local "black clergy" most prevalent in the press?

David Wilson, one of the plaintiffs in *Goodridge* who married his male partner after the ruling made it possible, made a more experiential argument about his entitlement to equality. When complaining about the black clergy statement calling for a constitutional ban, Wilson, a black man who is also gay, was quoted in the *Globe* arguing: "they are now discriminating against me . . . gays and lesbians were not enslaved, but they were certainly denied jobs, housing, health care, and marriage. That clearly steps on our civil rights."[50]

Byron Rushing, a black state legislator and active Episcopalian offered another critical response to the statement by Boston-based black clergy organizations opposing marriage equality. He told the *Boston Globe* "Martin Luther King Jr. is rolling over in his grave . . . they [clergy who signed the statement] are not acknowledging the responsibility [of] any people who have been able to struggle and gain civil rights, which is that you have to support others who are seeking civil rights."[51] Rushing's argument not only acknowledges the universal moral content in both movements for civil rights, but he also introduces the idea of a moral responsibility toward others that comes with the achievement of rights. It is a perspective that values the expansion of equal rights in the society as an intrinsic good that enables justice to prevail in our public practices. This process of expanding rights disciplines citizens to support the interests of their neighbors in realizing the benefits of just public practices.

In (2003–2005) U.S. debates about access to marriage and the authentic meaning of civil rights, there were a range of underlying race-based tensions about who was a legitimate spokesperson that deflected attention from essential concerns with the pursuit of justice in the society. Questions about the racial legitimacy of gay-rights activists simmered below the surface of the choices made by media outlets as well as political strategists about whose perspectives should be featured. Can gay-rights activists of any racial-ethnic background be viewed by the public as legitimate interpreters of the legacy of Martin Luther King Jr. and the historic achievements of the 1950s and 1960s Civil Rights Movement? Does the role of white supremacist repression in that history undermine the legitimacy of contemporary white activists as its interpreters? Can black gay Christian leaders be viewed by the public as legitimately representing black churches and communities when espousing gay-rights views?

Some anti-marriage-equality strategists counted on a refusal by black voters to acknowledge gay-rights advocates as legitimate interpreters of civil rights movement history. For instance, Sadie Fields a white southern leader of the Christian Coalition in Georgia, was quoted in the *New York Times* threatening Black Caucus members who initially voted against the constitutional amendment saying they "would have a lot to answer for come . . . fall" when upcoming elections were held.[52] Fields added, "If I was African American, I would be furious that homosexuals are comparing what they want to do with civil rights."[53] This comment, like so much of the anti-marriage-equality rhetoric already noted, carries the false assumption that there are no African American same-gender couples who desire the right to marry.

A *Boston Globe* columnist offered another example of this racially targeted, anti-marriage-equality strategy citing an anonymous voice message widely distributed to home answering machines in black communities in the Boston area in 2004. It said:

> Dr. Martin Luther King's dream is being violated . . . The civil rights movement is being compared to the same-sex marriage movement. If Dr. King was alive today, would he permit this?

> We must be the voice. We must stand up for what millions have died and suffered for, the dream of equality. Same-sex marriages will hurt our dream. More importantly, it will hurt our children.[54]

This propaganda not only presumes that the proper spokespersons for "our dream" but also the legitimate recipients of "the dream of equality" cannot include gay men and lesbians in black communities as well as their heterosexual allies in those communities. The message also seems to contain either the vicious insinuation that the children of gay and lesbian black community members do not deserve to be claimed as "our children," or the puzzling idea that it is hurtful to the children of black gay and lesbian couples if their parents are married.

In a bold calculation, the Family Research Council helped to sponsor a Massachusetts press conference that included Rev. Eugene Rivers from Boston and Reverend Gregory Daniels from Chicago. Daniels repeated his comment about his willingness to ride with the Klu Klux Klan at this Boston event. Their support[55] for this extremist form of violent white supremacy provided a dramatic illustration for the public of the degree of urgency black male ministers attached to banning same-gender marriages. For their opponents, it perhaps merely signaled the depth of the men's capacity for cynical collusion with white financial benefactors.[56]

In a subtler public appeal by anti-gay-rights activists, Randy Hicks, a white leader of the Georgia Family Council helped to organize a black clergy rally in the Atlanta area against "gay marriage." He pointed to African Americans at the rally and told an Associated Press reporter that they "can certainly be characterized as compassionate and caring, and they are concerned about things like discrimination."[57] The white racial identity of Hicks is not included in the story. Because of their racial identity, black clergy were seen as reflexively endowed with a commitment to oppose discriminatory public practices. They were, therefore, especially useful for convincing the broader public that limiting access to marriage to heterosexuals did not actually constitute unjust discriminatory public policy. Black clergy willingly contributed their moral authority as Christian ministers in support of this position. Accordingly, the same Associated Press story, noted that Bishop William Shields, an attendee at the black clergy rally declared: "I'm not here to discriminate against anyone. I'm here to stand on the word of God."[58] Again, the claim that "God is on our side" has been persuasively and routinely employed as a tool for Christian legitimation of discriminatory and bigoted acts against targeted groups of people throughout western history. The racial identity and attendant moral status of white Christian anti-marriage advocates was also being negotiated here. The status of blacks as historical victims of white Christian subjugation coupled with the status of conservative white Christians as the subjugators of blacks, granted black ministers the moral capital that was needed and serviceable to the anti-marriage-equality cause of white Georgians like Hicks.[59]

Georgia was unique in having the presence of historic, civil rights movement icons Coretta Scott King, Julian Bond, and John Lewis speaking out in favor of marriage equality.[60] Nevertheless, affirmations by these veteran black activists of the appropriateness of linking the 1950s and 1960s civil rights movement to the struggle to defeat the constitutional amendment against marriage equality had minimal impact on debates about this linkage. Their views were drowned out by press coverage of numerous local Georgia black pastors and others who labeled comparisons between the two struggles improper, claiming that any association with "homosexuality" was offensive and demeaning to the earlier civil rights movement. In Georgia, it seems that the power of homophobia was so thorough in its stigmatizing effect that it even rendered authentic heroes of the 1950s and 1960s civil rights movement inauthentic as spokespersons for their movement.

The competition over public legitimacy has significance that extends beyond media recognition of spokespersons to the deeper matter of who should be accorded moral credibility and respect in the society. Historically depicted in popular culture as singularly focused on sexual promiscuity, gay men and lesbians gain more than equality with access to legal marriage. They also receive what cultural theorist Judith Butler terms the "normalizing powers of the state."[61] For anti-gay-rights blacks, the normalized racial status won by 1950s and 1960s civil rights movement activists was somehow placed at risk by analogies between that movement and the gay marriage movement. At the same time, the moral capital accruing from hard-earned, increased acceptance among some white Americans enabled black anti-marriage-equality spokespersons to function as moral arbiters of sexual morality and of who deserves civil rights. Few in the press seemed to care about the deleted details from the so-called defense of "their black movement," such as its inclusion of a black gay leader (Bayard Rustin) and of white Christian and Jewish participants, its achievement of new federal protections against discrimination based on "sex" and "national origin," or black resistance to 1950s and 1960s civil rights movement leaders, especially among southern black clergy.

Ultimately, telling the truth about civil rights will require deliberate and nuanced historical memory. The promise that broadened civil rights held out for black citizens of all sexual orientations during the 1950s and 1960s is the same as it holds out for contemporary gay and lesbian couples of any race or ethnicity who want a marriage license. Each deserves complete equality of rights, respectful treatment, and protection under the law. Each should be fully supported in that entitlement by the common religious values of inherent human dignity and innate equal human worth. It is certainly questionable that such rights, respect, and protections are not achievable for socially stigmatized groups without battling dominant, institutionalized, supremacist notions that are supported by the majority of the nation's population who benefit from being treated as if they have innate moral superiority over members of those groups.

Appendix A: Examples of Civil Rights Rhetoric in 2004–2005 *Atlanta Journal–Constitution*

Statements in support of link between 1950s and 1960s Civil Rights Movement and 2004–2005 Marriage Equality Movement:

[In response to opponent:] "He is the perfect person to sell discrimination because he comports himself very nicely," said Arline Isaacson, co-chairwoman of the Massachusetts Gay and Lesbian Political Caucus. "And he doesn't seem hateful, even though every single thing he's working for is just that. "We're always cordial, and I hold no animosity toward him," she added. "But I hold animosity toward his views, and I hold animosity toward his working to take my civil rights away. I take more than umbrage at that. I resent it deeply."

—Matt Viser, "Ex-Georgia legislator leads foes of gay marriage," *Atlanta Journal–Constitution*, Feb. 15, 2004, A12

"This is the next chapter in our national civil rights movement," said Mark Shields, spokesman for the Human Rights Campaign in Washington. "But you don't get to the top of the mountain in a day. We have a long way to go in this country before we get to full equality for gay Americans."

—Dan Chapman, "Gay union pioneers send ripples south Canadians who wed expect wave of acceptance to sweep across United States," *Atlanta Journal–Constitution*, Mar. 4, 2004, A1

Last week, Lewis stood before a Senate committee in Washington, comparing the gay marriage movement to the civil rights movement he helped lead in 1965. "We have been down this road before in this country," Lewis, now a Democratic congressman from Atlanta, told fellow lawmakers. "The right to liberty and happiness belongs to each of us and on the same terms, without regard to either skin color or sexual orientation." There's no comparison between the violent clashes of the Southern civil rights movement and the recent joyous gay wedding marches in San Francisco and elsewhere. But Lewis isn't alone among civil rights leaders in saying today's gay marriage movement shares similarities with their own movement of the 1950s and 1960s. NAACP Chairman Julian Bond has called attempts to prohibit gay marriage "an attempt to write bigotry into the Constitution," although the National Association for the Advancement of Colored People hasn't taken a position on the issue.

—Bob Keefe, "Blacks' Old Guard Feels Link With Gays Lewis,
Coretta King Denounce Marriage Ban,"
Atlanta Journal-Constitution, Mar. 28, 2004, A11

"If Dr. King were here today, he wouldn't participate in this march," said U.S. Rep. John Lewis (D-Ga.), a veteran of the civil rights movement who marched alongside King. "During the civil rights movement, we were trying to take discrimination out of the Constitution."

—John Blake, "March Divides King Followers,"
Atlanta Journal-Constitution, Dec. 11, 2004, A1

"This is the same as civil rights," she said. "More parents need to stand up for their children." Initially distraught when Adam revealed several years ago he was gay, the Ellises became activists for embracing gay children.

—Kevin Duffy, "Parents Sad Over Ban of Gay Marriage,"
Atlanta Journal-Constitution, Nov. 11, 2004, 6JM

Statements that oppose link between 1950s and 1960s Civil Rights Movement and 2004–2005 Marriage Equality Movement:

Timmons took exception to some black lawmakers' claims during the House debate that the fight over the same-sex marriage ban echoes the African-American struggle in the civil rights movement. "Gay marriage has nothing to do with civil rights," he said. "Marriage has already been defined by God as being between one woman and one man. How can you take that and try to make it a civil rights issue? How can you discriminate against something that God said no to? God made the laws, and we obey his laws. That has nothing to do with discrimination."

—Jim Tharpe, "Pastors send 'clear' message Gay marriage weighs on black legislators," *Atlanta Journal-Constitution*, Mar. 1, 2004, B1

Although most of them said homosexuality is against their religion, many members of the African-American church said a constitutional ban might go too far. "The constitution should not be used as a tool to oppress anyone's rights," said the Rev. Isaac Mullins, 45, who was visiting the church to play piano there. "But I don't advocate gay marriage." With airplanes from nearby Hartsfield-Jackson International Airport flying overheard, Mullins said he does not agree with the comparison between the African-American struggle for civil rights and the efforts of gays and lesbians to marry. "A man or woman who is gay can walk around without anyone knowing they're gay," he said. "I don't have a choice; I'm black 24/7."

> —Etan Horowitz, Rhonda Cook, and Sonji Jacobs,
> "Churchgoers Air Views On Gay Issues,"
> *Atlanta Journal-Constitution*, Mar. 1, 2004, B6

But is gay marriage a matter of civil rights? Not really, said Bishop Donn Thomas, one of two dozen ministers who gathered in Atlanta last week to denounce same-sex marriage. "I do not see gay marriage as a civil right. I do not see gay marriage as a right, period," the bishop of Messiah's World Outreach Ministries said in a telephone interview. "This is not an issue of discrimination, it's not an issue of hatred or anger. It's an issue of morality, as we see it, rooted in the word of God." Thomas issued a statement supporting a statewide ban on gay marriage that the ministers plan to deliver to the Georgia Legislature. "To equate a lifestyle choice to racism demeans the work of the entire civil rights movement," the statement said. "People are free in our nation to pursue relationships as they choose. To redefine marriage, however, to suit the preference of those choosing alternative lifestyles is wrong."

> —Bob Keefe, "Blacks' Old Guard Feels Link With Gays Lewis,
> Coretta King Denounce Marriage Ban,"
> *Atlanta Journal-Constitution*, Mar. 28, 2004, A11

Bernice King, the Kings' youngest daughter, expressed how she felt her father would have responded while speaking at a church in Aukland, New Zealand, in October: "I know deep down in my sanctified soul that he did not take a bullet for same-sex unions."

> —John Blake, "March Divides King Followers,"
> *Atlanta Journal-Constitution*, Dec. 11, 2004, A1

Appendix B: Examples of Civil Rights Rhetoric in 2004–2005 *Boston Globe*

Statements in support of link between 1950s and 1960s Civil Rights Movement and 2004–2005 Marriage Equality Movement:

Gay marriage of loving people does not belittle the civil rights struggle. It gives it full blossom.

> —Derrick Z. Jackson, "Bible Lessons These Clergy Forgot,"
> *Boston Globe*, Feb. 11, 2004, A23

This week, NAACP chairman Julian Bond urged Massachusetts legislators to reject a ban on gay marriage. While declining to take a
position on the amendment, Bond connected the fight on Beacon
Hill to the civil rights struggle.

> —Frank Phillips and Raphael Lewis, "A Hunt For Middle Ground
> Travaglini Voices Confidence on a Marriage Accord Today,"
> *Boston Globe*, Mar. 11, 2004, A1

"Martin Luther King [Jr.] is rolling over in his grave at a statement
like this," said state Representative Byron Rushing, a Boston Democrat and an active Episcopal layman. "They are not acknowledging
the responsibility that any people have who have been able to struggle
and gain civil rights, which is that you have to then support others
who are seeking civil rights."

> —Michael Paulson, "Black Clergy Rejection Stirs
> Gay Marriage Backers," *Boston Globe*, Feb. 10, 2004, B1

"Their terminology and reasoning is similar to that of segregationists
and racists who have worked hard to keep blacks from attaining full
citizenship," said Jacquie Bishop, 39, of Boston. Pamela K. Johnson,
40, of Boston, who worships at the predominantly African-American
Union United Methodist Church in the South End, called the statement "hurtful."

> —Michael Paulson, "Black Clergy Rejection
> Stirs Gay Marriage Backers," *Boston Globe*, Feb. 10, 2004, B1

*Statements that oppose link between 1950s and 1960s Civil Rights Move-
ment and 2004–2005 Marriage Equality Movement:*

Many black ministers are indignant at any parallels to gay marriage
and the African-American civil rights movement. The Rev. Wesley
Roberts of Boston's Peoples Baptist Church said, "To equate what is
happening now to the civil rights struggle which blacks had to go
through would be to belittle what we had gone through as a people."

> —Derrick Z. Jackson, "Bible Lessons These Clergy Forgot,"
> *Boston Globe*, Feb. 11, 2004, A23

Most African-American ministers appeared unswayed by the notion
that gay marriage was a civil rights issue. After I wrote a column
praising state Senator Dianne Wilkerson and Representative Marie
P. St. Fleur for supporting gay marriage, more than one minister
informed me that it was the clergy who were truly representative

of the black community, while the lawmakers, and the media, were shamefully out of touch.

—Adrian Walker, "Calm After The Storm,"
Boston Globe, May 16, 2005, B1

On radios, a spot featuring a prominent black minister told listeners: "Same-sex marriage is no civil rights issue. . . . Same-sex unions are really about special rights for a special interest group."

—Yvonne Abraham, "Gay-Marriage Lobbying Builds Activists On
Both Sides Converge On State House For Crucial Session,"
Boston Globe, Mar. 10, 2004, B1

In another spot, the Rev. Eugene F. Rivers, pastor of the Azusa Christian Community in Dorchester, urges listeners not to "let lawmakers pretend this is about civil rights." This morning, a group of black pastors from across the country is to hold a press conference denouncing the comparison of the movement for same-sex marriage to the struggle for civil rights.

—Yvonne Abraham, "Gay-Marriage Lobbying Builds Activists On
Both Sides Converge On State House For Crucial Session,"
Boston Globe, Mar. 10, 2004, B1

At the State House, the simmering tension in the African-American community over the gay marriage issue erupted at a press conference. The session, organized by the Family Research Council, turned into a shouting match between a handful of gay marriage supporters and black pastors who reject the idea that gay marriage is a civil rights issue.

—Frank Phillips, and Raphael Lewis, "A Hunt for Middle Ground
Travaglini Voices Confidence on A Marriage Accord Today,"
Boston Globe, Mar. 11, 2004, A1

The half-dozen ministers argued that unlike race, homosexuality is a changeable lifestyle and that gays and lesbians don't deserve the same rights and protections as racial minorities. "There is no scientific data that says that anybody is born that way, and because they could not substantiate it through science, they've jumped on the civil rights bandwagon," said the Rev. Gerald Agee of the Friendship Christian Church in Oakland.

—Frank Phillips, and Raphael Lewis, "A Hunt for
Middle Ground Travaglini Voices Confidence on A Marriage
Accord Today," *Boston Globe*, Mar. 11, 2004, A1

Susan Gallagher, who identified herself as a health care worker from the South Shore, shook a large sign reading "No Civil Rights for Sodomites" at gay marriage supporters leaving the State House and added a few derogatory words.

> —Kevin Joy, "A Battle Just Begun For Both Supporters,
> Foes The Opponents Come Face To Face On Beacon Hill,"
> *Boston Globe*, Mar. 30, 2004, A6

The Rev. Jesse L. Jackson, who has stopped short of endorsing gay marriage in the past, yesterday said he opposed a proposed state constitutional amendment that would outlaw gay marriage and create civil unions. "We must measure human rights by one yardstick: Marry who you want to. And leave when you're ready," he said at a meeting with *Globe* reporters and editors.

Still, Jackson chafed at the idea—championed by some legislators and gay rights advocates—that the gay marriage fight is analogous to African-Americans' struggle for civil rights. Only blacks have had to contend with the legacy of slavery, Jackson said, adding that "some of the slavemasters were gay." "The gay civil rights issue is real," he said, but the analogy "is a stretch. It is diminishing of slavery to have that comparison."

> —Joanna Weiss, "Jackson Opposes Gay Marriage Ban Rejects
> Comparison to Blacks' Struggle," *Boston Globe*, Apr. 3, 2004, A5

The civil rights movement, though often invoked, isn't completely apt as an analogy for the gay marriage struggle, in that the discrimination African-Americans suffered, particularly in the South, was both more pronounced and less avoidable than that which homosexuals endure today.

> —Scot Lehigh, "A Trend Toward Acceptance of Gays,"
> *Boston Globe*, Feb. 27, 2004, A23

The three major associations of Greater Boston's black clergy, exercising their considerable influence within the minority community and asserting moral authority on civil rights matters, have shaken up the debate over same-sex marriage with their insistence that the quest by gays and lesbians for marriage licenses is not a civil rights issue.

> —Michael Paulson, "Black Clergy Rejection Stirs
> Gay Marriage Backers" *Boston Globe*, Feb. 10, 2004, B1

Notes

1. Lower-case letters are intentionally utilized in my references to the 1950s and 1960s civil rights movement in order to further an understanding of

the specificity of that movement as one movement in U.S. history that battled for civil rights for disenfranchised citizens, and thereby counter a misunderstanding of it as the only "civil rights movement" that can ever exist where activists struggle for civil rights unjustly denied groups of U.S. citizens.

2. For examples, see "Martin Luther King Jr.: He Showed Us the Way," *The Words of César Chávez*, César Chávez, Richard J. Jensen, John C. Hammerback (College Station: Texas A&M University Press, 2002); Sara Evans, *Personal Politics: The Roots of Women's Liberation in the Civil Rights Movement and the New Left* (New York: Vintage Books, 1979); Larry Isaac and Lars Christiansen, "How the Civil Rights Movement Revitalized Labor Militancy," *American Sociological Review* Vol. 67, No. 5 (Oct., 2002), 722–746.

3. Bob Keefe, "'Blacks' Old Guard feels link with gays; Lewis, Coretta King denounce marriage ban," *Atlanta Journal–Constitution*, March 28, 2004, 11A.

4. Frank Reeves, "Trouble for Gays in Black Churches; Pastors Say Bible Prohibits Homosexuality" *Pittsburgh Post–Gazette*, April 15, 2004, A1.

5. Michael Paulson, "Black Clergy Rejection Stirs Gay Marriage Backers" *Boston Globe*, February 10, 2004, Third Edition, B1.

6. World News Tonight with Peter Jennings, "A Closer Look: Same Sex Marriage" Steve Osunsami, ABC News, March 11, 2004.

7. Lynette Clemetson, "Both Sides Court Black Churches In Battle Over Gay Marriage," *New York Times*, March 1, 2004, A1.

8. See further analysis by Irene Monroe, an activist minister and scholar who publicly advocated for marriage equality during the struggles in Boston, of the opportunism of anti-gay-rights black ministers, "Between a Rock and a Hard Place: Struggling with the Black Church's Heterosexism and the White Queer Community's Racism" in Miguel de La Torre, *Out of the Shadows, Into the Light: Christianity and Homosexuality* (Chalice Press, 2009), 39–58.

9. Thomas E. Nelson and Donald R. Kinder, "Issue Frames and Group-Centrism in American Public Opinion," *Journal of Politics*, Vol. 58, No. 4 (November 1996), 1057, 1058. For a review of media framing literature, see Dhavan V. Shah, Douglas M. McLeod, Melissa R. Gotlieb, and Nam-Jin Lee, "Framing and Agenda Setting," in eds. R. Nabi & M. B. Oliver, *The SAGE Handbook of Media Processes and Effects* (Los Angeles, Sage, 2009), 83–98.

10. See Joe Bob Hester and Rhonda Gibson, "The Agenda Setting Function of National Versus Local Media: A Time-Series Analysis for the Issue of Same-Sex Marriage," *Mass Communication and Society* 10, 3 (2007), 299–317.

11. *Baehr v. Lewin*, 852 P2d 44 (Hawaii 1993).

12. Hawaii Constitution, Article I, § 23.

13. Linda Hosek, "Judge Grants Delay in Same-Sex Marriage Case," *Honolulu Star–Bulletin*, December 4, 1996, http://archives.starbulletin.com/96/12/04/news/index.html.

14. DOMA 28 United States Congress § 1738 C.

15. By the end of 1996, state statutes opposing equal access to marriage for gay and lesbian couples were passed by state legislatures in Utah, Arizona, Delaware, Georgia, Indiana, Illinois, Kansas, Michigan, Missouri, North Carolina, Oklahoma, Pennsylvania, South Carolina, South Dakota, Tennessee.

16. Ga. Code § 19-3-3.1 (a)(b).

17. Similar ballot measures prohibiting "same-sex marriage" were passed in Arkansas, Kentucky, Louisiana, Michigan, Mississippi, Missouri, Montana, North Dakota, Ohio, Oklahoma, Oregon, and Utah.

18. National Black Justice Coalition, "Same-sex marriage ban finds support: Blacks' unity splintering," 3 March 2004, http://nbjc.org/news/001001.html. Accessed 21 January 2011.

19. Andrea Jones, Patti Ghezzi, "Gay Marriage Debate: Down to the Wire Lobbying, Then Tense Wait for the Vote," *Atlanta Journal–Constitution*, April 1, 2004, A13.

20. Ibid.

21. Seth Goldman and Paul R. Brewer, "From Gay Bashing to Gay Baiting: Public Opinion and News Media Frames for Gay Marriage" in ed., Martin Dupuis and William A. Thompson, *Defending Same-Sex Marriage, The Freedom to Marry Movement: Education, Advocacy, Culture, and the Media* (Westport, CT: Praeger, 2007), 110.

22. Pamela Ferdinand, "Same-Sex Couples Take Vows as Law Takes Effect; Across Vermont, Dozens Celebrate Civil Union," *Washington Post*, July 2, 2000, A03.

23. *Goodridge v. Department of Public Health*, 798 N.E. 2nd 948 (Mass., 2003).

24. See Mary Bonauto, "Massachusetts: Cradle of Liberty," in ed., Mark Strasser, Defending Same-Sex Marriage, *"Separate But Equal" No More: A Guide to the Legal Status of Same-Sex Marriage, Civil Unions, and Other Partnerships* (Westport, CT: Praeger, 2007), 10.

25. *Opinions of the Justices*, 802 N.E. 2nd 569.

26. *Lawrence v. Texas*, 539 U.S. 558 (2003).

27. Sarah Kershaw and Judith Berck "Adversaries on Gay Rights Vow State-by-State Fight," *New York Times* (July 6, 2003): Sect. 1, 8.

28. Ibid.

29. http://www.whitehouse.gov/news/releases/2004/02/20040224-2.html. Retrieved from the Internet on October 9, 2008.

30. Lynette Clemetson, "Both Sides Court Black Churches In Battle Over Gay Marriage," *New York Times*, March 1, 2004, A1. Also see Chinta Strausberg, "Rev. Daniels: 'I'd Rather Ride with KKK,'" *Chicago Defender*, February 25, 2004, Vol. XCVIII, Iss. 207, 1.

31. Ibid. Also see "Paula Zahn Now," Aired March 1, 2004, Transcript, CNN.com, accessed from the internet October 20, 2008; Daniels repeats the statement at a Boston Press conference, see Eileen McNamara, *Boston Globe*, March 14, 2004, B1.

32. Lynette Clemetson, "Both Sides Court Black Churches."

33. Ibid.

34. Ibid.

35. ABC News transcripts, *World News Tonight with Peter Jennings*, "A Closer Look: Same-Sex Marriage," Reporter Steve Osunsami, March 11, 2004.

36. Ibid.

37. Ibid.

38. Ibid.

39. See A. Dang and S. Frazer, *Black Same-Sex Households in the United States: A Report from the 2000 Census,* (New York: National Gay and Lesbian Task Force Policy Institute and the National Black Justice Coalition, 2004).

40. Associated Press, "Massachusetts Lawmakers Reject Gay Marriage Ban," 14 September 2005, http://www.msnbc.msn.com/id/9341091/ns/us_news-life/. Accessed 20 January 2011.

41. Jim Tharpe, "Pastors Send Clear Message: Gay Marriage Weighs on Black Legislators" *Atlanta Journal–Constitution,* March 1, 2004, B1.

42. The mandatory separation of church and state in the United States is usually attributed to the Establishment Clause of the First Amendment of the Constitution: "Congress shall make no law respecting an establishment of religion, or prohibiting the free exercise thereof." For a summary discussion on its legal interpretation, see Ronald B. Flowers, "What is the Supreme Court Doing to the Establishment Clause?" *Lexington Theological Quarterly* 20, no. 3 (July 1985), 79–90; For a discussion of court interpretations of the separation of church and state in relation to same-gender marriage, see David W. Machacek and Adrienne Fulco, "The Courts and Public Discourse: The Case of Gay Marriage," *Journal of Church and State* 46, No. 4 (Autumn 2004), 767–785.

43. For example, see Teresa Watanabe, "Evangelicals differ on whether Palin's career fits biblical model; some believe her work outside the home has turned 'husband lead, wives submit' on its head," *Los Angeles Times,* October 1, 2008, B1.

44. Ron DePasquale, "Gay Debate Splits Black Community," *Chicago Tribune,* March 14, 2004, 10.

45. Michael Paulson, Globe Staff. "Black Clergy Rejection Stirs Gay Marriage Backers [Third Edition]." *Boston Globe,* February 10, 2004, http://www.proquest.com/. Accessed January 22, 2011), B1.

46. Nicholas Zamiska, "Clergy Coalition Offers Support For Same-Sex Marriages," *Boston Globe,* June 6, 2003, http://www.proquest.com/. Accessed January 22, 2011, B4.

47. "Religious Leaders Call for Support of Civil Marriage for gays and Lesbians," http://archive.uua.org/news/2003/030605.html. Accessed January 22, 2011.

48. Ibid.

49. Ibid.

50. Ibid.

51. Michael Paulson, "Black Clergy Rejection Stirs Gay Marriage Backers," *Boston Globe,* February 10, 2004, http://www.boston.com/news/local/articles/2004/02/10/black_clergy_rejection_stirs_gay. . . . Accessed from internet July 20, 2004.

52. Andrew Jacobs, "Black Legislators Stall Marriage Amendment in Georgia," *New York Times,* March 3, 2004, A11.

53. Ibid.

54. Adrian Walker, "Misusing King's Legacy," *Boston Globe,* April 29, 2004, B1.

55. The *Globe* report includes the observation that Rev. Rivers seemed a little uncomfortable with the assertion about the Klan by Reverend Daniels. Eileen McNamara, "A Hurtful Calculation," *Boston Globe,* March 14, 2004, B1.

56. Irene Monroe, "Between a Rock and a Hard Place."

57. Mark Niesse, "Black Clergy Rally to Dispel Comparisons Between Civil Rights, Gay Marriage" Associated Press, *Herald Sun*, March 23, 2004.

58. Ibid.

59. For a specific analysis of the role of race in the votes about marriage equality that took place in Georgia, see Thomas Chapman, Jonathan I. Leib, Gerald R. Webster, "Race, the Creative Class, and Political Geographies of Same Sex Marriage in Georgia," *Southeastern Geographer*, Vol. 47. No. 1, (May 2007), 27–54.

60. Bob Keefe, "Blacks' Old Guard Feels Link with Gays, Lewis, Coretta King Denounce Marriage Ban," *Atlanta Journal-Constitution*, March 28, 2004, A11.

61. Judith Butler, *Undoing Gender* (New York: Routledge, 2004), 105.

14

The Feminization of HIV/AIDS
and Passivity of Black Church Responses
in Denver and Beyond

Carroll Watkins Ali

The HIV virus first came to public attention in the United States in 1981. Initially, HIV/AIDS was thought of as a gay white men's disease. During the years 1981–1987, statistics supported that belief given that gay white men were 51 percent of those infected, while African Americans collectively represented 28 percent. However, by the year 2008 the numbers reversed. Currently, African Americans represent approximately 51 percent of those infected with HIV/AIDS, while gay white men comprise 29 percent of those infected.[1] One factor partly explaining these statistical shifts may be that a majority of resources were directed at HIV treatment and prevention for gay white men while the black community lacked resources and knowledge necessary for confronting the disease. Today, to their detriment, many African Americans continue to think of HIV/AIDS as a homosexual disease. Due to the ignorance and stigma about AIDS, the disease has spread in the black community regardless of sexual identity or preference as evidenced by the disproportionate numbers of heterosexual African Americans acquiring the HIV virus and living with AIDS. Moreover, the threat HIV/AIDS presents to the African American community through the disproportionate numbers of newly diagnosed cases of African American women and their children clearly refutes the idea that HIV/AIDS is a homosexual disease and signifies the urgency of the problem. This chapter will consider the feminization of HIV/AIDS in terms of its impact on the existential dilemma of heterosexual black women and the black community at large.

The chapter is also concerned with how African American churches are responding to the HIV/AIDS crisis, especially as it relates to prevention. It is not correct to suggest that black churches are doing nothing to combat HIV/AIDS, nevertheless, the notion that HIV/AIDS is a homosexual disease has stifled progress in stopping the disease. The bottom line is that often the level of HIV/AIDS awareness determines the level of activism. Stemming the tide of the current HIV/AIDS pandemic in black America will require a comparable level of engagement by black churches of the collective struggle against HIV/AIDS as they put forth in the collective struggle for civil rights. This chapter examines key examples of black church responses to HIV/AIDS—nationally, and especially within metro-Denver, Colorado, where I serve as the Director of the Greater Denver Interfaith Alliance.

Awareness and Responsiveness at the National Level

The combination of urban poverty and the HIV/AIDS pandemic affecting African American people disproportionately resulting in black people dying at increasingly alarming rates jointly poses a threat to the continued existence of blacks as a people. Statistical data provided by the Center for Disease Control supports the need for a large scale response to the problem: (1) African Americans as 12 percent of the country's population represent as high as 51 percent of those living with HIV/AIDS; (2) African American women are as high as 68 percent of the newly diagnosed cases of HIV among women of all racial/ethnic groups, and; (3) African American youth between the ages of 13 and 19 represent 15 percent of American youth but 66 percent of teens living with HIV/AIDS. Additionally, the numbers of infections are increasing annually. For example, it is estimated there were 68 African American living with HIV/AIDS in every 100,000 in 2005. By 2008, the numbers increased to 74 African Americans in every 100,000 living with HIV/AIDS. The death rates estimate that HIV/AIDS has been the third leading cause of death for all blacks between 25 and 34 and the first leading cause for black women between the ages of 25 and 34.[2] The statistics on Black HIV/AIDS infection nationally are dire, but black churches have generally not approached this matter as a crisis requiring an urgent response.

The Rev. Dr. Marvin McMickle, pastor of Antioch Baptist Church in Cleveland, points out that black churches have responded in some manner to AIDS, if only to hold funerals for those dying of the disease, and calls on black churches to respond more effectively to persons with HIV/AIDS that are sitting in their pews as well as those beyond church walls.[3]

During an interview for the August 24, 2006, ABC Primetime documentary, "Out of Control: AIDS in Black America," Rev. Dr. Calvin Butts, pastor of the Abyssinian Baptist Church of New York stated emphatically that black churches are not doing enough to respond to HIV/AIDS. The documentary strongly emphasized that "the church that took on civil rights has mostly been unwilling to take on AIDS," and spotlighted well-known religious leaders such as Rev. Jesse Jackson and Bishop T. D. Jakes for not making better use of forums at their disposal to raise awareness about HIV/AIDS and about the reality that black people are dying are in record numbers.

The reasons for not taking radical measures to save the black community from the AIDS pandemic are not readily explained by black churches. A common theme in analysis by scholars, however, is that black churches harbor a conservatism based on theological views of homosexuality as a sin and AIDS as God's punishment for the "sinner." In his book, *Their Own Receive Them Not*, Horace Griffin critically analyzes black church teachings on homosexuality as immorality and the effects that it has had on homosexuals who are Christian and upon black church life more broadly. Speaking specifically to a tendency by black churches to look the other way on AIDS, Griffin attests to his personal campaign to disabuse black pastors of the notion that AIDS is a homosexual disease and a punishment from God. As Griffin attempted to reframe HIV/AIDS as a health threat for anyone engaging in risky sexual behavior regardless of their sexual orientation, the resistance to a change in view on the part of these black pastors was quite evident:

> Though I shared these basic facts with the ministers, they would not take on board any factual information . . . Ministers resented any perspective other than AIDS as retribution to homosexuals, especially a perspective such as mine that humanized a group of black men for whom they cared very little, if at all. I had hoped this topic would challenge them to confront their discomfort and fears about sexuality and encourage them to rethink their notions about gender identity and black male difference.[4]

Womanist theologian Kelly Brown Douglas' posits that black church reluctance to engage the HIV/AIDS issue results from a black church theological disposition where discussions of sexuality have been regarded historically as "taboo."[5] Similarly, black theologians Anthony Pinn and Dwight Hopkins argue, "scholars involved in the study of Black religion must wrestle with sex and sexuality—and the erotic—if they are to actually present liberation as a mode of existence that frees the body and fully appreciates the body."[6] Ultimately, it is hoped that engagement in theological reflection and discourse on sex and sexuality will liberate black churches from their inability to wrestle with strategic responses that will provide for life-giving ministry to persons with AIDS.

Where black churches have evidenced responsiveness to HIV/ AIDS, perhaps the best examples come from black churches within the United Church of Christ (UCC) denomination. A cadre of leaders within predominately black UCC congregations (and within a UCC umbrella group called United Black Christians, which represents the denomination's 70,000 African American members) has been instrumental in driving the agenda of the White House policy on AIDS prevention. The congregations themselves practice compassion and approach AIDS as a major health issue churches must approach through educational, public policy, and social service interventions. A congregation that has been especially active on these issues is City of Refuge United Church of Christ in San Francisco.

City of Refuge United Church of Christ founded by Bishop Yvette Flounder, addresses the AIDS pandemic comprehensively, especially through its nonprofit organization, the Ark of Refuge. Services of the Ark of Refuge include housing, direct services, education, and training for persons affected by HIV/AIDS, and residential houses for persons who are HIV infected. For example, the Walker House in Oakland provides direct services to persons recovering from substance abuse who are also living with HIV, while the Restoration house in San Francisco is the first residential facility of its kind serving African American women who have a dual-diagnosis for mental health and substance abuse issues. The Ark of Refuge also provides programs for HIV/AIDS education and prevention/intervention that are also directed at the faith community.[7] Bishop Flounder has also participated in planning and advisory committees for the White House and Center for Disease Control on HIV/AIDS matters.

Perhaps the leading advocate of black church responsiveness to the AIDS crisis has been a national faith-based, nonprofit organization called Balm in Gilead, based in Richmond, Virginia. Balm in Gilead has worked consistently since its inception in 1989 to mobilize black churches as centers of support for people with HIV/AIDS.[8] The founder and CEO of Balm in Gilead, Dr. Pernessa C. Seele, is one of the nation's most prominent voices on issues of HIV/AIDS and other health disparities. In an interview for an article on AIDS and the role of the Black Church, Seele states that her "goal is to have every Black pulpit in the Unites States addressing HIV and AIDS. . . . I believe that every Black pulpit must empower and educate black people about HIV/AIDS and that includes encouraging people to get tested."[9] The Balm in Gilead has engaged over 20,000 black churches around the country through a national Call to Action on HIV/AIDS and through providing technical assistance to black churches on responding to the disease. Since 1989 Balm in Gilead has also convened members of black churches annually for the "Black Church Week for the Healing of AIDS," and numerous congregations have participated in Balm in Gilead's national "Week of Prayer for the Healing of AIDS" every March.[10]

When asked for her assessment of Balm in Gilead's progress with black churches, Seele acknowledged, "while a lot of progress has been made through the Balm in Gilead's dedication to the struggle against HIV/AIDS, in some ways things do not seem a whole lot further along in the black church's response to AIDS" than when she began her work in 1989. "We should be further along dealing with the rate of response equal to the rate of the epidemic," said Seele. She estimates that "approximately 85 percent of pastors are aware of the concern and want to do something about it, but just don't know what to do or how to go about it. In fact, many of them are in pain about the concern, but don't know how to have the conversation because the norm has been to be silent. Prayer and healing ministries get the biggest response as demonstrated through the National Week of Prayer for the Healing of HIV/AIDS."

Regarding the feminization of HIV/AIDS, Seele points out that talking about the heterosexual dimensions of the HIV/AIDS problem helps make the conversation with black churches easier. Nevertheless, says Seele:

> we cannot stop there and cannot win the battle by compart-mentalizing who the virus is attacking. The problem with heterosexual Black women acquiring the disease dispropor-tionately will continue because the Black church is still a male dominated community that does not want to have the conversation on the other side of the issue, which is Black male sexuality. Homosexuality is just a "smoking mirror." Yet, we cannot address heterosexual African American women without addressing the homosexuality and bisexuality of Black men.

Seele's suggestion for black churches is "to develop strong ministries through which black men can talk about their sexuality."[11]

Nevertheless, Balm in Gilead has developed partnerships with important black church networks that have the potential of moving black churches much further along in their responsiveness to HIV/AIDS. A strong ally in Balm in Gilead's work has been the Rev. Dr. W. Franklyn Richardson, Senior Pastor of Grace Baptist Church in Mount Vernon, New York and Chairperson of the Conference of National Black Churches (CNBC). Grace Baptist Church, a highly influential congregation within the National Baptist Convention, USA Inc., and beyond, and the CNBC, a social policy organization supported by nine African American denominations, provide crucial platforms for Richardson's consciousness-raising efforts on HIV/AIDS. Richardson states that "the overall passivity and ignorance" among black churches on HIV/AIDS results from what he refers to as "Bad Bible." The internal response of black churches has been to" use the Bible to support the premise that HIV/AIDS is a disease sent from God to persecute homosexuals and to show God's disapproval of the behavior of gay people." "So there is no outrage," says Richardson, and "quite often just the opposite is true—there is applause—and publicly, silence is the normative way of dealing with not only HIV/AIDS but also anything pertaining to sex." When asked what it will take to move black churches toward openly addressing the threat of HIV/AIDS, Richardson replied: "It is going to take an educated pulpit, because the pulpit sets the culture of the Black Church and guides the public discourse." Specifically, says Richardson, black churches will need to overcome stigmas around gender and sexuality that compound black church difficulties in responding effectively to the HIV/AIDS crisis.

Richardson contends that, ultimately, the HIV/AIDS pandemic is a civil rights issue that has become a "disaster for Black people." It is a disaster because black church approaches to the issue have "rendered HIV/AIDS invisible" while playing into an historical devaluing and silencing of issues related to human sexuality in general and to women's quality of life issues. Moreover, the silence on HIV/AIDS is crippling black people and potentially contributing to black genocide. Richardson acknowledges that as the chairperson of CNBC, he is in a position to drive a national agenda that ultimately makes HIV/AIDS prevention a priority for black churches. He is "hopeful that the CNBC will purpose to take responsibility to awaken all sectors of the Black Church to unite."[12]

Black Church Responsiveness to HIV/AIDS in Greater Metropolitan Denver

The number of African Americans who reside in the greater metropolitan area of Denver is approximately 120,000, comprising approximately 12 percent of the metro area population. Specific to the city and county of Denver, African Americans make up only 5.88 percent of the population but account for 14.5 percent of those living with HIV/AIDS and 12.3 percent of newly diagnosed cases in 2008.[13] African Americans living in Denver are disproportionately affected by health disparities across the board. In metro-Denver, fifty additional African Americans are diagnosed with HIV each year in comparison to ten whites and sixteen Latinos. Annually, there are seven African American deaths from AIDS per hundred thousand African American deaths. By comparison, the rate is 1.5 AIDS-related deaths by whites per hundred thousand white deaths, and 2.7 AIDS-related deaths by Latinos per hundred thousand Latino deaths.[14] Although the Office of Health Disparities, Colorado Department of Public Health and Environment does not break this figures down further to describe what is going gender-specific as it pertains to HIV/AIDS statistics, a needs assessment done by the Greater Denver Interfaith Alliance in 2006 indicated that African American women represented 30 percent of newly diagnosed cases of HIV and all of them acquired the virus through heterosexual intercourse.[15] In term of poverty rates, 31.9 percent of children living in poverty in Denver are African American.[16] It is also significant that while African Americans are 4 percent of Colorado's population (with most living in Denver), they make up 20 percent of the state's prison population.[17]

In Denver there is a need for movement-level activism on the part of black churches if the fight against HIV/AIDS is to be won. Two faith-based organizations in Denver took up aspects of this challenge, the Greater Denver Interfaith Alliance and the Metro Denver Black Church Initiative (which became known in 2005 as the Center for African American Health).

The Metro Denver Black Church Initiative dates to the mid 1990s as a program under a local foundation known as the Piton Foundation. It incorporated as nonprofit organization in 2001 with a social outreach mission to Denver's low-income populations primarily through local black churches. Initially there were over 80 local churches involved in the outreach in one form or another and it has been said that the membership was as many as 113 churches, representing the diversity of black churches in Denver. By 2003 a consensus among the member pastors was that the health and wellness of Denver's black community was top priority, and the organization became the Center for African American Health (CAAH) with a mission "to improve the health and well-being of African Americans, who have higher rates of illness, disability, and premature death from diseases such as cancer, diabetes, and cardiovascular disease." Unfortunately HIV/AIDS and mental health issues were not included as priority health issues along with the other leading health issues listed above. Many would argue that HIV/AIDS and mental health issues rank high on any list and are of major concern to the overall health of African Americans especially because historically they have been so stigmatized that a great wall of deadening silence has been built up around them. Under the direction of its executive director, Grant Jones, CAAH is making a huge impact on the African American community as indicated by the thousands that show up at the Center's various health fairs. It remains a successful model for outreach and intervention in the African American community.

Jones maintains that black churches are institutions with "preeminent" influence over "the mission, purpose and core values" of the African American community at large and that they are essential to black social advancement. Nevertheless, Jones attributes the seeming inability of black churches to galvanize a collective struggle against HIV/AIDS to: (1) the fact that black churches are better at "fighting against something" than "fighting for something;" (2) a general lack of knowledge on the part of black church leaders about the fact that the HIV/AIDS pandemic is a threat to the health and well-being of black people as whole; and (3) the size of the HIV/AIDS problem and the limitations on clergy leaders' time, resources, and energy.

In terms of CAAH's decision not to include HIV/AIDS as one of the major health issues receiving priority by the Center, Jones acknowledges that it was his own "tentativeness about how to address HIV/AIDS in the black church context that was the deciding factor. . . . At the time, I did not think I could get 10 percent of the initiative's member pastors to condone an agenda that included HIV/AIDS as a health issue. Hence, I was unwilling to allow the controversy over the issue of HIV/AIDS to prevent the Metro Denver Black Church Initiative from addressing all the other critical health issues facing black people in Denver."[18] Considering the large amount of previously nonexistent services CAAH has provided to Denver's African American community, it appears that Jones accurately assessed the situation in determining his approach. It was the right call at the time, but Jones admits that it is not his final call on the HIV/AIDS issue. It is notable that the newly elected Board chairperson, Jeff Fard, is a well-known activist against AIDS.

The Rev. Dr. Robert Woolfolk, pastor of Agape Church and a former president of the Greater Metro Denver Ministerial Alliance, agrees with Jones about the divisions building among the organizations black member-churches when HIV/AIDS prevention was raised as a priority. Dr. Woolfolk says, "It is times like those that make you wonder what it is going to take just to do ministry?" Yet, despite the stiflingly slow progress made by black churches in addressing HIV/AIDS in Denver, Woolfolk has not shrunk from the issue. That is why he was one of the co-founders and is the current co-chair of the Greater Denver Interfaith Alliance.[19] "Due to the multitude of critical concerns facing Denver's Black community," Woolfolk says, "I was "willing to work with whoever was willing to work in the faith community context regardless of religious persuasion. That is what our circumstances call for in facing this battle against AIDS here in Denver and the whole country."[20]

The Greater Denver Interfaith Alliance (GDIA) is a not-for-profit organization founded in 2001. GDIA's first collaborative project was concerned with increasing the number of housing units available in the greater Denver area to low-income persons as well as to persons living with HIV/AIDS. Since that time, GDIA's programs have evolved to encompass additional social concerns for at-risk populations in greater Denver pertaining to disparities in economic development, education, health, housing, mental health, substance abuse, and the overrepresentation of racial/ethnic groups in the Juvenile and Criminal Justice Systems and Child Welfare System. Essentially, GDIA serves as a catalyst for coalition building and network development across faith traditions and between community organizations, service providers, and governmental entities for purposes of resource development, expansion, and coordination on behalf of Denver's at risk populations.

In 2005, GDIA applied for a federal grant from the Department of Health and Human Services for substance abuse and HIV/AIDS and hepatitis prevention in Denver's communities of color.[21] GDIA was awarded a five-year grant to implement a pilot program for HIV prevention in minority communities. Although the funding came during the Bush Administration, these funds were allocated under the Clinton administration in response to an agenda pushed by the Congressional Black Caucus to specifically address the disproportionate numbers of black people in this country acquiring the HIV virus and dying from HIV/AIDS and disparities in health care resources available to blacks. As lead agency on the project, known as "Project Redemption," GDIA targeted the disproportionate numbers of heterosexual black women acquiring HIV/AIDS, and the sometimes related issue of black men and women returning to Denver from prison. This was intended to deal with two urgent issues adversely affecting the "survival and liberation" of American blacks: (1) the threat of the HIV/AIDS pandemic; and (2) the mass incarceration of African Americans. Strategically, heterosexual African American women were also made a priority because of the widespread belief that HIV/AIDS is a homosexual disease, despite that fact that unassuming heterosexual blacks are rapidly acquiring the disease. The program, which has been sustained after its federal funding cycle, draws connections between substance abuse, HIV/AIDS, and the prison reentry population as variables contributing to the increasing numbers of heterosexual African American women diagnosed with HIV.

Project Redemption, which was initially comprised of twenty-seven community and faith-based organizations, service providers, and local and state governmental entities, offered two evidence-based interventions to address each of its target populations. The SISTA Project, which stands for "Sisters informing sisters on the topic of AIDS," was implemented for heterosexual African American women, while "Holistic Health and Recovery Program" was an evidence-based program implemented for the prison reentry population. Focusing on women, the SISTA Project begins with enrollment in an intense six-week intervention to raise awareness and provide tools for HIV/AIDS prevention. In order to be in compliance with federal funding, the women were surveyed before and after engaging the course content. In short, these assessments revealed a great deal of ignorance about HIV/AIDS among women participating in the program. The baseline questionnaires indicated that more than 50 percent of the women were not aware of the ways in which they could be infected with the virus and/or the threat and connections between substance abuse and at-risk sexual behavior. The exit questionnaires demonstrated, however, that approximately 87 percent of the women retained knowledge of how to avoid acquiring or transmitting the disease.

Women of various backgrounds and income levels participate in the program. Each participant is tested for the HIV virus and, while most welcome the opportunity to know their status, some resist testing, perhaps because they already know they have the disease. To date, of the 250 women that have come through the program in the past three years, six have openly disclosed their HIV positive status.[22] Referring to GDIA's emphasis on providing services to women, GDIA co-founder, co-chairperson, and resident Imam of the Northeast Denver Islamic Center, Imam Abdur-Rahim Ali, states:

> The increasing numbers of African American women that are becoming infected is very concerning. There are far reaching consequences for the African American community and the next generation, when women become endangered species. We have only begun to see the social problems that will occur in the near future, if we don't take measures on a larger scale. GDIA has intentionally targeted African American women, their children and the reentry population in effort to positively impact the lives of those showing the greater risks.[23]

Initially, the SISTA classes were held at GDIA until churches and mosques (in response to GDIA outreach initiatives) began opening their doors so that classes could be held in "houses of faith"[24] This was a major victory for GDIA because of the resistance that had to be overcome on both sides—the congregations and the program participants. The stigma against persons with HIV/AIDS among Denver's black religious communities remains strong, even as the women in the program remained resistant to entering houses of worship where they have felt devalued or disrespected as women. In some cases, women simply did not perceive the church as a comfortable environment to have open discussion on the topic of AIDS, given the stigmatization of HIV/AIDS within many of these contexts.

Having also partnered with health practitioners in direct service provision,[25] GDIA is beginning to provide training to black congregations so that they can offer on-site HIV testing. The hope is that there will be increasing importance placed on knowing ones HIV/AIDS status, and African Americans will make a habit of openly going to their local church or mosque for confidential HIV/AIDS screening. GDIA health consultants, Byron Conner, MD and his wife Alfredia Conner, RN, have deployed to churches in an effort to partner with them in establishing on-site ministries for HIV-infected persons and their families and to provide community testing. After encountering numerous church ministries throughout the country, the Conners agree that "it is most often the pastors of the churches that are most responsible for stifling the Black Church's response to HIV/AIDS." They say that "the pastors are often apathetic, openly hostile and outright oppositional to addressing HIV/AIDS regardless of whether it is gay men or heterosexual women who are the subject of increased rates of acquiring the disease." The Conners say that they have also "witnessed many pastors intentionally misuse the influence that they have with their congregants by interjecting stigmatizing messages into their preaching. Our greatest concern is the children because many are sexually active. Yet, the Black Church refuses to speak about the need for protection beyond abstinence for fear it will appear that it is condoning sex. It is hard to understand how the church reconciles turning a blind eye and a deaf ear to the reality."

Despite criticism and opposition to GDIA's HIV education and prevention activities and its technical assistance to local congregations, GDIA's persistence has helped motivate the establishment of HIV/AIDS ministries by faith groups in Denver. Most of GDIA's momentum in driving the public discourse came from month-long events scheduled each year beginning in early November and leading up to World AIDS Day, which always falls on December 1st. The events usually begin with a Pre-World AIDS Day dinner and end with a leadership conference for the faith community on World AIDS Day. The rest of the year, GDIA is intentional about keeping the issue of AIDS in front of the community by recognizing all of the dates on the national calendar that deal with raising awareness about AIDS, including the Balm in Gilead's National Week of Prayer for the Healing of HIV/AIDS in March and National HIV/AIDS Black Awareness Day in February.

Moreover, GDIA's success in mobilizing Denver's faith community in the fight against HIV/AIDS has resulted from building partnerships with individuals, congregations, associations, conferences, and other interfaith contexts. Imam Ali has been a strong promoter of interfaith responses to HIV/AIDS. He states: "The concerns of all faith leaders should be the same as we attempt to minister to God's people, and HIV/AIDS is one of the gravest concerns facing Black people right now." Imam Ali's commitment to mobilizing faith communities on HIV/AIDS issues is both principled and practical. He points out: "even Muslims, are looking to the Black Church, as the largest institution in the black community, to take a leading role in addressing the well being of the masses of black people in this country—across faith traditions. An interfaith approach can only strengthen the struggle."

Black churches are clearly viewed by many as occupying a strategic place in the struggle against AIDS, but equally clear is that black churches have not lived up to those expectations. Although it might be argued that some may expect too much of black churches in this regard, it is important that black churches fully recognize the extent to which persons struggling against HIV/AIDS may be depending upon them to provide leadership on this issue. The accounts of three Denver women affected by HIV/AIDS may personalize the urgencies in ways that reinforce the importance of black church engagement of the issues.

Three Courageous Women Living with HIV/AIDS:

The stories of three Denver women infected with HIV illustrate the dilemmas HIV-infected women have experienced in their relationships with black churches.[26]

Penny

Penny was diagnosed with the HIV virus approximately twenty-five years ago shortly after her husband became extremely ill and died very quickly of AIDS. At the time they were both students studying for their master's degrees. Penny says she hardly had time to think of herself because her husband's demise happened so suddenly. However, before her husband died Penny says they tried to come to terms with how he may have become infected. At the same time, they were also learning that a lot of the people with whom her husband had used heroin intravenously were dying. So they deducted that intravenous drug use and sharing infected needles is how he contracted the HIV virus.

Penny is a very bright resourceful woman, who with the help of her personal network of friends began to identify resources and navigating the systems that helped her get ahead of the disease's affect on her own health. "The medical resources and the funding are there," says Penny, "if you know how to find them, but you have to do your research. Clearly the disparities are obvious when it comes to black people and even more so if you are a black woman with AIDS." Currently, Penny is in the process of starting a consulting business for AIDS advocacy and education, which she has named, "An Issue of Blood," which is a take on the biblical story of the woman with the issue of blood that touched the hem of Jesus' garment.

Regarding black churches, Penny quickly states, "The Black Church is simply not a safe place for women to be able to say, "This is who I am— naked and unashamed." Although Penny was not involved in a church at the time she got her diagnosis, her experience as she has outreached to black churches has been very discouraging. More recently, Penny made a decision to leave her church in order to engage activism to provide awareness about HIV/AIDS. Penny states, "Obviously, the Black Church should be the first part of the puzzle, but instead it is the last part of the puzzle. It needs to be the catalyst for bring resources together so that it can take care of its own."

In the final analysis, Penny says that the "Black Church is doing an injustice because it is not practicing love and not preaching the fullness of God's word. Love is education and knowledge is power. Our people 'perish for lack of knowledge.' Love is saving people's lives and empowering people. This is what the business of the Black Church should be about." Penny makes her point quoting St. Francis: "At all times preach the Gospel, and if you have to, use words."

Sallie

Sallie was diagnosed with AIDS three years ago, which could possibly mean that she had been infected with the virus many years before she tested. She is well aware that she acquired the virus through sexual transmission and pretty much knows who transmitted the disease to her despite the fact that she had always been in the practice of using protection. So she is convinced that the man who infected her had knowingly and intentionally exposed her to the disease without her knowledge.

Today, Sallie looks and feels great because she has been taking good care of herself and she says she "expects to live a long time." She has become certified to facilitate the same evidence-based HIV/AIDS intervention program (SISTA Project) that she participated in while she was enrolled in the Greater Denver Interfaith Alliance HIV/AIDS prevention program. She is also engaged in other projects aimed at raising awareness, including the AIDS Alliance for Children and Family Services located in Washington DC.

Although Sallie had not been involved in a church for several years by the time of her diagnosis, she says she has always had a "personal relationship with God." She did not come back to the church until after hearing her current pastor preach a sermon in which it was as though he was speaking just to her. His words were, "Some of you have been in stages of life that brought no changes. Don't trust me. Trust the Lord." Sallie said these words made her "get up and come from the back pew to front of the church."

After a suicide attempt, Sallie shared with her pastor that she had AIDS because she "knew that she could trust him, too." Previously, only Sallie's children and several other family members knew her status. Interestingly, there is only one other person in the church—an elderly woman—that Sallie has shared her status with because she is not yet ready to share it with the rest of the congregation. Sallie says she is "not ready for people to 'change on her' once they find out." Therefore, she is going to "pick her time—a time when she is definitely at her strongest and looking so much at her best that when she tells people they will tell her that she is lying." She wants them "to see the Lord's might manifested in her and hopes that they won't have to ask for forgiveness."

When asked about the role of black churches, Sallie responded, "The church could be such a force for comfort and education, if it would get God's word right." Her view is that the fact that the numbers of black women are becoming infected is increasing has not made an impact on black churches. "The response is still the same. The concern is still more about how you may have gotten HIV/AIDS than helping you deal with it," says Sallie. When asked, "What would you say to the collective Black Church?" Sallie replied, "I would ask them would you touch Jesus if he had AIDS and you knew he was infected?"

Melissa

Melissia shared that she acquired the HIV virus "doing the most natural thing that there is—having a baby." During delivery she was given infected blood through transfusion. She has been living with HIV/AIDS for twenty-seven years. Her twenty-seven-year-old daughter is not HIV positive, but carries the "trait" and tests every six months to ensure that she knows her status.

Life was very hard for Melissia after her diagnosis and for years to come due to the media coverage around her case in light of the fact that she acquired the virus in the hospital and was a woman—a black woman at that. Things got increasing worse with each day: The state stepped in to remove her children from her custody for "their protection;" She was moved to an isolated ward that she referred to as "a leprosy colony." After her husband tested negative, he filed for divorce, leaving her to fight for her life alone. Her only settlement was mandatory health care for the rest of her life, which at the time she felt grateful for as long as her children were placed in the care of their grandparents. There was never any outreach from black churches. Melissia says that although she was raised in the church and had attended many churches, "the Black Church became nonexistent to her." She says she "relied totally on her one-on-one relationship with God."

Although Melissia had never used drugs prior to these life occurrences, she started using drugs when she could not get help. It was hard for her to get and keep a job because people continued to recognize her name and her face from all the media coverage. Eventually she succumbed to spending time with the "wrong people and using crack cocaine as a means of numbing her pain and of providing income. It took going to jail and encountering a dedicated social worker to help get her straight again." She learned that she was qualified to receive social security and was put in touch with some of the resources available for HIV/AIDS-infected people. These resources came primarily through established "AIDS projects" in the nonprofit sector that were state and federally funded. However, it soon became very clear to her that "the majority of the resources were geared towards white gay men and that her needs as a black woman were considered last."

Ten years ago, Melissia's oldest daughter brought her to the church she was attending and disclosed to the ministry couple in leadership that she had HIV. At first, these pastors would not accept her in the church. It was not until a woman, who had befriended Melissia and her daughter and who was also a valued leader in the church, stepped forward to advocate on her behalf that the pastors relented. Yet, it was agreed that Melissia's HIV status would not be disclosed to members of the congregation. Melissia, refused to be shut down because she had nothing to be ashamed of. Today, Melissia takes pride that she has become a leader in this church with responsibility for food ministry. She exclaims, "Imagine that I have AIDS and I am the one handling their food!"

Melissia said she stayed in the church because she wanted to address their ignorance and lack of understanding about HIV/AIDS. She wanted them "to know that their hugs give life to her skin." She says, "if she can face this disease and go the distance to fight it, the least they can do is be in her corner. It is the church's responsibility to love me; to feed a word from God into my spirit to tell me that I am more than a conquer—this is what I need to get up and fight." Melissia goes on to say, "It is the misunderstanding of God's words that 'steals, kills and destroys.' Until the Black Church gets that right, it does not matter whether I am a woman or a gay man, things are going to remain as they are."

Among the personal stories of these three courageous women, there is clear recognition that initially there was little response, if any, from the black church to their life-threatening and altering dilemma resulting from their infection with the HIV virus. Notably, each of these women, in turn, saw the need to remain in the church arena to help raise awareness about HIV/AIDS and to advocate for those living with the disease. Clearly as African American women they all speak to the way in which black churches have failed them and their children. They also speak to how black churches can respond more effectively by providing care and service that is consistent with Biblical mandates. Surprisingly, none of these women feel as though black churches are any more apt be concerned for them as women than they are for gay men who have HIV/AIDS, because black churches in their lack of understanding about HIV/AIDS have seen it as a moral indictment of the person infected rather than as a health disaster for the black community as a whole.

Conclusion

Although there is an urgent need for black church engagement on HIV/AIDS issues, it appears that black churches are passive and, at times, resistant to responding to the urgency of the situation. Despite the increasing feminization of AIDS in black communities, many black churches have not moved much beyond their reluctance to responding to what they consider to be a gay male disease that can be reasoned away as God's wrath against homosexuals.

Lack of understanding is one explanation for the slow responses of black churches, but so too are factors such as lack of capacity and diversity of church policies, politics, and history, as well as the convoluted ways churches approach issues of sex and sexuality. Consequently, black churches have been unable to mobilize a unified and sustained response to the HIV/AIDS crisis. Clearly, black churches need to find ways to facilitate broad dialogue and HIV/AIDS response networks. In the meantime, existing national and local efforts need to continue to be as responsive as possible in raising the awareness in black communities and caring for those living with HIV or AIDS. Examples of courageous black churches and organizations offering ministries working to positively impact HIV/ AIDS prevention help point the way. We need also to understand as Dr. Martin Luther King, Jr., did that it is our divisiveness and a lack of tenacity that is holding the struggle back.[27]

Notes

1. http://www.cdc.gov/nchhstp/newsroom/doc/fastfacts-MSM-Final508 COMP.

2. It must be noted that the statistics indicate differing figures depending the date of the year and the topic that the fact sheets or graphs are addressing. Often one has to do the math to make sense of the numbers and what they are actually saying. See the following Center for Disease Control Web sites for the estimates I used to summarize data ranging from 2004 to 2008: http://www. cdc.gov/hiv/topics/aa/resources/factsheets/aa.htm; http://www.cdc.gov/hiv/toppics/ women/resources/factsheets/pdf/women.pdf; http://www.cdc.gov/nchhstp/news room/doc/fastfacts-MSM-Final508COMP; http://cdc.hiv//resources/factsheets/ youth.pdf; http://www.kff.org/hivaids/uploads/6089-3.pdf.

3. McMickle, *A Time To Speak*, 45.

4. Horace Griffin, *Their Own Receive Them Not* (Cleveland: Pilgrims Press, 2006), 167.

5. Kelly Brown Douglas, *Sexuality and the Black Church* (Maryknoll, New York: Orbis Books, 1999), 89.

6. Ibid., 6.

7. http://www.arkofrefuge.org.

8. www.balmingilead.org.

9. Pernessa C. Seele, "AIDS and The Role of the Black Church," *Inside Grace* (Fall/Winter 2007), 12.

10. Ibid, 12.

11. Comments from Pernessa Seele come from author's telephone interview with her conducted April 16, 2011.

12. Comments from W. Franklin Richardson come from author's interview with him conducted at Grace Baptist Church, Mount Vernon, New York, March 17, 2011.

13. Denver TGA Demographic data. See http://www.scribd.com/ doc/18051065/denver-TGA-Demographic-data-CY20081.

14. *Racial and Ethnic Health Disparities in Colorado 2009*, Office of Health Disparities Colorado Department of Public health and Environment, 57.

15. Data from presentation "Colorado HIV/AIDS Epidemiological Data," Colorado Department of Public Health and Environment, March 2006.

16. http://www.fresc.org/download/income%20and%20poverty%20% metro%20Denver.pdf.

17. http://www.ccjrc.org (Colorado Criminal Justice Reform Coalition).

18. Comments from Grant Jones come from author's interview conducted at the Center for African American Health, Denver, Colorado, March 29, 2011.

19. Dr. Woolfolk's wife, Eddie Woolfolk, is his ministry partner and also a co-founder of Greater Denver Interfaith Alliance.

20. Comments from the Rev. Dr. Robert Woolfolk come from author's interview at the Greater Denver Interfaith Alliance, Denver, Colorado, March 30, 2011.

21. The application was made specifically to HHS's Substance Abuse and Mental Health Services Administration, Center for Substance Abuse Prevention.

22. In addition to the opportunities for empowerment, education and support provided by Project Redemption to prevent substance abuse and HIV/AIDS infection, GDIA also offers support services for the reentry population in terms of transitional housing, individualized case management, health screening services, life and job skills training, other family services, and referrals to community resources, as well as education and awareness trainings and HIV screening for the African American community at large.

23. Comments from Imam Abdur-Rahim Ali come from author's interview conducted at the Greater Denver Interfaith Alliance, Denver, Colorado, April 1, 2011.

24. I want to acknowledge those houses of faith in Denver that were front-runners in partnering with our efforts to impact HIV/Prevention: Friendship Baptist Church of Christ Jesus (Pastors Paul and Dallas Burleson), New Hope Baptist Church (Rev. Dr. James Peters/ Rev. Ambrose Carroll), Park Hill Seventh Day Adventist Church (Rev. Lister), Shorter A.M.E. (Rev. Dr. T. Tyler), Campbell Chapel A.M.E. (Rev. Dr. Regina Groff), United Church of Montbello (Rev. Dr. James Fouther), New Covenant Christian Church (Rev. Reginald Holmes), Anchor of Hope (Rev. Kenneth Roberts), Agape Christian Church (Rev. Dr. Robert Woolfolk), and the Northeast Denver Islamic Center/Masjid Taqwa (Imam Abdur-Rahim Ali). Another frontrunner to step up with our efforts at strategic planning was New Beginnings Cathedral of Worship (Rev. Lewis Brown, Sr.) in Aurora, Colorado.

25. GDIA's medical team, Byron Conner, MD and Mrs. Alfredia Conner, RN have spent countless hours consulting and providing health services to this endeavor and the African American community of Denver.

26. Comments from Penny, Sallie, and Melissia come from author's interviews with these three women at the Greater Denver Interfaith Alliance, Denver, Colorado, March 31, 2011; April 6, 2011; April 15, 2011.

27. See Aldon D. Morris, *The Origins of the Civil Rights Movement: Black Communities Organizing for Change* (New York: Free Press: 1984), 43.

15

Black Churches and African American Opinion on Immigration Policy

R. Khari Brown

Introduction[1]

This chapter assesses the impact clergy have on the immigration attitudes of African Americans. U.S trade policies with Mexico between 1986 and 1994 contributed to the dramatic increase in the ethnic diversity of American cities and subsequent contact between native-born blacks and Hispanic immigrants, the largest immigrant group in the United States.[2] Between 1980 and 2004, Mexican immigration increased by fivefold to 10.2 million in 2004. Many of the poor and working-class Hispanic immigrants who find their way to urban areas are responding to trade policies, the 1993 North American Free Trade Agreement (NAFTA) in particular, that make it difficult for them to lead a quality life in their native countries. NAFTA effectively integrated the markets of Mexico, the United States, and Canada, thereby making it easier for capital inputs to flow across these borders. While U.S. factories are able to produce cheaper goods by locating in countries with lower operational costs, these policies have been costly for Mexican workers, small- and medium-sized businesses, and, the poor. U.S. transnationals in Mexico often undercut suppliers by importing their own capital and materials. In addition, these companies often pay less than the cost of living in areas in which their plants are located.[3] These practices have had the effect of weakening local economies and governments' capacity to provide services, which, in turn, encourages Mexican emigration. Many of these migrants land in urban American communities where they compete with poor and working-class blacks for low- and semi-skilled jobs.

The position taken on immigration by the National Baptist Convention, USA Inc. (NBCUSA), the oldest and largest black denomination in the United States, highlights the conflict between black churches' theological commitment to fighting for the oppressed and their historic role in advocating for black Americans.[4] In, "Immigration and Mission Matters: Framing Our Response," Rev. Charles E. Mock, the executive secretary of the Home Mission Board of NBCUSA, maintains that national boundaries are artificial, political constructions that should not limit access to a quality of life befitting all God's children. Nonetheless, Mock also spoke to the realities of persistent black poverty and increasing competition over jobs and wages between blacks and immigrants.[5]

Economic competition with immigrants is a real concern for many black churchgoers. National data reports that blacks are more fearful than are whites of immigrants taking desirable jobs from Americans.[6] Blacks are also more likely than whites to say that they or a family member have lost a job, or not gotten a job, because an employer hired an immigrant worker.[7] These experiences are consistent with research that suggests that employers prefer immigrants over native-born blacks because they believe that immigrants have a greater work ethic and are willing to work for less pay under worse conditions.[8] Some scholars argue that the above conditions contributed to immigrants having had a depressing effect on black wages over the past twenty years.[9] Therefore, in many respects, prophetic black churches are increasingly caught between a theology that espouses helping strangers in need and meeting the needs of their disproportionately poor congregants who are increasingly competing with immigrants for jobs and wages.

During the 2000s, black church leaders and groups largely have been absent from nationally coordinated marches and conferences that pushed for increased freedom of movement and access to work, social services, and education for immigrants. Apart from the NBCUSA, black church leaders have not offered official statements or passed resolutions on this issue. The silence of black church leaders and groups on the immigration issue may be suggestive of the priority black churches place in battling poverty-related ills within low-income black communities. Their absence may also signal a hesitancy to take prophetic stands on issues that they believe will threaten the already precarious economic position of their congregants and African Americans as a whole.

Because of the lack of discussion on immigration among African American clergy leadership at the national level, the position that many local African American clergy may take on this issue is unclear. It is also unclear if the immigration-related political cues that some clergy deliver during sermons have any impact on their congregants' immigration attitudes. By political cues, this study refers to persuasive messages delivered by political leaders in an effort to inform and shape the policy attitudes of followers. It is particularly important to assess the impact of clergy cues on such attitudes because few citizens have the time and perhaps interests to thoroughly research the pros and cons of the policy issues of the day.[10] In addition, because of blacks' relatively low level of education and their isolation within communities lacking both resources and civic institutions, black churches are key sources of political information for many blacks.[11]

At this point, there is no comprehensive theory that explains how religion impacts the immigration attitudes of racial/ethnic minority groups. System-blame theory may provide some assistance in this regard. System blame suggests that structural forces, such as a history of oppression, unfair laws, or lack of policy attention are responsible for racial inequality.[12] There is evidence that politically conscious black churches reinforce such attitudes among African Americans by emphasizing power inequities between blacks and whites and its relation to racial identity.[13] The most referenced example of black church leaders delivering system-blame cues is evidenced when Civil Rights Movement churches point to the federal government's failure to enforce the Bill of Rights as a primary cause of black oppression.[14] It is plausible that some blacks hearing political sermons and/or announcements highlighting the disadvantaged position of blacks may make cognitive connections to immigrants. The relatively high levels of poverty in black communities combined with African American perceptions that immigrants are taking jobs may contribute to an interpretation among some blacks that immigrant economic maneuverings are representative of an antagonistic structuring of society against blacks.[15] Under this scenario, immigrants represent another external force threatening the economic life chances of African Americans. The following discussion intends to move beyond what has been mostly speculation within scholarly literature about the relationship between exposure to political cues from clergy and African American immigration attitudes.

Religion and Immigration Attitudes

Gordon Alport's theory of prejudice suggests that, for dominant groups, religion serves a dual role in promoting and challenging racial/ethnic prejudice.[16] On the one hand, members of dominant religions are more prejudiced than are members of minority religions. The more religiously involved people are, however, the more open they are to out-groups.

Alport argues that highly religious persons tend to have an intrinsic commitment to a faith's core teaching of love and compassion.[17] In contrast, members of dominant groups that are marginally attached to religion tend to claim religious identification for social status purposes. Consistent with Alport's theory of religion and prejudice, a growing body of research suggests that Protestants have more conservative immigration attitudes than do Jews, Mormons, and other minority religious groups.[18] In addition, the more individuals attend houses of worship, the more supportive they are of legalizing immigrants and the less supportive they are of limiting the number of immigrants to the United States.[19] Given the research done on religious context and congregant attitudes, clergy cues are likely to inform the immigration attitudes of congregants. This body of work largely suggests that clergy have a substantive impact on the ideology and policy attitudes of their congregants.[20]

Nonetheless, the role that religion plays in shaping the immigrant attitudes of African Americans remains unclear. As mentioned earlier, the role of political black churches in reinforcing a system-blame perspective among African Americans offers the most from which to glean. These churches reinforce awareness among blacks of their common racial experience and identity as a marginalized group and call attention to the power inequities between blacks and non-blacks.[21] In doing so, blacks come to recognize the role played by institutions such as the legal system, government, and economic systems, in limiting black economic mobility. Even if clergy do not specifically speak on immigration, discussing a need to mobilize against candidates and policies that attempt to weaken opportunity structures for African Americans may contribute to some blacks seeing immigrants as an obstruction to black mobility.

Implicit in assumptions about exposure to clergy political messages influencing black immigration attitudes is that congregants pick up on and are influenced by political cues in general delivered by clergy. It is likely that congregants are willing to consider the policy arguments put forth by their clergy leadership because of the social capital that exists in most congregations. Social capital refers to the connections among individuals and the norms of reciprocity and trustworthiness that arise from them.[22] These social networks increase awareness of opportunities that may have a positive effect on individual and social group well-being. Because Americans are able to choose their congregations, congregations are, for many, a source of friendships and social support with people of shared of interests and backgrounds.[23] Moreover, to the extent that churchgoers are encouraged by their clergy and fellow congregants to consider a given policy, many give it thought trusting that their clergy are acting in their best interests as well as that of their church community and larger society.[24] In addition to the role of trust and obligation, inducements from fellow congregants to consider a given set of policy issues are often effective because such appeals are often culturally relevant.[25] That is, politically conscious clergy often make policy arguments within the contexts of common songs, communication styles, and religious narratives that hold special meaning to their ethno-religious group. Taken together, this may lead one to believe that the more political messages that blacks hear from their clergy, the more critical they will be of the presence of immigrants in this country.

The following study will help to clarify many of the assumptions made in the preceding paragraphs.

Sample

This study utilizes the 2004 National Politics Study (NPS) to test the assumption that exposure to political messages from clergy may heighten African Americans' concern with immigrants. The Program for Research on Black Americans of the University of Michigan's Institute for Social Research launched the study in September 2004 and concluded it in February 2005. All of the 3,309 interviews were conducted via telephone and in either English or Spanish, depending upon the preference of the respondent. The national sample of interviewees was comprised of persons eighteen years of age or older. The overall response rate was 31 percent.[26] In total, 756 African Americans, 919 non-Hispanic whites, 757 Hispanics, and 503 Asian Americans were interviewed. An additional 404 Afro-Caribbean respondents were also interviewed. The present chapter, however, is primarily interested in the African American sample.

Measures

To assess immigrant attitudes, respondents were asked to report whether or not they believe: (1) that immigrants take jobs away from people who were born in America; (2) that the number of immigrants from foreign countries permitted to immigrate to the United States should be decreased; and (3) that there should be increased spending to patrol the border against illegal immigrants. Respondents' exposure to political messages in their houses of worship is measured by (1) the extent to which they were encouraged by their clergy to take some action on a political issue and (2) the extent to which their clergy encouraged them to vote for a certain candidate. The current study also accounts for frequency of worship attendance, denominational affiliation, college education, family income, gender, and southern residence.[27]

Results

The bivariate and multivariate data presented in Tables 1 and 2, respectively, largely suggest that exposure to political messages from one's clergy contributes to blacks maintaining critical immigration attitudes. More specifically, the more political messages that blacks hear from their clergy, the more likely they are to believe that immigrants take jobs from Americans, to support a reduction in the number of immigrants in the country, and to support the patrolling of borders to keep illegal immigrants out of the country. By and large, African American's levels of worship attendance, denominational affiliation, college education, family income, gender, and southern residence have no real bearing on their immigration attitudes.

The probability estimates reported in Figure 1 further illustrate the relationship between exposure to political messages from clergy and critical immigration attitudes. These estimates are based upon the logit regression analyses listed in Figure 1.[28] Figure 1 makes it fairly clear that as blacks move from not hearing any political messages from their clergy to hearing both types of messages, the more critical they become of immigrants. In sum, exposure to politicized messages by clergy tends to heighten black concern about the immigrant presence.

Discussion

The current study builds upon research that point to the impact of clergy on the policy attitudes and political ideology of their congregants.[29] This study goes a step beyond such studies, however, by assessing the impact

Table 1. Relationship between Exposure to Political Messages from Clergy and African American Immigration Attitudes: Chi-Square Analyses: Cross-tabulations

	Immigrants Take Jobs from Native Born Americans*	Support a Decrease in Immigrants**	Support Patrolling Borders to Keep Illegal Immigrants Out #
0 Political Messages	47.46	27.59	52.13
1 Political Message	55.56	34.44	60.00
2 Political Messages	60.24	39.76	62.65
N=	756	756	756

#<.1, *<.05, **<.01

Table 2. Relationship between Exposure to Political Messages from Clergy and African American Immigration Attitudes: Logit Regression Analyses: Odds Ratios

	Immigrants Take Jobs from Native Born Americans	Support a Decrease in Immigrants	Support Patrolling Borders to Keep Illegal Immigrants Out
Political Messages	1.306*	1.345*	1.279*
	(0.148)	(0.157)	(0.146)
Controls			
Church Attendance	1.018	0.927	1.097
	(0.070)	(0.069)	(0.076)
Black Protestant[37]	1.587**	1.254	1.011
	(0.245)	(0.207)	(0.156)
College Graduate	0.578**	0.839	0.886
	(0.578)	(0.157)	(0.151)
Family Income	1.000	1.000	1.000
	(0.000)	(0.000)	(0.000)
Age	1.003	1.002	1.004
	(0.006)	(0.006)	(0.006)
Women	0.908	1.299	0.541**
	(0.150)	(0.232)	(0.090)
South	0.920	1.138	1.000
	(0.149)	(0.197)	(0.162)
Weight	1.000	1.000	1.000#
	(0.000)	(0.000)	(0.000)
N	756	756	756

#<.1, *<.05, **<.01; (Standard errors are in enclosed)

of clergy cues on the out-group attitudes of a racial/ethnic minority group. By and large, African Americans who are members of congregations in which clergy encourage them to take political action tend to have unfavorable attitudes toward immigration. At its core, the social and cultural capital of clergy within the life of the congregation translates into a strong ability for influencing the immigration attitudes of congregants. It stands

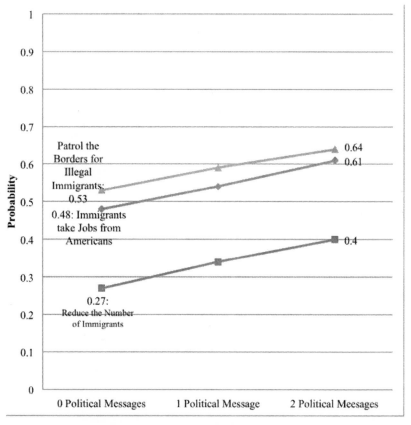

Figure 1. Probability Estimates based upon Table 1 Regressions of the Relationships between Exposure to Political Messages from Clergy and African American Immigration Attitudes

to reason that congregants are open to the policy arguments put forth by clergy because they trust that their clergy are acting in their best interests, and because clergy arguments are delivered in a manner that resonates with the sociocultural experience of blacks.[30]

While the social and cultural capital resources found within congregations likely account for the influence of politically conscious clergy on African American immigration attitudes, the system-blame cues delivered by clergy likely influence the *direction* of such attitudes. The system-blame approach emphasizes the significance of structural forces, such as limited access to jobs, quality education, and quality legal representation in the relatively poor socioeconomic standing of African Americans.[31]

Black clergy who engage in political mobilization from the pulpit often frame the need for political mobilization by using such cues. From the Civil Rights Movement to local grassroots political movements today, activist black church leaders have often framed the necessity of political engagement around a need to prophetically challenge economic, legal, and governmental systems that restrict African American life chances.[32] The current study suggests that the extent to which congregants hear political cues from clergy, congregants likely interpret such cues in a manner that places some blame on immigrants for the relatively poor socioeconomic condition of African Americans. To be clear, this study cannot definitively state that the clergy are directly linking immigrants to the relatively poor socioeconomic position of blacks. However, past research has found that, even when specific policy issues are not mentioned, clergy are effective in influencing the ideological worldview of their congregants.[33] And so, even if clergy do not preach on immigration, blacks are open to applying system-blame cues transmitted from their clergy to their beliefs about immigrants.

A tension seemingly exists between the prophetic theology of activist black churches aligned with oppressed groups and the way in which political messages heard from clergy inform African American immigration attitudes. This tension may stem from the lack of critical discussion among clergy leadership that links Western economic exploitation of developing countries to immigration by the global poor to the United States and, consequently, to the competition between immigrants and the black working poor for jobs and wages. The lack of such critical discussion probably has much to do with the inadequate organizational resources of many black denominational bodies.[34] Unlike the Catholic, mainline Protestant, and Evangelical churches, black churches do not have national and/or statewide offices dedicated to researching the implications of public policies for their congregant base and their theological principles.

In the absence of such a global perspective and discourse, some local church leaders likely transmit to their congregants a myopic view that places immigrants, and not multinational corporations and pro-business trade policies, as responsible for blacks' relatively poor socioeconomic standing. Therefore, rather than blacks and immigrant groups seeing themselves as potential coalition partners, both groups see themselves as competing against one another for jobs, political appointments, and control of community institutions—as a recent study of relations between blacks and Hispanic immigrants makes clear.[35] This social reality makes it difficult for social justice oriented faith groups to forge black and Hispanic congregation-based political alliances in efforts to improve economic and educational opportunities within these communities.[36]

In sum, this study suggests that political cues from the clergy have a consistent impact on black immigration attitudes. The anti-immigration attitudes that such cues reinforce are likely linked to African Americans picking up on system-blame political messages from their clergy and applying them to their perceptions of immigrants and immigration policy. Therefore, while politically active black churches are often perceived by blacks as serving a social justice function, some may do so by emphasizing racial group interests that, at times, pit blacks against immigrant groups.

Notes

1. A version of this chapter was previously published in *Review of Religious Research*, December 2010.

2. Douglas S. Massey, "Borderline Madness: America's Counterproductive Immigration Policy" in Carol M. Swain (ed.) *Debating Immigration* (New York, NY: Cambridge University Press, 2008), 175–188; Raúl Delgado Wise and James M. Cypher, "The Strategic Role of Mexican Labor Under NAFTA: Critical Perspectives on Current Economic Integration," *The ANNALS of the American Academy of Political and Social Science* 610, 2007: 119–142.

3. Ibid.

4. Charles E. Mock, *Immigration and Mission Matters: Framing Our Response*. Home Mission Board of the National Baptist Convention, USA, Inc., 2006; Available at http://www.nationalbaptist.com/images/documents/605.pdf.

5. Ibid.

6. Carroll Doherty, "Attitudes Toward Immigration" in *Black and White*, Pew Research Center for the People & the Press (April 2006). Available at, http://pewresearch.org/pubs/21/attitudes-toward-immigration-in-black-and-white.

7. Ibid.

8. Harry J. Holzer, *What Employers Want: Job Prospects for Less-Educated Workers* (New York, NY: Russell Sage Foundation, 1999).

9. George J. Borjas, Jeffrey Grogger, and Gordon H. Hanson, "Immigration and African-American Employment Opportunities: The Response of Wages, Employment, and Incarceration to Labor Supply Shocks," *NBER Working Paper* No. 12518, 2007. Available at http://www.nber.org/papers/w12518.

10. Philip E. Converse, "The Nature of Belief Systems in Mass Publics" in,*Ideology and Discontent*, ed. David Apter (New York: Free Press, 1964); Anthony Downs, *An Economic Theory of Democracy* (New York: Harper & Row, 1957); Donald R. Kinder, "Diversity and complexity in American public opinion" in *Political Science: The State of the Discipline*, ed. Ada W. Finifte (Washington, DC: The American Political Science Association, 1983).

11. Frederick C. Harris, *Something Within: Religion in African-American Political Activism* (New York, NY: Oxford University Press, 1999); C. Eric Lincoln and Lawrence E. Mamiya, *The Black Church in the African-American Experience* (Durham, NC: Duke University Press, 1990).

12. Laura A. Reese and Ronald E. Brown, "The Effects of Religious Messages on Racial Identity and System Blame among African Americans," *The Journal of Politics* 57 (1), 1995: 24–43.

13. Ibid.

14. Aldon D. Morris, *The Origins of the Civil Rights Movement: Black Communities Organizing for Change* (New York: Free Press, 1984).

15. Doherty, 2006.

16. Gordon W. Alport, *The Nature of Prejudice* (Cambridge, MA: Addison-Wesley, 1954).

17. Ibid.

18. Robert Eugene Brenneman, Faith and the Foreigner: Exploring the Impact of Religion on Immigration Attitudes. Master thesis, Graduate Program in Sociology, Notre Dame University, 2005. Available at http://etd.nd.edu/ETD-db/theses/available/etd-04142005-165951/unrestricted/BrennemanR042005.pdf; Benjamin R.Knoll, And Who Is My Neighbor? Religion and Immigration Policy Attitudes, *Journal for the Scientific Study of Religion* 48(2), 2009: 313–331.

19. Brenneman, 2005; Joseph P. Daniels and Marc von der Ruhr, "God and the Global Economy: Religion and Attitudes Towards Trade and Immigration in the United States," *Socio-Economic Review 3*, 2005: 467–489; Knoll, 2009.

20. Brenneman, 2005; Daniels and von der Ruhr, 2005; Christopher P. Gilbert, *The Impact of Churches on Political Behavior: An Empirical Study* (Westport, CT: Greenwood Press, 1993); Robert Huckfeldt, Eric Plutzer, and John Sprague, "Alternative Contexts of Political Behavior: Churches, Neighborhoods, and Individuals," *The Journal of Politics* 55 (2), 1993: 365–381; Gregory A. Smith, "The Influence of Priests on the Political Attitudes of Roman Catholics," *Journal for the Scientific Study of Religion* 44 (3), 2005: 291–306; Thoroddur Bjamason and Michael R. Welch, "Father Knows Best: Parishes, Priests, and American Catholic Parishioners' Attitudes Toward Capital Punishment," *Journal for the Scientific Study of Religion* 43: (1, 2004): 103–118.

21. Reese and Brown, 1995.

22. James Samuel Coleman, "Social Capital in the Creation of Human Capital," *American Journal of Sociology* 94, 1998, (supp.): S95–S120.; Robert D. Putnam, *Bowling Alone: The Collapse and Revival of American Vommunity* (New York: Simon & Schuster, 2000).

23. Robert Joseph Taylor and Linda M. Chatters, "Church-Based Informal Support among Elderly Blacks," *Gerontologist.* 26, 1986: 637–642.

24. R. Khari Brown and Ronald E Brown, "Faith and Works: Church-Based Social Capital Resources and African American Political Activism," *Social Forces* 82 (2), 2003: 617–641.

25. Harris, 1999;

26. This is comparable to the median response rate (30%) reported in Robert Groves's 2006 study of over 200 response rates in thirty-five published articles. Robert Groves. "Nonresponse Rates and Nonresponse Bias in Household Surveys," *Public Opinion Quarterly* 70 (5), 2006: 646–675.

27. Missing values for family income were imputed from an imputation procedure that organizes missing cases by patterns of missing data so that the

missing-value regressions can be conducted efficiently. The imputations did not significantly or substantively alter the analyses.

28. Odds ratios derived from logit regression analyses are employed to test the above hypothesis. This study also utilizes predicted probability estimates based upon the logit regression analyses to further illustrate the relationship between clergy messages and immigration attitudes. The probability estimates are based upon the following formula; $Pr(y = 1|X, \max xk) - Pr(y = 1| X, \min xk)$, in which Y represents immigration attitudes and X represents exposure to political messages.

29. Brenneman, 2005; Daniels and von der Ruhr, 2005; Gilbert, 1993; Huckfeldt, Plutzer, and Sprague, 1993; Smith, 2005.

30. Harris, 1999; Lincoln and Mamiya,1990; Mary Pattillo-McCoy, "Church Culture as a Strategy of Action in the Black Community," *American Sociological Review* 63, 1998: 767–784;

31. Reese and Brown, 1995.

32. Harris, 1999; Pattillo-McCoy, 1998; Morris, 1984.

33. Smith, 2005.

34. Hans A. Baer and Merrill Singer, *African American Religion: Varieties of Protest and Accommodation* (Knoxville, TN: University of Tennessee Press, 2002).

35. Nicolas C. Vaca, *The Presumed Alliance: The Unspoken Conflict Between Latinos and Blacks and What It Means for America,* (United States of America: Harper Collins Publishers Inc., 2004).

36. Mark C. Warren, *Dry Bones Rattling: Community Building to Revitalize American Democracy* (Princeton, NJ: Princeton University Press, 2001); Richard L. Wood, *Faith in Action: Religion Race, and Democratic Organizing in America,* (Chicago, IL: University of Chicago Press, 2002).

37. Individuals that affiliate with historically black Protestant denominations serve as the reference denomination category and are compared against all others.

16

Religious Others and A New Blackness in Post-9/11 California

James Lance Taylor

The devastating September 11, 2001 attacks in the United States intensified the pariah status of Muslims and numerous other religious
minorities in the country. This is a dynamic traceable to the surveillant
experiences of the African American organization, the Nation of Islam,
more commonly known as the Black Muslims.[1] With a statewide population of more than one million Muslim residents—500,000 in southern
California alone—California is home to the country's largest overall Muslim population. California's Muslim population, which is less than 4 percent of the state's general population, consists primarily of immigrants and
their American-born descendants. Nationally, African Americans constitute the largest segment of American Muslims at nearly 40 percent, dwarf-
ing South Asian Muslims (Indian, Pakistani, Bangladeshi, Sri Lankan, and
Afghan) which are almost 25 percent of the national Muslim population
and approaching three times the roughly 15 percent American Muslim
population from Arabic-speaking countries of the Middle East and North
Africa. Altogether, estimates range from 2.5 million to 8 million adherents
to Islam in the United States.[2]

The widely discussed routine of "Driving While Black" or brown
(DWB) emerged with the first Clinton Administration's expansion of the
conservative-inspired "War on Drugs" in the 1990s and gave rise to the
nomenclature, "racial profiling." The automobile and pedestrian stops
common for decades in the lives of ordinary African Americans as pre-
texts for discriminatory policing have since expanded to other populations, including Latinos and, especially, to men thought to be Muslims.
In anti-profiling legislation, Congress defines it as "the practice of a law

enforcement agent or agency relying, to any degree, on race, ethnicity, national origin, or religion in selecting which individual to subject to routine or spontaneous investigatory activities or in deciding upon the scope and substance of law enforcement activity following the initial investigatory procedure, except when there is trustworthy information, relevant to the locality and timeframe, that links a person of a particular race, ethnicity, national origin, or religion to an identified criminal incident or scheme."[3] But these practices, whether formalized or informal, are more common at state and local levels where most investigatory and policing entities do not necessarily acknowledge patterns of racial and religious profiling as accepted policy or practice.[4] The black male-targeting "War on Drugs" also laid groundwork for the Muslim-targeting "war on terrorism" that emerged in the 2000s.

Long-standing U.S. Protestant patterns of discriminatory group attitudes and relations concerning native-born and foreign-born Muslims as well as Indian Hindus, Pakistani Muslims, and Punjabi Sikhs (most of whom are originally indigenous ethnic Indians with comparatively disparate religious beliefs) have given way to increased legal discrimination and vigilante violence by private citizens. For a number of reasons, African American Protestant churches in the region have not strongly supported most interfaith alliances. Thirty years after the Jonestown, Guyana massacre of hundreds of the Bay Area's disenchanted black church members in the Peoples Temple Movement, the horror of 1978 may factor in the hesitance of black church leadership to partner in contemporary alliances (some in which Jim Jones previously participated) aimed at fighting systematic mistreatment of Muslims and Sikhs in the region.

The Black Origins of Islam in America

In the United States, Islam was black before it was Sunni. The earliest known Muslims to arrive on the American continent were free African traders and African slaves imported by Spanish explorers in the seventeenth century.[5] As late as 1860, roughly 40,000 Muslims were among the Africans enslaved in the United States.[6] Factors that began repositioning views of and by Muslims in the United States included Edward Wilmot Blyden's nineteenth-century writings and thought (for example his 1884 *Christianity, Islam, and the Negro Race*)[7], the early twentieth-century initiatives of Marcus Garvey's United Negro Improvement Association movement, Timothy "Noble" Drew Ali's Moorish Science Temple, and Ahmadiyya Muslim immigrants from India.[8] In historicizing Islam in the United States, scholars ignored these American adaptations in part because these unconventional versions were not viewed as authentically Muslim.[9] The steady immigration of Muslim populations to European and North American countries since World War II (and especially after the 1965 Immigration Act) made immigrant Muslims and their interpretations of Islam somewhat more tenable to the American public, especially in comparison to Elijah Muhammad's Nation of Islam (NOI) with its exotic and less acceptable adaptations. With origins based in the general shift in self-conscious racial attitudes among migrants and in the post-World War I/New Deal era literary movements referred to as the "New Negro" movement[10] and the "Harlem Renaissance," Islam emerged institutionally in the United States during what historian Gayraud Wilmore identifies as a twentieth-century "dechristianization of black radicalism."[11] As Wilmore argues, opiatic African American Protestantism was sharply critiqued by syncretistic urban cults and other non-Christian alternatives competing for the religious loyalties of the 1.5 million newly dislocated masses in Northern, Midwestern, and West Coast cities. Against the grain of mainstream African Americans commitments to the "double victory" against racial fascism abroad and racial apartheid in the United States, the NOI openly supported the Japanese cause during World War II, resulting in the indictment and three-year imprisonment of NOI leader, Elijah Muhammad.[12] According to historical descriptions of the September 1942 arrests:

> the Muslims were charged with evading the draft and influencing others to do so, and also with maintaining seditious relations with the Japanese government. The latter indictment more or less petered out. The Islamites would be likely to feel at least passive sympathy for any nation of colored people at war with the "blue-eyed Caucasian devils," but the government failed to prove that there was any active link between the Nation of Islam and the nation of Japan.[13]

The NOI's core identities were centered in intersections between race, Black Nationalist philosophies, and Islam, which was a mixture viewed with great suspicion within America. Since J. Edgar Hoover's pursuit of Marcus Garvey and the UNIA after World War I,[14] Black Nationalism has been feared and associated with widespread militancy and violence, treasonous disloyalty to the United States, and "black supremacy." From these early encounters with Black Nationalism, Hoover remained obsessed with what he regarded as "Black nationalist hate groups," as evinced in the surreptitious Counter-intelligence Program (COINTELPRO) initiated by the FBI and CIA on an ongoing and ad hoc basis as early as 1955 out of an obsession with Communist infiltrations of Negro organizations.[15] The

Nation of Islam later propounded millenarian prophesies predicting the
destruction between 1965 and 1984 of the United States, (considered by
the Nation of Islam as the epitome of the Western world).[16] These highly
racialized introductions of Islam into the U.S. context initially made it
as quintessentially "un-American" as incarnations of Islam connected in
recent years to anti-Western terrorism.[17]

Malcolm X was key to bridging these early *political* variants of
Islam in the United States with traditional Sunni Muslim practices and
understandings of the Qu'ran.[18] Prior to September 11th nearly all immigrant Muslims viewed the NOI's racial critiques, and even its reformed
Sunni rendition under the guidance and leadership of Imam Warithuddin
Muhammad, as counterfeit and heretical.[19] The path to al-Islam, which
Malcolm X first traversed amid his 1964 break from NOI, was not accepted on terms Muslim immigrants sought to impose in their unfamiliarity
with the unrelenting racial landscape in the United States.[20] Although
Malcolm X traveled to Saudi Arabia in 1959—a detail that runs counter
to claims in his autobiography that he encountered "white" Muslims there
for the first time *after* his 1964 break with the Nation of Islam—his later
travel to African and Arab Islamic nations exposed him to Sunni Islam.[21]
In preparation for Elijah Muhammad's *hajj* to Mecca at the invitation of
Afro-Arab nationalist Gamal Abdel Nasser of the newly emergent United
Arab Republic and Egypt, Malcolm X was permitted to meet with Nasser
and future Egyptian President (Muhammad) Anwar el Sadat. Revolution-
ary Egypt's recognition of Elijah Muhammad and the Nation of Islam pro-
vided a legitimacy that troubled many Muslims in the region, rival African
American groups such as the Moslem Brotherhood (which considered
Muhammad's teachings a perversion of authentic Islam), and government
officials in the FBI and U.S. State Department.[22] Nasser deeply resented the
United States and Europe for their assistance to Israel in the 1948 Arab-
Israeli war. Learning of the NOI's existence through an FBI propaganda
effort to highlight NOI's unorthodox teachings, Nasser saw an opportunity
to work with, not against, NOI. Nasser thought NOI could be instrumental in spreading Islam in West and Sub-Saharan Africa, which Elijah
Muhammad rejected in lieu of a vision of forging "an Islamic empire in
America instead."[23] Against this backdrop, young Muslims from abroad
confronted Malcolm X on his "un-Islamic" teachings on race and politics
in the United States while his relationship with Elijah Muhammad and
his inner circle of ministers deteriorated, combining to lead Malcolm X
to look to Muslim scholars and authorities such as Dr. Mahmoud Youseff
Shawrabi.[24] Shawrabi, sensing Malcolm X's sincerity, urged him to make
the *hajj* in his own right.[25] In the midst of Islam's greatest missionary
push (*da'wa*) in the United States, Malcolm X's probing for a comprehen-

sive understanding of Islam and for ways it might be coupled with Black Nationalism and/or Pan Africanism served equally to influence immigrant Islam's reading of the American scene. Meanwhile, some of the same confrontational Arabic students established the most important intellectual segue for Islam at the University of Illinois, Champaign-Urbana by creating the Muslim Student Association (MSA) along the lines of the identity studies movement resonant on many U.S. campuses.[26] The impact these Arabic students had on America's most popular Muslim empowered the *da'wa* that was to implant Arabic versions of Sunni Islam more firmly in the United States.

Still, Nation of Islam loyalists insist Malcolm X's embrace of Sunni Islam is inextricable from Elijah Muhammad's American-made version. Despite widespread rejection concerning the NOI among most Muslims in America, whether African American or immigrant, Curtis sympathetically insists, the "Sunnification" of Islam did not begin with the 1975 death of Elijah Muhammad. Rather, "it had started years before as they adopted various elements of Afro-Eurasian Islamic traditions and incorporated them into their religious narratives, ethics, and ritualized activities. . . . Wallace Muhammad's Sunni reformation may have been a dramatic break with the past, but it was also a remarkable perpetuation of already established African-American Islamic traditions."[27] Warithuddin Muhammad's reformation, which began immediately after the death of Elijah Muhammad, might be understood as following the path which he and Malcolm X envisioned for the future of Islam in America, modeled after Malcolm's Muslim Mosque Incorporated established in 1964.[28]

Challenge to the NOI's adaptation of Islam (its inception as a Black Nationalist entity) was heightened in the post-Civil Rights era when large segments of African American Muslims embraced the puritanical Saudi Arabian Wahhabi interpretation of Islam known to "avow a universalism which holds that color, race, ethnicity, and national differences are inconsequential. *Asabiya* (nationalism) was considered *haram* (forbidden), and it was acceptable to proclaim loyalty only to the umma or community of Muhammad, the Messenger of God."[29] The homogenizing tenets of Wahabbism (Salafism) have often been uttered with Saudi Arabic accents and with an ideological commitment to "purifying" the international *umma* of the Sufist tendencies of tolerance and pluralism. A staple of international relations among thinkers and scholars (muftis) in the *umma* of Islam is the interpretation that *Dar Al-Islam* can be at peace with non-Islamic states and societies that have favorable treaty relations with Islamic polities. States and societies friendly to Islam were viewed as part of the "house of alliance" (*Dar al-'Ahd*), and at variance with the "house of war" (*Dar-al-harb*)—meaning a country without a peace treaty with Islamic states, which then becomes an object of "jihad . . . until it is conquered, converted, or joins the Dar-al-'Ahd."[30] Islamic scholar, Sherman (Abdul Hakim) Jackson, insists that an immigrant Islam draped in a "false universalism":

> enshrines the historically informed expressions of Islam in the modern Muslim world as the standard of normativeness for Muslims everywhere. In fact, it equates its *understanding* of Islam itself with a simple, unmediated *perception* of an undifferentiated ontological reality. On this approach, "true Islam" can only assume one form anywhere it goes. And in the process, Immigrant Islam's interpretations are effectively placed beyond critique via the tacit denial that they are in fact interpretations. In short, Immigrant Islam does not interpret; it merely *transfers* "true" Islam from one location to the next (emphases original).[31]

There is a thoroughgoing tension between the heterodox African American renderings of al-Islam that emphasize an essential black particularity and imported versions of Islam that avoid such racializations. Oakland's much heralded Imam, Faheem Shuaibe, a former NOI member who embraced the khalifa of Warithuddin Muhammad, has written:

> African American Muslims have a role to play when it comes to the widespread Islamophobia (an irrational fear of Islam) that is prevalent in the West. The unfortunate fact is that some Americans see Muslims as a disease to be rooted out. However, as is the case with immunisation, the "disease" can sometimes also be the source of a cure. . . . African American Muslims are a sign of how Islam can take a vanquished people and turn them into productive and active participants who help to shape their political and social environment. They are a people that have faced discrimination and fear before and are equipped to play a significant role in pushing back against a new incarnation of cultural discrimination and misunderstanding—Islamophobia.[32]

The "policed" aspects of the black experience might inform the experience of others who, especially after September 11th, have been incorporated into the "domestic enemy" trope aimed at previous groups. Gardner C. Taylor, considered the "dean of African-American preaching," points to this dynamic in a post-9/11 speech: "I come out of a community in which, in my childhood, people, some of whom had known the awful indignity of slavery . . . that community and those who are sympathetic with that community, those who have entered vicariously into the experiences of that community, are perhaps alone competent, to some extent at least, to deal with what has happened to our country."[33] Often lost on those propounding a purportedly "true" immigrant Islam is that NOI's version of Islam, by all accounts, was imported by W. D. Fard Muhammad in 1930 likely from Pakistan.[34] This was just one of the major impediments to strong interfaith and interracial alliances between African American religionists and immigrant religionists before the 2001 attacks. But there are others.

After the Civil Rights Movement forged the space and political will in Congress to pass the 1965 National Origins Act (NOA) permitting an unprecedented influx of Asian and Middle Eastern immigrants, Arab immigrants in particular were registered in the column of "white" by the NOA and related legislation. Jackson rightly notes how, prior to September 11th, black American Muslims—the Hanafi, Salafi, Dar Al-Islam, American Society of Muslims (mostly former Nation of Islam adherents), Jama 'at al-Tabligh, two Sufi groups,[35] and independents—understood that while

> . . . American whiteness operated to authenticate and enhance the position of immigrant Muslims, it continued to exert the nearly opposite effect on them. . . . This would remain the case . . . all the way until the events of September 11th 2001, which resulted in an anti-immigrant backlash that carried unmistakably racial implications.[36]

Moreover, the real or imagined ubiquity of immigrant Muslim and Arab petty bourgeois proprietors as parasitic liquor "dealers" and "pimps" in impoverished African American urban communities, (operating beneath placards reading *Masha'Allah,* meaning roughly, God has willed it), has been yet another impediment to minority group solidarity across ethnic and religious lines. This prompted violence from members of the late Yusef Bey's offshoot version of the NOI in Oakland, California in 2007 where members violently attacked Arab Muslim merchants as violators of strict alcohol prohibitions within Islam and as exploiters of the black community.[37] A Bay Area Muslim activist, Samina Faheem Sundas, who founded American Muslim Voice, recounted how two incidents on and after the 2001 attacks shocked her into an awareness of the potency of intersections between race, Islamic identity, and ethnic hostilities.[38] Her first realization of this came when a white man observed Sundas's tears in reaction to the horrors on 9/11 and said: "what are you crying for, America is for white people!" Her second realization came when an African American male student responded to a speech she was giving in southern California on the need for cross-cultural understanding between Muslims and others with the accusation: "where were you when we needed you, where were you?!" The implication here was that the student was placing on her the burden of pre-9/11 immigrant Muslim indifference toward African Americans. There was obvious prescience in Elijah Muhammad's perspective that in Anglo-Protestant U.S.A., Islam would be "racialized" in its own terms, or it would be racialized by others, even when its adherents were considered "white," as recent immigrant Muslim populations would tragically learn.

9/11 Backlash: A New Site of Blackness

As several million law abiding immigrant Muslims, Arab Americans, Punjabi Sikhs, and Christian Armenians have learned, Islam symbolizes not just a decades-long alternative religious tradition among African Americans, it has become a new site of "blackness" for immigrant adherents and suspected adherents in post-9/11 America. The presence of the South Asian Ahmadiyya Islamic tradition predates non-Muslim South Asian traditions by several decades in the United States, but procrustean inclinations of its Protestant religious and cultural heritage tend to conflate disparate, often conflicting immigrant cultural groups into a single, homogenous body. Discrimination toward Hindus, Sikhs, and other religious populations, is more than a case of "mistaken religious identity"; rather, it conveys a general jingoistic sentiment within American culture. Even allowing for the fact of the NOI's historically embattled presence in the United States, Muslims (and since September 11, those thought to be Muslims) have reaped the antipathies of a general anti-Islamic ethos.[39] Mohommed A. Muqtedar Khan insists, "this attitude that Islam is a major threat to the West in the post-communist era alienates many American Muslims, putting them on the defensive and creating barriers that discourage their assimilation."[40] Nowhere was this more salient than in the 2008 Democratic Primary and General Election campaigns of then-U.S. Senator Barack Obama (D, Ill.) whose patrilineal familial ties to Islam in Kenya and stepfather's adherence to Islam in Indonesia became the filter through which much anti-Muslim, anti-Islamic feeling was expressed.[41] Islam is viewed by many critics today as an anti-Jewish, anti-Christian, "alien, oppressive, extremist, or terrorist religion"[42] not fit for Constitutional guarantees afforded other traditions.

A series of events bracketed by the 1979 Iranian Revolution and the 2001 attacks crystallized the pariah status of Muslims in the United

States—forcing them to negotiate the terrain Elijah Muhammad's interpretation of the faith adapted in Jim Crow America. The prospect that
committed jihadist individuals and organizations are present in the United
States (ranging from Hamas, Hezbollah, the Muslim Brotherhood, Pal-
estinian Islamic Jihad, and al-Qaeda), and accounts of attacks abroad in
Madrid, London, India, Indonesia, and Africa since 2001, have made the
chant "Allahu akbar" (God is great) an object of national anxiety, and
has cast Islam as bent on the destruction of Western civilization and
liberal democracy. A cabal of anti-Arab and anti-Muslim propagandists
and investigative journalists in the United States and abroad has tended
to generically implicate all Muslims in terrorism. These commentators
have claimed, for example, that since the 1990s "international terrorist
organizations of all sorts had set up shop in America" (mostly of Arabic,
Pakistani, Afghan, and American Islamic origins) and that "America is
part of an interconnected world of terrorists."[43] People who "look like
Muslims" in airports have been arbitrarily deplaned, if allowed to board
at all. Several hundred Transportation Security Administration (TSA)
workers in California, most of them of Filipino descent, were fired as a
result of new rules after the attacks requiring TSA workers to be U.S. citizens.[44] For months in 2007, the Islamic Center of the East Bay (Antioch,
California), which serves several hundred Muslim men and women, was
subjected to vandalism, a "drive-by" shooting, and threats until it was
destroyed by arson in August of that year.[45] Muslim women donning
hijabs became especially vulnerable. In November of 2008, leaders of the
country's largest Muslim Charity, the contested Holy Land Foundation
(HLF) for Relief and Development were convicted of financing Hamas.[46]
Thousands of non-citizen students at U.S. universities were detained and/
or deported for minor green-card and visa violations. Advocacy organizations have highlighted increased patterns of violence against Muslims and
other groups since the attacks. For instance, the Muslim Public Affairs
Commission reports increases in anti-Muslim violence, once the second
least commonly reported form of intergroup violence but since 9/11 the
second *highest* form of violence among victims of religious motivated
violence (which is an increase of 1,600 percent).[47] Five days after 9/11
the murders in Dallas of Waquar Hasan (a Pakistani on a non-immigrant
visa) and in Mesa, Arizona of Balbir Singh (a Sikh immigrant) epitomize
the arbitrariness of jingoistic vigilantism. In October 2006, Alia Ansari,
an Afghan immigrant mother of six was shot by an assailant in heavily
Muslim populated Fremont, California while wearing her *hijab*.

The civil rights struggles of Sikh immigrants and American Sikhs
preceded anti-Muslim sentiment in post-9/11 America.[48] Sikhs first came
to the United States in 1910, by way of British Columbia, Canada, with

roughly 6,000 settling in northern California.[49] The draw of migrant work opportunities in Stockton, California made it the center of life in the United States for Sikhs in the first of three waves of twentieth-century Sikh immigration to the U.S. Other Bay Area cities such as San Francisco and Berkeley were attractive to Sikhs seeking professional degrees at local universities during the 1920s and 1930s. But it was in Stockton, five years after the first Sikhs arrived, that a site was established for the first *gurdwara* (translated "house of the guru" which is a Sikh place of community worship). A second *gurdwara* was formed in El Centro in the Imperial Valley of southern California in 1948 and today there are more than thirty which serve over 250,000 Sikhs.[50] Much of the discrimination Sikhs have experienced in North America has been related to the wearing of the *kirpan* (sword) and turbans.[51] Their pursuit of Khlasa, the imagined homeland of Sikhs, led Sikhs to view themselves as the army of God (Kartar) and violence could be employed when nonviolent means to the establishment of Khlasa failed.

Perennial ethnoreligious conflicts, animosities, and resentments of the Indian homeland have tended to carry to North America, yet these often hostile groups have also been conflated with others as presumed threats to the United States. This is especially true of Sikh immigrants and Pakistani Muslims, the former having been at variance with Muslims in the Indian subcontinent since the first decade of the seventeenth century when Islamic Moguls viewed Sikhs as an internal threat to their authority.[52] Khan writes:

> in India, Pakistan, Afghanistan, and Saudi Arabia [violence] erupts frequently in the form of riots or discriminatory practices, just as in other parts of the Muslim world ethnic differences lead to riots between Sindhis and Punjabis in Pakistan, Pashtuns and Uzbeks in Afghanistan, Arabs and non-Arabs in Sudan, Berbers, and Arabs in Algeria . . . Far from being united as an American Muslim community that seeks to establish itself, American Muslims are allowing the identity politics of the Muslim world to fragment them into various sectarian groups.[53]

In 2002, Peter Kirsanow, a fascistic African American attorney and Bush appointee to the U.S. Commission on Civil Rights, warned: "If there's another terrorist attack, and if it's from a certain ethnic community or certain ethnicities that the terrorists are from, you can forget civil rights in this country." He warned of a *Korematsu* moment in which "not too many people will be crying in their beer if there are more detentions, more stops and more profiling," and that "there will be a groundswell of public opinion to banish [their] civil rights."[54] Statistical data on patterns of arrests, detentions, interviews, deportations of Arabs and Muslims and surveillance of mosques in the United States have been elusive as the U.S. Justice Department and local agencies do not voluntarily collect or report such data.[55] But according to the Migration Policy Institute, the U.S. Justice Department activated the National Security Entry-Exit Registration System (NSEERS) program in 2002 with two components that ultimately led to the registration of more than 110,000 mostly male individuals from 149 countries and yielded eight terror suspects.[56] In June 2008, the San Francisco-based coalition, Muslim Advocates, urged Senate Judiciary leaders to "hold hearings on interrogations and searches by the Department of Homeland Security (DHS) and Customs and Border Protection (CBP) of law-abiding Americans returning from international travel."[57]

If removal and internment of the Bay Area's Japanese population during WWII (vis-à-vis President Roosevelt's Executive Order 9066) is in any way instructive, the fragile Muslim presence in the United States is indeed in jeopardy of being quarantined should another catastrophic attack be attributed to Muslims. Expanded federal and state police powers as demonstrated in the massive garrisoning of FBI agents who arbitrarily interrogated hundreds of thousands of immigrant, naturalized, and native-born American Muslims after the 2001 attacks (via what were officially classified as "voluntary" interviews) could portend such an eventuality.[58]

Immigrant Muslims, their American born descendants, and other non-Christian religious minorities within the contemporary United States are in a comparable position to early twentieth-century Negroes of whom W. E. B. DuBois morosely inquired: "how does it feel to be a problem?" Nevertheless, these "religious others" have only barely supplanted the "African-American menace," especially when considering that in nearly all of the alleged "homegrown" terrorist plots between 2007 and 2009, the "face" of terrorism has not been of Arab or Pakistani Muslims but, rather, of African Americans or West Indian immigrants.[59] Since 9/11, African Americans and Latinos in southern California continue to be subject to disproportionate and selective profiling as compared to other residents.[60] In Palo Alto, California, for instance, a brief firestorm of protest followed a November 2008 statement by its chief of police in which she declared to an audience concerned with a spate of robberies: "when our officers are out there and they see an African-American, in a congenial way, we want them to find out who they are." In her comments she especially emphasized the need to profile any African American young man "wearing a do-rag." These comments seem almost gratuitous given that the one suspect arrested for the crimes happens to be white.[61]

Amid widespread public pressure, the Civil Rights Division of the U.S. Justice Department conceded the existence and use of pre-9/11 profiling practices targeting especially African Americans and people of

Mexican, Central, and South American descent, and gained agreements
from egregious offenders such as the Los Angeles Police Department and
the New Jersey State Police. An official consensus emerged at the turn of
the century with George W. Bush and Attorney General John Ashcroft
publicly declaring racial profiling to be "wrong" and promising to "end
it in America." Subsequently during the summer of 2001, Senator Russell Feingold (D-WI) and Representative John Conyers (D-MI) sponsored
the End Racial Profiling Act of 2001. The goal of the legislation was to
abolish the practice of profiling; authorizing judicial enforcement of that
ban by the federal government; requiring state and local law enforcement
agencies to collect traffic stop and other law enforcement data; and establishing institutional safeguards against profiling as a condition of federal
funding. Unfortunately, the consensus collapsed with the World Trade
Center buildings and the legislation was never passed. Today foreign-born
individuals make up about 35 percent of the California's population, but
they constitute only 17 percent of its adult prison population. African
American men, constituting less than 4 percent of the state's population
represent the lion's share of prisoners, with U.S.-born men (ages 18–40)
institutionalized at a rate that is 10 times higher than that of foreign-born
men (4.2% to 0.42%). Despite fears and concerns over terrorist extrem-
ism (now stereotypically associated with Arabs or Muslims) it has been
African Americans and not foreign-born individuals from Asian countries
with large Muslim populations that have been disproportionately subject
to arrests and incarceration in California.

Despite the Bush administration's condemnation of racial and religious profiling, the Applied Research Center (ARC) based in Oakland,
California has itemized numerous abuses of authority by federal and local
officials and argues:

> the administration has conflated immigration with crime, ter-
> rorism and national security, institutionalizing this approach
> in 2003 with the creation of the Department of Homeland
> Security. Subsequently, the creation of Immigration and Cus-
> toms Enforcement (ICE) within the DHS has led to a dramatic
> increase of workplace raids and deportations from about 186,000
> in 2001 to 277,000 in 2007; an increase that began during
> President Clinton's second term (70,000 deportations in 1996
> to 114,000 the following year).[62]

ARC co-sponsored a series of "The Public's Truth" forums in major
cities in 2003 which provided individuals of African American, Middle Eastern and Arabic, Mexican, Sikh, Indian, Japanese, and Filipino

descent to share their experiences. Subtitled "Stories of Racial Profiling and The Attack on Civil Liberties," the Bay Area forum focused on individual accounts of discrimination in the areas of hate crimes, without-cause-firings, workplace attire and headdress discrimination, and police harassment.[63] Apparently, the illegal practice of religious profiling has not supplanted racial profiling; rather, the two have fed off each other.

Islam and Other Religious Minorities on Jericho Road: Black Church Responses[64]

In most metropolitan areas, there are hundreds of little-known church leaders and congregations that serve meaningfully in the shadows of more prominent ministers, large congregations, and broader ecclesiastical alliances. A general overview of black clergy interventions on behalf of "religious others" in California reveals instances of effective faith-based networking with African American elected officials and with churches large and small. Nevertheless, as was the case with black religious leaders and elected officials in the aftermath of 9/11, black leaders in California were viewed as secondary spokesmen at best because their political views on international matters were often seen as in opposition to mainstream national concerns.[65]

Whether referring to Martin Luther King and the Southern Christian Leadership Conference, Jesse Jackson's Rainbow Coalition, or even Louis Farrakhan's "coalition of the subaltern" (leading up to the Million Man March), African American religious elites have emphasized interfaith means to eradicating social injustice. Civil Rights activism and subsequent black religion-based collective actions did not result from mobilizing a majority of African American denominations and congregations but from intensive efforts from a minority of African American religious leaders and congregations.

Locally, Bay Area African American churches have had to adapt to a rapidly transformed theatre in which their main constituencies are increasingly stratified by gender, socioeconomic status, and age, and are heavily affected by numerous downturns and negative patterns within urban contexts. Some of these difficulties include community violence, the proliferation of "crack" cocaine and other drugs, alcoholism, individualism, HIV/AIDS, and economic distress that set in long before the economic collapse of 2008. Black Power and Hip-Hop activists are just two manifestations of a mode of secularization that grew out of the black church's "success" in the Civil Rights Movement, foregrounding institutional declines in black churches' once powerful hold on many aspects of African American life.

The narcissistic "wealth and prosperity gospel" that pervades hundreds of megachurches is of a considerably different morality and social orientation than that represented by King's critiques of capitalism or Black Theology's critiques of white supremacy in the churches.[66] Still, talk of the death of the black church would be presumptuous as its adaptation to new realities portends more promise locally than at a broad national level.

Northern California has a vibrant ecumenical and interfaith community, forged in support of earthquake preparation and recovery, same-sex marital rights, environmental issues, health, workers' and union rights, housing rights, peace and nonviolence, religious common ground, prison ministries, homelessness, and immigration policy. The region's ecumenical and interfaith infrastructure is vast, progressive, and "hyperplural,"[67] but these networks tend to be "apolitical," single-issue oriented, dominated by one of the Abrahamic traditions (with other faiths operating as junior partners),[68] ad hoc, moving from one crisis to another, and led by older white progressives and liberals.

There was no preexisting interfaith infrastructure in the region prior to the 2001 attacks that could in turn assist in the struggle against Islamophobia. Not only are interfaith alliances opposing Islamophobia recent, but they are hampered by what seems to be a pact of silence on the part of Muslim leaders and organizations in the region.[69] Also, the alliances tend to operate on a kind of "trickle down" approach to ecumenical and interfaith work, held together less by a desire for mass movement or educating ordinary people about the tenets of Islam than by pastor-to-pastor and leader-to-leader collegiality.

There have been a few noteworthy ministers who have supported these coalitions, but they have been exceptions more than the rule among Bay Area clergy. Individual leaders such as J, Alfred Smith, Sr. (Allen Temple Baptist Church, Oakland), Amos Brown (Third Baptist Church, San Francisco), Dorsey Blake (Church for the Fellowship of All Peoples, San Francisco), Phil Lawson (Interfaith Program Director for East Bay Housing Organizations), Calvin Simmons, (Greater St. Paul Baptist Church, Oakland) Rev. Ken Chambers, Jr. (former pastor of West Side Missionary Baptist Church, Oakland who was awarded the National Council of Churches President's award two months after the 2001 attacks), Rev. Michael Yoshi (Japanese-American pastor of Buena Vista United Methodist Church in Alameda), Clarence Johnson (Mills Grove Christian Church, Oakland) and Imam Faheem Shuaibe (Masjidul Waritheen, Oakland/San Francisco) are listed as allies, board members, former presidents, and partners on many Bay Area interfaith council rolls and Web sites.[70] All of these clergy except for Rev. Yoshi are African American. Each has been allied variously with the Northern California Interreligious Conference, Islam Networks Group, Applied Research Center, Greater Richmond Interfaith Program,[71] Interfaith Coalition for Immigrant Rights, Interfaith Council of Contra Costa County, California Council of Churches, the Graduate Theological Union's Center for Islamic Studies, the California Interfaith Power and Light Alliance, East Bay Housing Organizations (EBHO), Temple Sinai of Oakland, and Foundation Alliance with Interfaith to Heal Society (FAITHS) of the San Francisco Foundation.

Despite involvements in broader California ecumenical and interfaith organizations by individual black clergy, there have been no institutional formations or interfaith coalitions initiated specifically by black churches with the exception of an African Immigration advocacy group, Priority Africa Network. The purpose of this group has been to give voice to African immigrants, many of whom are Muslims, during the fierce immigration debates of 2006 and after. Amos Brown, pastor of Third Baptist Church and former San Francisco Supervisor[72] responded to a question about the involvement of African American churches in interfaith alliances supportive of Muslim concerns with what seems to be a consensus. Specifically, he retorted, "they are not doing a thing!"[73] Allen Temple Baptist Church of Oakland is one of the very few African American fellowships that have allied with efforts to increase interfaith understanding and to combat religious discrimination against Muslims. Similarly, Antioch Baptist Church of San Jose, (formerly pastored by J. Alfred Smith, Jr. who has recently replaced his father as pastor of Allen Temple), has been yet another. Antioch Baptist church is the oldest black Baptist congregation in California's second largest city. It has supported Muslims mainly in alliance with the Islam Networks Group (ING) of San Jose. The ING too tends to be exceptional, defying the general tendency of interfaith non-engagement between African American Protestants and Immigrant Muslim groups. The ING has steadily forged pluralistic alliances with a wide array of faith and cultural traditions—Jewish, mainline Protestant, Catholic, Buddhist, Unitarian, and independent nondenominational fellowships beginning formally in the late 1990s. Its activities took on added significance after the 2001 attacks. The most visible black clergyman in the Bay Area on these issues has been East Bay Housing Organizations' Phil Lawson, (brother of civil rights leader, James Lawson, who worked closely with Martin Luther King, Jr.). Lawson's involvement in Bay Area interfaith alliances is unmatched by any single individual. He has carried the integrationist commitments of the Civil Rights Movement into his systematic advocacy for others languishing at the religious, sexual, class, and racial margins of American society.[74]

Generally, African American religious leaders—Christian or Muslim—have not instituted strong anti-profiling alliances with immigrant

Muslim groups beyond annual commemorations of the 9/11 attacks and interfaith networking among religious elites that have not necessarily translated into heightened grassroots consciousness or support. A partial explanation has to do with the importunate state of the communities which many African American church leaders service. Reverend Lawson, who has worked closely with Muslim leaders, expressed in an interview that immigrant "Muslims need to understand that the black community is the Gaza Strip of the American Empire; the black community is under assault."[75] In the Bay Area, black churches constitute less than 5 percent of the hundreds of religious institutions in the region.[76] Moreover, the crisis mode of many African American churches affected by black population decline, widespread and banal community-level violence (e.g., Richmond, East and West Oakland, East Palo Alto, and the Bayview-Hunter's Point section of San Francisco), and ministerial divisions has persisted even before the 1978 Jonestown, Guyana massacre shook the foundations of African American churches.[77] An overwhelming majority of those who belonged to the Peoples Temple in San Francisco and Los Angeles and that later died in Guyana were African Americans disenchanted with local churches. In this regard J. Alfred Smith, Sr., notes, this tragedy ". . . stops my brothers and sisters in the black clergy in the Bay Area from giving a voice to the grief, to the sense of betrayal, and to the internal struggle to understand how we played a role in the success of Jim Jones in our midst."[78]

The Peoples Temple tragedy in 1978 exposed major ecclesiastical fractures that have persisted throughout the post-Civil Rights era.[79] Before leaving for Guyana, Jim Jones and the Peoples Temple participated in ecumenical and interfaith alliances with the San Francisco Council of Churches (in 1972 its name was changed to Northern California Ecumenical Council, and in 2000 to the Northern California Interreligious Conference). Rebecca Moore and her colleagues note, "in the Bay Area of the 1970s, black churches were expressive of two different strands of the black Christian tradition." One strand was the conservative and evangelically motivated majority of congregations with a largely "otherworldly" emphasis. The other strand was epitomized in the Alamo Black Clergy, which included Jim Jones-ally Rev. Cecil Williams of Glide Memorial United Methodist Church. It had a strong social justice orientation rooted in the Black Theology tradition born of Black Power. Moore and her colleagues argue further: "San Francisco itself was less affected by the Civil Rights movement than by the secular 'New Left' political movement; most black churches were influenced by neither."[80] Most of the ministers and churches that were moved toward interfaith alliances in support of Muslims and religious others in light of the 2001 attacks have been leaders who emerged from the ashes of Black Power's own domestic enemy status.

Conclusion

This chapter focused on the plights and coalition challenges of immigrant Muslims in a war and national security milieu shaped powerfully by the events leading to and following the 2001 attacks on the United States. Home to the nation's largest Muslim and Sikh communities, (as it was to most Japanese Americans during World War II), the state of California provides students an opportunity to imagine if the past is prologue to a future where clear social and legal biases target an otherwise heterogeneous people for suspicion of national disloyalty based on salient cultural characteristics.

The coalition challenges are manifold—particularly those posed by the internal and external dynamics of African American versions of Islam, Immigrant Muslims, Sikh Indians, and African American Christian churches. With a few very noteworthy exceptions, it appears that the strongest interfaith and ecumenical alliances in the region have been forged, not by African American churches and ministerial alliances well positioned to confront official misconduct such as "racial profiling," but with Japanese Buddhists and Christians who have not forgotten the nadir of World War II. Scholars of Japanese removal and internment have asked the question, "*how could we have interned 120,000 Japanese Americans during World War II?*"[81] Interspersing the study of the balance between national defense and security and individual civil liberties for citizens and non-citizens is the account of how a majority of descendants of Japanese ancestry were removed by the War Relocation Authority of the federal government from their homes and community in San Francisco's "J-Town" district (later known as the Fillmore "Harlem of the West" among African American residents and others) following the 1941 attacks on Pearl Harbor. With short notice, they were shuttled and later interned in military camps throughout the Western United States and held for years.[82] State claims of "military necessity," and national security trumped the civil liberties of Japanese Americans and Japanese nationals alike. A consensus formed within the major branches of government reinforced by social and racial discrimination aimed at Japanese individuals in northern California (some 150,000 Japanese Americans and nationals in Hawaii were never affected by the executive order authorizing removal and internment)[83] leading one Congressionally-funded study to conclude, "the broad historical causes which shaped the decisions were race prejudice, war hysteria and a failure of political leadership."[84]

For its liberal and progressive tendencies, the San Francisco Bay Area, like the nation at large, promoted and passed racially discriminatory laws and pacts regarding South and Southeast Asians and Middle

Eastern populations as far back as Chinese Exclusion beginning in 1882. As University of California historian Ronald Takaki points out: "Chinese migrants found that racial qualities previously assigned to blacks quickly became 'Chinese' characteristics. . . . White workers referred to the Chinese as 'nagurs,' and a magazine cartoon depicted the Chinese as a bloodsucking vampire with slanted eyes, a pigtail, dark skin, and thick lips. Like blacks, the Chinese were described as heathen, morally inferior, savage, childlike, and lustful . . . and their depravity was associated with their physical appearance, which seemed to show 'but a slight removal from the African race.'"[85] When religious others and people of Arab and South Asian descent encountered U.S. wartime prejudice and hostility in the early twenty-first century, they found themselves in the precarious position once reserved for Native Americans, fugitive slaves, Chinese "coolies," Nisei and Sensei Japanese, New Left radicals, Communists, African American people, and groups such as the Nation of Islam and the Black Panther Party.

In order to participate fully in *Al-Islam* in the West and the interfaith "beloved community," it may be the experiences of these groups that best inform the plight of discrete minority populations subject to official surveillance and individual vigilantism. The cultural capital and instruments of resistance which African Americans have employed, including Elijah Muhammad's version of Islam and the Christianity of African American churches can be critical entrées into sustainable coalitions suited to post-9/11 political realities.

Notes

1. See Arna Bontemps and Jack Conroy, *Any Place But Here* (New York: Hill and Wang, 1966); C. Eric Lincoln, *The Black Experience in Religion* (Garden City, NY: Doubleday Press, 1974).

2. See Kenneth Wald and Allison Calhoun Brown, *Religion and Politics in the United States*, 5th ed., (Lanham, MD: Rowman and Littlefield, 2007); and Yazbeck Haddad and John L. Esposito, eds., *Muslims on the Americanization Path?* (Oxford: Oxford University Press, 2000).

3. In particular, the practice stands in violation of the Due Process and Equal Protection Clauses of the 14th Amendment, and Title VI of the 1964 Civil Rights Act that prohibits discrimination based on race, color, or national origin for entities that receive federal aid.

4. According to *Drug War Chronicle* (formerly The Week Online with DRCNet) online newsletter, in 2003, the California Highway Patrol (CHP) announced a series of reforms to settle a racial profiling lawsuit brought against it by the American Civil Liberties Union (ACLU) of Northern California. The federal class-action lawsuit was filed in 1999 after a San Jose-area drug interdic-

tion operation searched a car driven by a Latino lawyer, part of what the ACLU called a pattern of law enforcement activity where "race and racial stereotyping had become a proxy for criminal activity." According to ACLU researchers who studied the more than one million traffic stops made by CHP in the state's central and coastal divisions in 2000 and 2001, Latinos were pulled over three times as often, and blacks 1.5 times as often, as white drivers. Please see http://stopthedrugwar.org/chronicle-old/277/chprofiling.shtml.

5. See Anthony B. Pinn, *Varieties of African American Religious Experience*, (Minneapolis, MN: Augsburg Fortress Press, 1998), 113; Ernest Allen, Jr., "Identity and Destiny: The Formative Views of the Moorish Science Temple and the Nation of Islam" in *Muslims on the Americanization Path?* eds., Yvonne Yazbeck Haddad and John L. Esposito (Oxford: Oxford University Press, 2000), 164.

6. See Allan Austin, *African Muslims in Antebellum America: Transatlantic Stories and Spiritual Struggles* (New York and London: Routledge, 1997), 22. Austin is cited in Sherman A. Jackson, *Islam and the Blackamerican: Looking Toward the Third Resurrection* (Oxford: Oxford University, 2005), 34. Jackson insists that Austin's number of 11 million overestimates the number of black people in the country by 2 million more than the 1900 U.S. Census estimate of 9 million (see fn. 40 on p. 204).

7. See Edward W. Blyden, *Christianity, Islam, and the Negro Race* (Baltimore, MD: Black Classic Press, 1994).

8. See, C. R. D. Halisi, "Blyden's Ghost: African American Christianity and Racial Republicanism" in *New Day Begun: African American Churches and Civic Culture in Post-Civil Rights America*, ed., R. Drew Smith (Durham, NC: Duke University Press, 2003); Sherman A. Jackson, *Islam and the Blackamerican: Looking Toward the Third Resurrection* (Oxford: Oxford University, 2005); Edward E. Curtis IV, *Islam in Black America: Identity, Liberation, and Difference in African-American Islamic Thought* (Albany, NY: State University of New York Press, 2002); Richard B. Turner, *Islam in the African American Experience* (Bloomington, IN: Indiana University Press, 1997).

9. Richard B. Turner, *Islam in the African American Experience*, 1997; Yvonne Yazbeck Haddad and John L. Esposito, eds., *Muslims on the Americanization Path?* 2000; Curtis, Edward E. Curtis IV, *Islam in Black America: Identity, Liberation, and Difference in African-American Islamic Thought*, 2002.

10. I use the term Negro throughout this article as a chronological referent indicating the names of organizations, pre-Civil Rights leadership and political activity, and as used in common language of the period preceding Black Power in 1966. Thus, I do not use the term interchangeably with black or African American, which have since replaced it in common usage. The United Negro College Fund is one of the few organizations that continues to use the term that has otherwise become obsolete.

11. Gayraud S. Wilmore, *Black Religion and Black Radicalism: An Interpretation of the Religious History of African Americans*, 3rd ed. (Maryknoll, NY: Orbis, 2003).

12. C. Eric Lincoln, *The Black Experience in Religion*, 1974, 25.

13. Arna Bontemps and Jack Conroy, *Any Place But Here* 1966, 224. Consistent with the many other reversals to his father's theological and social teach-

ings, during the Desert Shield action and the subsequent Desert Storm Gulf War several decades later, Warithuddin Muhammad would enthusiastically support the George H. W. Bush administration's actions in the region.

14. Garvey was targeted for violation of the "white slavery" Mann Act for traveling abroad with his future wife (but then secretary) Amy Jacques Garvey (although she was clearly "Negro"), tax evasion through the foundering but highly influential Black Star Line, and finally federal mail fraud violations.

15. Karl Evanzz, *The Messenger: The Rise and Fall of Elijah Muhammad* (New York: Pantheon Books, 1999), 169.

16. Originally set by Elijah Muhammad for 1965, the Islamic apocalypse— at least in the form of insurrectionist violence—would not be forthcoming. The epitome of the Nation's "separatist" inclinations was reflected in its self-determina- tion ethos and in a plethora of business ventures including restaurants, bakeries, and grocery stores. The chief source of revenues aside from these efforts was the hawking of the organization's newspapers, whiting fish, and bean pies by the para- military Fruit of Islam (FOI) and the women spread across every major city in the country extending from Massachusetts to California and North to South. Please see, Claude Clegg III, *An Original Man: The Life and Times of Elijah Muhammad* (New York: St. Martin's Press, 1997), 72.

17. Given the centuries-old tensions between Islam and the West from Islamic domination of Europe to the First Crusades at the beginning of the second millennium (CE), to the collapse of Islamic Spain at the hands of the Christian *conquistadors,* and the defeat of the Ottoman Empire in World War I, being coupled with race made the introduction of Islam to America doubly contestable. Please see Sherman A. Jackson, *Islam and the Blackamerican: Looking Toward the Third Resurrection,* 2005, 39.

18. See Louis A. DeCaro, Jr., *On the Side of My People: A Religious Life of Malcolm X* (New York: New York University Press, 1996); Edward E. Curtis IV, *Islam in Black America: Identity, Liberation, and Difference in African-American Islamic Thought,* 2002; William R. Sales, Jr., *From Civil Rights to Black Liberation: Malcolm X and the Organization of Afro-American Unity* (Boston, MA: South End Press, 1994).

19. Yvonne Yazbeck Haddad and John L. Esposito, eds., *Muslims on the Americanization Path?* 2000, 273–274, 276.

20. Because of African American Muslims, including the Nation of Islam, legal challenges in the local jails and state and federal prisons related to Muslims' rights to *halal* meals, *Salat* (prayers) and *Jummah* Friday services were settled issues by the time Immigrant Muslims arrived in the United States.

21. Karl Evanzz, *The Messenger: The Rise and Fall of Elijah Muhammad* (New York: Pantheon Books, 1999), 214.

22. Ibid., 200.

23. Ibid., 199, 213.

24. Edward E. Curtis IV, *Islam in Black America: Identity, Liberation, and Difference in African-American Islamic Thought,* 2002, 90–91.

25. Curtis notes Shawarbi's sponsorship and introduction of Malcolm X to anti-Nasserite Islamic authorities in the region of the Middle East. Specifi- cally, he taught Malcolm X the details of Sunni Islam, and provided him with

an introduction letter and a copy of Abd al-Rahman Azzam's classic defense of Islam against the West, *The Eternal Message of Muhammad*. A son of Azzam's was married to the daughter of Saudi Prince Faysal (see Edward E. Curtis IV, *Islam in Black America: Identity, Liberation, and Difference in African-American Islamic Thought*, 2002, 93–96).

26. Ibid, 93.

27. Edward E. Curtis IV, *Black Muslim Religion in the Nation of Islam: 1960–1975* (Chapel Hill, NC: The University of North Carolina Press, 2006), 185. Curtis appears to be referring in this quote to the African and Amhadiyya movement of Islam from India that arrived early in the USA—this chapter does mention this Eurasian movement on pages XX and XX of Chapter 4 in this text.

28. Along with one of his older brother's Akbar, Wallace D. Muhammad studied with Muslim scholars while attending university in Saudi Arabia and would emphasize those teachings even among the Nation of Islam faithful— especially rejecting the notion that Elijah Muhammad was "the last messenger of Allah," or Allah's Holy Apostle. Wallace Muhammad and others sided with Malcolm X in the disputes that emerged after Malcolm X's suspension from the Nation of Islam for suggesting that the November 22, 1963 assassination of JFK was a case of retribution for the purveyance of anti-black violence in America, historically. He famously called the assassination as a case of "chickens coming home to roost." He was expeditiously suspended and his career in the Nation of Islam was effectively over.

29. Yusuf Nurrudin, "African American Muslims and the Question of Identity: Between Traditional Islam, African Heritage, and the American Way" in *Muslims on the Americanization Path?* eds. Yvonne Yazbeck Haddad and John L. Esposito (Oxford: Oxford University Press, 2000), 225.

30. Mohommed A. Muqtedar Khan, "Muslims and Identity Politics in America" in *Muslims on the Americanization Path?* eds. Yvonne Yazbeck Haddad and John L. Esposito (Oxford: Oxford University Press, 2000), 94.

31. Sherman Jackson, *Islam and the Blackamerican: Looking Toward the Third Resurrection*, 2005, 12.

32. In Shuaibe's estimation, the African American Muslims' role as vanguard cannot be subordinate to Arab cultural hegemony anymore legitimately than Western and North American Christianity was to the Black collective it first encountered in slavery. See Faheem Shuaibe, "Islamophobia: We Shall Overcome," *African American Muslims Series* of the *Common Ground News Service*, July 5, 2008. The CGNS can be accessed at www.commongroundnews.org.

33. Frederick J. Streets, "African-Americans and Middle East Bridges" in R. Drew Smith, ed., "Black Clergy and U.S. Policy in the Middle East and North Africa," *The Review of Faith and International Affairs*, Vol. 6, Number 1 (Spring 2008), 56.

34. Claude Clegg III, *An Original Man: The Life and Times of Elijah Muhammad* 1997; Karl Evanzz, *The Messenger: The Rise and Fall of Elijah Muhammad*, 1999.

35. Sufi scholars included leaders of the four Sunni schools of thought. They are Imam Malik, Imam Abu Hanifa, Imam Shafi'i and Imam Ahmad Ibn Hanbal. These Imams are represented in the four schools of Fiqh (Law).

36. Sherman Jackson, *Islam and the Blackamerican: Looking Toward the Third Resurrection*, 2005, 16.

37. This sect gained far more notoriety for its connection to the brutal slaughter of well known local African American journalist Chauncey Bailey whose murder stunned the Bay Area in 2008. Bailey was killed execution style after investigating the group's many financial troubles. Yusef Bey established several businesses in the Oakland, especially the Your Black Muslim Bakery establishment. The legal problems of this offshoot group of Black Muslims are too numerous and longstanding to list here. In August 2011, the defendants charged in Bailey's murder were sentenced to life without parole.

38. Person-to-person telephone interview with Samina Faheem Sundas conducted by the author November 18, 2008. Sundas Sundas founded the grassroots organization American Muslim Voice in direct reaction to hostilities aimed at Muslims since September 11th 2001. She has also founded Global Peace Partnership, a partnership of American Muslim Voice, Global Peace Partners and Peace Alliance.

39. Among the clamoring over the first Muslim elected official in the twenty-first century being sworn into office "on the Qur'an" (Koran) and not the Bible, Minnesota Congressman Keith Ellison (5th District, Minnesota), who is also the state's first African American elected to Congress, silenced many critics by using the personal Koran of Thomas Jefferson while taking the oath of office.

40. Mohommed A. Muqtedar Khan, "Muslims and Identity Politics in America" in *Muslims on the Americanization Path?* eds.,Yvonne Yazbeck Haddad and John L. Esposito (Oxford: Oxford University Press, 2000), 95.

41. Called a "terrorist" by some opponents, Obama's "cosmopolitan" racial composition betrayed an ambidextrousness that enabled critics and opponents to depict him as an alien threat as Black *and* Muslim, his Swahilian middle name—Hussein, was mocked repeatedly to cue xenophobic anxiety in post-9/11 society. At no point during his campaigns, where even after the nearly fatal insertion of Christian Black nationalist theologian and Pastor of Obama's former congregation Trinity United Church of Christ into the campaign, more than 1 in 10 people in some polls continued to spout, "he is a Muslim," has Barack Obama "defended" the right of any would-be Muslim, such as his friend and colleague Keith Ellison (5th District, Minnesota), to run for or hold office in the United States. At least two incidents, one related to an Ellison speech on behalf of Obama being canceled and another, related to the removal of two or more *Hijab*-wearing young Muslim women during a campaign photo-opportunity, were brought to light.

42. Yvonne Yazbeck Haddad and John L. Esposito, eds., *Muslims on the Americanization Path?* 2000, 9.

43. Propaganda independent films such as "Obsession: Radical Islam's War Against the West" have run unchallenged on the major American cable networks (2006). Discredited journalist, turned "terrorism expert" Steven Emerson—who attributed the Oklahoma City attacks to that city's Islamic community in 1995—through his Investigative Project, and the likes of former 1960s New Left radical turned arch conservative David Horowitz have gained notoriety and the ire of Muslim groups across the United States where Horowitz has engaged in McCar-

thyist hunts for "Islamofascists" mainly in the faculties on college and university campuses. See Steven Emerson, *American Jihad: The Terrorists Living Among Us* (New York: The Free Press, 2002), 9.

44. Separate incidents on Greyhound buses in the summer of 2002 resulted in an African American man with the surname Muhammad being removed from a bus in Cincinnati, Ohio just weeks after a 29-year-old American of Middle Eastern descent was removed for attempting to move to the front seat of a bus. These incidents were preceded by a throat slashing attack of a Greyhound bus driver in Tennessee by a 29-year-old Croatian Muslim Army veteran named Damir Igric that resulted in the deaths of six people, including Igric.

45. Hillary Costa, "Islamic Center Celebrates Resurrection after Arson," *Oakland Tribune*, June 27, 2009, A9.

46. In December 2001 HLF was designated under Executive Orders 13224 and 12947 as a charity that provided millions of dollars of material and logistical support to Hamas. HLF, originally known as the Occupied Land Fund, was established in California in 1989 as a tax-exempt charity. Other charities targeted were the Global Relief Foundation and Benevolence International.

47. In conjunction with the Muslim Public Affairs Commission, the Los Angeles County Commission of Human Rights created the Hate Crimes Prevention Department three months after the attacks in order to handle the heightened volume of reported incidents.

48. See Gurinder Singh Mann, Paul Numrich, and Raymond Williams, *Buddhists, Hindus, and Sikhs in America: A Short History* (Oxford: Oxford University Press, 2008), chapters 7–9.

49. With its Hindu derivation, Sikhism emerged in the late fifteenth century based on the teachings of the first of ten "gurus" (teachers) named Nanak in the principle Sikh city, Punjab located in the Northwest section of India. The followers of Guru Nanak became known as Sikhs (disciples). Sikhism rejects polytheism, belief in angels or spirits and embraces the belief in and worship of the deity Kartar (also called Patishah or Sahib). Kartar created and rules the universe based on the principles of justice and grace. The principle goal of all human beings is to achieve *mukti* (liberation), which enables one to become unified with Kartar. Commitments to other-centeredness, family, community, recognition of Kartar's power in the universe and in creation, hard work, and Sikh scripture (several hundred poems written by Guru Nanak called *Guru Granth Sahib*) form the core of Sikh religious belief and cultural practices.

50. Sikh enthusiasm for the United States would be steady until the Great Depression adversely affected migrant labor. In the interim, however, Congress passed the Asiatic Barred Zone Act of 1917 barring immigration from East Asian and Pacific Island countries, reinforcing the to Chinese Exclusion Act, resulting in a decline of the Indian population to less than 2,500 by 1940. The low point of early Sikh life in the United States came in the 1923 Supreme Court case *Bhagat Singh Thind v. United States*, in which Thind, a former U.S. soldier in World War I who legally entered the United States, sought citizenship and the right to be considered white. The ruling followed the *Ozawa v. United States* case, where the same court ruled that a light-skinned native of Japan could not be counted

as "white" by equating it with Caucasian. The rejection by lower courts and the Supreme Court signaled the ongoing "alienness" of Sikhs and all other South Asians until the Luce-Celler Bill.

51. In 1994 California Governor Pete Wilson vetoed a state senate bill which would have permitted Sikh children in California's school systems to wear the ceremonial knives. But the main object of physical violence, social derision, and job discrimination has surrounded the wearing of the Sikh turbans; especially for Sikh children. See Gurinder Singh Mann, Paul Numrich, and Raymond Williams, *Buddhists, Hindus, and Sikhs in America: A Short History*, 2008.

52. Ibid., 101.

53. See, Mohommed A. Muqtedar Khan, "Muslims and Identity Politics" in Haddad and Esposito, 2000, 91. The December 2008 Mumbai (Bombay), India massacre of nearly two hundred Indians and Westerners, attributed to Pakistani Muslims with ties to contested Kashmir, further exacerbated longstanding and often violent tensions between India and Pakistan and their expatriated nationals. Pakistani Muslims disagree with their Indian Muslim cohorts on Kashmir as fiercely as they do with Hindus and others.

54. *Koremastu* refers to the Supreme Court challenge to World War II era Japanese removal and internment; many of the 120,000 internees were from the San Francisco Bay Area. Please see Eric Yamamoto, Margaret Chon, Carol L. Izumi, Jerry Kang, and Frank H. Wu, *Race, Rights, and Reparation Law and the Japanese Internment* (New York: Aspen Law and Business, 2001).

55. In 2002, for instance, Attorney General issued an interim regulation forbidding any state or county jail from releasing information about INS detainees housed in their facilities.

56. Please see http://www.migrationinformation.org/USFocus/display.cfm?ID=116#1. The Special Registration component of the program required individuals from age 25, mostly Arabic and Muslims countries to register with the INS within a designated time. Those countries are: Iran, Iraq, Libya, Sudan, and Syria; Afghanistan, Algeria, Bahrain, Eritrea, Lebanon, Morocco, North Korea, Oman, Qatar, Somalia, Tunisia, United Arab Emirates, and Yemen; Pakistan and Saudi Arabia and Bangladesh, Egypt, Indonesia, Jordan, and Kuwait.

57. This letter was addressed to Committee Chair Patrick Leahy and Ranking Member Arlen Specter. The organizations that formed the coalition included Asian Law Caucus, American-Arab Anti-Discrimination Committee, American Civil Liberties Union, Association of Physicians of Pakistani-descent of North America, Bill of Rights Defense Committee, Center for National Security Studies, Defending Dissent Foundation, Electronic Frontier Foundation, Fairfax County Privacy Council, The Freedom and Justice Foundation, Friends Committee on National Legislation, Liberty Coalition, NAACP Legal Defense Fund, Inc., Mexican-American Legal Defense and Educational Fund, MAS Freedom, Muslim Advocates, Muslim Bar Association of New York, Muslim Consultative Network, National Lawyers Guild, National Council of La Raza, People for the American Way, Privacy Times, Privacy Journal, South Asian Americans Leading Together, Sikh Coalition, Unitarian Universalist Service Committee, U.S. Bill of Rights Foundation. The full letter can be viewed at http://www.muslimadvocates.

org/documents/Coalition_sign_on_letter_re_invasive_border_interrogations_
SJC.pdf. Moreover, included in a long list of grievances based on the anecdotal
experiences of many individuals is the instance of an attorney in California who
". . . was interrogated by CBP agents at San Francisco International Airport upon
her return to the U.S. from a trip to visit overseas relatives. Upon establishing
her citizenship status, she thoroughly answered initial questions about her travels
and identity. Nevertheless, without any reason to believe that this U.S. citizen was
carrying prohibited items or was otherwise engaged in unlawful activity, the CBP
agent arbitrarily insisted on searching her luggage, seized her digital camera and
reviewed the images—reflecting pictures from her travel with her family, as well
as various photos taken in the United States prior to her travel. The agent interrogated her about the identities of the people in her travel photos, their location,
and her relationships to them. The CBP agent then posed questions about her
political views of candidates in the 2008 presidential election.

58. Some estimate that nearly 500,000 American Muslims were interviewed
by the Federal Bureau of Investigations, constituting nearly 1 out every 4 Muslim households following the attacks. Of the 28,000 interviewees detained, only
39 had been charged or convicted of a crime. I would like to acknowledge the
assistance of an advanced undergraduate student, Jordan Chase, for pointing this
data out in one on one discussion and in an undergraduate paper for my fall 2008
Religion and Politics class at the University of San Francisco. Please see, John M.
Buchanan, "Consequences," *Christian Century*, 21(124) (October 16, 2007), 3.

59. The June 2006 arrests of members of a syncretistic Hebrew-Israelite,
Christian, and Moorish Science Temple Islamic group calling itself the "Seas of
David," in the largely impoverished Liberty City section of Miami, Florida brought
the Black militant-radical Islam linkage full circle as they were added to the long
list of "homegrown terrorist" cells for expressing little more than street corner
resentment of the American government and talk of a "full ground war" that
would result in the deaths of "all the devils" possible. Seven black men, five of
them native-born Americans, were charged with conspiring to support al Qaeda
(the base), to wage war against the United States and to use explosives to damage
or destroy the Sears Tower and the FBI building in Miami. The federal indict-
ments allege that these individuals sought $50,000 and various weapons, training,
firearms, vehicles, radios, binoculars, bullet-proof vests, and military boots. No
hard evidence of a serious plot has yet to emerge. Florida was also home to about
15 of the 19 hijackers on September 11th 2001, including Mohamed Atta. In addition to the "Seas of David" defendants, the arrests of four *older* black men with
ties to Guyana and Trinidad and Tabago for an alleged plan to attack gas lines
across New York City in June 2007 is an example. Another, as recently as May
2009, resulted in the arrests of four African American Muslims with links to an
obscure group identified as Jaish-e-Mohammad for allegedly plotting to bomb a
Jewish synagogue in the Bronx. In each of the noted cases, the alleged plots cited
not much more evidence than resentments for U.S. military presence in Islamic
lands as interpreted by unnamed FBI "informants." Authorities also concede that
in each case, the accused had "no capability," "no training," to actually carry out
an attack and "no connections" to Al Qaeda. Jose Padilla, an American "enemy

combatant" who was arrested in Chicago in 2002 for allegedly planning a "dirty bomb" attack in the United States in support of al Qaeda, also attended a mosque in Broward County in the early 1990s. See Steve Emerson, *Jihad Incorporated* (New York: Prometheus Books, 2006), 74.

60. A 2008 ACLU study conducted by Yale University economist Ian Ayers found disproportionate patterns of minority contact, stops, "frisks," searches, and arrests even when controlling for factors such as crime rates in neighborhoods, the number of police officers in a neighborhood, weapons or drugs recovered as a result of the arrests when compared to the yield of stopped white residents. The rate of stops of African Americans by the Los Angeles Police Department based on its 2006 single-year (July 2003–June 2004) self-study showed that African Americans are stopped at a higher rate than white and Latino drivers and pedestrians combined. The same is true of patterns of arrests following pretextual stops. The study found that when police officers of the "same race" stopped African Americans and Latinos, the patterns of arrest declined. It is also pertinent that African Americans are cited at *lower* rates than whites and Latinos, but the chief investigators of the study attribute this to the detail that ". . . black residents are stopped so much more often that black residents still get citations at nearly twice the rate of whites and Hispanics do." They conclude from this, that African Americans residents are not the beneficiaries of leniency on the part of the LAPD officers, "but that African Americans are more subject to stops without justification where no ticket could be issued" justifiably. Please see, "Racial Profiling and the LAPD: A Study of Racially Disparate Outcomes in the Los Angeles Police Department" at www.yale.edu/ayres/.

61. Victims of the street robberies in Palo Alto variously described their assailants as being black, Latino, white, or Pacific Islander males. Chief Lynne Johnson subsequently modified her comments, suggesting that her original intention was to order her officers to interrogate any "suspicious African-American adult males." The other groups were not mentioned.

62. The president and executive director of the Applied Research Center is Rinku Sen, co-author of the book, *The Accidental American: Immigration and Citizenship in the Age of Globalization* (Berrett-Koehler, 2008). The ARC held a "Facing Race" conference at the Oakland Marriot City Center hotel in November of 2008. ARC is not a religiously affiliated organization.

63. Of course, the most widespread policing tools at the federal and local levels is implementation of two installments of the Uniting and Strengthening America by Providing Appropriate Tools Required to Intercept and Obstruct Terrorism Act (USA PATRIOT Act I and II) as well as the Clear Law Enforcement for Alien Removal (CLEAR) Act. Where the former would expand arbitrary federal police powers by lowering probable cause standards and expanding spying, surveillance, and harassment provisions, the CLEAR Act binds local law enforcement to report to immigration officials any encounters with undocumented individuals at the risk of losing federal funding.

64. The story of the "Man of Samaria," more commonly labeled the "Good Samaritan," is in some ways analogous to the precarious predicament of Muslims in the United States, especially after the 9/11 attacks. The parable in Luke 10:

25–37 invokes questions of religious piety, "racial," cultural, and religious antipathies, and the exercise of cross-cutting religious compassion for the victims of arbitrary violence and matters of religious law and duty that were brought to bear in answering the question, "who is my neighbor?"

65. R. Drew Smith, "Black Denominational Responses to U.S.–Middle East Policy Since 9/11," *The Review of International Affairs* 6, no.1 (Spring 2008), 5–16.

66. See Anthony Pinn, *The Black Church in the Post-Civil Rights Era* (Maryknoll, NY: Orbis, 2002).

67. Richard E. De Leon, *Left Coast City: Progressive Politics in San Francisco, 1975–1991* (Lawrence, Kansas: University Press of America, 1992).

68. For instance, one respondent in a one on one interview conducted on July 7, 2009 in Alameda expressed reluctance in supporting the San Francisco Interfaith Council due to its refusal to make advocacy statements against the early 2009 violence in Gaza Strip. On another occasion there was a panel on mutual understanding between Christians and Jews, that excluded Muslims.

69. In writing this article the author attempted to make contact with dozens of Muslim scholars, leaders, and organizations which resulted in only a handful of actual interviews. Non-Muslim coalition partners likewise expressed how a general sense of fear and suspicion, particularly engendered by Bush-era surveillance instruments, pervades the lives of many Muslims and organizations.

70. Other key individuals and congregations include Rev. Calvin Jones, Jr., Providence Baptist Church of San Francisco; St. John's Baptist Church of Richmond; and Sojourner Truth Presbyterian Church of Richmond.

71. GRIP, which focuses chiefly on homelessness, has one of the interfaith community's only African American female Board of Directors members, Ms. Naomi Williams, who represents St. John's Missionary Baptist Church of Richmond. She also serves on the Black American Political Action Committee (BAPAC). She has served in many local housing and violence prevention efforts in Richmond. Created in 1967 in response to urban riots, GRIP now has a 3 million dollar facility in Richmond and is in transition from an interfaith advocacy group to a social service provider with now-independent offshoot social service providers such as a rape center, day care center, food pantry that feeds 6,000 people per month, community housing, and violence prevention.

72. Brown was appointed to the San Francisco Board of County and City Supervisors by then-Mayor Willie Brown. He has also served as chairman of the National Baptist Commission on Civil Rights and Human Services and a member of the governing board of the National Council of Churches of Christ. Brown was defeated in a largely anti-Willie Brown referendum election in December of 2000 losing to Gerardo Sandoval who received 61.7 of the vote while Amos Brown received 38.3. He also heads the city's NAACP branch.

73. For instance, Brown identified himself and Rev. Dorsey Blake of The Fellowship of All Peoples Church (founded by Howard Thurman under the aegis of A. J. Muste's Fellowship of Reconciliation) as the only even occasional supporters among African American pastors of the San Francisco Interfaith Council, which was originally created in response to the 1989 Loma-Prieta earthquake. Blake agrees.

74. In addition to serving as the resident pastor of the Easter Hill United Methodist Church in Richmond (1992–2003), Lawson served as president of the Northern California Ecumenical Council (now Northern California Interreligious Conference (NCIC)), G.R.I.P., Interfaith Coalition for Immigrant Rights, California Council of Churches, F.A.I.T.H.S., Priority Africa Network, Northern California Religious Leaders in Conversation, East Bay Housing Organizations, and several others.

75. Face-to-face unstructured interview with Rev. Phil Lawson, Oakland, California, Monday July 27, 2009.

76. Based on 2000 U.S. Census. Please see The Association of Religion Data Archives at www.thearda.com/mapsreports/reports/counties/06075_2000. asp. Please note that African American churches are *not* counted in this data source.

77. Rebecca Moore, Anthony B. Pinn, and Mary R. Sawyer, eds., *Peoples Temple and Black Religion in America* (Indianapolis, IN: Indiana University Press, 2004). For instance, East Palo Alto, just two miles from affluent Palo Alto where Stanford University is located, experienced serious crime and poverty, especially during the 1980s and early 1990s. In the early 1990s, East Palo Alto had the highest per capita murder rate in the country with 24,322 people, and 42 murders, equaling a rate of 172.7 murders per 100,000 residents. Richmond, California and the other heavily African American populated Bay Area towns and San Francisco City districts have also experienced high rates of per capita violence. Please see, http://www.stanfordalumni.org/news/magazine/1998/janfeb/articles/epa.html.

78. J. Alfred Smith, "Breaking the Silence: Reflections of a Black Pastor" in *Peoples Temple and Black Religion in America,* eds., Rebecca Moore, Anthony B. Pinn, and Mary R. Sawyer (Indianapolis, IN: Indiana University Press, 2004), 94.

79. Mary R. Sawyer, "The Church in Peoples Temple" in *Peoples Temple and Black Religion in America,* eds., Rebecca Moore, Anthony B. Pinn, and Mary R. Sawyer (Indianapolis, IN: Indiana University Press, 2004), 180–189. Tensions among prominent African American Christian leaders and churches, including Amos Brown of Third Baptist Church, and local Nation of Islam leaders concerning a controversial Redevelopment Agency gentrification project in the city's predominantly Black Bayview Hunters Point in 2007 exacerbated relations. The anti-gay marriage Proposition 8 further divided the African American Christian churches of San Francisco among themselves.

80. Rebecca Moore, Anthony B. Pinn, and Mary R. Sawyer, eds. (Indianapolis, IN: Indiana University Press, 2004), xii.

81. Eric Yamamoto, Margaret Chon, Carol Izumi, Jerry Kang, and Frank H. Wu, *Race, Rights, and Reparation: Law and The Japanese American Internment* (New York: Aspen Law and Business, 2001), 32. Emphasis is in original text.

82. Ibid., 36–37.

83. Ibid., 39.

84. Ibid., 40.

85. Ronald Takaki, *Strangers From A Different Shore: A History of Asian Americans,* 1989, cited in Eric Yamamoto, Margaret Chon, Carol Izumi, Jerry Kang, and Frank H. Wu, *Race, Rights, and Reparation: Law and The Japanese American Internment* (New York: Aspen Law and Business, 2001), 8.

Contributors

Carroll A. Watkins Ali is the executive director of the Greater Denver Interfaith Alliance and has a private pastoral psychotherapy practice. She earned her PhD in Religious and Theological Studies at the University of Denver and Iliff School of Theology and is the author of *Survival and Liberation: Pastoral Theology in African American Context.*

R. Khari Brown is an associate professor in the Department of Sociology at Wayne State University. His research interests include the intersections between race, religion, and social activism. He is currently working on a series of articles that investigate the impact social-political messages heard in church have on the political behavior and policy attitudes of black, white, Asian, and Hispanic Americans.

Katie Day holds the Charles A. Schieren Chair in Church and Society at the Lutheran Theological Seminary at Philadelphia. As a sociologist, with degrees in social ethics and theology, she teaches courses that draw heavily on both the social sciences and social ethics. Her research interests have included extensive studies in African American congregations, cross-cultural volunteerism, and faith-based involvement in economic development, community organizing, and social services. Her recent publications include *Difficult Conversations: Taking Risks, Acting with Integrity* (2001).

Omari L. Dyson is an assistant professor of Curriculum Instruction in the Department of Teacher Education at South Carolina State University. Dyson earned his PhD in curriculum instruction at Purdue University in 2008.

Juan M. Floyd-Thomas is associate professor of Black Church Studies at the Vanderbilt University Divinity School and core faculty of History and Critical Theories of Religion area in the Graduate Department of Religion.

355

He is author of *The Origins of Black Humanism: Reverend Ethelred Brown and the Unitarian Church*, 2008, and co-author of *Black Church Studies: An Introduction*, 2007, as well as several journal articles, book chapters, and other publications.

Judson L. Jeffries is professor of African American and African Studies at Ohio State University. Prior to going to OSU he was an associate professor of political science, homeland security studies and American studies at Purdue University. Jeffries has published widely on the Black Panther Party. He earned his PhD in political science at the University of Southern California in 1997.

Maurice Mangum is an associate professor of political science at Texas Southern University and editor of the *Ralph Bunche Journal of Public Affairs*. His specialty area is African American politics, with a focus on the impact of religion and race consciousness on the political attitudes and political behavior of African Americans. He has published in many outlets, most notably *Political Research Quarterly*, *Policy Studies Journal*, *Politics and Religion*, and *Journal of Black Studies*.

Steve McCutcheon is a former member of the Black Panther Party, having served in both Baltimore and Oakland for a period of ten years. McCutcheon earned an Associate of Arts degree in social science at Laney College and a B.A. in Applied Psychology at City University in Bellevue, Washington. Currently, he teaches at Carl B. Munck elementary school in Oakland, California.

Larry G. Murphy is professor of the History of Christianity at Garrett-Evangelical Theological Seminary. He is editor *of Down by the Riverside: Readings in African American Religion* (New York University Press, 2000) and co-editor of *The Encyclopedia of African American Religions* (Routledge, 1993). He is also author of *African American Faith in America* (2002) and *Sojourner Truth: A Biography*, 2011.

James R. Ralph, Jr. has taught at Middlebury College since 1989, where he is currently the Rehnquist Professor of American History and Culture and the Dean for Faculty Development and Research. He is the author of *Northern Protest: Martin Luther King, Jr., Chicago, and the Civil Rights Movement* (Harvard University Press, 1993).

Rosetta E. Ross is professor of Religious Studies at Spelman College in Atlanta. Her research and writing explore the role of religion in black women's activism, focusing particularly on the Civil Rights Movement.

She is author of *Witnessing and Testifying: Black Women, Religion, and Civil Rights.*

David K. Ryden is a professor of political science at Hope College. He has authored, co-authored, or edited six books, including *Sanctioning Religion?: Politics, Law, and Faith-Based Public Services* (2006); *Of Little Faith: The Politics of George W. Bush's Faith-Based Initiatives* (2004); *The U.S. Supreme Court and The Electoral Process: Perspectives and Commentaries on Contemporary Cases, Revised and Updated Edition* (2002), and *Representation in Crisis: The Constitution, Interest Groups, and Political Parties* (1996).

R. Drew Smith is scholar-in-residence at the Morehouse College Leadership Center and is co-convener of the Transatlantic Roundtable on Religion and Race. He has edited multiple volumes and written numerous articles, chapters, and reports on African American and African religion and public life and is currently writing a book under contract with Columbia University Press on contemporary black clergy activism.

Clarence Taylor is an associate professor and chair in the Department of Politics and Black and Hispanic Studies at Baruch College and professor of History at the Graduate Center, CUNY. He is the author and editor of several books including the *Black Churches of Brooklyn* (Columbia University Press 1994) and *Knocking at Our Own Door: Milton A. Galamison and the Struggle to Integrate New York City Schools* (Columbia University Press, 1997).

James Lance Taylor is an associate professor in the Department of Politics at the University of San Francisco. He teaches in the areas of American Politics, Black Politics, Political Leadership, and Race & Ethnic Politics. His most recent book is entitled: *Black Nationalism in the United States: From Malcolm X to Barack Obama*, 2011. He has served as president of the National Conference of Black Political Scientists.

Traci C. West is professor of Ethics and African American Studies at Drew University Theological School. She is the author of *Wounds of the Spirit: Black Women, Violence, and Resistance Ethics* (1999), *Disruptive Christian Ethics: When Racism and Women's Lives Matter* (2006) and editor of *Our Family Values: Same-sex Marriage and Religion* (2007). She is an ordained clergy member of the United Methodist Church.

Yohuru R. Williams is an associate professor of History at Fairfield University and is the chief historian and vice president for Public Education and Community Outreach at the Jackie Robinson Foundation in New

York City. He is the author of *Black Politics/White Power: Civil Rights Black Power and Black Panthers in New Haven* (Blackwell, 2006) and *Teaching U.S. History Beyond the Textbook: Six Investigative Strategies, Grades 5–12*, Corwin Press, 2008). He is the co-editor of *In Search of the Black Panther,* (Duke University Press, 2006) and *Liberated Territory: Toward a Local History of the Black Panther Party* (Duke University Press, 2009).

Index